Ecstasy Unlimited

"Ecstasy Unlimited"

On Sex, Capital, Gender, and Aesthetics

Laura Kipnis

Foreword by Paul Smith

University of Minnesota Press
Minneapolis
London

An earlier version of chapter 2 appeared as "Refunctioning Reconsi-dered: Toward a Left Popular Culture" in *High Theory/Low Culture*. Copyright 1986 by Laura Kipnis. An earlier version of chapter 4 ap-peared as "Feminism: The Political Conscience of Postmodernism?" in *Universal Abandon? The Politics of Postmodernism*. Copyright 1989 by the Regents of the University of Minnesota. An earlier version of chapter 6 appeared in *Wide Angle* 11, no. 4. Copyright by Johns Hopkins University Press. Reprinted by permission. An earlier version of chap-ter 7 appeared in *Social Text 15*. Copyright 1986 by Social Text. Reprinted by permission. Chapter 8 originally appeared in *Cultural Studies*. Copyright 1991 by Routledge.

Thanks to David Kaplan and Editel, Chicago, and to Larry Logman for the photos in chapters 3, 5, and 7.

Published by the University of Minnesota Press
2037 University Avenue Southeast, Minneapolis, MN 55455-3092
Printed in the United States of America on acid-free paper

Library of Congress Cataloging-in-Publication Data
Kipnis, Laura.
    Ecstasy unlimited : on sex, capital, gender, and aesthetics / Laura Kipnis.
        p.   cm.
    Includes bibliographical references and index.
    ISBN 0-8166-1996-4 (acid-free paper)
    ISBN 0-8166-1997-2 (pbk.: acid-free paper)
    1. United States—Popular culture. 2. Aesthetics. 3. Political culture—United States. I. Title.
E169.12.K47   1993
306'.0973—dc20   92-19139
                                                            CIP

Contents

To Myra and Len

Foreword
Paul Smith

THE MAIN PROPOSITION running through Laura Kipnis's
work—the one that for me at least holds together her
essays and the videos represented here—is an idea that might at first
sight be construed either as an oxymoron or as a pleonasm. What Kipnis's work calls for and strives toward—essentially, a contestatory
postmodernism—would be a pleonastic notion for some in that it is
possible today to imagine that everything radical and effective in cultural politics derives from postmodernism's having discarded the
pretensions and dictates of the programs and the so-called grand narratives of the traditional left. On the other hand, the notion could be
thought an oxymoron. There are those who reckon that the term "postmodernism" itself describes exactly a cultural condition that has dis-
pensed almost utterly with any radical oppositional politics and has
opted instead for a certain kind of complicity with the seemingly in-
domitable creative processes of transnational capitalism.

But there resides one of the difficulties, or even one of the contradictions, of the cultural formations that we have come to know as postmodernism, and equally of the discourses and debates that both engage
and help constitute it. There is a difficulty, that is, in discerning what
could indeed count as effective opposition or resistance in the current
context where capital appears to reign supreme, installing its ideological presuppositions and its unjust practices at more and more points
across the globe. This is a situation that, at the cultural level at least, has
been noted by many of postmodernism's commentators. While there is
a fashion for the kind of theory that will proffer postmodern cultural

practice as being in and of itself resistant and oppositional in relation to hegemonic formations, other kinds of theory will claim that it has, to the contrary, authorized a deep complicity at the level of cultural politics. Hal Foster, for instance, has been led to distinguish between a radical and a conservative postmodernism, and the same kind of partition informs Pauline Rosenau's survey of the postmodernist debates. Meaghan Morris has assailed the dominant strands of postmodern thinking, whose celebratory analyses she sees as disregarding the material and political issues that the old left narratives were intended to address. Christopher Norris, noting the same lacuna in much postmodern theory, has tried to deploy deconstructive philosophy as a way of supplying the ethical and political program that he sees lacking in postmodernism. One of the best anthologies of critical analyses of postmodernism, *Universal Abandon?*, demonstrates effectively a variety of the ways the question of the politics of postmodernism can be addressed and perhaps answered. These are but several examples of the many available indications that the articulation of the terms "postmodern" and "politics" is still a matter for great and lengthy debate, and that the question of whether or not embracing the conditions of the postmodern necessarily entails an abandonment of oppositional practice is still a crucial one.[1]

The work that Laura Kipnis offers in the present book has a distinct relation to this debate and its history, intervening there in a way that is almost unique and, in my view, salutary. It is not simply that Kipnis's video work gives rise to and arises from a set of fully articulated theoretical positions (I can think only of the filmmaker Trinh Minh-Ha as peer to Kipnis in this regard), nor simply that Kipnis so convincingly deploys the academic essay to resonate with and to inform her video practice. While these habits are impressively executed and help produce a coherent body of work exploiting both registers, it is what one might call (using prejudicially a weighted vocabulary) the *tendency* of Kipnis's work that I find most congenial. That is, both the writing here and the videos consistently demonstrate that they are themselves practices that must be construed as political; the political is imbricated in the practice and the theory to produce struggle and opposition. Clearly, Kipnis is not of the view that the postmodern entails an elision of the political or of political desire. Rather, it is for her a set of cultural formations in which political desire must be formulated and played out over and over again through the acts of theoretical and artistic production. The politics of the postmodern cannot, that is to say, be presignified or made to fit a predictive or prescriptive program. Contestation must be produced, then, from within the context of the postmodern and its formations, and must take the measure of the specific nature of those formations in order to be effective.

The effort to enact this production—at both the theoretical and the practical levels—would seem to involve at first a certain kind of theoretical housecleaning, an effort to clear away some of the erstwhile oppositional certitudes and developed programs that guide traditional and modern political thinking and practice. Thus Kipnis devotes a certain amount of energy in this book to interrogating what is at stake in the relationship of the *modernist* project to the political. One of her fundamental complaints is about the way the aesthetics of modernism finds its expression as a set of political assumptions and practices that she suggests can no longer be viable. She is particularly incensed, for example, by the way modernist literature and art practice become a seminal site for the construction of a politics. How this construction works is nicely explicated in her essay, "Aesthetics and Foreign Policy." There she shows how modernist aesthetic paradigms, offered as self-evident and true, inform an imperialist discourse of the North and direct it as a political weapon against the culture and political system of Cuba, imposing those paradigms as a quintessential version of "first world perception." Similarly, in "Looks Good on Paper," Kipnis analyzes the way in which the politics of what is often called "French Feminism" are intimately tied to a modernist aesthetic: she suggests that "the policies of *écriture féminine* and its practice of displacing revolution and politics to the aesthetic take us right back to that very modernist tradition that these continental theorists are presumed to transcend."

Kipnis's arguments against the modernist conflation of politics and aesthetics are the beginning of what makes her own work properly *postmodernist*. This is not, I stress, a postmodernism that authorizes the elision of politics, but one that feels its very root in a political argument and recognizes the ensuing struggle. One of Kipnis's strengths in this regard, it seems to me, is that, unlike so many of her contemporaries, she does not assume that merely to glimpse the political logic that the modernist project installed authorizes us to abandon the problematic. Quite to the contrary: it may just as easily be the case, as she implies, that hegemonic culture depends upon the perpetuation of those paradigms whose residual (at least) presence in dominant discourses is indeed one mechanism to inhibit oppositional politics in the postmodern. The residual forms of modernism obviously provide a powerful structure on which to rest the imperatives and the practical ideologies of "late" capitalist culture. Postmodernism cannot, then, simply pretend to be blind to this problematic, nor to somehow anarchically sweep it under the rug. What distinguishes Kipnis's practice in this context is the conviction that the postmodern constitutes the continuation under new conditions of a familiar struggle against capitalist hegemony.

So this is a postmodernism that recognizes that it cannot sever its relations with the modernist political problematic, even though it simultaneously and consistently refuses to recognize the validity of the modernist tendency toward the aestheticization of the political (which is the modernist solution to the political problems it raised for itself). Kipnis sees this aestheticizing process as also the root of the prescriptive "grand narratives" of modernist politics; the aesthetic modernist notion of the avant-garde, for instance, has its analogue in the vanguardism of the traditional left. Her work thus points toward what we could call a "postaesthetics" that, as I understand it, would more nearly involve a continued struggle to politicize the cultural forms of the present. In that sense she offers the postmodernist debate a politics lesson, while at the same time sternly rejecting the pretensions of the old left.

This moment of "postaesthetics" demands a concomitant rejection of the notion of the avant-garde, one of modernism's most potent tropes. If Kipnis's view of the aestheticized politics of the modern is akin to the critiques that someone like Perry Anderson has made of contemporary theory,[2] her view of how that aestheticization operates in art discourse elaborates upon the multiple critiques of the avant-garde that postmodernist writers have produced. As I have suggested, the critique of aesthetic avant-gardism and the rejection of political vanguardism go hand in hand for Kipnis, since they are two sides of the same coin, each subventing the other. Central to the critique is the claim that the avant-garde is essentially a form of elitist high culture and thus stands diametrically opposed to popular culture. The modernist fetishization of the avant-garde has usually inhibited the kind of political intervention into the popular that Kipnis sees as crucial and indeed inevitable.[3]

Thus, in the first essay of this collection, "Repossessing Popular Culture," Kipnis begins to make the case for the intervention that her own work comes to constitute. Her task of articulating what she dubs a "contestatory postmodernism" begins as she endorses Brecht's notion of "refunctioning," a tactic whereby the elements of the culture are taken up; exposed in their contradictions, absences, and silences; and appropriated to oppositional use. This is anti-avant-gardist in the sense that "Repossessing" claims that it is useless at this point to try to deal with the popular as it were from above; rather, one must work with what is already to hand, already out there, and engage it in a struggle for meaning and hegemony. Most important for me, the notion of refunctioning maintains here a link to a Marxist tradition, by way of Brecht, while updating that tradition. The basic insight—a postmodernist one to be sure—is that the signs in circulation in our cultures are

not fixed in their meaning and cannot simply be critiqued by oppositional practice; rather, they must be appropriated and elaborated in the
service of a political desire. The conviction that cultural signs and practices are still open to contestation and appropriation is the practical ten-
et by which Kipnis operates.

Kipnis's point that the left often tends to cede popular culture to
commodity culture rather than seeing it as an access to hegemony is
well taken. The left and its imaginary have often been guilty of disdain-
ing the popular because of its site of production — the commodity culture that she mentions. In that context her project of refunctioning becomes essential. The need is to refunction what is there, what is at hand
and available in a culture made possible by capitalism, so as to transform the shape of the culture and its political tendencies — that project
needs to be engaged without assuming the right to dictate or prescribe
either the shape of change or the activity of audiences and agents. Yet
at the same time, there is a need to avoid the risk that many postmodernist apologists run when they simply genuflect in front of the pleasure
of audiences and agents and thereby subvent the political quietism that
always stands quite close to the operations of postmodern discourse.

It might be objected here that this kind of intervention (akin to what
Fredric Jameson recommends as the project "to undo Postmodernism
homeopathically by the methods of Postmodernism")[4] might not constitute a totally sufficient strategy, even for an avowedly politicized
postmodern practice. Even while it is necessarily the case that contestation is a contingent phenomenon and always a matter of specific context and discourses, it still might be premature to discard completely
and forever the political paradigms of the older left. That is, there is
perhaps still a need to recognize the place and effect of the modernist
elements embedded in the postmodern, and to retain a way of thinking
those residues in their actual specificity, rather than in their putative
outmodedness. It could be that postmodern culture is just one more
stage in capitalism's creative processes and that it has the ideological
effect (akin to that of, for instance, the church in industrial capitalism)
of obfuscating the social relations and the material bases of the culture.
At any rate, it might still be the case that the kind of contestation
produced in the modernist paradigms still has a target, be it residual
modernism or modernism as a structure that postmodern culture has
the effect of hiding. Indeed, when Kipnis herself recognizes that the
economic system is "asynchronous," composed of unevenly developing structures, it seems tolerably clear that the same can be said of the
cultural formations in which the economic is imbricated. Popular culture in this sense is still shot through with paradigms that are not postmodernist. One might think, as examples, of the utter fascination that

classic narrative structure still exerts, or the way in which the ideologies of realism or authorship still reign in popular culture, or, at other registers, how certain institutions of articulated political organization, like unions and political parties, still subsist in and alongside the cultural elements of postmodernism.

This is to say no more than that postmodernism is not the definitional constituent of contemporary cultures (even if it might be what Raymond Williams would have called an emergent paradigm) and that it exists only in conjuncture with (and even as the product of) equally powerful formations. In that sense a contestatory postmodernism can perhaps only ever be partial. Even though it seems to me right to suggest that we cannot seek resistance to hegemonic culture beyond the present conjuncture — as Kipnis says, there is no outside to the dominant forms and ideologies of culture — there are still modes and even concepts within the grand narratives and the modernist paradigms that can and do have purchase on contemporary cultural formations (Kipnis indeed shows this in her essay "Aesthetics and Foreign Policy"), and this recognition would have implications for oppositional practice.

One might make this argument around any number of the concepts and practices of an older-style leftism; one such might be the notion of solidarity. There is room for a critique of that notion in that in the discourses of the left it has usually come with a presignified idea of the nature of the agent presumed capable or apt to construct solidarity. But even that critique is countermanded in Marx by the insistence that classes are forged in and through struggle, and not the other way around. Contestation and resistance can come from anywhere (even if they cannot be said to be everywhere), and part of the task of any political discourse is to recognize this. Kipnis's work and her arguments certainly do not prejudicially decide the agent of contestation or direct that agent from any vanguardist position. But the issue of solidarity and alliances — the issue, that is, of a pragmatic politics of action and change — then gets to be much more problematic as it is left to one side.

A case in point is Kipnis's relation to feminism. The video, *A Man's Woman*, poses the problem of the relation between women's political desire and the impulse to construe a solidarity among women as feminists; the video could be criticized for depicting such a disjuncture between the two urges that solidarity among women is compromised. Kipnis is certainly not hesitant about expressing her deep irritation at various feminist projects and discourses on the grounds that their relation to popular practices is distant, limited, and stifling, and in the end often constitutes yet another aestheticization of political issues. This view emerges in several places, but one can take as examples Kipnis's complaint about feminism's refusal to think beyond the immediately objectionable and vulgar characteristics of a cultural object such as *Hustler* magazine and her satirization and interrogation of various kinds of feminist discourse in *A Man's Woman.*

One fault she sees in these discourses is of course their vanguardism, or their claim to speak from some great height both about and for all women. Against that kind of feminism Kipnis poses what can be called women's ressentiment, the rage and discontent of women (all the more visible, ironically enough, now that feminism has become "post-feminism"),[5] leveled against not only the conditions of their existence or against men, but also against those vanguardists, those feminists who appear to want to speak for all women. The juxtaposition of women's ressentiment and feminism itself is clearest in *A Man's Woman,* where the voices of women in the street (to put it that way) are valorized at the video's opening, while avant-garde feminism is satirized, for example, through the academic figure (a thinly disguised portrayal of Julia Kristeva)[6] whom Kipnis's reporter interviews. While it is true that the video's narrative does not endorse the quest for power of the right-wing ideologue, Clovis Kingsley, it is clear that she offers a response to women's anger that cannot simply be dismissed or critiqued and that feminism has certainly not effectively accommodated. Clovis's importance is that she can "tap elemental currents of resentment, fear, and anger running beneath the surface of American society."

The way Kipnis amplifies this sort of ressentiment in much of her work recalls Meaghan Morris's powerful reminder that the foregrounding of aggressivity as a political element is something all too often avoided in postmodern critical strategy. Morris comments that much of that work leaves little space "for an unequivocally pained, unambivalently discontented, or momentarily *aggressive* subject." She goes on to suggest that this strategy is a deliberate attempt to discredit the voices of, among others, "grumpy feminists and cranky leftists," and thus she points a finger at the general function of postmodernism as an elision of inconvenient voices, angry voices.[7] What is interesting about Kipnis's work, however, is that even while it certainly critiques certain feminisms and leftisms, it does attempt to locate the kind of aggressivity of which Morris speaks and to take it up into her interventions. In that sense Kipnis's work maintains and respects an element of political anger in a context where it is frequently forgotten, discredited, or elided.

All the same, I think it is still legitimate to ask what the practical consequences are of discovering these kinds of ressentiment and counterposing them to the assumed failures of older political paradigms. That is, one still might ask what kind of organized politics women (or any of us) can engage in, given this postmodern rejection of the familiar *or-*

ganizational strategies. How are solidarity and mass political action to be considered or theorized in everyday life in the postmodern space? The question of solidarity, alliances, or the articulation of political res- sentiment into a mass political force still seems to me something to be desired. I do not mean to suggest that there are *no* channels for political ressentiment in our cultures — from the ever-growing efficacity of les- bigay activism to the electoral articulation of women's anger in the wake of the Anita Hill–Clarence Thomas confrontations, such channels can be seen in operation. Rather, I am simply suggesting once more that the utter rejection of the older paradigms is perhaps too hasty.[8]

Nonetheless, even if *A Man's Woman* might be understood as an ar- gument against existing feminism or as an exposé of feminism's lack of connection with women's ressentiment, it must also be grasped as an attempt to show that which tends to exceed the old political paradigms, fall outside of them, and threaten to compromise them under current conditions. In that sense the video operates, like much of Kipnis's work, by turning attention to those symptoms of the postmodern that still need to be accounted for or formulated if we are to talk about a postmodern political problematic. This tactic can, of course, make for some discomfort, since it threatens old certitudes and refuses to coun- tenance a fixed or prescriptive political perspective in the old way. But, as Kipnis suggests, "there is no guarantee that counterhegemonic or even specifically antibourgeois cultural forms are necessarily also going to be progressive." Rather, a first principle in the political context is to resist the temptation to police the popular or subsume its significance to a given program. The tactic must be, then, to intervene there in order to join the struggle over meanings that the postmodern invites.

This is certainly the strength of Kipnis's position, this double move- ment of locating the discourses of resistance in Northern capitalist cul- ture and subjecting them to an often inconvenient maneuver that will force them to recognize the difficulties of their articulation with other strands or elements of resistance. This strategy leads Kipnis to adum- brate some of the political and cultural issues that are the most pressing right now. One of the most telling instances of her procedures in this respect is the opening to her essay on *Hustler* magazine. There she juxta- poses two discourses: first the feminist antagonism of "disgust" in rela- tion to such material, and second the point of view of the working-class male porn consumer whose "fantasy life here is animated by cultural disempowerment in relation to a sexual caste system and social class system." Beginning with the latter insight, she convincingly elaborates a view of *Hustler* discourse as itself antagonistic, resistant, and situated in opposition to the entrenched privilege of the elite classes under capitalism, and, she notes, "It's fairly clear that from *Hustler's* point of view, feminism is a class-based discourse." In that way she sketches out a sort of war of positions wherein two opposing discourses are antagonistic to each other as well as to hegemonic discourses. Here again Kipnis has espied elements of ressentiment, and without automatically or uncritically celebrating them she takes them seriously in terms of what they signify—or to put it another way, in terms of the struggle in which they are implicated and the disruptions they effect. Here what is disrupted is a too complacent feminist ideology of norms, moralism, and modernist values; what is reinstalled is what exceeds that discourse—a concern for the economic and class bases of *Hustler's* antagonistic discourse. Kipnis suggests that feminism misses something important when it deploys a "totalizing theory of misogyny," and the implication there again is that the totalizing or universalizing move is always inadequate to the conditions that postmodernism helps constitute.

There is a similar kind of juxtaposing of two problematics in Kipnis's most recent video, *Marx: The Video,* a work that itself follows on the first video represented here, *Ecstasy Unlimited.* Both videos explore the tensions that arise when considering the body and sexuality in relation to the economic and cultural conditions in which they are implicated. In *Ecstasy* Kipnis watches how capitalism and sexuality "interpenetrate": "Would it surprise you to learn that your sex life functions according to the laws of the market?" the script asks. Kipnis offers a critique of this interpenetration in order to suggest that a critical interrogation of "our mode of sexuality is to begin to criticize the mode of social organization that produces it." The early video critiques the capitalist process of the commodification of sexuality—the selling of the orgasm—and is in a sense a pessimistic vision of how capitalism deploys sexuality as a means of social control.

The same kind of pessimism permeates *Marx: The Video* in the sense that its fundamental proposition is that the oppositional discourse of Marxism, with its stress on political economy, is shot through with an unexamined discourse of the body; the body and sexuality are thus offered as that which exceeds this oppositional discourse. Again here Kipnis offers a certain kind of discomfiting critique of a resistant discourse, this time Marxism. There is no denying the humor with which Kipnis explores this theme as she depicts the body of Karl Marx struggling to control its symptoms; the body is offered, then, as that which Marxism symptomatically elides but which returns as sexual and hysterical symptoms—the ultimate return of the repressed. It is, to use the terms in which Kipnis describes the body in *Hustler's* discourse, too, "a body threatening to erupt at any moment." Kipnis's exploration of this constitutes a kind of rebuke to both Marxism and feminism for being unable to see their commonality in the question of the body and sexuality, and the video becomes a kind of essay on the repression of the body in Marxist discourse and on feminism's relative lack of success in thinking the body in economic terms.

A similar tactic marks Kipnis's work around another of the pressing issues provoked by postmodernism's relation to the political—the issue of postcolonialism and the complexities of utterance in that context. In "The Phantom Twitchings of an Amputated Limb" Kipnis discusses a couple of postcolonial representations—the movies *Passage to India* and *Out of Africa*—and shows how they confront or attempt to disavow the history of colonialism. Her problematic is the way in which popular culture represents the vicious history of colonialism by construing it as a pathology; what she notes is the way that pathology is displaced onto female bodies or onto femininity in general. In other words, the scandal of colonialism is converted to the scandal of female sexuality in these films. Here again Kipnis has taken the measure of two different discourses as they come into collision: the discourse of postcolonialism in these films is compromised by its symptomatic difficulties in dealing with female sexuality.

All of these essays and videos have similar aims, then, in that they articulate antagonistic moments one with another, exploit the gaps between different discourses, and refunction the materials that are at hand in the context where postmodernism operates. This is not a set of aims that can always and necessarily be carried out by Kipnis or anyone else. But this is not to criticize this work, which, as I have suggested, is unusual for its tendency and consistent in its desire to advance the struggle for contestatory and antagonistic cultural forms and practices. But as Kipnis herself is aware, the art-worker or the critic-intellectual is always both a bearer of and an effect of the contradictions of the culture, and is one whose job it is to read and report those contradictions rather than to suppress or deny them. The lesson of this is that the effort of intervention is not a war that can be won once and for all, but an almost endless series of battles, cutting across many different discourses and never being able to preapprove any of them. Kipnis's rejection of the modernist paradigms, her remarking of forms of resistance that have not been accommodated into those paradigms, her disapproval of the vanguardism and aestheticizing procedures of an older left, her critique of current feminism, her understanding of the discourse of the postcolonial situation in the North—these all contribute to the complexification, and at the same time the clarification, of the (dis)juncture between the terms "postmodernism" and "politics." The sometimes uncomfortable descriptions of the terrain that Kipnis offers are offset by her positive enactment of the refunctioning project, by her foregrounding of the strands of ressentiment that are too often elided from political analysis, and by her recognition of the complex relation of the body and of pleasure to the signifying modes in which we operate. Her practice, which becomes properly postmodern in its isolating and rejecting the wiles and lures of the modernist modes, is exemplary in all these ways, and the importance of her interventions resides in her effort to correct the situation where we are impelled to proclaim that "what is crucially lacking is a postmodern political discourse."

Acknowledgments

I 'D LIKE TO THANK a sort of mobile ad hoc institution and its participants, who met every summer and provided an ongoing context for me when I was formally institutionless: the Marxist Literary Group (known euphemistically as "The Institute for Culture and Society")—and I'm especially grateful to its then doyen, Fred Jameson, who generously shared with us his early work-in-progress on postmodernism, the impact of which has made a permanent dent on my own work. Other less ephemeral institutions provided financial support: the Society of Fellows of the University of Michigan gave me a three-year fellowship, during which much of this work was done; Britain's Channel Four (thanks to my commissioning editor Rod Stoneman) funded *A Man's Woman*; and the University of Wisconsin–Madison Graduate School funded *Marx: The Video* while I was on the faculty there. And thanks to my former colleagues in the Department of Communication Arts, who were always exceptionally congenial and supportive. I've also had grants from the Regional Fellowship Program of the NEA for *Ecstasy Unlimited* and *Marx: The Video*. I've benefited enormously from discussions about my work with audiences in different parts of the country, and I'm grateful to all the people who have at various times invited me to screen tapes, including Susan Leonard of the South Carolina Arts Commission, which sponsored a ten-day tour through the South with *A Man's Woman*—it was hair-raising at times, but enlightening.

The essays here were all written for conferences or edited volumes: thank you to Colin MacCabe who insisted that I produce a theory of the work I was doing in video, which led to my first essay and my dual identity as video artist–theoretrix. Thank you for invitations to deliver or write papers from Jonathan Arac, Paul Smith, Andrew Ross, Larry Grossberg, Cary Nelson, and Paula Treichler, and for discussions and editorial first aid on them; thanks also to the *Social Text* collective. I'd especially like to thank Lauren Berlant, who struggled through multiple drafts and rough edits of much of the work here, Constance Penley, Mindy Faber and the girls at Video Data Bank, Rick Maxwell, and my parents, whose homes I've seized as locations for various productions and who only complained a little when a field monitor got dragged over a laminate sideboard (dad) or an extra heisted an Instamatic camera from a desk drawer (mom). I'm grateful to Biodun Iginla, of the University of Minnesota Press, who suggested this collection. And most of all, my love and gratitude to Steve Rodby for putting up with my shifting obsessions — from crime to carbuncles — for the last ten or twelve years, and for making this work possible in so many ways, not to mention doing the music for all my tapes. My thanks seem puny in comparison to his contribution to this book, and my debt enormous.

Videotape Distribution Information

The videotapes can be purchased for $49.95 each from:

The University of Minnesota Press
Attn: Customer Service Department
2037 University Ave. SE
Minneapolis, MN 55455-3092
1-800-388-3863

CHAPTER 1

Introduction
Crossing the Theory/Practice Rubicon

THIS IS A COLLECTION of critical essays and scripts for videotapes written over the last decade. Although it becomes evident in juxtaposing the two that actually what I've been doing is dealing with much the same issues in two different media and within two disciplines, I've sometimes had the impression that there's an element of the talking horse about the theory-wielding artist. If you're a product of art schools, as I am, your image of an artist, even though Conceptual Art may have hit the fan by the time you became a student, was still, at least in part, someone like Jackson Pollock, for whom theory consisted of simply burping in people's faces at the Cedar Bar. (And in my formative art school years the gendered aspect of these images wasn't particularly a question on the table.) Whoever thinks the Romantic image of the artist is dead obviously doesn't circulate through the art world much, and part of its legacy is the residual and unspoken postulate that too much thinking leads straight to bad art.

On the other side of the great theory/practice divide, as an occasional visitor to the world of academic theory one can feel like something of a mascot, invited for your entertainment value and never quite sure if you're really getting it. (Are people laughing behind your back?) Crossing over between two worlds at least has the benefit of allowing an ungenerous critical distance on both—or a sort of *unheimlich*-ness in two homes—which this work must certainly reflect. My approach to cultural theory is very much from the point of view of someone also engaged in producing representations, and one of the main reasons I've kept on writing cultural theory is the sense of profound irritation I've felt at the various critical and feminist theories of representation in circulation. My feeling was that, generally, theorists had little considered the implications of their particular theories for *aesthetic practice*, yet theory was having distinct implications in terms of how audiences received my work. One constantly has the experience, traveling around and screening your work, of being confronted with the most au courant theory of representation and your own deviations from it. I've been berated for having too much closure and thus trafficking in masternarratives; for having too little closure, thereby not enforcing political critique; for not having positive images of women; for not having utopian moments; for constructing fixed identities for my audience; for my work being *too* pleasurable rather than deferring pleasure until after the revolution; for being both overly psychoanalytic and hostile to psychoanalysis; for representing the female body and thus eliciting the dreaded male gaze; for challenging dominant conventions and thus being elitist; and any number of other theory-driven complaints. Sometimes I just cackle silently to myself as I imagine theorists behind the camera, stymied as to what sort of an image their particular master-theory would allow them to produce—or, once produced, who they could possibly compel to watch them.

So to some extent I started writing theory as a defense, in order not to be mute object for someone *else's* theory. But at the same time it was a historically overdetermined move. More than anything, what these scripts and essays reflect is the overwhelming influence of theory on artists and the art world throughout the last fifteen years. When I started art school in San Francisco in 1975, structuralism and semiotics were just starting to have an impact on local artists, particularly in the area of photography. Arriving at art school as a figurative painter, I had, the first semester, a required modern art history class with a charismatic Freudian-Marxist body builder (widely reputed to be heavily into S & M on the side). Whatever the exact nature of this early influence I'm not capable of saying (I should add that I was too intimidated to ever actually speak to this instructor); all I can say is that this particular constellation of concerns—Marx, Freud, the body—were to become, and still remain, the primary concerns of my work. The course itself was an immersion in the radical art of the time—Conceptual Art, Body Art, Performance Art—people who shot and crucified themselves and called it art, Europeans who cut off their penises and claimed it was art, Vito Acconci masturbating in an art gallery for art—I shortly became convinced that painting was an archaic form and groped around with other media. At the same time West Coast feminist artists were strewing art galleries with bloody Tampax and rage, and there were certain imperatives for a woman artist to situate herself in relation to gender and its effects. In the Whitney Museum studio program in New York and at Nova Scotia College of Art where I went to graduate school, Marxism and later poststructuralism were both heavily influential. Mary Kelly, my graduate adviser, and visitors like Claire Johnston, among others, brought psychoanalytic theory and the issues British feminists had been working through to bear on questions of gender. (And perhaps I should add that my own entry to the growing body of feminist theory wasn't through writers like Adrienne Rich or Mary Daly, as it seems to have been for women of my generation who came out of the humanities, but through feminist art history and, later, Marxist-feminist theory.)

I suspect that this formation isn't unusual, and that many artists who came out of similar institutions at the same time felt these same sorts of influences, although they may have taken different forms in their work. I don't want to suggest, however, that theoreticist art or artists are the dominant breed in our time. At professional art gatherings, for example the Society for Photographic Education conferences, the influx of theory generates outraged howls of pain and antitheory guerrilla actions. It's not an uncontested terrain. In any case, and for many reasons—perhaps something to do with the Freudian-Marxist body builder—the kind of transferential relation that I've had with theory may have been stronger than that of other artists with similar formations, but this is work, I think, very much *of* a particular time and place—which I'll be designating throughout the book as postmodernism—rather than some sort of individual inspiration. The pressure that I felt to come to grips with and to master theory, to be able to traffic in a critical as well as an aesthetic vocabulary, was, I think, widely felt.

These video scripts largely concern the attempt to develop an aesthetic language—and a language for video—that deals with the politics of everyday life. In her acknowledgments to her book *Purity and Danger*, after citing an array of professors and anthropologists, Mary Douglas thanks her husband for inspiring her work: "In matters of cleanness his threshold of tolerance is so much lower than my own that he more than anyone else has forced me into taking a stand on the relativity of dirt."[1] This acknowledgment delights me because it sums up something about the way I, too, work, which is primarily out of vexation, or being uncomfortable or bothered. To put it in more theoretical language, what I've worked to develop is a political-aesthetic practice whose inception is the points of tension and contradiction of everyday life. I can offer a sort of origin tale as an example. The genesis of one of my earliest tapes, *Your Money or Your Life* (1982), came when I was walking home through dark Chicago streets at about 3:00 A.M. from a cocktail waitressing job in a jazz club. I suddenly realized that, as on every night I walked home—because I didn't want to squander my tips on a taxi—I was completely terrified. This particular night I simultaneously realized two additional things—first, that this condition of terror, which I was accustomed to taking for granted, was not necessarily a natural condition. The second was that the faces I imagined jumping out of bushes ready to steal my night's tips belonged to black men. This horrified me—my head was full of racist images, which I refused to believe were authored by me, but which somehow had become my lived experience: there they were. After about a year spent working through and scripting this interior imagery, the resulting tape analyzed the current discourse on urban crime as a primary site for the reproduction of racist ideologies, through the suppression of economic motives for crime, and through the hysterical rhetoric and coded speech and images of popular media. One section of the tape simulated a TV game show called "Textual Analysis" in which contestants were asked to analyze a *Time* magazine cover story on urban crime that consistently emphasized the racial aspect of crime while offering absolutely no information on, for example, unemployment among the group—young black men—it singled out as responsible for the urban crime wave. Contestants were also asked to analyze the graphics and rhetoric of the article, which consistently typified black men in language that emphasized jungles and crazed animals—certainly nothing discernibly human. The general theme of the tape was that the rampant individualism, profit motive, and even the violence of urban street crime aren't so very different from the ethos of American Big Business, but that members of the underclass have few opportunities for white-collar crime. Crime is spread across all social classes, but only one class bears the brunt of criminalization.

This tape formulated an aesthetic position I'd follow in subsequent tapes—an essayistic form, a mélange of dramatic and documentary sequences, and an appropriation of forms and idioms of popular culture (there was also a rap song in the tape sung by the mugger about the ways that consumerist ideologies work on the underclass). In ways that are not always so direct or easy to relate, the subsequent tapes too arose from moments of discomfort, *frisson*, pain—moments that I assume are social experiences, rather than completely individual. So, in that I take these sorts of moments as, to varying degrees, typifying a social and historical lived experience at the intersections of social contradictions —racial, sexual, economic, gendered, national, and bodily—this work describes the role of the artist as a bearer, an effect, of those contradictions, whose task is to read and report on them. The discourse of the tapes—their intellectual work—is to produce theories about the ways in which what seems, subjectively, most private and freely chosen is structural, economic, and political, and actually chooses us.

One thing that I can say clearly chose me was a postmodern aesthetics, and reading the essays against the scripts will make clear—as it becomes clear to me in retrospect—that what both are engaged in is staking out and producing a left postmodernism in theory and aesthetics. What postmodernism has meant to me is the possibility of a popular political art, and the first essay, "Repossessing Popular Culture," was written to outline in more general and theoretical terms the aesthetic position of *Your Money or Your Life*. To a large extent this aesthetic was also a reaction against the political art of the time, which tended to be, I thought, self-righteous, humorless, and pietistic. While I don't intend to hold these tapes up as examples of a successful solution to the problem of a popular political aesthetic (my fascination with theory has definitely limited the audiences for my tapes), each, in different ways, grapples with the problem of how to be popular and *critical*, popular without, at the same time, being simpleminded. What I've worked to resist, in each case, are what I believe have been simplistic politicized aesthetic practices — positive images (whether of women or labor or minorities), correct images, humorless didacticism (I suppose I've tried for funny didacticism instead), ridiculing the stupidity of political enemies (well, usually), political piety, and the elitist antipopular tactics of the avant-garde. This work takes the position that there's no place to speak from *outside* dominant forms and ideologies: from outside commodification, from the natural body, or from the vanguard. And on the contentious subject of positive images, we should note that this is now a favored representational mode of a self-congratulatory and socially obfuscating liberal entertainment industry. There are probably more African-American women judges in one week of prime-time television than in the entire American judiciary — a simulacrum of racial equality absent the demand to actually achieve it.

In theory, too, what ties these essays together is the position that the task of a politically engaged theory is to articulate the possibilities of a popular political resistance and contestation, taking one's direction from existing political movements and struggles. What these essays largely attempt to do is intervene in current theoretical debates to artic-ulate the places where theory falls prey to antipopular moments, retrenchments, and displacements — where theory produces represen-tations of a political terrain that work to defeat the possibilities of con-testation: in the repeated tendency toward modernist aestheticism in both left and feminist theories of representation and aesthetic practices ("Repossessing Popular Culture," "Looks Good on Paper"); the tropes of misogyny in popular representations of postcolonialism ("Phantom Twitchings"); the coded traces of class interests and enforcement of bourgeois bodily norms in the feminist antipornography movement ("Reading *Hustler*"). What these essays also attempt to hold in the bal-ance is that theory here means first-world theory. What I've attempted is a symptomatic reading of the tropes of first-world interest — the way first-world aesthetics and its foreign policy uncannily echo each other in "Aesthetics and Foreign Policy," the question of why psychoanalytic film theory limits its account of castration to the individual subject in "Phantom Twitchings" — and a symptomatic reading of the repetitions and preoccupations of current first-world theory. What does it mean to dwell so repeatedly on "the popular," "the subject," "the margin," representation, even "pornography," when these preoccupations can be read, symptomatically, as retrenchments against crises of power and authority in other spheres?

The theoretical movement of both the essays and the tapes is largely out of and through Marxism, toward an interplay of Marxism and fem-inism, and in the end, back to Marx himself — but Marx after feminism, after psychoanalysis, and after the collapse of Communism. These essays also arise from a kind of knee-jerk resistance to critical orthodoxies. As a feminist and a feminist artist, one of my aversions is the climate of orthodoxy and the litmus tests around issues of representation within feminism. Part of my orneriness about it comes from having been made an occasional target of it, particularly over my tape *A Man's Woman*, which attempts to raise the difficult question, "Why is the Right so popular with women while feminism's popularity declines rapidly?" When it was screened at the American Film Institute, it prompted a walkout by some offended feminists in the audience, and the lack of willingness to openly debate the issue was chilling. (I will say, as a loyal feminist and leftist, that one sometimes gets the uneasy feeling that when the Left and feminists do come to power, show trials of the heterodox will shortly follow.)

The influence of Foucault also puts into question for me the easy assumption of identities and identity politics. *Ecstasy Unlimited* looks at the way sexual identity gets produced in relation to forms of power and surveillance (this tape was written in 1983–84, before the impact of AIDS on sexual ideology was widespread). Issues around the status of identities and the critiques of essentialism have also put into question for me many of the assumptions of American feminism, and the political consequences of its focus on victimization. The essay on *Hustler* magazine, which I fear may be read as the complete abandonment of feminism, is for me anything but. In much the same way that *Your Money or Your Life* was an attempt to work through the way that racism becomes imbricated into private lived experience, the *Hustler* essay (along with *"Ecstasy Unlimited"*) attempts to work through how sexuality is constructed and lived. Posing the question, "Why am I so disgusted and offended by *Hustler* magazine?" necessarily involved putting into question many of the tenets of American feminism—which both legitimate, and in fact, *demand* those responses of disgust and offense—by putting them into a historical and political context. My response to the porn debates is also conditioned by the fact that I also work at producing representations, and ones that aspire to political effects. If images *did* so simply and immediately lead directly to actions, as antiporn feminists claim, if reception of images *could* be guaranteed to have particular effects, the work of political artists would certainly be a lot easier. It's not at all clear to me why the pornography industry along with the consciousness captains of consumer capitalism are so much better at mobilizing fantasy than we are; I only know that I don't particularly want to be part of a movement that sees its task as crushing fantasy and patrolling desire.

Given the time period in which I've been engaged in producing representation, and given that my work has often lifted (and "refunctioned") the most suspect, most pleasurable elements of popular culture — narrative, porn images, stereotypes — one of the first objects of my critical ire as a theorist, was, of course, Laura Mulvey's visual pleasure essay, which probably more than any other single work has shaped the discourses I've worked within.[2] My objection to it was that its critique and its call to destroy the pleasures of narrative film leave open only the possibility of a modernist and elitist avant-garde countercinema as a political antidote to the power of the male gaze — it seems to suggest, as I say somewhere, luring the masses to *Riddles of the Sphinx* as the only permissible form of feminist representational politics.

The attempt to rethink some of Mulvey's positions informs most of these essays in one way or another — the suggestion of avant-garde practices as correctives, its ahistorical account of castration, and, in the later work — the *Hustler* essay and *Marx: The Video* — the foundational theory of the male gaze. It would be worth it, first of all, to situate Mulvey historically, to keep in mind that her theory of the gaze was in relation to a historically specific period of filmmaking, classical narrative cinema, and to a particular organization of the industry, and finally that it was anchored in a particular form of diegetic organization — the male hero who becomes the ego ideal for the male spectator. So it would be possible to detail changes in the industry — a greater number of women directors, producers, and writers and an increased number of independently made films, for example — as well as changes in narrative form and structure, the production of different sorts of plots and images, and the recent trend toward the sexualization of the male body, to put into question whether Mulvey's theory is still viable in relation to current cinema and aesthetic practices.

This seems to me an important project. Feminist film theory has produced many challenges to Mulvey within its own discipline — the thorny issue of the female spectator, along with, for instance, questions such as whether the male gaze is necessarily aligned with sadism or whether it may be, instead, masochism that's the structuring fantasy.[3] But outside film theory the term "male gaze" (along with its companion term "objectification") has filtered down through aesthetic theory and practice, through feminist art history and criticism, even to some extent into the culture at large, as omnipresent theoretical givens. One finds everywhere, even in feminists who are virulently antipsychoanalytic, the reliance on some version of "the male gaze" as a cornerstone of a feminist aesthetics; the male gaze seems also to have become imbricated in general theoretical usage with a Foucauldian theory of panoptic vision to produce a theoretical brick wall of a monolithic, determinate male gaze.

The question raised for me is whether this represents the field of male power in such a way as to simply naturalize that power. To some extent, the gaze becomes monolithic because the dialectical basis of Mulvey's argument gets repressed in its common usage — what gets left behind, outside film theory, is castration. Whether you see that metaphorically or psychopolitically, or whether you're orthodox in your adherence to the Oedipal narrative, what has to be retained, I believe, is the dialectic of the gaze — that it doesn't originate in male power but in male fear, or repressed knowledge, of disempowerment and loss. So the male gaze isn't simply a triumphal exercise of power, it's compensatory; it is not simply masterful but also pathetic. Men may control the industry, but they don't *have* the phallus. Even Mulvey, while certainly not unpsychoanalytic, sometimes seems to conclude that the gaze actually accomplishes its mission — which would be to suppose that repression *can* be complete and successful. And this would be one place to hope that there *is* a political metaphor to psychoanalysis, to argue, with Freud, that repression can never completely succeed.

The widespread dissemination throughout feminism of gaze theory has had profound consequences in constructing aesthetic theories and corresponding practices based on the gaze as determinate of all meaning. So, for example, Janet Wolff in her book *Feminine Sentences* poses the question, "Can women's bodies be the site of feminist cultural politics?" — a question prompted by the theoretical assumption that women's bodies are inevitably appropriated as an object for the male gaze, whatever the intentions of the woman involved.[4] Wolff gives an example of a protest by a group of Dublin women over a particular swimming area, in which, to protest male domination of the beach, the women invaded the area, took off their bathing suits and swam nude. Wolff concludes that the protest was ineffectual because it invited male lechery, captured in a newspaper photograph of the action in which men and boys can be seen staring and laughing at the nude women. The conclusion that the protest was ineffectual is clearly theory-driven — derived from the theoretical premise that the male gaze is determinate of meaning. So the deployment of theory works here to foreclose the possibility of the popular struggle these women have engaged in. For Wolff, the leering men have won — a priori — and the women's challenge to them is written off as political naiveté, as if the job of the feminist theorist is to rebuke the naiveté of the nontheoretical classes.

Given this sort of deployment of the theory of the gaze I'd argue that one of its effects has been to deprive feminists, and women who pay attention to feminist theory, *of* a possible critical aesthetics of the body; what we've been deprived of is a theory of female resistance — a way of theorizing the cracks, fissures, the *failures* of the male gaze. Wolff, in her conclusion to the essay, does suggest one possibility for a critical feminist politics of the body — modern dance. I don't think it's only because I'm severely bored by modern dance that this seems to me an ineffective solution. If academic feminist critics invariably turn to the most rarefied forms of high culture as political correctives, where does that leave the majority of women? And I'd add that the assumption of the gaze as determinate and all-powerful has contributed to the lack of attention to class in feminist theory (discussed at length in chapter 8, "Reading *Hustler*," which attempts a reading of pornography not anchored in a theory of the male gaze). Treating the male gaze monolithically neglects the fact that not all men do have equal social power. In much the same way, looking to high culture for a feminist aesthetics seems designed to protect feminism as a preserve of the academic elite.

A number of women artists and performers — both in the art world and in popular culture — *are*, in practice, creating a resistant politics of the body that ignores feminist dicta around the issue of the gaze, risking the stereotypical identification of woman and body to counter the grip of misogyny over bodily meaning. There are two categories of work I find interesting in this context. The first produces an excess of visibility around the body rather than attempting to veil it, subvert the gaze, or deny pleasure — this is work by women who, at the same time, refuse any position of subjection. I'm thinking of, say, performance artist Annie Sprinkle, part of whose repertoire includes lying spread-eagled on the stage and inviting the audience to look into her vagina using a speculum. Karen Finley's work, more confrontational than Sprinkle's, also uses similar tactics of inviting looking rather than coyly refusing it. Neither of these women assume that the male power to look is such a determinate power as to dictate the meaning and reception of their work. Rather, I think their position is that through engaging with the male gaze and through producing excess rather than prohibition they can throw a wrench into any sort of comfort zone that scopophilic looking affords, and that male looking, in itself, isn't the final word on anything. To engage the male gaze is not automatically to be annihilated or subjected by it.

But I think that some of the most interesting examples of a politics of the body are in popular culture, by women who in one way or another say "fuck you" to both the male gaze and its theoreticians. Madonna gets raised in this context, but I'm thinking more of female comediennes like Judy Tenuta or Roseanne Arnold. Both fall into a category feminist academics have lately ventured into — the possibility of an aesthetics of the female grotesque.[5] But feminist academics too often seem to look to high culture for their examples. Both Tenuta and Arnold are full of rage against men, both turn conventions of the proper on their head, both use parodic techniques to indict and invert hierarchies of gender, and both are enormously popular, which—I suppose it's graceless to say—is more than can be said about feminist theory these days.

Female rage and discontent are more and more pervasive in the culture at the same time that feminism has lost its popular audience. These elements are up for grabs politically, open to articulation by the Left, the Right, and the ultra-Right. There's some evidence that they're being most effectively articulated by consumerism, deploying psychographically based market research techniques. *American Demographics* reports that when the McCann-Ericson ad agency wanted to find out why Raid roach spray outsold Combat insecticide disks in certain markets, their research revealed that, not surprisingly, female consumers see roaches as men. "A lot of their feelings about the roach were very similar to the feelings that they had about the men in their lives," says marketing executive Paula Drillman. The article explains: "The act of spraying roaches and seeing them die was satisfying to this frustrated, powerless group. Setting out Combat disks may have been less trouble, but it just didn't give them the same feeling. 'These women wanted control,' Drillman says. 'They used the spray because it allowed them to participate in the kill.' "[6]

It's a long way from modern dance to roach spray, and it's the task of a popular feminist aesthetics to bridge the gap. If we don't, someone else will. The squeamishness about consumer culture, popular representation, popular sex, and the body leaves the field open for guys in suits: the Right and the businessmen. This tendency to turn to high culture and high theory for political answers ignores what's going on in front of us. Roseanne scratching her crotch while singing the national anthem at a San Diego Padres game, a parodic gesture that invited presidential excoriation by George Bush—isn't this a female politics of the body that refuses the name of feminism? It's interesting that both Roseanne Arnold and Karen Finley have attracted governmental condemnation, as has *Hustler* publisher Larry Flynt on any number of occasions—all on "taste" issues. Something *is* at stake in these debates over representation, something *is* at stake in enforcing bourgeois bodily norms and conventions—and in developing contestatory aesthetic practices and strategies that work from the popular but, unlike current popular culture, work toward resistance of the dominant.

CHAPTER 2

Repossessing Popular Culture

IN SEPTEMBER 1990 the *New York Times*, ever the cultural augur, announced the death of postmodernism after a decade's reign over the art world, noting as evidence the exhaustion of pomo's favored gestures of "stereotypes, repetition and media-derived experience," then pounding the nail into the coffin with its assessment that "appropriation and pastiche seem old hat."[1] While the haunted souls of the art world may have moved on to new and better idioms — "spirituality," suspects the man from the *Times* — perhaps we should interrupt the eulogy to point out that the corpse is still twitching. If you see postmodernism as having been reflected in the art world rather than created there you might look a bit further afield than West Broadway before announcing, so precipitously, its demise. And so if the aesthetic realm is not simply an autonomous sphere of passing fads and aesthetic tics, but is somewhat more intertwined with what is sometimes called "everyday life" — whether knowingly or not — the *Times* might be just a bit more attentive to the fact that the sorts of practices of appropriation and repetition it insists on reducing to art-world style *continue* to typify the signifying practices of so many other spheres, from mass culture to official political discourse itself. You don't have to be a lit crit or an art worker these days to be preoccupied with the circulation of signs whose meanings are subject to contestation — you could be Roger Ailes or even the Ayatollah Khomeini. And this should be of particular interest to those engaged in formulating a contestatory culture, as I would argue that any strategy for a cultural-political practice has to take its direction from the structure of which it is a moment (it is provisional), and that what postmodernism has to tell us about oppositional practices is that being ahead of one's time, or avant-garde, is definitely passé. The purpose of this essay, then, is to outline the structural possibilities offered for an oppositional cultural practice at the present moment: to assess the possibilities given within the current conjuncture — which I'll be describing as postmodern — for cultural politics. Part of this argument entails describing why it is that the possible moment of a political and contestatory *modernism* — or any cultural politics that seeks some ground of autonomy, whether outside the present, outside the commodity, or, arguably, from outside dominant modes of representation — is no longer viable.

Brecht coined the phrase "functional transformation" (*Umfunktionierung*) to convey his position that intellectuals and artists shouldn't merely supply the production process but, rather, should attempt to transform it, along the lines of existing political struggle.[2] The fact is that capitalist culture is capable of assimilating even the most "revolutionary" sorts of themes without ever putting its own existence and continuation into question. Brecht dismissed as "hacks" and "revolutionary hacks" those artists who maintain an unwitting complicity with the political forms they aspire to transform by continuing to supply "new effects or sensations" for public consumption and entertainment, innovations that are immediately lapped up by the dominant and dominating culture in a feeding frenzy of the new. The sort of practice Brecht was suggesting, transforming what is already there—what I'll call "refunctioning"—should be quite recognizable to us here in what is known as late capitalism—or even more appropriately, media capitalism—because it seems so similar to what has, in fact, been a dominant cultural and discursive strategy in the production of social meaning for at least the last decade. This sort of practice gets described or denounced in numerous ways, but contrary to the Brechtian expectation, it now seems to make its appearance all over the political spectrum. However, let me start out by describing an early and paradigmatic example of refunctioning as a form of contestation before getting into its reappearance, in a seemingly apolitical guise, as the privileged signifying practice of postmodernism.

Toward the end of the seventies, almost overnight, it seemed, nearly every stop sign on the north side of Chicago was transformed by local women's groups (presumably at night and with stealth) to read "STOP RAPE," by the addition of the word "RAPE" spray-painted in reflective white paint directly under the word "STOP." The signs would remain in this altered state for a short time, until the city sent work crews out to obliterate the word "RAPE" with red paint, thus terminating the sign's brief career as a tool of feminist agitation and returning it to its prosaic function in traffic control. Sporadically, midnight spray-painting campaigns would renew the ongoing struggle between the city and women's groups for this highly visible site of address with its guaranteed audience, but the city's resources triumphed and there are very few STOP RAPE signs to be found anymore. In the mideighties, though, this same tactic was taken up by another movement (which continues to deploy it to this day), whose members affixed to stop signs *printed* stickers that read "U.S. INVOLVEMENT IN NICARAGUA" or "U.S. SLAUGHTER IN CENTRAL AMERICA." These stickers, designed expressly for stop signs (and apparently with very strong glue), transform the interpellation of the signs to read "STOP U.S. IN-VOLVEMENT IN NICARAGUA" or "STOP U.S. SLAUGHTER IN CENTRAL AMERICA." (Historians of left aesthetics will want to note the introduction of mechanical reproduction into this particular form of agitation.)

Using the term "interpellation" here deliberately invokes Louis

Althusser's contention that the mechanism of all ideology is the inter-pellation, or hailing, of individuals as ideological subjects.[3] To cite the example of the bland and ubiquitous stop sign as an instance of ideolog-ical interpellation may seem eccentric (its elimination is not on even the most ultraleft program so far as I know, since even ultraleftists in this day and age fear gridlock; however, the intrepid free-enterprise anar-chists of the Libertarian party have, in fact, announced their opposition to the stop sign).[4] But the STOP of the stop sign does uncannily echo Althusser's own ironic demonstration of the role of "recognition" in the process of constituting ideological subjects: the policeman who yells, "Hey, you there!" to the individual who cannot fail to *recognize* herself as the subject of the interpellation and automatically, guiltily, turns around. To simply stop at a stop sign then — a constant and automatic act for those of us with private transport — is to recognize oneself as the subject of the interpellation and to be ("always already") engaged in an ongoing process of transformation, from mere individual to legal-juridical subject. This example of the stop sign is even more apt in that it makes grimly clear the inseparability of ideological interpellation and agencies of state repression. As anyone who has ever been caught run-ning a stop sign discovers, the entire array of what Althusser calls the Repressive State Apparatuses stands ready to enforce this interpellation should one fail to heed it. (And in Chicago it really is the *entire* array: periodically reports emerge of traffic violators routinely subjected to strip searches by particularly zealous defenders of the peace; in Los An-geles, enforcement includes savage beatings by armed, crazed bands of police-thugs.)

This struggle over the (stop) sign exemplifies political contestation precisely at the level of ideological interpellation. These anonymous agitational acts of appropriation and transformation enact a struggle over, and within, an ideological terrain, between a dominant discourse (Althusser regards the legal system as a part of both the Ideological and the Repressive State Apparatuses) and an oppositional discourse. To view a stop sign as something worth struggling over may seem politi-cally unambitious, but there are two interesting implications here for a theory of a left popular culture. First, the prior interpellation, the "STOP" of state power, is mere "raw material." It derives its meaning only in relation to its articulation within a particular discourse, and in specific relation to the other elements of that discourse. It doesn't have a preassigned, essential meaning, and, moreover, its meaning can't be reduced to an expression of its class or national origins. The second im-plication, then, is that these raw materials can be appropriated and transformed by oppositional forces in order to express antagonisms and resistance to dominant discourses — a process also suggested by the phrase *disarticulation-rearticulation*, which occurs in the writing of the Argentinean Marxist, Ernesto Laclau.[5] In Laclau's terms, the stop sign is disarticulated from the discourse of which it was formerly a part, and is rearticulated to a competing or antagonistic discourse. The important point here is that *any* of the materials of dominant culture can be subject to this process.

But why insist that this sort of refunctioning practice is either typically postmodern or quintessentially Brechtian? Or to ask the question in a more ass-backwards way, what is the break signaled by the "post" of postmodernism a break from? As the *Times* points out, an engagement with "media-derived experience" is typical of postmodernism. If we rephrase this as "an engagement with the experience of dominant culture," perhaps the point becomes clearer. What the *Times* fails to note is that while this new attention to media may describe the sort of historical turning point, specifically the *rejection*, that Pop Art and its postmodern successors marked from the modernist formal preoccupations of the previous part of the century, this localized account doesn't particularly weigh the sense of *shock* that all forays of both mass culture *and* mass-produced objects into high art have created throughout the century — from Synthetic Cubism, Surrealism, the work of Duchamp, on through Pop Art to the present. Mass culture crossover, or, in Brecht's terms, transforming what is already there — and what is more always already there than the media (now more than ever)? — always threatened to throw into disarray the founding assumptions of the traffic in high culture, from the sanctity of individual authorship — and all that it guarantees for the market in cultural objects — to the class divisions inherent in the spatial and monetary distinctions between mass and high culture (if not the spatial and monetary distinctions between their different audiences).

To think about why it is that mass culture so troubles high art it might be useful to look at the term "mass" itself, which, whether standing alone or paired with its buddy, "culture," is a term situated in contradiction. It carries sedimented and contrary implications, alluding as it does to that dubious entity "the people" — a presence coded variously: from the pejorative connotations of "low" or "vulgar" to the suggestion of a positive political and social force — a people acting together in solidarity, as in the *levée en masse* of the French revolution.[6] In that this current and contradictory usage became fully available in the mid-nineteenth century, with industrialization and the birth of modern class society in western Europe, the term arrives clearly burdened with a weighty historical residue: not only the evocation of the urban proletariat, but also, then, implicitly the proletariat's conditions of formation — that is,

the economic ascendancy of the bourgeoisie and its attendant consolidation of political power. There are two things to say about this: first,
the terms "mass" and, concomitantly, "mass culture" have a particular
set of connotations specific to capitalist society that can't be evaded. (Or
rather, the evasion is symptomatic, indicative of the sort of genial
ahistoricism practiced by cultural conservatives of the *New Criterion*
stripe.) Secondly, arguments, positions, and theories about mass *culture*
are inevitably coded ways of talking about class.

These two points might shed a different light on the last decade's
flurry of theoretical (and artistic) interest and investedness in popular
culture, as well. Theory is never autonomous: critical discourse is not
only a site of production of cultural meanings, but is itself a product
of the conditions it theorizes; transformations outside theory deserve
as much serious attention as is traditionally paid to the internal transformations and minutiae of intellectual history. The exponential
growth of mass culture *studies* has occupied the same theoretical moment as what, in the decade prior to the collapse of Communism, was
commonly referred to as the "crisis in Marxism" or the "crisis on the
Left." The conjuncture of these two discursive spaces has a kind of
poignancy, assuming a historically mediated reading of the term
"mass": it connotes, in retrospect, something of a political denouement,
with two historical moments as, roughly, bookends, or mirror images.
In the first is the emergence of the urban proletariat, the seeds of the
working-class movement, and socialist theory — all the previously
mentioned sedimentation of the word "mass" — which marked the
opening up of a determinate political space. In the second moment, that
of the last decade, post-Marxism (as if anticipating the events of
1989–91) edges out the working class as the "privileged subject" of history and the anticipated agent of social transformation (not so coincidentally, just as union busting, declining wages, and capital flight
were the dominant economic trends of the eighties). Here we find the
emergence of mass *culture* as the privileged subject of left academia,
hand in hand with the loss of any sort of previous assurance about what
might be called the political subject, and, with the closing down of that
earlier set of political possibilities, a groping and stumbling through the
murk of the present toward new political forms.

The last decade's theoretical preoccupation with popular culture
marked a major shift from a period when mass culture was either not
worth discussing or only worth denouncing. Whether it was mass cultural forms or contents being indicted, whether it was "kitsch" or "de-
based means-ends rationality" being dismissed, the practices of popular
culture seemed incapable of being adequately theorized in the modernist era. Equally, mass culture content was banished from high art style

during the modernist heyday. The acceptability of introducing content from mass culture into high art has been an art-world given at least since Pop Art, which might be said to have terminated modernist cultural hegemony. The work of artists like Cindy Sherman, Dara Birnbaum, David Salle, and so many others working in the area of what the *Times* calls "media-derived experience" is familiar enough not to require elaborate description here. This cultural transformation—the crossing of the previously uncrossable chasm between high and mass culture, evidenced in this keen and nervous attention to mass culture in the current production of both high culture and high theory—is a decisive feature of the postmodern, and is decisively different from the treatment of popular culture during the reign of modernism.

By invoking modernism's relation to the popular here, I want to begin to sketch out a sort of preliminary periodization of approaching the popular. Its current approachability—the inundation of scholarly books on the subject, the plethora of conferences and journals, a rewritten canon within universities, *and* the focus on popular forms on the left and in the art world—this burgeoning approachability is not only characteristic of *postmodernism*, but seems to indicate a certain urgency to theorization in this historical configuration.

If theory isn't autonomous, but there is a degree of interpenetration of theory and the object it theorizes, then transformations in the object itself (say, the field of culture) are what make possible transformations in our knowledge of that object. Peter Burger's *Theory of the Avant-Garde* offers a corollary: he argues that only "the full unfolding of the constituent elements in a field" makes possible "an adequate cognition of that field."[7] A further corollary is that these new theoretical developments always cart along with them a rewritten history: the conditions that allowed Marx to theorize capital—the emergence of the urban proletariat, the universal commodification of labor, and the reduction of difference to the common denominator of exchange value— simultaneously allowed precapitalist economic formations to be construed. Precursors of present developments only come into view at certain moments; they're discovered in retrospect rather than being already known. This would account for the last decades's spate of retheorizations of modernism (Burger's book being one); modernism comes into view differently through the emergence of postmodernism.

An onslaught of theorization works perhaps like a symptom: its etiology can be uncovered by working backward from its given components to discover its presuppositions. "The task is . . . simply to discover, in respect to a useless idea and a pointless action, the past situation in which the idea was justified and the action served a purpose," as Freud writes. One presupposition of intensified theorization about popular culture has been suggested: the shift from a refusal to an embrace of the popular in theoretical discourse marks a break between modernism and postmodernism. We might then, speculatively, surmise that the "purpose" of the "symptom" can be found in the paradigm of *transition* and the compensatory structures this puts into play. Evidence for a link between theorization and transition can also be found in Michael Taussig's *The Devil and Commodity Fetishism in South America*.[8] Based on Taussig's fieldwork, the book details the appearance of a particular set of mythic beliefs, or theorizations, which have arisen "at a particularly crucial and sensitive point of time in historical development" in distinct areas of rural South America. Regions of both Colombia and Bolivia are undergoing the transformation from what is often referred to as "traditional society" to "modern" or "industrial society" — from peasant-cultivator, use-value-based societies to societies of landless wage-laborers based on exchange-value. Local peasants have become proletarianized, often through violence and appropriation of land; they are driven to seek employment for wages in the sugar plantations of Colombia and tin mines of Bolivia.

An explanatory mythology has arisen independently in both these societies based on the figure of the devil, who is invoked "as part of the process of maintaining or increasing production." In Colombia, certain workers, it is believed, have entered into secret pacts with the devil to increase their production and earn more money. These contracts, though, are said to ultimately destroy those who enter into them, for devil's money is barren: if spent on such capital goods as land or livestock the land will become sterile and the animals will sicken and die. In Bolivia, Indians create work-group rituals to the devil, whom they believe to be the true owner of the tin mines. Although the devil is assigned the central role in sustaining production, he is seen as a "gluttonous spirit bent on destruction and death." In both Bolivia and Colombia, while the devil is held to be the mainstay of production, this production is believed to be ultimately destructive of life. (And note that where the mysterious workings of capital are concerned how similar is the content of these myths — or theorizations — and the quasi-populist anti-big-business sentiments that permeate our own popular culture: our ambivalent fascination with devilish figures like Donald Trump, J. R. Ewing, and other assorted moguls, oil barons, and robber-tycoons.)

Late capitalism is not so much a postindustrial society as one marked by the complete industrialization of all segments of society.[9] Even the most "advanced" economic system, however, is composed of a discontinuous series of structures that develop unevenly — they are asynchronous. The area of high culture, for example, lags far behind, say, industry in capital penetration and mechanization, though these days we see all sectors subject to an increased penetration of capital and heightened mechanization. In the art world this sometimes appears as style: it's not much of a stretch to read the industrialized elements in the work of Warhol, the Minimalist sculptors, or the current *succès de poseur*, Mark Kostabi—to name but a few forward thinkers who have managed to merge Fordism and high culture—as the distant rumblings of the infrastructure around the perimeter of circled wagons erected by high culture, with its traditional disdainful autonomy from the hoi polloi and their dirty little assembly lines. Elements of older modes of production coexist with anticipations of future modes of production, with the result that different areas in any social order, are, at any given moment, at quite different stages of development.

This suggests that observations or theories about one sphere of one social formation at a particular developmental stage might aptly be applied to a different sphere of a distinct social formation at a comparable stage of development. So to return to Taussig's fieldwork, a structurally similar relationship might exist between an outbreak of *theory* and social transformation in two dissimilar social formations. Taussig's fieldwork on the mediation of oppositions found in devil beliefs in South America—a set of practices at first glance quite distant from Western academic popular culture studies—might offer a paradigm for understanding current theorizing on popular culture as, in Taussig's words, the mediation "between two radically distinct ways of apprehending or evaluating the world of persons and things."

Like Michael Taussig, I'm concerned with tracing a *transition* between two points: a transition of industrialization and capital penetration. The transition outlined here, however, is in this social formation, and specifically in the sphere of culture: we might describe it as the historical moment running roughly from the point where Walter Benjamin notes the erosion of "aura" in painting as a correlate of proliferating photographic technology, to a current point, postmodernism, which has often been defined, following Guy Debord, as the complete commodification of the image sphere.[10]

In Debord's argument, the "spectacle" is the commodified form of the image. Like the commodity, it disguises what it really is—relationships between persons and classes—into an appearance of the objective and the natural. The spectacle is the capitalist colonization and monopolization of the image; it subjugates people to its monopoly of appearance and proclaims: "That which appears is good, that which is good appears."

So while for Althusser the nature of ideology is, following Jacques Lacan, *specular*, mirrorlike—the interpellated subjects recognize them-

selves in a mirrorlike relationship with dominant ideology — for Debord ideology is *spectacular*: the spectacle is "the existing order's unin-
terrupted discourse about itself, its laudatory monologue." The privileged ideological form is, though, in both cases, the representation.

We hear an awful lot about the politics of representation these days — so
much that one might be forgiven the impression that the representation
is now the sole locale of the appearance of the political. One way of accounting for this new theoretical fixation is Debord's self-reflexive
point that it is precisely that the spectacle has now become the universal
category of society as a whole that both allows and provokes his own
understanding of it as a category. But again, contemporary developments like these never arrive unescorted, but are accompanied by a rewritten history. This new awareness of the status of representation and
its new approachability inevitably raise the question of its previous un-
availability to analysis and of the *cordon sanitaire* erected around the
popular in the modernist era. So postmodernism, it appears, not only
allows, but dictates, a deconstruction of the binarism upon which modernism was enacted and of the problem of value that programmed the
high culture/mass culture split.

The most interesting question in regard to the binary opposition
high culture/mass culture is, What is or was the ideological investment
in its maintenance? That the dominant stylistic gesture of the postmodern is the increasing interpenetration of high culture and mass culture seems to indicate the attenuation of that ideological function, both
institutionally and within individual cultural texts. Dismantling its
ideological scaffold affords a rereading of modernism as constituted and
produced solely within that split, and existing only so long as it could
keep its Other — the popular, the low, the regional, and the impure — at
bay. We might then, from this new historical vantage point, redefine
modernism as the ideological necessity of erecting and maintaining exclusive standards of the literary and artistic against the constant threat
of incursion or contamination, and the partial success of this project as
what is generally given to us as the unity, modernism. What didn't conform was excluded from consideration. Without the binarism high/low
in place — a displacement that can be staged only after the emergence of
the postmodern — it's unclear whether modernism as such ever existed
at all. (The ongoing project of feminist art history to provide an alternative account of the period is a simultaneous assault, and if the politiciza-
tion of the literary canon by multiculturalists is any precedent, the academic field of modern art history is also going to have some rough
waters ahead.)

It's pretty difficult to avoid the social implications of the terms high and low. If the adventures of the high/low culture dialectic are read against the dialectic of social classes, the narrative of transgression and suppression, rebellion and restoration that emerges suggests that the "political unconscious" lurking beneath the veneer of culture might not be unrelated to the larger ongoing drama of struggles between social groups engendered by class society. At roughly the same moment at which we can mark the emergence of the "modern" in the visual arts, the *Salon des Refusés* of 1863, where Manet showed his *Olympia* — a contemporary prostitute painted in the pose of Titian's *Venus of Urbino* — at just about that same moment Matthew Arnold was earnestly erecting barricades *against* such incursions in his proclamation — the founding statement of modern academic criticism — that criticism should deal only "with the best that is known and thought in the world." This symbolic Arnold-Manet one-on-one set the stage for a century of contestation, not only between critical discourse and the "artistic text," but within the field of artistic practices, as well. Throughout the period we know as modernism, work that was greeted with "shock" (or work that fulfilled its avant-gardist mission) was work that introduced elements of the popular, the low, or elements untransformed by the artist's hand into the temple of Art: Synthetic Cubism, which used newspapers and wallpaper in painting to destroy painting as a "unified field"; Duchamp's readymades (including the infamous signed urinal); and the series of shocks and aesthetic aggressions gleefully administered by Dada and Surrealism, to name a few examples.

Clement Greenberg, the preeminent American theoretician of modernism, dismissed what he called "kitsch," which he opposed to the true "avant-garde"; he dismissed Synthetic Cubism to champion Analytic Cubism; and he termed Surrealism a "reactionary tendency" for introducing "outside" subject matter. Greenberg's teleology of art, reflected in his deployment of terms such as "reactionary" and "avant-garde," decreed a triumph of the pure over mixed parentage: it is cultural miscegenation that excited his shrillest and most dictatorial denunciations. He was still fighting these dragons throughout the sixties and well into the seventies. When confronted with proto-postmodernism in the form of Minimalism, Greenberg condemned it as "lacking aesthetic surprise," and he hoped to deal the death blow to Pop Art by dismissing it as "Novelty Art."[11] In culture rewritten as a binary field where quality battles crassness and the rightful inheritor contests the interloper, what else is being preserved, enforced? Yet in spite of Greenberg's protestations, the Other always threatened to close in, as if he were James Bond trapped in one of those tiny rooms where the walls are slowly closing together, and there he stands, heroically, pectorals straining, holding them apart by sheer muscle power mere seconds away from being squashed like a bug.

Even in recent serious retheorizations of modernism, the opposition high culture/mass culture remains in place. In order to posit the existence of this aesthetic field at all, the same exclusions seem necessarily to operate. Peter Burger's *Theory of the Avant-Garde* attempts to rewrite the unity, modernism, into two opposing fields: "aestheticism" and its superior rival, "the avant-garde." Burger's first point is that the emergence of aestheticism and its challenge by the avant-garde are developments in the *institutional* status of art and that the styles and contents of individual works — traditionally the site of art-historical endeavors — can only be understood through the mediation of the institution of art. His next move is to attempt to reclaim the political radicality of the term "avant-garde" against critics like Greenberg who collapse it unproblematically into modernism. For Burger, "aestheticism," emerging in the late nineteenth century, denotes art that claims autonomy from the concerns of everyday life: form transpires to reflect this autonomy, becoming the sole content of art. In Burger's narrative, the avant-garde movements of the twenties began to question this autonomy and rebel against the enforced social impotence of art determined by its institutional status. But their move to reinsert art into the praxis of daily life failed, and Burger derides what he calls "post-avant-garde art" (singling out Warhol as the baddest bad guy) because this work revives techniques and procedures invented with political motives by the real avant-garde and now cynically appropriates them for a renewed aestheticism.

Interestingly, though, Burger manages to locate popular culture exactly where the Frankfurt School did, even while pointing out that the relation between high and mass culture (or in his words, "serious" and "pulp") is not adequately thematized in their writings. He recognizes that Adorno's separation of high culture and mass culture passively accepts the separation that is established within, and establishes, the institutions and marketplaces of art and literature, yet Burger, too, upholds the distinction in his own dismissals of the popular. His only direct attention to mass culture yields a somewhat familiar point about the relation between the development of photographic technology and the end of representation in painting (another example of the way in which high art within this period was forever running scared from the popular).

Another interesting attempt at revision of modernist history is Mary Kelly's "Re-Viewing Modernist Criticism."[12] Like Peter Burger, Kelly upholds modernist categories of the popular even while attempting to dismantle modernist ideology. She argues that modernist critical discourse functions to construct, out of disparate art practices, the category of the *artistic text*, the purpose of which is to express the essential creativity of the artistic subject. In painting, it does this by conjuring evidence of the human hand, of human action, to mark the subjectivity of the artist in artistic gesture: "It is above all the artistic gesture which constitutes, at least metaphorically, the imaginary signifier of 'Modern Art.' " The *work* of modernist critical discourse is to recover artistic subjecthood from essentially abstract work, and in a form that is fundamentally identical with the category of the bourgeois subject.

But according to Kelly, the production of the subjective image, imperative for modernist painting, is unfeasible for narrative film because "the cinematic apparatus is employed to remove the traces of its own steps," while in painting, on the other hand, "the painterly signifier is manipulated precisely to trace a passage, to give evidence of an essentially human action, to mark the subjectivity of the artist in the image itself." The end result is "a radical asymmetry in their respective modes of address."

So the opposition high culture/low culture is again upheld, here on the basis of the production of artistic subjecthood: the "trace of a passage, or the artistic gesture" recoverable only, says Kelly, in high art. That "the cinematic apparatus is employed to remove the traces of its own steps" is certainly true of the continuity system in general and the classic Hollywood film in particular—the object texts of most contemporary film theory. But it is increasingly less self-evident in regard to contemporary film, and it should be emphasized that, in general, film theory as we know it emerged in a retrospective relation to the mass forms of the modernist era—classical narrative cinema. Current cinema, though, regularly displays a variety of the formal devices of discontinuity and rupture associated with avant-gardist high art, including direct address, nonseamless modes of editing, "making strange," and so on. Current mass culture has no fear of baring the device. (I should note here that I'm equally uninterested in investing these acts of baring the apparatus with value as in giving political weight to other sorts of materialist practices in writing or film, or attempts to break with ideologies of closure and identity through similar formal disruptions.)

Moreover, Kelly obviously knows, although she doesn't address it in her argument, that "auteur theory" is the most widespread informing theory in popular discourse on film, constructing the lowly movie *as* artistic text, effacing the reality of collaborative production by asserting the director as privileged artistic subject, recovering temperament, creativity, and subjectivity from the filmic text in the authorial gesture *and* giving it a signature. In addition, the discourse on and of popular culture saturates us with information precisely *on* the constructedness of the motion picture, including regular "behind-the-scenes" TV documentaries on the making of movies, like "The Making of *Gandhi*" or the now classic "Making of *The Deep.*"

The techniques of modernist subjectification and the discourse of the artistic subject are not even confined to cinema, the high end of low culture: these devices are at work in TV commercials, as well. Ben Yagoda claims, only somewhat facetiously, that the only place avant-garde theatrical techniques can still be seen is not on the New York stage, but in TV ads. He finds "an ingenious appropriation of Pirandello's musings on appearance and reality" in a commercial where a man can't decide if he is listening to a live singer or a Memorex recording of one; he discusses the dilemma with an announcer who, it turns out, is on tape himself. And in those toilet paper ads that show characters "who seem to possess a hidden socially unacceptable urge to squeeze the merchandise," he sees the Ionescesque comedy of the absurd: "People with ridiculous values were engaged in a ridiculous activity, which for comic effect was treated as though it were absolutely normal." And there's the one where "a woman about to buy the high-priced spread is cruelly browbeaten by fellow shoppers, stock boys, and the assistant manager — the Theater of Confrontation such as it hasn't been seen since the '60s."[13]

As for the artistic subject, auteur theory is not only a marketing technique in commercial cinema ("auteurs" now include such cinematic luminaries as Russ Meyer, the director of soft-porn epics like *Vixen* and *Beyond the Valley of the Dolls*, and Roger Corman, the oft-touted genius behind New World Pictures), but even applies now to commercials themselves. *Esquire* magazine and others have run fawning cover stories on Joe Sedelmaier, the director-auteur of the classic Federal Express commercials and the Wendy's "Where's the Beef?" commercials, applying to him all the phrases *Cahiers du Cinéma* once did to John Ford. And the Sedelmaier commercial *is* instantly recognizable through characteristic and unique authorial gestures in his use of camera, the frontality of his mise-en-scène, his ironic approach to sound (sound tracks often dominated by tuba), and signature idiosyncratic casting and direction of actors. *Esquire* describes him as too much his own man to go to Hollywood.

So if critical discourse produces the artistic subject for works of high art, as Mary Kelly writes, popular discourses do the same for mass culture. And let's not forget that the discourse of advertising itself is now permeated by this same rhetoric of imagination, rebellion, creativity, and free expression once associated with the figure of the artist. To become the quintessential artistic subject you don't have to paint your masterpiece, but only consume the right stuff. This language, originating in contestation, emanating as it does from the Romantic invention of the artistic subject at the moment that nascent industrialization threatened those forms of individuality, has now at least filtered down through the class system to achieve a sort of universality of artistic rebellion. So why should the language of artistic subjecthood be conserved only for the rebellions of the petite bourgeoisie? Since the kinds of claims that were once confined to the realm of high culture are now freely made with regard to commodified culture and commodities themselves, it becomes harder and harder to draw the kinds of distinctions between high culture and mass art that Burger and Kelly still maintain—not to mention the fact that the world of high culture is hardly immune from the imperatives of the market. It becomes less and less feasible to offer high culture as a potentially more critical and contestatory realm less marked by the shame and onus of commodification. And as these distinctions become harder and harder to enforce, so too do the class distinctions they buttress.

The calls by Habermas and others for a contestatory modernism are nostalgia-ridden disavowals of the knowledge that there is no transcendent, privileged cultural space on which to stand that is *outside* capitalist reification. There is particularly no such space that can be guaranteed strictly through particular cultural, aesthetic, or textual practices: not through a refusal or disruption of the signifying practices within which subject positions are said to be constructed, as suggested at different times by *Tel Quel, Screen,* or the cultural ministry of Lacanian psychoanalysis and its feminist wing, all of which promise, as Colin MacCabe has written, "the absolutely new and the absolutely different, right up to the gates of the university campus."[14]

I've been discussing the conjunction of a number of breaks: between modernism and postmodernism; between the remnants of an image sphere of use value and one completely permeated by commodification; between the previous unapproachability of popular culture in both high culture and high theory and its current urgent ubiquity. This aggregate set of transformations meets, I'd like to suggest, the criteria Peter Burger outlines in *Theory of the Avant-Garde* for the possibility of a genuinely contestatory political art: one whose potential critical role isn't neutralized in advance by its institutionally determined autonomy from everyday life.

The set of structural possibilities and structural limits that postmodernism makes available is a field of possibility that antagonistic social forces attempt to appropriate and utilize in opposing ways. By way of demonstration, let me offer a second example of refunctioning — one on the other end of the political spectrum from the opening example of the transformed stop signs — an antiabortion artwork by an artist named Mary Cate Carroll, which became newsworthy when it was barred from an invitational show at her alma mater, a college in Virginia. Here is the piece described in the artist's words: "a 5' x 5' collage of a mother and father sitting on their couch. In the mother's lap is the outline — in red dotted lines — of a baby without any features. There is a door built into the middle of this baby and when you open that door there is a jar inside. A real jar, not a painting of a jar. In the jar, in formaldehyde, is a saline-aborted male child. A real five-month old fetus, not a painting of a fetus."[15] The title of the work is *American Liberty Upside Down.*

The piece obviously borrows from the favored tactic of antiabortionists who have effectively transformed the fetus into a semiotic weapon and are prone to assaulting women attempting to enter abortion clinics with its image in so-called "rescue operations." Carroll describes the inception of the work this way: "It seemed logical to me to find a fetus and put it in the painting." The controversy began when the college told her she couldn't show the piece unless she replaced the real fetus with a drawing of a fetus or some other artificial substitute.

The public hue and cry about the artwork ran the gamut from "What is art?" to the citation of laws concerning the uses to which dead bodies may or may not be put. (This last, Carroll considered a triumph: the college invoked a state ordinance against exhibiting dead bodies as the grounds for its censorship, yet the Supreme Court opinion legalizing abortion — as of this writing still tenuously in place — defines a fetus as "not a person." Carroll attempted to make a court case out of the contradiction, hoping that a court decision *would* actually declare her fetus a dead person.)

On the "What is art?" question, an art teacher at the college weighed in with her opinion that Carroll's piece *can* be considered a work of art. "However," she says, "the contents of a bottle that was placed on a shelf within the framework of the painting, namely a second trimester fetus, cannot by any standards be called a work of art." She affirms the right of artists to express themselves freely, but goes on, "I do not consider human tissue to be an article of mixed media. . . . What would the next step be following the display of a human fetus in a painting today? Would it be perhaps placing some other offensive morsel of human tissue, chosen by the whim of the artist, in a painting tomorrow?"

The hysterical edge provoked by Carroll's piece testifies to the agitation-potential of self-consciously political strategies to eliminate the distance between art and the world. This strategy alone doesn't guarantee the reception of the work, though, and Carroll's piece seems not necessarily to have worked as she intended: Nat Hentoff claims that the piece was censored for the "quintessential, visceral reason that some folks found [the fetus] disgusting," rather than because it was an automatically convincing antiabortion argument. Carroll's work wielded the fetus as if it were, in itself, an objective correlative of antiabortionism, as if it were, as T. S. Eliot describes the term, "the formula of that *particular* emotion" through which that emotion can be immediately evoked. For Eliot, the success or failure of a piece of art rests on the "adequacy" of the symbol or situation to the state it is meant to evoke.

The image of the fetus, deliberately detached from the mother, deliberately shunting aside the maternal body, is, in Eliot's terms, a fairly adequate symbol. It has been a difficult image to contest. Prochoicers have rallied with a counterimage—the bloody coat hanger—and attempted to shift the ground of the argument back to the body of the woman and to contest the sentimentality of the fetus imagery with the cold reality of the consequences to women of illegal abortions, of no choice. The antiabortion movement's strategy, and it is a sophisticated strategy, has been to transform the fetus into an ideological element and appropriate it to their own discourse, performing their ideological interpellation in the name of, even in the voice of, the fetus.

Hegemony isn't imposed, it's won. While a single image can't make or break a political struggle, while unconscious processes are certainly mobilized in the reproduction of capitalist and patriarchial relations, the issue of how the popular imagination is captured is at the heart of the struggle for hegemony. The question, then, for the radical democratic Left, and for radical aesthetics, is of producing a *popular* culture. Left theorists have regularly opposed the conflation of the terms "mass culture" and "popular culture," arguing pristinely that mass culture is *capitalist* culture rather than one that is truly popular (which in the Old Left imagination seems to consist of sitting around a campfire and playing homemade musical instruments, far from the evil corrupting pleasures of commodity culture). While the left argues terminology, the terrain of the popular is simply ceded *to* commodity culture. Like the antiabortionists' arrogation of the fetus, popular culture works by *transforming* elements from the culture at large—not through inventing or imposing arbitrary materials on a stunned and passive populace. It's not merely a siren song luring the masses onto the rocks of capitalist capitulation, it makes itself effective by appropriating meaningful cultural elements as its "raw materials" and transforming them in such a way that they express a capitalist hegemonic principle.

Ernesto Laclau makes a similar analysis of the structure of populism. Populism, a political mode often associated with the transition from a traditional to an industrial society, has, in Laclau's analysis, striking resonances with the sphere of culture in advanced Western economies.[16] In Laclau's structural reading, populism isn't defined through its particular class basis or specific stage of economic development, but through its mode of address—a series of "popular interpellations" that develop the antagonism between the people and the power bloc. In that the mass of "mass culture" still does contain echoes of "the people"—at the very least in its demographics—Laclau's analysis of populism might give us culturalists some insight into, or even better, some access to, the effectivity of popular culture, not as an instrument of domination, but as access to a counterhegemony.

A class becomes hegemonic not through its capacity for sheer domination, but through its ability to appropriate visions of the world and diverse cultural elements of its subordinated classes, but in forms that carefully neutralize any inherent or potential antagonism and transform these antagonisms into simple *difference*. Classes only exist as hegemonic forces to the extent that they can absorb the popular into their own discourse, but in such a way that "the people" as an oppositional force are neutralized.

Hegemony is always in process. Yet this *is* a process with cracks and openings. Dismissing popular culture as merely an instrument of capitalist domination rather than a site to be struggled over simply cedes the territory of popular interpellations to capitalism. The theory of postmodernism presented here argues for a different cultural practice, one of appropriation, of transformation, of refunctioning. Certainly much of the success of capitalist hegemony comes from its exclusive claim to those elements in the culture that are socially meaningful (like narrative) and its transformation of those elements into the basis of the continuing appeal of an existing social order. According to Laclau, for dominated classes to win hegemony they must precipitate a crisis in dominant ideology, stripping the connotative power from its articulating principles. For this to happen the implicit antagonism of popular culture and popular interpellations must be developed to the point where the contradictions between "the people" and the power bloc are unassimilable.

Much capitalist popular culture obviously already expresses populist antagonism to "the system"—antigovernment, anticorporate, and antitechnology themes are far from rare. A left popular culture would undertake to articulate the antagonistic moments *already* there in popular culture into moments when radical democracy gets presented as an unassimilable option *against* the the dominant. Laclau refers to this as the "ideological class struggle": it aims to provoke a crisis of dominant ideology and a crisis in the ability of the system to neutralize its dominated sectors: this, in Laclau's account of populism, precipitating a more general social crisis. Precisely because those contradictions can never be *totally* absorbed by any dominant class discourse, the articulation of an antagonistic moment characterizes populism, and the more radical the confrontation with the system, the less possible it is for a class to assert its hegemony without populism.

The imperative to produce a left *popular* culture accounts for the emphasis here toward conscious experience and the fact that my argument locates the work of popular culture somewhat closer to the level of the conscious subject than do many recent theorizations of mass culture. The focus on the intersections of the unconscious and the repressive social order, and on legitimation secured at the level of signification through the subject-effects of narrative and visual pleasure, represents the cultural and political field in terms that effectively foreclose in advance the significance of any cultural practices other than the most ultramodernist (read *elitist*) — those which are generally unpleasurable and clearly unpopular. I'm neither intrinsically against strategies of rupture, distance, or textuality nor theoretically biased in favor of ego psychology or American revisionism over psychoanalysis. I wouldn't want to dismiss important psychoanalytically derived theories on production of the subject within popular cultural forms. Rather, the focus on conscious experience is provisional, part of a provisional strategy for a provisional radical postmodernist popular cultural politics.

This vision of a left popular culture seems not so far from what Laclau calls populism, a political mobilization posing a challenge to capitalist hegemony, and without which no such challenge can be made. My aim is toward formulating a strategy for the *production* of a left popular culture rather than toward fostering critical strategies that provide *readings* of the antagonisms inherent in already existing popular culture. This has marked the general limit of left involvement with popular culture: the rendering of interpretations that are produced and that circulate within the circumscribed domains of high culture and high theory. Much of this work is content to locate what it describes as moments of resistance and stop there. We need to produce those moments ourselves.

Both theorists of modernism and theorists of the unconscious have recoiled from popular culture. Attempts to interpret the popular from within these categories have yielded arcane and academicist interpretations that impute diminished intellectual or political credibility to its audience. Attempts to defy the popular via modernist or neomodernist aesthetic practices have produced an endless array of baffling and elitist sterilities. Postmodernism makes available the means to approach popular culture — and thus its audience — differently, to wrest its very popularity away from the dominant culture, in the process transforming it into a popular and *contestatory* mode of political address. Neither interpreting nor defying popular culture is enough; the point of the populist intervention outlined here is to change it.

CHAPTER 3

Ecstasy Unlimited
The Interpenetrations of Sex and Capital
(1985)

FADE UP:

1. A phone rings and a recorded phone sex message comes on. A woman listens.

A FEMALE VOICE: *(from the phone)* Thank you for calling "Speaking of Sex." Today we're going to share with you some fantasies others have acted out in the "erotic theater."

A MALE VOICE: *(from the phone)* A common scene for many women is to be a teacher — she needs to discipline a male student. To do so, she puts him under her desk and continues with her teaching. At this point the student becomes quite mischievous, breathing, kissing and caressing his teacher's legs. Any desk or table can serve as a prop. The acting can be quite simple. Try explaining a historical fact, or basic addition or subtraction. For the student, he needs to obey his teacher's order to go under the desk. The rest is up to his imagination.

FEMALE VOICE: That's all for today. Call again tomorrow for more "Speaking of Sex."

CUT TO:

2. A Darkened Interrogation Room

A glaring naked bulb shines directly in the face of a bedraggled, beaten-up look-ing, unshaven MAN. He sits at a long bare table, shirt unbuttoned, his head in his hands. Loud interrogating, echoing questions are barked at him by an OFF-SCREEN VOICE.

OFF-SCREEN VOICE: Are you sexually satisfied?

> When was your first time?
>
> Are you orgasmic?
>
> Are you multiorgasmic?
>
> Was it good?
>
> What turns you on?
>
> Are you a good lover?
>
> Have you ever been attracted to a member of the same sex?
>
> Do you suffer from premature ejaculations?

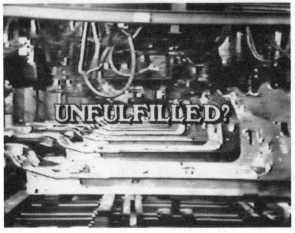

Could you handle a hush-hush affair?

Do you really like oysters?

Does your smile say SEX APPEAL?

Have you ever been impotent?

Are you a latent homosexual?

Is your deodorant soap effective?

Do you need sex therapy?

Is your spouse having an affair?

At this last question the MAN shudders violently.

TITLE: ECSTASY UNLIMITED
THE INTERPENETRATIONS OF SEX AND CAPITAL

3. An Auto Assembly Line

FEMALE NARRATOR: *(voice-over)* Are you sexually unfulfilled? There's no use trying to hide it. We see it in the way you nervously tap your fingers, the way you cross and uncross your legs, the rigidity with which you hold your cold, unfulfilled body. Hey, get with it! The body-racking, mind-blowing blockbuster orgasm is within every modern woman's reach, says *Cosmopolitan*. Perhaps you have a boner for your pet collie? Well, "Bow-wow," says the *Playboy* Advisor. Enjoy a little pain with your pleasure? Any practice between consenting adults is all right with the author of *More Joy of Sex*. For what used to be called sexual aberrations you can now find instruction manuals. How reassuring that even the perversions are under the administration and control of experts.

Perhaps you suffer from "masturbatory orgasmic inadequacy?" Not to worry. Teaching women how to masturbate pleasurably is the life's work of San Francisco sex therapist Lonnie Barbach. Think of it! Before this new era of sexual openness you could have been masturbating wrong and not even known it!

Sexual fulfillment isn't only your right, it's your obligation. Commit yourself to hunting down sexual satisfaction, to pursuing it, rooting it out from whatever nook or crevice it might be hiding in. Be a foot soldier in the war for sexual liberation, fight the good fight for freedom from repression.

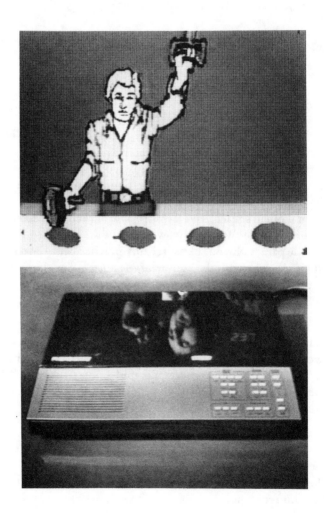

(confidentially)

Yes, *I* am a woman whose quest is sexual pleasure, whatever the price. I am a sexual adventurer, expanding the frontiers of pleasure, extending the horizons of desire, fulfilling the Manifest Destiny of sexuality.

What a radical concept! Our own sexuality offers us liberation here on earth, in our own lifetime. Whether you're a Democrat or Republican, whether you're an industrialist or on welfare, whether you're a struggling young artist or have vast holdings in South Africa, you too can be liberated. Why bother to demonstrate, contribute to Amnesty International, or try to change the system when you can now achieve liberation in the privacy of your own bedroom?

4. A *Sesame Street*-style Animation Sequence of the Letter *L*

(A MALE ADULT VOICE reads the letter and word; CHILDREN'S VOICES IN UNISON read the definition.)

A worker performs a repetitive task on an animated "Modern Times"-type assembly line.

ADULT VOICE: L is for LIBERATION . . .

CHILDREN'S VOICES: Yet another of the many achievements of liberal capitalism!

5. A Telephone Answering Machine

The PHONE MACHINE sits on a desk. A telephone rings once and the machine clicks on.

PSYCHIATRIST: *(from the phone machine)* Hello, this is Dr. Foreman. I'm in a session and can't take your call right now. Please leave your name and a short message and I'll get back to you just as soon as I can.

The PSYCHIATRIST can be seen as a reflection in the cover of the answering machine, smoking a cigar. The machine BEEPS and the message is this song — sort of new wave, a woman's voice.

DOCTOR, DOCTOR, I need a session,
I've been naughty, please hear my confession,
My sex life stinks, can't get no satisfaction,
DOCTOR, DOCTOR, show me some action.

DOCTOR, DOCTOR, listen please,
I need you so bad it's like a disease.
Help me, know me, cure me, show me,
lead me to . . . ECSTASY, UNLIMITED ECSTASY.

Yes, sex is an eight-billion-dollar-a-year business,
now that's what I call cataclysmic.
So whatever it costs, it's worth what you pay,
Because business and pleasure's the American way.
Revolution and business now have the same mission.
Be patriotic, without inhibitions.

If pleasure makes money, why moralize?
Where else is there such a fine compromise?
Let's fight the fight to end repression.
We know sex is the answer, now what's the question?

I WANT IT, I CRAVE IT, I NEED IT—
ECSTASY, UNLIMITED ECSTASY.

6. Psychiatrist's Office

The camera lingers on a large photo of a red high heel posed seductively on a zebra-skin rug hanging on the office wall. A WOMAN is lying on the couch, in session with the MALE PSYCHIATRIST seen only from behind.

FEMALE NARRATOR: The psychoanalytic tradition offers us the concept of sex as that which is repressed. For Freud, it was the price we pay for civilization. Wilhelm Reich thought that sexual repression was essential for insuring workers' submission to the authority of the class system, and that sexual fulfillment was incompatible with an obedient work force. Later he changed his mind and decided that sexual repression could be overcome through psychotherapy.

But suppose that it isn't the *repression* of sexuality that works to secure the status quo, but rather that sexuality is *produced*—in forms that work in conjunction with the existing power structure. In that case, what we take for liberation might instead be authority disguised as freedom, and an affirmation of the existing social order. Your sexual-

ity would be the libidinal structure of consumer capitalism. The genitals are organs of history.

PSYCHIATRIST: When did you first start feeling this way?

TITLE: SUPPLY-SIDE SEXUALITY

7. Documentary Interview with Michael Kapec, Manager of "The Pleasure Chest," a Sex-Toy Chain
(Note: This is a transcript of an unscripted interview.)

MICHAEL: Business has been real good for the last year, year and a half. The economy in the nation seems to be up, retail's been up. So there's more money to spend. People are beginning to spend more on each other. As opposed to taking the family out to dinner, a husband and wife will come in here and buy an intimate lotion or a cream or a vibrator or something a little more explicit and take it home and spend a lot of time with each other.

Footage of various sex products in the store.

NARRATOR: In advanced capitalism our lives are subordinated to the laws of the market — not only, as in the nineteenth century, in the sphere of work and production, but also in consumption, in recreation, culture, art, education, and personal relations. All that is left is the dream of escape — through sex and drugs, which are, in their turn, promptly industrialized.

Capital works to complete its conquest of the world by reaching down into the last remaining private zones of individual life to penetrate the few enclaves of precapitalism. Capital has finally discovered sexuality as a prime site for investment and speculation, as a major outlet for venture capital, one of the last remaining regions of the world with a "Secure Investment Climate." The United Fruit Corporation is already making plans to pull out of Central America and concentrate on sexuality, where American business interests can operate at a higher profit margin with far fewer risks from local insurgents. Multinational corporations are plowing research and development money by the billions into sex, and its robust growth has given corporate America a renewed optimism. The invention of the G spot alone grossed millions. Sexual timesaving devices have become a necessary part of every household. New erogenous zones are

being discovered and patented every month. President Reagan has proclaimed the beginning of a "New Renaissance in America."

MICHAEL: By and large, business has been very, very good.

8. *Sesame Street* **Animation of the Letter** *P*

A somewhat phallic drill drills the letter into the ground as dollar signs erupt like oil being struck.
A MALE VOICE leads the children in unison.

ADULT: P is for PENETRATION . . .

CHILDREN: To stick one thing into another thing. To enter the interior of. To obtain a share of the market. To arrive at the truth or meaning of: Capital Penetration!

A shot of money being counted in slow motion.

NARRATOR: *(in a singsong voice)*

Sex liberation, say the radicalized,

is very subversive, but not of free enterprise.

We spend eight billion a year on sexual titillation.

More than the total GNP of many other nations.

ROLLING TEXT:
GROSS NATIONAL PRODUCT IN BILLIONS OF DOLLARS

SYRIA	7.0
BANGLADESH	6.7
SUDAN	5.8
ZAIRE	5.0
BURMA	4.8
KENYA	4.8
UGANDA	4.4
TANZANIA	3.8
ETHIOPIA	3.7
AFGHANISTAN	3.5
SRI LANKA	2.8
MOZAMBIQUE	2.1

MADAGASCAR 1.9
NEPAL   1.5

9. The Sugar Shack — a Male Strip Club for Women — Night *(documentary footage)*

MALE STRIPPERS gyrate as giggling WOMEN stuff money into their jock-straps.

NARRATOR: Sexual liberation, as brought to you by liberal capitalism, has even abolished gender oppression. No discrimination here. Women can now seize their pleasure in the same ways men tradition-ally have. We have sex shows for women, phone sex for women — anything you want, doll.

As capital penetrates sexuality, sexuality becomes industrialized. As sexuality provides an outlet for capital investment, capital logic penetrates every bedroom. The central organizing principles of capitalism and the workplace are extended into the sphere of sexuali-ty: rationalization and exchange relations come to dominate your sex life.

But don't think what I tell you, think for yourself.

TITLE: WOULD IT SURPRISE YOU TO LEARN THAT YOUR SEX LIFE FUNCTIONS ACCORDING TO THE LAWS OF THE MARKET?

10. An Old *Playboy* Centerfold

An arrow points to the WOMAN's crotch, which is labeled "SUPPLY," and another arrow points to her head, which is labeled "DEMAND."

NARRATOR: Current economic thinking assures us that we must devote ourselves most vigorously to "stimulating the supply side." Because when the supply side is sufficiently stimulated, demand will reach new heights. This is also known as "trickle-down theory."

11. *Sesame Street* **Animation of the Letter** *M*

The STATUE of LIBERTY being whipped.

ADULT VOICE: M is for MARKET DISCIPLINE . . .

The sound of the CRACK of a whip and a pleasurable MOAN.

TITLE: ON DEREGULATION

12. A Bar—Night

An intimate conversation between CLIFF and TRISH.
They hold hands, coo at each other.

CLIFF: What's it worth to you?

TRISH: Nothing ventured, nothing gained.

CLIFF: A bird in hand is worth two in the bush.

TRISH: What's the bottom line?

CLIFF: Your loss is my gain.

TRISH: A wife is an investment in the future.

CLIFF: My last relationship didn't pay off.

TRISH: Just cut your losses and run.

CLIFF: You get what you pay for.

TRISH: Nothing comes cheap.

NARRATOR: *(voice-over)* There are only two kinds of people these days. The first kind believe in free sex with a regulated economy. And the rest believe in a free market with no sexual expression outside the family.

PSYCHIATRIST: And which kind are you?

13. The Sugar Shack

The MEN gyrate, WOMEN look admiringly on.

NARRATOR: Well, I read in *U.S. News and World Report* that the sex business does an eight-billion-dollar-a-year trade. But then I read in

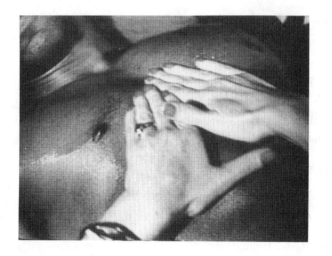

Time magazine in April '84 that the sexual revolution is finished, and that "there is growing evidence that the national obsession with sex is subsiding." Does this mean that more people are paying for sex and fewer people are doing it for free?

TITLE: YOUR PLEASURE IS MY JOB

14. A Massage Parlor—Day

A FEMALE MASSEUSE and her MALE CUSTOMER. He lies stretched out on a massage table. On the wall is a huge photo blowup of a pair of female hands.

NARRATOR: *(voice-over)* Massage parlors and telephone sex are the latest advances in prostitution. You *could* call them the mating ground of a current mode of production and a current mode of sexuality. These new forms of prostitution are produced by spaces in the laws on prostitution: sexual intercourse for money is highly illegal, manual sex is semilegal, and committing acts of autoeroticism while someone talks dirty to you over the telephone is completely legal. So this must be what the Law has in mind for us.

"Prostitution is too slow," says San Francisco porn king Jim Mitchell. He thinks the future is in "dry-rub" sex like peep shows and phone sex services. "To take your pants off takes too long," he says. "The future is assembly-line sex."

MASSEUSE: *(to camera)* I see myself as a professional with a job to do. So, first off, I'll politely ask all sorts of questions like, have you ever been to this or any other massage parlor before, which might indicate his experience in having to shell out money for "special services." Or I ask him what he does for a living, like you'd ask any other date. That gives me an idea of what kind of cash he might have on him and what he might be willing to spend. At the same time, I'll be looking over his body and deciding just what I might and might not be willing to do for him, "sizing up the job" just like with any other service. Then I'll start to massage his chest to get him a bit excited, and usually by the time I've gotten around to rubbing his legs, he'll be pretty excited, and I can smile and ask if there's anything else he'd like me to do.

MASSEUSE: So what do you do for a living, honey?

CUSTOMER: Me? Work at the Ford plant—on the line.

MASSEUSE: So, do you like it?

CUSTOMER: Like it! I stand on my feet for eight hours a day and do this—

(he makes an in-and-out pulling gesture identical to the one she's making over his body at bottom of frame)

all goddamn day long.

MASSEUSE: *(with a double take at her own hand doing same thing)* Well, it's a living, I guess.

CUSTOMER: Living is hardly the word for it; I feel like a goddamn machine. It's probably only a matter of time before they get a machine to replace me anyhow—management says labor is pricing itself out of the market.

MASSEUSE: Yeah, soon we'll all get replaced by machines.

CUSTOMER: Yeah, why should they even put out to buy a machine when they can just turn me into one instead? You know, I used to do this and this—

(he makes two different hand gestures)

Now they got me doing just this—

(first gesture)

and another guy doing that.

(second gesture)

There's specialization for you.

15. Auto Assembly Line Footage, Workers on the Line

NARRATOR: Specialization: the increasing division and degradation of labor within the production process to increase the productive power of capital. It is the lifetime confinement of workers to partial operations that stunt and distort their human capacities. In late capitalism all human institutions are subject to this process. When you become an appendage of the machine in the production process, the logic of the production process extends to the rest of your life, as well. When

machines dominate the human, the human becomes mechanized
. . . and did you think sex was exempt?

16. Massage Parlor

MASSEUSE: Yeah, I know what you mean. It used to be that I'd give
massages and guys would want me to talk dirty to them, too. Now
they've got phone sex for talking and all I do is give massages. I hardly have to talk anymore; I think this is the first conversation I've had
in weeks. Well that's progress, I guess. I think of massage parlors as
like fast food. It's mechanized, it's impersonal, it doesn't taste great,
but it gets the job done.

CUSTOMER: Yeah, but a job's a job. At least you can take your time
here—where I work they're always trying to get you to work faster,
faster. Even your body ain't your own anymore. Now the company
wants to hook us up to these electrodes that would give us a mild
electric shock if we slow down the line, but the union's fighting it.

MASSEUSE: You know, that sounds just like here. I probably shouldn't
tell you this, but there are hidden cameras in all the massage rooms
so the manager can check up on how long we're taking with each
customer. He analyzes our technique and gives us pointers about
how to get the guy off quicker. So listen, is there anything "else"
you'd like me to do?

CUSTOMER: Ahhh . . . don't stop. Whatever you do for twenty dollars, do it.

MASSEUSE: For twenty you can get a "local."

17. A Montage of Porn Magazines

NARRATOR: Marcuse wrote that the localization of erotic pleasure in the
genitals and the desexualization of the rest of the body is a precondition for transforming the body into an instrument of labor. It is socially necessary that the libido become concentrated in one part of the
body, leaving most of the rest free for work. The libido takes up less
space, less time, and is incapable of eroticism beyond—

(coming noises from customer)

localized, genital sexuality.

18. Massage Parlor

CUSTOMER: *(loud orgasm noises, then a sigh)* That's good enough for me, babe.

MASSEUSE: There you go, hon.

A shot of a CAMERA mounted on the wall.

MASSEUSE: *(yelling at camera)* Ya see, Irving. Four-forty flat.

(to herself, wiping her hands on a towel)

What I want is to get me one of those phone sex jobs. Less mess.

19. A Montage of Lips, Phones, a Man Lying on Bed Talking on Phone

SONG: "CALLING ORGASM CENTRAL" *(sung like a jingle)*

> I shop at Orgasm Central,
> For value and price,
> At Orgasm Central,
> the salesgirls are so nice.
> They tell you what you need to hear,
> they whisper dirty things in your ear.

ANNOUNCER: Want a hot time with your telephone? Want more satisfaction than you ever dreamed possible?

> Give me a charge,
> and charge it to my Mastercard.
> *(ring, ring)*
> Give me a charge,
> and charge it to my Mastercard.

TITLE: THE GENITALS AS A FREE-ENTERPRISE ZONE

20. A Well-Furnished Living Room

On the wall is a large photo blowup of a phone, and a pair of red pouty lips speaking into it.

TWO WOMEN are sitting on the couch chatting. The OWNER of the phone sex service, genteel, fortyish, speaks to the MASSEUSE from the previous scene.

OWNER: We're selling a product here—orgasms. I used to work in a massage parlor myself, so messy. Then I got the idea—let them pay for their own towel service—after all, they can do it just as well as we can. So I scrimped and saved, I worked my fingers to the bone, until finally I saved enough to go into business for myself. Then I opened "Orgasm Central."

21. *Sesame Street* Animation of the Letter O

The animation is of a package tied with a bow, labeled orgasm; it hops around until it explodes.

ADULT VOICE: O is for ORGASM . . .

CHILDREN: A product of human labor, produced for a system of exchange, sold for a price and appearing on the market as a commodity!

ADULT: O is for ORGASM . . .

CHILDREN: The epitome of all human experience!

22. Phone Sex Owner's Living Room

OWNER: It's a new industry, so exciting to be in on the ground floor! There are fortunes to be made here. It's an old idea but a new product. It's the commodification of the obscene phone call. Before, no one profited but the phone company, and every woman with a phone was being exploited for free sexual labor. Now everyone gets their share. There's a big potential market in the perversions. It's an idea whose time has come.

23. Auto Assembly Line

NARRATOR: If the orgasm is now a commodity—that is, a product of human labor traded on the open market—then what is true of all commodity production is also true of the orgasm—that these products of human labor come to dominate the producers them-

selves, that, as Marx wrote, "Man's own deed becomes an alien power opposed to him, which enslaves him instead of being controlled by him."

24. Phone Sex Owner's Living Room

SNEAK UP MUSIC — "America the Beautiful" — until it swells.

OWNER: *(inspirational)* You see, I have a dream, a vision: the conquest of sexual scarcity. Isn't it a great society where all you need is a charge card to overcome the antithesis between the anarchy of desire and organized polite society?

Freud, for one, thought it couldn't be done, that sex couldn't be tamed — he heightened our sense of its perils and its opposition to the values of civilization, the sense of the demonic element in human sexuality. But we've shown that old Victorian fuddy-duddy. In this country no one shall be in want. The sex industry epitomizes Progress with a capital P. And that's what made America great: the conquest of nature and the progressive conquest of scarcity.

The music ends abruptly.

(She continues, very businesslike.)

The men call us and tell us what they want. The most popular thing lately is men who want to be used as a toilet — that happens every fourth or fifth call. We charge thirty-five dollars a call and you get seven for each one.

MASSEUSE: Only seven?

OWNER: Well, I do have my overhead, dear.

25. A Cityscape

NARRATOR: Now, progressive companies have started allowing their employees a "sex break" instead of a coffee break. "In our day and age," they explained in an interview on *60 Minutes*, "there's *no* reason why sex, properly scheduled, can't be compatible with the dictates of the total worker productivity environment."

Two male hands enter the frame, one labeled "Management" and the other labeled "Labor." They clasp hands and shake.

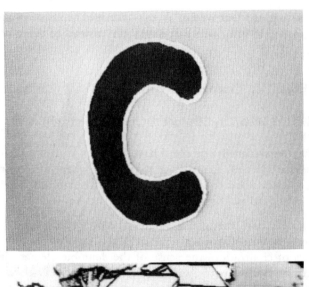

TITLE: YOU GET WHAT YOU PAY FOR, SO YOU MIGHT AS WELL PAY FOR WHAT YOU GET

26. *Sesame Street* Animation of the Letter *C*

A MAN lovingly strokes a sportscar.

ADULT: C is for COMMODITY FETISHISM . . .

CHILDREN: Just you and the object you love!

27. The Bar—Night

CLIFF: *(gazing into Trish's eyes)* The way I look at it, it's not what you make a year, it's what you *buy* that makes you what you are. And you see, that's what makes America a classless society—it's not who your old man was, it's what you make of yourself—where you shop, what you spend. That's democracy for you—freedom to buy the best, equal opportunity in spending. Discrimination? Don't talk to me about it—nobody stops them from going into a store and putting down their money just like the next guy! Sexual inequality? Don't make me laugh, honey! Show 'em your green stuff and you're just as good as a guy any day. That's what makes this country great. And *that's* why I went into advertising—it's the pulse of democracy.

CUT TO:

28. Trish's Foyer

Following the date, TRISH and CLIFF stand at her doorway exchanging good-nights.

TRISH: Well, thank you so much, I really had a wonderful time. Dinner was just marvelous.

CLIFF: I'm glad you enjoyed yourself.

TRISH: I hate for the evening to end so soon. Would you like to come in for a nightcap?

CLIFF: Well, thanks, but I have an early morning, and, uh, I have to get home and feed the cat. . . .

TRISH: Look, I don't usually say this type of thing but I really find my-self very attracted to you and, well, I'd like to go to bed with you tonight.

CLIFF: *(hesitating)* Uh, that's very flattering, uh, but, you know, well, I just don't really think we're right for each other.

TRISH: *(hurt)* Don't you find me attractive?

CLIFF: No, no, it's not that at all, you're very attractive.

TRISH: *(her voice rising)* Well, then what, do you think I'm too pushy?

CLIFF: No, no. Here, well—

(fumbling in his pocket)

let me give you something.

TRISH: Give me something? You don't have to give me anything and anyway you already paid for that lovely dinner.

CLIFF: No really, I want you to have this.

(He opens his wallet.)

TRISH: But this is a hundred dollar bill! I don't understand!

CLIFF: Shhhh . . . don't ruin the moment.

He begins kissing her passionately.

FREEZE FRAME OF THE COUPLE

A ROD SERLING VOICE: *(voice-over)*
We present for your approval, one advertising executive.
His mission in life is to convince the populace that certain
products lead directly to sexual fulfillment. He gives objects
the characteristics of human beings.
He attributes human relations to objects.
He objectifies his own relationships.
He makes merchandise into objects of the libido.
Objects of his sexual desire become merchandise.
He objectifies his sexual relationships.

His sexual relationships are relations of commerce.
He can't get it up unless he pays for it — the perfect consumer.

29. Cliff's Bedroom — Night

CLIFF is lying on the bed talking on the telephone. His American Express card is lying on the nightstand beside him.

On the other end is the former MASSEUSE. We see her in her kitchen. While she talks she stirs a pot on the stove.

MASSEUSE: *(very sultry voice)* Now just relax . . . trust me, we're going to have a hot time together tonight. . . .

CLIFF: I trust you. After all, you're a professional, and I say sex is best left to professionals. At least if you pay for it you know what it's worth. This is the age of specialization — I don't sell sex, you don't sell detergent. When I want sex I go to an expert. Boy, did I have a disaster last night. She wouldn't let me pay for it and that's exactly what it was worth, nothing, zip, nada. My only problem is that my drive, you know, is bigger than my wallet. The more I pay, the more satisfaction I get, but I just can't afford the amount of satisfaction I need on my salary. I guess I could pay less and do it more, but I'm into quality. I could pay more and do it less, but I'm into frequency. Well, that's why McDonald's has sold ten billion burgers, I guess — you can't afford to eat at Lutèce every night.

TITLE: DISORDERS OF DESIRE: THE BODY AGAINST THE MACHINE

30. A Bar — Night

CLIFF and his friend ANDY lean against a pinball machine.

CLIFF: Listen, man, did I have a hot time last night. Let me give you the number of this gal. She's terrific and not too high-priced.

ANDY: *(coughs, embarrassed)* Well, thanks, but I'm not really interested.

CLIFF: Not interested! My god, if you were in my business! I spend all day each day figuring out how to jack people up about this or that new product. Sometimes I get so turned on I can hardly stand it. I mean, the whole idea is that you promise them more satisfaction than

can ever be fully provided — if desire were totally satisfied, the economy would fall apart and yours truly would be on the street selling pencils.

31. *Sesame Street* Animation of the Letter *A*

An animation of people with televisions for heads.

ADULT: A is for ADVERTISING . . .

CHILDREN: A controlled mobilization of instinctual energy. The scientific management of the libido!

32. The Bar

CLIFF: It's a good thing telephone sex was invented to pick up the slack in the production-consumption cycle, otherwise I'd be walking around with a perpetual hard-on.

ANDY: I don't seem to have that problem.

CLIFF: Listen, man, have you ever tried paying for it? It makes all the difference in the world, let me tell you. It's like the thrill of riding down the street in a Porsche and waving to the poor slobs waiting for the bus. What a high — paying for what you could get anywhere for free.

ANDY: Look, I just find I'm not very interested in sex lately. Well, hell, it's been almost three years now, it just . . . well I just can't get worked up about it anymore. Gettin' old, I guess.

CLIFF: Jeez, man, that's unnatural. You're missing out on one of the great delights of living. You ought to see someone about this. See a professional. They're high-priced, but they're worth it. Someone who'll talk to you. . . . You know, a sex therapist.

33. A Car Radio

SLICK ADVERTISING VOICE: *(voice-over)* If you're experiencing sexual dysfunction problems, our sensitive, trained male and female surrogates, supervised by certified sex therapists, can help you on the road to a healthy, satisfying sex life. Call Sexual Enlightenment Counseling Services Incorporated TODAY for a no-cost consultation.

TITLE: PSYCHOLOGY, THE SCIENCE OF A RULING CLASS
DETERMINED TO EXAMINE THE INDIVIDUAL IN ALL HIS
OR HER MANY FACETS, IS CALLED ON TO UNDERSTAND
THE REPUDIATION OF SEXUAL PLEASURE

34. Sex Therapist's Office — Day

There is a large photo blowup of an ear on the wall.

ANDY: *(speaks directly to the camera)* It all started about three years ago.
I was dating this gal who worked in marketing relations. We got
along great, but in bed she would say things like, "Come to where
the flavor is," "Darling, flick my Bic," "Take it off, take it all off." I
think she used to watch a lot of TV. I told her it distracted me, but
she said it turned her on. Finally we had to stop seeing each other.

So then I started dating a very high-powered corporate headhunter.
At first everything was okay, but then, you know, during sex, I
started hearing these voices in my head saying things like, "Where
a man belongs," "An awesome display of power," "This is no place
for the inexperienced," "Outperform the competition," "Just point
and shoot," "The taste of success" — you know, that type of thing. It
pretty much ended things for us.

After a while I met a woman, through friends, a financial analyst. She
consented to have sex while wearing our own personal stereo head-
phones. She wanted to hear the Stones. I played Barry Manilow. I
tell you I really blasted it, but I couldn't get those damn voices out
of my head: "We build excitement," "Rich smooth taste," "Taste the
good life. . . . "

That was the last time I had sex. What could I do? You'd have to be
blind and deaf not to encounter all those voices screaming their messages at you every single day — billboards, magazines, radio, TV.
. . . Once I heard them I couldn't get them out of my mind. And
I just read they're going to sell advertising space in airport toilet stalls
— the toilet: the last private space, the only remaining sanctuary! But
there's an untapped captive audience just sitting there — it was only
a matter of time. So mostly now, I stay at home and watch TV. I've
just lost my sexual desire. I guess I'm a pretty sad case, huh?

MALE SEX THERAPIST: No, Andy, you're not unusual at all. Lack of sexual desire now affects about 20 percent of the population, we esti-

mate. We call it Inhibited Sexual Desire, or ISD for short. *Time* magazine even did a story on it.

ANDY: If it's got an acronym and it's in *Time* magazine it *must* be important. I never realized there were so many like me; I thought I was alone.

THERAPIST: I think we can help you here, Andy. What we do is teach you new skills, train you to respond to sexual cues in a different fashion. Of course, sex therapy isn't cheap, but we can work something out. How were you planning to pay—Visa, Mastercard, or Blue Cross?

35. *Sesame Street* Animation

A phallic drill drills for dollars.

CHILDREN'S VOICES: PENETRATION, ishy oshy ation. CAPITAL PENETRATION!!

36. The Auto Assembly Line

NARRATOR: *(voice-over)* Capital expands not only into sexuality, but even into the mind in its quest for profit. Even the unconscious is now an industry, and a productive industry. It's certainly no accident that the unconscious was invented at the same moment as Henry Ford's first production line. Indeed, the unconscious was invented *as* a producer—of errors, symptoms, dreams—and we can know it only insofar as it is productive—a good worker.

Ford's invention of the production line spawned an industry that allows a corporate elite to get rich off the backs of labor. Freud's invention of the unconscious has spawned an industry that allows a therapeutic elite to get rich off the misery of their patients. You *could* say that what Ford is to the auto industry, Freud is to the consciousness industry.

37. Sex Therapist's Office

ANDY: I wish I knew why sex doesn't interest me.

THERAPIST: Our feeling here at Sexual Enlightenment Counseling Incorporated is that the current form of sexuality in our society is the

only form of sexuality available to us. And the healthy individual is the man or woman tailored to fit the system. To change sexuality you'd have to change the entire social system, since another social system would, of course, produce a different form of sexuality. But who has time to change the system? And most of us are having too good a time to want to. So our program is designed to teach you to adapt and enjoy. Nobody likes a party pooper, Andy. It's time to get with it.

ANDY: Yeah, I see your point.

THERAPIST: We use sexual surrogates in our program, Andy. Let me tell you about it.

NARRATOR: *(voice-over)* We're persuaded to a current form of sexuality from all directions. Is lack of sexual desire the only possible rebellion against the social engineering of sexuality?

TITLE: THE BEDROOM AND THE WORLD

38. The Pleasure Chest—Interview with Manager
(Transcript of an unscripted interview)

MICHAEL: When Pleasure Chest opened twelve years ago as a corporation, the S & M aspect was probably the biggest selling part of the merchandising retail store itself. All of the leathers, the S & M equipment, the bondage and dominance equipment, they all have our labels in them, and that's what we were primarily known for. They do, consistently, keep up a high percentage of the business here as well as a lot of other things. I think that people talk about it more openly now, as opposed to when we did open several years ago. There was a point when people would not ask for leathers, but now we can proudly display them.

39. Montage

A series of EXTREME CLOSE SHOTS:

   A BELL RINGING
   WOMEN'S FEET running
   A WHITE NIGHTGOWN dropping to the floor
   MEN'S FEET running

Red ink poured on a SHEET
A MAN'S FINGERS fondling a cigar
The stain on the SHEET
THE BELL RINGING

NARRATOR: *(voice-over)* Freud wrote about a woman who suffered from a peculiar obsessional manifestation. Many times a day, without knowing why, she would run from her own room into the next room, take up a particular position there beside a table in the middle of the room, ring the bell for her housemaid, and then run back into her own room. Whenever Freud asked the woman, "Why do you do this? What sense has it?" she answered, "I don't know."

During the analysis, the key to her behavior emerged. More than ten years before, she had married a man much older than herself, and on the wedding night he was impotent. Many times during the night he had come running from his room into hers to try once more, but every time without success. The next morning he said angrily, "I should feel ashamed in front of the housemaid when she makes the bed." He then took up a bottle of red ink that happened to be in the room and poured its contents over the sheet, but not in the spot where a stain would have been appropriate.

The woman then told Freud that the tablecloth on the table that she repeatedly ran and stood next to also had a large stain upon it. She would position herself next to the table in such a way that the maid who had been sent for could not fail to see the stain. There appeared to be an intimate connection between the traumatic scene on her wedding night and her present obsessional action.

Her obsessional action was shown to have a sense. It was a representation, and a repetition, of the earlier significant and traumatic scene. But her action had an intention, too. She was not simply repeating the scene, she was continuing, and at the same time correcting, it.

40. *Sesame Street* Animation of the Letter *C*

CHILDREN'S VOICES: C is for the compulsion to repeat . . .

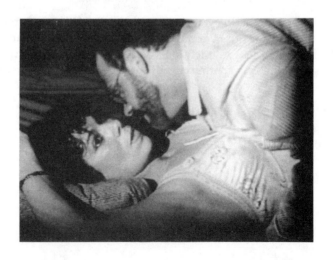

41. The Pleasure Chest — Interview
(Transcript of unscripted interview)

MICHAEL: People are coming out of their closets and respecting and ap-
preciating the feel, the smell, the sensuality of leather, of bondage
equipment. Whether it's used or whether it's not used — because there
are many adaptations — you can use leather as a placebo, not necessarily inflict pain but threaten with it, lay it on the bed. It can all be
part of a costume, or it can be functional.

TITLE: POLITICS BELOW THE BELT

42. Montage — A Series of Porn Reaction Shots

NARRATOR: *(voice-over)* Looking at contemporary sexuality, what sense
can we derive from these widespread psychosexual repetitions? Are
you turned on by military paraphernalia, uniforms, Nazi regalia? Do
S & M scenes, golden showers, scatological amusements titillate you?
Does leather make your blood run hot? Do you like to wear hand-
cuffs and be chained to a bedpost during sex? Do you crave being
hurt, whipped, spanked, kicked, stepped on? Do you own sex aids
that resemble instruments of torture? Do you think you've been
naughty and need to be punished?

Girls: Isn't it unfeminine to initiate? Do you like those "baby-doll"
outfits in bed? Does your guy say you emasculate him 'cause you
make more money than he does? Or 'cause you want to get on top?
It's true: Studies quoted in *The American Couple* show that the less
power a heterosexual woman has in her relationship, the more likely
it is that the couple will have sex in the missionary position. So, guys,
if you want dinner ready on time, better not roll over.

43. *Sesame Street* Animation of the Letter *M*

*A cartoon man lying on top of cartoon woman. She struggles to overturn him and
get on top herself.*

ADULT: M is for the MISSIONARY POSITION . . .

44. The Sex Therapist's Bedroom — Night

*The SEX THERAPIST, dressed in pajamas, lies on top of HIS WIFE in their
bed. A large photo of RONALD REAGAN looms over them on a rear wall.*

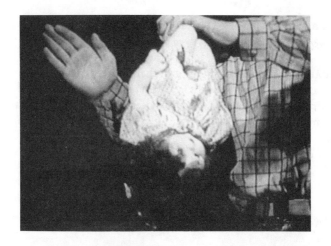

WIFE: *(to camera)* We all know that a man who can *only* make love to his wife while he's on top is expressing his identification with world-wide domination and patriarchy.

45. A Man Spanks a Doll; A Woman's Boot Steps on a Man's Face

NARRATOR: *(voice-over)* Do you think that you *chose* your sexuality, like you go to the supermarket and *choose* your brand of detergent? You over there, licking the boot, stop for a minute and listen. Oh, you can't stop? Liberal capitalism wants you to think that you chose it, but really, *it* chose *you.*

46. A Car Radio

SLICK ADVERTISING VOICE: Would you like to have longer orgasms? Training in Extended Sexual Orgasm—ESO for short—is now available to help you achieve deep, continuous orgasms lasting thirty minutes to an hour. Call Sexual Enlightenment Counseling Services Incorporated TODAY for a no-cost consultation!

47. Sex Therapist's Bedroom

A postcoital conversation.

SEX THERAPIST: I had a new patient today, another desire disorder. Seems like it's getting more and more frequent. Poor guy. Lucky we don't have that problem.

HIS WIFE: You're so right, darling. I think being able to share our sexual fantasies with each other has really helped us to renew our sex life.

SEX THERAPIST: *(lasciviously)* Tell me your sexual fantasies.

HIS WIFE: *(coyly)* Well, sometimes I like to fantasize that we're being watched. . . .

INSERT: *Still of a PORNO PEEP SHOW*

The idea of domination really turns me on. . . .

INSERT: *Still of POLICE VICIOUSLY BEATING PROTESTERS*

I think I'd like to be tied up. . . .

INSERT: Still of POLICE ARRESTING UNDOCUMENTED WORKERS

I like to fantasize that I'm powerless . . .

INSERT: Still of a long, winding WELFARE LINE

that if I'm not a good girl, I'll get hit . . .

INSERT: Still of a Latin American MOTHER *holding photos of missing relatives*

that I'm being humiliated . . .

INSERT: Still of a SOUTH AFRICAN ANTIAPARTHEID PROTEST

restricted . . .

INSERT: Still of LATIN AMERICAN SOLDIERS ARRESTING MAN

cheated . . .

INSERT: Still of BLACK SOUTH AFRICAN WORKERS

lied to. . . .

INSERT: Still of BLACK PRISONERS *in an American jail*

But my favorite fantasy of all is that a right-wing fundamentalist minister —

INSERT: Still of JERRY FALWELL

lies awake in bed at night fantasizing about ways to put my body under his complete control.

TITLE: THE LOSS OF A SENSE OF HISTORY IS FANTASY'S GAIN

48. S/M Paraphernalia

NARRATOR: Pleasure isn't fixed, it's malleable. So why not turn your reality into your pleasure? If surveillance technology is everywhere, become an exhibitionist. If you have no power, get aroused by submission. If the world shits on you, become a coprophiliac.

Freud thought that certain fantasies might have once been real occurrences in another time and place—

INSERT: *Still of SOLDIERS AND TANKS of some right-wing Latin American regime*

actual traumatic events whose memory is elaborated and concealed by fantasies. Perhaps our fantasies function. as a way of mastering those traumatic occurrences that have proved impossible to master politically.

49. *Sesame Street* Animation of the Letter *C*

ADULT: C is for the COMPULSION TO REPEAT . . .

50. Montage—Porn Clips, Women's Reaction Shots

PSYCHIATRIST: *(voice-over)* The patient does not remember anything of what she has forgotten and repressed, but *acts* it out. She reproduces it not as a memory but as an action; she repeats it, without, of course, knowing that she is repeating it.

51. Rolling Text: The Words "Radical," "Liberation," "Progress," "Rebellion," "Subversion," "Political"

NARRATOR: Current sexuality presents itself in a *radical* pose—of liberation, of a battle against the forces of repression, of progress, rebellion, and a subversion of the existing order. Certainly there's no other area of human experience that some proclaim as subversive, that others accuse of subversion, that is practiced daily by so many. In no other area is such an explicitly political language used to describe daily life. Politics has moved underground. Sex has become a way of "thinking about" and acting politically in our current situation.

PSYCHIATRIST: But how does this apply to your own experience?

52. Montage of Stills of S/M Paraphernalia and News Stills—Soldiers with Dead Bodies, Police Taking Prisoners, Welfare Lines, Mothers with Photos of the "Disappeared"

NARRATOR: Perhaps it is the inscription on the first-world body of third-world *tragedies* of the body—torture, political imprisonment, apartheid, starvation. It is the inscription on our bodies of bureaucratization, official surveillance, political powerlessness, the fetishization of the commodity, and the corresponding objectification of the person. These strange eruptions of the body can be read like a book, and when we do read them it's the narrative of the political that we'll find there.

The commodified ecstasy of the thirty-minute Extended Sexual Orgasm gives us the means to forget, for thirty minutes, the sexual torture supported by our tax dollars in other parts of the world. How long can you make the amnesia last? And if you manage to forget it, do you really think it *stays* forgotten?

TITLE: IN THE PENAL COLONY

NARRATOR: Kafka wrote about a prison system with a unique method of dispensing justice. This system employed an elaborate apparatus that tortured and executed the convicted criminal, by inscribing on his naked body, with hundreds of long sharp needles, his criminal sentence. "HONOR THY SUPERIORS!" the prisoner will have written on his body until he is dead.

At the sight of the prisoner, the explorer asks, "Does he know his sentence?"

"No," says the officer. "There would be no point in telling him. He'll learn it from his body. He deciphers it from his wounds. Then the judgment has been fulfilled."

TITLE: WHAT DO WE LEARN FROM OUR BODIES?
        WHAT CAN WE DECIPHER FROM OUR WOUNDS?

53. Slow-Motion Montage: Bell Ringing, Feet Running, an Ink Stain on a Bedsheet

NARRATOR: For Freud, sex was the *hidden* root of the symptom. For us sex is the visible symptom. We're still compelled to *repeat* what we can't master, what is too painful to face. Sexual practices could be our symbolic resolutions, our compensations, for unmastered political and historical reality. Politics is displaced onto the sexual, and the sexual is produced as political.

Freud wrote that the construction of the symptom is a substitute for something that *didn't* happen, something consciousness should have received information of, but didn't. Out of an interrupted process the *symptom* emerges. Out of the repression of politics comes the production of this symptomatic sexuality.

PSYCHIATRIST: How long have you had the feeling that you were being watched?

54. *Sesame Street* Animation of the Letter *S*

An animated eye that grows bigger and bigger in the frame.

ADULT: S is for SURVEILLANCE . . .

CHILDREN: The military-industrial complex loves you so much it can't take its eyes off you.

55. A Subway Station

The shot is like the black-and-white output of a surveillance camera—a very slow tilt up and down a WOMAN'S BODY. Then cut to the camera itself, mounted high on the wall, panning the station.

WOMAN'S VOICE: *(very chirpy)* "Life in These United States"—this amusing anecdote is provided as a public service by the *Reader's Digest.*

Visitors to this country's urban areas are said to find the atmosphere impersonal and the people reserved. If this is true there *are* exceptions, as I discovered in Washington, D.C. I was about to make my first trip on that city's new subway system, and while we waited at the station my friend pointed out a couple of closed circuit cameras high overhead that were silently scanning the area. When the lens tracked past us again I waved at it.

Suddenly the camera reversed itself—and didn't stop until it was

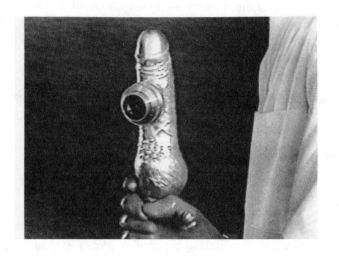

pointing right at me! Then it nodded up and down several times as if waving back.

The camera tilts up and down the woman's body.

Embarrassed, I feebly waved again. Amid the chuckles and smiles of people around me, a warm bass voice came over the PA system. "Hi there," it said.

56. A Lab Technician in White Coat Holding Huge Dildo with a Camera Lens Affixed to It

NARRATOR: In the last two decades the well-known sex research team of Masters and Johnson have observed more than *ten thousand* orgasms under laboratory conditions in St. Louis, Missouri. They have employed sophisticated technological means such as cardiographs, brain wave monitors, and other measuring devices to measure heart rate, blood pressure, and respiratory rate. But their supreme innovation was to have invented an electronically powered artificial phallus made of plastic and designed for intravaginal observation and photography.

CLOSE-UP into the dildo's camera lens.

At the same moment that Masters and Johnson were conducting this intravaginal scrutiny . . .

57. Car Interior—Night

A MIDDLE-AGED MAN is behind the wheel. He's a real nerd type, collar buttoned all the way up and a furtive air about him. He's cruising through an urban area late at night, past porn stores and all-night diners. He yawns, surveils the street through binoculars, drinks coffee, and makes notes. These scenes are intercut with pages from Cohen's book.

NARRATOR: A sociologist from the City University of New York named Bernard Cohen, a former consultant to the NYPD *and* the Rand Corporation, was writing a book on "female heterosexual street prostitution" in midtown Manhattan. In it he extols the virtues of the everyday automobile as a tool of observation and surveillance in social research. Professor Cohen is puzzled that in this technologi-

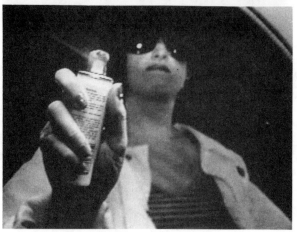

cal age, the auto isn't used more often for *just* this type of work. His research method, he writes, is to follow the routes used by cruising "johns," who, of course *have* already discovered the automobile as an aid in their own quests to track down female street deviance.

BERNARD COHEN: *(voice-over)* I entered my car, left the safety and confines of my home and university and drove around the city streets at all hours of the day and night. I quickly discovered that a car and street observation go hand in hand.

Prostitutes frequently attempted to solicit my business. They spelled out numerous details including price, place, and amount of time for services.

An important issue in this type of field research is safety. About 4:00 A.M. in the vicinity of Bowery and Delancy Street a prostitute approached my car and attempted to solicit my business while I was waiting for a traffic light.

A PROSTITUTE approaches his car and he shuts the window on her hand.

BERNARD: When I declined she suddenly pulled an object from her handbag and sprayed me with mace. Only a small quantity penetrated because simultaneously I made an evading movement and closed my window. The burning and choking sensation in my throat lasted about one and one-half hours even after several glasses of water, obtained in a nearby restaurant.

On a number of occasions prostitutes spilled coffee and banged my car—

A WOMAN throws liquid at the car window and tries to grope at him through the window.

presumably because I declined their solicitations. . . . Once a prostitute remarked that I was a police officer and then leaned through the car's front window to frisk me for a gun. Close contact of this kind can result in physical harm.

58. A Camera Lens Staring into Camera

ROD SERLING VOICE: *Reader's Digest* honoring the human face behind surveillance technology . . .

The rotating dildo with camera lens.

Masters and Johnson and their all-seeing, all-knowing phallus . . .

BERNARD COHEN in his car.

intrepid sociologist Bernard Cohen on the Bowery at 4:00 A.M. eyeing prostitutes from his car . . .

TITLE: A PRICK + A CAMERA = HARD SCIENCE

59. A Screen Full of Blinking Eyes

NARRATOR: The forms of surveillance have become so regular, so mundane, so ingrained in the texture of daily life that we hardly notice them. Official surveillance has become internalized in our habitual confession and display. For Casanova, the best moment of love was following your lover up the stairs to the bedroom. Foucault thought the best moment of love is when your lover leaves in a taxi. But for me, the real best moment of love is when you get to tell your shrink about it the next day.

PSYCHIATRIST: Yes, go on.

TITLE: THE ANALYST IS A BIG EAR

60. A Big Ear

NARRATOR: I could tell you about myself endlessly, I crave self-revelation. "Buxom bisexual divorcée, 38, intelligent, feminine, financially secure, likes movies, nature, ballroom dancing, Bach and fine wine, Proust and Willie Nelson, wants children." That's me. And you? "Short, white, balding successful male, 180 pounds, Ivy League graduate, loves bike riding, brunch, cuddling, closeness, and Wittgenstein, seeks dominant female for afternoon liaisons."

We narrate ourselves in personal ads that read like police dossiers. Any distinguishing marks? We identify ourselves the way the all-seeing eye of the surveillance camera would, to an unseen interrogator. We confess our desire, speak our need to the reading gaze.

All right, I admit it, I'm a dyke.

PSYCHIATRIST: I sense that you're feeling hostile.

61. Psychiatrist's Office

NARRATOR: I define myself via my sexuality — what would I be if I didn't? I am what I do in bed. I transform my desire into advertising, by wearing the identifying markers of it: keys in this pocket, handkerchief in that one. I narrate myself in terms dictated by my sexual preferences — you'll know who I am by the dog collar around my neck and the slit up the front of my skirt. Sexual identity is now the essential component of the "self"; it occupies the place once held by "soul."

PSYCHIATRIST: When did you first start feeling this way?

NARRATOR: But this notion of sexual identity arises largely in reaction to attempts to inhibit sexual expression. Isn't there some irony in the fact that this solidified and rigidified notion of sexual identity is then *produced* by those forces that would restrict sexual expression? The more attempts that are made to restrict sexuality, the more consolidated sexual identity becomes. Now it seems all we can imagine as political intervention is restricting access to pornography or restricting access to abortion. Our notion of politics is confined to the terrain of the individual body.

Isn't defining yourself by your sexuality doing the work of the experts and surveillors for them? Isn't it participating in and continuing the "grand tradition" of Krafft-Ebing, Freud, Havelock Ellis, Kinsey, and police everywhere, of sexual classification — as identity, authority, knowledge, and social control? Only now we've internalized it, and reproduce it. We confess as a lifestyle and pay money to have ourselves interrogated. We are our own sex police.

ROLLING TEXT:

Our sexuality is not repressed, it is produced, and in forms custommade to our social order.

The paths to pleasure are frequently not pretty, but they are our pleasures. Instead of either denying them on the one hand, or glorifying them on the other, we can try to understand them.

Our sexuality is produced in the form of a commodity; our fantasies

are repackaged and sold to us as products in porn stores; our desire has the grammar of consumer capitalism, and those sexual forms will exist as long as those social forms exist.

The irony is in having us believe that our "liberation" is in the balance.

Instead, we can say of sex what was once said of religion: that our pleasure is the sigh of the oppressed creature, the heart of a heartless world, and the soul of soulless conditions. It is the opium of the people.

To do away with the illusion that we have chosen these pleasures is to demand new choices.

The call to abandon illusions about a condition is the call to abandon a condition that requires illusions.

Thus, to critically question our mode of sexuality is to begin to criticize the mode of social organization that produces it.

FADE TO BLACK

CHAPTER 4

Looks Good on Paper
Marxism and Feminism in a Postmodern World

THE POLITICAL FORTUNES of Marxism seem to be on the wane lately in the industrialized West, Soviet-style Communism having finally accomplished what the combined forces of the FBI, the CIA, and the National Association of Scholars had only fantasized. Though long before 1989 the phrase "Marxism lacks a theory of the subject" had often echoed through the shabby halls of Left theory — particularly in later years as better-dressed post-Marxists scratched out narratives of crisis, decline, and aftermath — as regime after regime crumbled overnight, it was clear that it wasn't merely the failure of Soviet economic policies we were witnessing, but the failure of eastern-bloc states to have ever achieved the sort of continuing hegemony over their populations that the advanced capitalist regimes enjoy, despite continuing economic crisis. In the decade of postmortems to come it seems likely that, particularly among those who were not already post-Marxists pre-1989, these events might renew discussion of what has widely been seen as the lack of consideration of subjective factors in orthodox Marxist theory. Often, psychoanalytic theory was offered up as a provisional remedy: although initially and officially rejected by a stalwart orthodoxy wielding such epithets as "bourgeois practice," it was periodically taken up as a prosthetic device for this politically disabling missing limb (as feminism has, in its turn, been called upon to supplement Marxism's missing theory of gender). This unlikely alliance of the theory of praxis and the talking cure, advanced initially by the Frankfurt School, came, more recently, with Althusser's loose appropriation of a Lacanian theory of the subject, to offer the crucial missing link, a theretofore unwritten theory of ideology. It was a theoretical renovation that would revitalize a decade of Marxist culturalism, while breakaway factions abandoned class altogether for the uncharted waters of sexuality, language, and other signifying practices, the political implications of which psychoanalytic theory appeared to offer access to.

The similarly fraught relations between feminism and psychoanalysis can be organized into a comparable narrative. The early repudiation of the psychoanalytic as a prescription for patriarchy (and Freud as patriarch personified) yielded to what might be called a homeopathic approach — poison in small doses as a temporary remedy, one whose curative powers, however, run the risk of producing in the healthy the symptoms of the disease. That this latex-gloved appropriation of psychoanalysis as a "political weapon" might have ceded, at least in some corner of academic feminist theory, to a transferential relation as interminable as analysis itself is nicely documented by Jane Gallop in her book *Reading Lacan*.[1] Gallop's book can also be read as a cautionary narrative on how the initial political imperative behind the psychoanalytic remedy became displaced in the intellectual frissons of continental theory. Like tourists seduced, or anthropologists gone native, those tentative forays into Freud-land for accounts of the gendered subject and narrative pleasures seem to have resulted in permanent residence—while oppositional elements have, in the meantime, pitched their tents in object relations and set to work constructing the countertheory of the powerful mother. As with Althusser for Marxists, the influence of Lacan in feminist theory seems to have hit feminist culturalism the hardest—particularly literary and film theory.

Despite these brief, tendentiously comparative historical sketches, this essay is not going to be another attempt to effect a rapprochement in what's been described as "the unhappy marriage of Marxism and feminism." I want instead to attempt to account for a shared theoretical moment or conjuncture: the moment in which a political orthodoxy turns heterodox and cohabits with what seemed, initially, the enemy. The narrative of the mésalliance turned true love is, of course, a powerful one in our culture—we have only to look to classics like *It Happened One Night* for an analysis of its structural conditions of possibility, for an account of how the carefully erected exclusion falls. (And it hardly needs pointing out that the tale of the feminist romance with Lacan itself strongly suggests the Harlequin formula: the hero may be, on the surface, rude, sexist, and self-absorbed, but it is he alone who knows the truth of the heroine's desire.)

This recourse to psychoanalysis (which provides no theory of social transformation and historically offers no evidence of political efficacy) in both Marxist and feminist theory seems to take place at a particular theoretical juncture: one marked primarily by the experience of political catastrophe and defeat. The political appropriation of psychoanalysis appears to signal, then, a lack—of a mass movement or of successful counterhegemonic strategies. The disastrous absorption of the European working-class movements into fascism, the decline of the political fortunes of feminism (outside the university) from those boisterous years when it seemed on the verge of becoming a mass movement—these are the events that have preceded the respective detours through the psychoanalytic. Notwithstanding Russell Jacoby's proviso that it's "the mystique of success that generates the fiction of defeat," the recourse to psychoanalytic theory appears to be implicated in just this dialectic of defeat, in that the appropriation of psychoanalysis seems precipitated by, and *indicates*, subjective factors recalcitrant to the particular social transformations at issue in the master theory.[2] The political use value of psychoanalytic theory would thus seem to be its updated account of the organization or etiology of *consent* to patriarchal or capitalist orders, which, as with the formation of the symptom, can now be seen to have its own characteristic form and specificity comparatively independent of its genesis. It indicates a theoretical shift away from the Gramscian "spontaneous consent" obtained in civil society, a conscious and rational acting-out of interest, and toward a theory of *unconscious* structures of consent negotiated in the suturing effects of various processes of signification, in the specularity of ideology, or in the very construction of gendered subjects. Any given assimilation of psychoanalytic theory to a political formulation can also be seen as an index of the chasmal distance between leftist theory-wielding intellectuals and popular consciousness. Discursively grafting on psychoanalytic theory ties the people into a radical political logic, filling a "space left vacant by a crisis of what . . . should have been a normal historical development"; it functions to close the gap left by the absence of a revolutionary subject.[3]

Where there is a vehement political rejection of psychoanalytic theory — as in American radical feminism, which repudiated psychological explanations of women's behavior, stressing instead that these are "always and only a rational, self-interested response to their immediate material conditions, i.e. their oppression by men"[4] — it appears to coincide with a denial of consent as a political factor, in favor of an insistence on coercion as the truth of political oppression. And a persistent criticism of cultural feminism, radical feminism's successor, has been its focus on coercion and its emphasis on women's status as victim.[5] For a popular feminist theorist like Andrea Dworkin, pornography, rape, and violence against women are the central and absolute determining instances not only in *all* women's lives and psychology, but in civilization as a whole. In women's studies programs, generally the American academic cognate of cultural feminism, we also see the rejection of psychoanalysis, as in, for example, the emotionally charged debate over Freud's repudiation of his seduction theory and the feminist insistence on sociological data of real rape and incest — real victimization — rather than the mere fantasy of seduction posited in the Oedipal theory, with its disturbing corollary, the sexual child.[6]

We can see that a psychoanalytically inflected political theory constructs a particular and specialized theoretical object, as well — it changes the nature of the object it analyzes. A filmic or literary text has to be construed as a symptom-producing entity in order to be an adequate object of psychoanalytic inquiry. It must operate completely differently from, say, the Lukácsian object text — which is required to reflect or disclose an anterior reality and is held responsible for how it does or doesn't disclose that reality. If the theoretical object prescribes a set of theoretical strategies, it simultaneously describes a field of political possibility. Then implicit in the constitution of a theoretical object (for psychoanalytic feminists, a psychic topography of oppression as opposed to, for cultural feminists, external structures of coercion) is also a representation of a political terrain. As with all representations, there is an appearance of transparency here: the textual operations of its own production and organization of meaning are effaced. So, as with any representation, this is a strategy of containment as well as of possibility. To put it another way—the way a psychoanalytic critic might— this discursive field is structured by its absences and its repressions: it is equally a product of the territory it *can't* represent. What emerges in the constitution of the theoretical object, then, is a dialectic of the representable and the nonrepresentable, or, in other words, an aesthetics.

Psychoanalytic theory was taken up at similar points by both Marxists and feminists, particularly in reference to culture. The question I want to pose is, How does this change the way a radical political theory constitutes its object? Or, what happens when you graft on psychoanalytic theory as a third term to the field of aesthetics and politics? I believe you get a topography that lays out something like this. Both Marxist and feminist positions that *reject* the political appropriation of psychoanalysis seem to favor a realist aesthetics, which is often seen as having direct political effectivity: socialist realism, obviously; Lukácsian critical realism (Lukács referred to Freud as a "devastating influence"); images-of-women criticism and the positive-images-of-women campaigns; the feminist appropriation of the realist novel and its project of inventing woman as full speaking subject; and the politics of the antipornography movement, which relies on an aesthetics of reference to constitute its political object.

The characteristic mark of a political appropriation of psychoanalytic theory, however, seems to be the affiliation of politics and aesthetic modernism: strategies of negation, rupture, inwardness. Modernism and psychoanalytic theory go way back; many theorists of modernism have found it impossible to theorize the twentieth-century avant-garde unless through Freud's theory of dreams and the unconscious. For other writers it's the same, only in reverse: for Edward Said, not only is the attitude of modern writers toward the text an essentially Freudian posture, and modernist antinarrational textuality the textual solution of the Oedipal tangle, but Freud's *Interpretation of Dreams* is itself a protomodernist text.[7] And Dominick LaCapra has pointed out that the distinction between high, mass, and popular culture closely resembles and may in certain respects have *shaped* Freud's topology of id, ego, and superego, in that, in certain periods, high culture becomes aligned with official state culture in a hegemonic formation that tries to "establish a shared superego . . . extending to other sections of society and culture"—an observation that's quite relevant to the problematic and repetitive tendency toward modernist aesthetics in twentieth-century political movements, which I'm getting to.[8]

The conjunctions of Marxism and modernism are less mutually constitutive, but equally well known. What I want to add to the picture is the pertinence of the appropriation of psychoanalysis and its particular thematics of the subject to these various Marxist modernisms: initially for the Frankfurt School and culminating in the Althusserian moment of *Screen*, in which Brecht was adopted as the heir apparent of Lacan and a Barthesian criterion of the writerly text was taken up as an antidote to the regime of phallic vision and the reproduction of the bourgeois subject.

However, the current *re*-articulation of modernism by feminist theorists working at the intersections of deconstruction and psychoanalysis suggests that there is, perhaps, something compulsive about this repetitive tendency toward cultural modernism in marginalized vanguard political movements, and something repetitive in the compulsive way this triangulation seems to appear again and again.[9] One explanatory strategy might be to see the appropriation of psychoanalysis by both Western Marxism and current feminism as an epiphenomenon of a general tendency to turn and return to modernism itself—a tendency problematic if regarded, as I'll be suggesting, as part of a larger impetus toward the aestheticization of the political. If psychoanalytic theory is seen as propelling politics toward aestheticization, specifically toward a modernist aesthetics, the postmodernist critique of modernism might be a starting point in evaluating the consequences of this gesture. It might also aid in generating a theory of whatever it is that is buried and at work in first-world radical theory at this juncture, which keeps manifesting itself, symptomatically, rashlike, as the repetitive conjunction of politics, modernism, and psychoanalytic theory.

The problem of aesthetics and politics has been central to an understanding of the shortcomings of existing theories of political transformation. The brunt of Perry Anderson's critique in *Considerations on Western Marxism* is his assessment that Western Marxism devolved into an aesthetic theory dissociated from the political; its central concerns became philosophy, and its theorists, professional philosophers with little concern or interest in practical politics. Particularly after the war, their orientation was increasingly toward academia, which became both refuge and exile from the brute realities of political struggle outside the university gates. In their work, they maintained a "studied silence" in the areas central to the classic traditions of historical materialism: economics, politics, and class struggle. According to Anderson, the very form of the Western Marxist tradition, in fact, took shape precisely through the displacement of mass practice: theory became "an esoteric discipline whose highly technical idiom measures its distance from politics," a charge that Anderson levels to varying degrees against all the denizens of Western Marxism, including, of course, the prescriptive modernism of the Frankfurt School, up to and through Althusser's theory of theoretical autonomy.[10]

The historical alliances of Marxism and modernism help to explain the ensemble of modernism and radical politics today. In fact, the late reception of Frankfurt School theory in France probably goes some way to accounting for the fact that the return to modernism has featured so prominently in the work of theorists like Kristeva, Cixous, Irigaray, and Wittig. That these writers have often been classified as *postmodern* is indicative of the confusions in mapping the affiliations of poststructuralism and postmodernism—given that the policies of *écriture féminine* and its practice of displacing revolution and politics to the aesthetic take us right back to that very modernist tradition that these continental theorists are presumed to transcend.[11] In addition, their repudiation of representation, subjectivity, and history clearly set up the same antinomies with the *popular* that constituted aesthetic modernism from its inception. In this version, however, rather than merely advocating a modernist cultural practice, a modernist aesthetic practice is enacted in the theory itself—political theory has now emerged as aesthetic expression per se, rather than being confined, as for earlier theorists, to the theory of aesthetic expression.

This new aestheticization of theory seems to be prefigured in Walter Benjamin's well-known warning about the "aestheticization of politics" and his counterprescription that "we" politicize aesthetics. Lurking here is a suggestion that this configuration of politics and aesthetics is not simply a characteristic of fascism, and its reversal not just a prescriptive for left culturalists, but that the configuration of the two is a structural particularity of capital in crisis, signaling the crisis of modernity. The consequence of this particular configuration of aesthetics and politics is, as Anderson points out, the transformation of theory into an autonomous, disconnected activity. In Anderson's critique of a Western Marxist tradition divorced from politics, seeking refuge from political defeat in high culture, we see a theory no longer able to constitute its political object; in the rejection of mass practice, so neatly condensed in Adorno's own rejection of the New Left, theoretical practice becomes an autonomous moment, a moment later made explicit by Althusser, who saw theoretical practice as its own criterion with no need for verification from anywhere. The post-Marxist critique of Marxism as fully implicated in the *grand récits* of modernity, and suffering from the same epistemological crisis, suggests that the crisis of Marxism and the decline of modernism are particularly intertwined. It's quite disturbing, then, to find the same configuration of politics, aesthetics, and theoretical autonomy that characterizes later Western Marxism operating in current feminist theory.

The earliest feminist appropriations of psychoanalysis for a political aesthetics (work carried out in the same milieu that produced Juliet Mitchell's 1974 defense of Freud, *Psychoanalysis and Feminism*) can be found in Pam Cook's and Claire Johnston's writings in *Screen* in the early seventies and later in Laura Mulvey's influential "Visual Pleasure and Narrative Cinema" (1975), in which psychoanalysis is taken up to demonstrate "the way the unconscious of patriarchal society has structured film form." From its inaugurating moment, this argument was made in the service of a modernist countercinematic practice — Mulvey is herself, of course, such a practitioner — and *against* mass culture, which is now repudiated not on the basis of its commodification, as it was for the Frankfurt School, but on the grounds of its phallocentrism, the critique that will be leveled against all forms of realist representation, including language itself. The political contradictions of this kind of left-aesthetic vanguardism seem clear enough. If the analysis of scopophilia in dominant cinema produces remedial cultural practices whose only audience is the traditional audience of high culture, it suggests — what? Somehow luring the masses to *Riddles of the Sphinx* as a future political program?

A postmodernist critique of modernism sees modernism as constituted by its binary opposition to popular culture; the popular, modernism's antinomy, is fully present, a "present absence," in any consideration of modernism. So it's against the "mass" of mass culture that the modernist program directs much of its oppositional energies. This suggests right off that any politics that devotes itself to refining a modernist poetics is likely to involve a gap between a popular and a vanguard political position, and that the consequences of an aestheticism that hinges on increasing self-reference and autonomy from everyday social life might be an increasing distance between radical theory and mass politics. So the turn and return to modernism suggests a spiraling aesthetics of defeat: the rejection of and by the popular compounded by a gravitation toward the hermetic.

What can we say about a feminist appropriation of psychoanalysis that works to reestablish relations of hierarchy in art, reinvesting in high culture while inveighing against a popular audience for its pleasure? Although one contradiction of this position is that from the standpoint of modernism, mass culture tends to be coded female,[12] it's also the case that the "radical political weapon" of psychoanalysis leads into an aestheticizing tendency in feminist theory that's essentially neo-Kantian: a conservative reinvestment in aesthetic autonomy that has provoked, in other quarters, the classification of poststructuralism as "New New Criticism." And with this particular invocation of the aesthetic, one might suspect that the transcendental subject can't be far behind. Interestingly enough, it was Adorno, in his aesthetic writings, who pointed to the similarity in matters aesthetic between the two seemingly antithetical thinkers who form the axis of psychoanalytic modernism, Kant and Freud. For both, Adorno points out, the work of art exists *only* in relation to the subject, but also, both, by "placing works of art squarely into a realm of psychic immanence . . . lose sight of their antithetical relation to the non-subjective." Adorno, with his quirky dialectics, explains the mutual blindness this way:

> Perhaps the most important taboo in art is the one that prohibits an animal-like attitude toward the object, say a desire to devour it or otherwise subjugate it to one's body. Now the strength of such a taboo is matched by the strength of the repressed urge. Hence, all art contains in itself a negative moment from which it tries to get away.[13]

This suggests that a political aesthetic that attempts to break with forms of address that it characterizes as reaffirming the subject's imaginary coherence at the same time, in fact, itself *hinges* on this subjectivity, which the aesthetic field is itself constituted by (a universal subjectivity according to Kant), and that this mutual interdependence of subject and aesthetic isn't in any way hindered by a repertoire of modernist techniques now recycled as the break with the scopophilia of visual mass culture and the phallocentrism of language. It's precisely this gap between a radical dismantling of the subject and the conservative, aestheticist, and antipopulist aesthetic practices that this dismantling puts into circulation and would seem, in fact, to dictate that I want to explore.

It's clear that the question of subjectivity has been at the epicenter of current reformulations of modernism. Within what can broadly be called current left theory—Marxism, feminism, and left poststructuralism, "the subject" is a rubric that now seems to determine just what political questions we may ask.[14] This "subject" we know by its traits: it is split; it speaks; it is gendered; it is social; or it is a linguistic effect; it is castrated; and it thinks it knows so much. Alternatively, we have its obituary, as narrated by Baudrillard, among others: it is occultated, disappears, and dies. Given that discourse is also productive, it's hard not to see this theoretical proliferation of the subject—its production as a site of attention, investigation, and speculation—as symptomatic of some kind of necessity. Its insistent visibility, which provides a certain bolstering of the category itself, provokes the question of what exactly it is that the subject needs bolstering against—its fragmentation in the chop-shop of late capitalism, or perhaps some glimmer of self-knowledge that the necessary historical precondition for a critique of the subject is the loss of its legitimating function? What other political determinations can account for such excessive visibility of a category that operated precisely from a blindness to its own determinations, whose greatest desire was to turn itself into an effect of nature? This subject that drops its veils one by one to reveal its naked status as construction, rather than nature, bares everything *except* the answer to its insistent appearance: if everywhere we look the subject is all that is visible, what is it that is hidden?

Inasmuch as the subject is itself an ideological category, the question of its current hypervisibility must be profoundly political; notwithstanding that the field of the visual, as Lacan makes clear, is itself bound up with the constitution of subjectivity. Visibility is a complex system of permission and prohibition, of presence and absence, punctuated alternately by apparitions and hysterical blindness. Let's suppose, initially, that this visibility of the subject, so necessarily tied to the loss of its legitimating function, is another dynamic of the closing off of the political space of modernity, in which consolidation of political power took place under the banner of Enlightenment rationality and reason. In the "centered subject," with its synecdochical relation to the political centrality of the West, lay a mandate to make the rest of the world its object: of conquest, knowledge, surplus value. Then, in the recent appearance of the category of the "de-centered subject" perhaps lurks a synecdoche of the decline of the great imperial powers of modernity, the traumatic loss of hegemony of the West, which here in the psychic economy of the United States, we have continually reflected back to us in compensatory fantasies like *Rambo*, *Red Dawn*, and Ronald Reagan.

What is interesting about this waning modernity is the theoretical crisis it engenders, in which the traditional narratives of liberation fall under suspicion, opening a theoretical void that these various modernisms attempt, but are unable, to fill. What is crucially lacking is a postmodern political discourse. I want to attempt to trace this symptomatic gap as it's manifested in first-world feminist theory, which seems to be suspended between an emergent postmodern political logic and a residual modernism.

It's now common, in feminist theory, to distinguish broadly between Anglo-American feminism on the one hand and Continental feminism on the other. I'd like to suggest that these distinctions are primarily between competing theories of representation, which can be summarized by the posture of each toward the signifier. Terry Eagleton has observed that the history of Marxism itself follows the Saussurean trajectory of the linguistic sign: "First we had a referent, then we had a sign, now we just have a signifier," and according to Eagleton's schema, this final moment, the autonomy of the signifier, is identified with Althusserian Marxism.[15] These successive moments of the sign seem to occur simultaneously within current feminist theory, with the divisions drawn primarily according to *nation* rather than diachronically, and with the culminating moment of the autonomy of the signifier associated, for feminism, with Lacan rather than Althusser.

What's generally called American feminism generally relies on a theory of language as transparency. This entails a belief in a recoverable history, in authored productions, in the focus on speech over language, in the conscious over the unconscious, in experience over theory, and in the phallus as a biological, rather than a symbolic, entity. In this camp, it's a short trip from a sign to a referent, and this produces, as sites of political engagement, the struggle for the terrain of the realist novel, the demand for access to the discourse of subjectivity, the possibility of an isolated sign or image as a potential site for political action, and in general, a politics of reformism. (Most of these positions are exemplified in the antipornography movement.)

Continental or poststructural feminism, in general, follows the Saussurean division of the sign; emphasizes the materiality of the signifier; privileges the synchronic over diachronic, structure over subject, signification over meaning; and asserts that women have no position from which to speak. Its focus on the priority of system marks the unconscious as the privileged area of exploration, and modernist rupture as the privileged aesthetic practice. In intellectual history terms, the priority of both psychoanalytic theory and modernist aesthetics in poststructural feminism might be seen as a by-product of the Saussurean legacy of the synchronic, the jolt of which is felt from Lévi-Strauss to Lacan.

It's been the contention of poststructural feminists that naming the female sex as the political subject of feminism reproduces the biological essentialism and the binary logic that have relegated women to an inferior role. This produces, as a site of political attention and engagement, a "space" rather than a sex: the margin, the repressed, the absence, the unconscious, the irrational, the feminine—in all cases the negative or powerless instance. Whereas "American feminism" is a discourse whose political subject is biological women, "Continental feminism" is a political discourse whose subject is a structural position—variously occupied by the feminine, the body, the Other.

From these radical insights of Continental feminism we move to the practice of *écriture féminine*, which, in posing a counterlanguage against the binary patriarchial logic of phallogocentrism, was an attempt to construct a language that enacts liberation rather than merely theorizing it—for Cixous, the imaginary construction of the female body as the privileged site of writing; for Irigaray, a language of women's laughter in the face of phallocratic discourse; for both, private, precious languages that rely on imaginary spaces held to be outside the reign of the phallus: the pre-Oedipal, the female body, the mystical, women's relation to the voice, fluids.[16]

This is, once again, the assertion of a political praxis through essentially modernist textual practices, which relegates the analysis of the symbolic construction of alterity into an aestheticism that closes off referentiality like blinders on a horse: in this notion of literary "productivity," the text itself operates as an ultimate meaning.[17] The attempt to straitjacket those marginal spaces into the text seems an essentially defensive maneuver, safeguarding against their escape beyond the confines of *écriture* into wider social praxis by limiting the dissemination of these forms of knowledge to the consumers of avant-garde culture.

What would it mean to find these operations now in literary confinement, these procedures held to deconstruct binarisms, dismantle phallocentrism, and decenter subjects, *outside* writing, to suspend the orthodoxy that reality and history are simply texts, while retaining the radical insights of feminist deconstruction? It's worth noting that another theoretical discourse, dependency theory in economics (which is closely linked in time frame to poststructuralism), in which the object of attention is not textual, but is rather the connection between economic development and underdevelopment in the unequal exchange relations of first to third world, tells a story very similar to that of poststructural feminism in its account of the mechanisms by which a dominant term comes to repress a secondary term. And in this telling, the deconstruction of these binarisms is anything but a symbolic practice.[18]

A narrative has emerged in postmodern theory that reads something like this. Feminism is the paradigmatic political discourse of postmodernism: its affirmation of the absence, the periphery, the Other—spaces in which the position of women is structurally and politically inscribed—rating more current political credibility than Marxism, a patriarchial discourse of "mastery/transparency/rationalism," a master code issuing from a transcendent point of view, the path that leads from "totality to totalitarianism, from Hegel to the gulag."[19]

A slightly different narrative might be pieced together from these same elements. If Marxism is viewed as the radical political discourse of modernity, and feminism as the radical political discourse of post-modernity, it can be seen that each functions as a dominant articulating principle through which other, disparate political struggles enunciate the possibility of political transformation. According to crisis-in-Marxism theories, Marxism's ambition to unify isolated working-class struggles into a mass movement of the proletariat has hampered its ability to provide articulations for new and emerging political positions — given transformations in the nature of labor and in the types of world geopolitical struggles of postcolonialism — in addition to its perceived inability to seriously theorize the subalternity of women.

The emergence in feminist theory of the periphery, the absence, and the margin implies a theory of women not as class or caste, but as colony — and this was in fact an analysis made early on in American feminism (and earlier still in Simone de Beauvoir's depiction of woman as Other) by women in SDS casting their controversial break with the male-dominated New Left in the political rhetoric of the day (1967): "As we analyze the position of women in capitalist society and especially in the United States we find that women are in a colonial relationship to men and we recognize ourselves as part of the Third World."[20]

What this analogy (whose genealogy can be traced back through the New Left, the relation of the New Left to the black power movement, and the crucial influence on black power by African decolonization movements) suggests is that the theoretical emergence of these political spaces now being described by Continental feminists parallels the narrative of the decline of the great imperial powers of modernity, the liquidation of the European empires, and the postcolonial rearrangements of the traditional centers on a world scale. It is France, after all, that has produced an influential body of theory based on the centrality of castration in the construction of human subjectivity. Perhaps this is why the American reception of Lacan has been primarily as a literary theory: to confine this disturbing knowledge to the text and recycle it through the recuperative apparatus of literary humanism, rather than allowing the emergence of France as the world capital of theory to perhaps be read as the sequel of its own political decentering and loss of mastery — in the war, in Indochina, in North Africa.

Yet, much of European postwar decolonization took place out of practical and economic necessity more so than out of ideological conviction: the colonial mind persists long after its political and economic structures have been dismantled. Continental feminism offers a radical structural analysis of operations it prefers to call phallogocentrism, but then retreats from the implications of its own analysis into the autonomy of the text, seizing on a modernist refusal of reference to enact its ambivalence. Continental feminism would seem to be the most potentially radical current in contemporary political theory, freeing itself from the essentialism, reformism, and liberal tradition of American feminism. Yet, it also seems beset by the same conjunctural elements associated with the depoliticization of Western Marxism, prone to aestheticization, theoretical autonomy, and a deliberate distance from political praxis. It identifies the structural position of a new political subject, inscribing itself into that moment, and is then paralyzed by this knowledge and by its own first-world status, hysterically blind to the geopolitical implications of its own program—and legitimately so, because the knowledge offered here is not benign. It is that real shifts in world power and economic distribution have little to do with *jouissance*, the pre-Oedipal, or fluids, and that the luxury of first-world feminism to dwell on such issues depends on the preservation of first-world abundance guaranteed by systematic underdevelopment elsewhere and by the postponement, by whatever means, of the political decentering that will mean the close of that historical epoch.

This essay was first written during the week of the U.S. bombing of Libya, so euphemistically presented to us by our ruling powers as a "surgical strike." This phrase, along with Reagan's memorable diagnosis of Qaddafi as "flaky," brings to mind another form of surgical strike, the lobotomy, so often performed with icepicks and on women, following the diagnosis of irrationality. Here we have Qaddafi, cast in the role of Frances Farmer, with the United States in the role of psychiatric surgeon. (That the colonial is coded female has been clear enough even without the *N.Y. Post*'s artist's rendering of Qaddafi as a woman.) Our network news these days is full of irrational Libyans and irrational Palestinians, needing a little frontal lobe job, and its own ideological mission is now admitted so freely that CBS's latest slogan for its news is "We keep America on top of the world." The diagnosis of national aspirations that don't coincide with the master plan of the West is "psychopathology," which demands a "cure"—the full array of state repressive apparatuses: for Libyans, bombs; in the case of women, rape, battery, confinement; and medical and psychiatric abuse—repressive apparatuses in a familial guise.

As was seen in the last decade's hysteria over "international terrorism"—the ultimate conspiracy theory into which our government once managed to fuse the Soviet Union, Islamic fundamentalism, the Sandinistas, and Palestinian nationalism—the reaction to any decentering telos is symptomatic blindness rather than insight: there is an unwillingness and inability to fully comprehend this phenomenon of shifts in power and spheres of influence, and of new forms of political struggle in which civilian tourists are held responsible for the actions of their governments. When retaliation is taken, as has been announced, for "American arrogance," *this* is the postmodern critique of the Enlightenment; it is, in *fact*, a decentering; it's the margin, the absence, the periphery, rewriting the rules from its own interest.

By associating feminism with other political struggles and with a particular historical space, I don't mean in any way to efface gendered oppression or actual historical women in the name of some putatively greater oppression. The rise of the current women's movement paralleled (and, according to some more unreconstructed elements, caused) the decline of the black power movement in the United States, suggesting a metonymy of struggle within this historical space. If feminism *is* read as a decolonizing movement, allied with other decolonizing movements, this is, in a sense, to say that the Right is right when it identifies feminism as a threat to the "American way of life." Yet, this latent knowledge of the political stakes produces the impasse that I think we currently see in feminist theory: after the critique of liberal reformism, after the dismantling of the biologistic but uplifting fable that women will, given the chance, construct a nonhierarchical political utopia, the political options are indeed narrower. It's either "out of the mainstream and into the revolution" or out of the revolution and into the text. On the local level, the decline of the narratives of liberation of modernity and the retreat from the political implications of postmodernity have left the field wide open for the Right, which has successfully fought on the terrain of popular interpellation: controlling the terms of popular discourse; arrogating the terrain of nature, family, community, and the fetus; not hesitating to appropriate and rearticulate a traditionally left rhetoric of liberation and empowerment. It is striking that Phyllis Schlafly's antifeminist manifesto, *The Power of the Positive Woman* (1977), opens with the question, "How are women to acquire power in the world?"[21] In fact, Schlafly modeled herself into one of the most effective political figures outside electoral politics in the United States by using the rhetoric of disenfranchisement to mobilize radical feminism's Other — suburban housewives — into an effective political force. By manipulating the classism and other exclusions operating in feminist discourse of the seventies to marshal fear and *ressentiment* among women who saw feminism as elitist and the ERA as a threat to their tenuous hold on any corner of empowerment in the world, Schlafly created a grass-roots movement that turned the expected ratification of the ERA by liberal feminists into a crashing defeat.

What this suggests is that the insights of a left postmodernism's renegotiation of the popular are relevant to a feminist theory that is increasingly unable to interpellate a popular audience or capture a popular imagination. Instead, the avant-gardist strategies of negation that have been proffered as a counterforce to the technics of popular culture end up producing their own Other — the "mass" of mass culture that resides outside the vanguard elite, outside the intelligentsia, and outside the university. If the popular is seen as an access to hegemony rather than an instrument of domination, what follows is a postmodern strategy of struggle over the terrain of popular interpellation, an acknowledgment that hegemony is won rather than imposed.

But this again mistakenly presumes that "we" are only the subject of political transformation, rather than the object. The hypervisibility of the subject, the symptom that introduced this etiology of current theory, parallels its deconstruction on the world stage. The neomodernist desire to locate the space of the margin and the absence within the text — to hold that theory has autonomously arrived at the point at which it achieves recognition of the periphery — is simply to theorize again from first-world interest, to display a hysterical blindness to the fact that the periphery has forced itself upon the attention of the center. To the extent that any deconstructive theory prioritizes the autonomous text, it maintains this blindness, it reinvents and reinvests in the centrality of that center. To the extent that a feminist theory discovers these crucial spaces in textual rather than in political practice, it indicates the resistance of first-world feminists to the dangerous knowledge that in a *world* system of patriarchy, upheld by an international division of labor, unequal exchange, and the International Monetary Fund, we first-world feminists are also the beneficiaries.

CHAPTER 5

A Man's Woman
(1987)

FADE UP:

1. An Aerobics Studio   Day/Interior

A number of leotarded female bodies move in and out of the frame. We hear inter-mingled women's voices.

VOICE 1: . . . so finally he rolls over and tells me that he's never had this problem with anyone else before and he thinks that I threaten his masculinity in some way.

VOICE 2: The Dutch treat. That's what feminism has done for women. We still make sixty cents on every male dollar but now we're expected to pay for our own damned dinner.

VOICE 3: . . . told me he'd never felt like this about anyone else before, so we go to bed together and then of course he never calls again.

VOICE 4: Men are shits. And you have to formulate a politics that accounts for that. A strategy.

VOICE 5: Castration at birth?

ROLLING TEXT:
The program you are about to see is purely fictional. Any resemblance between the characters portrayed here and actual persons such as Phyllis Schlafly, Marabel Morgan, or Anita Bryant is purely coincidental. No connection is intended or should be inferred.

CLOVIS KINGSLEY sits at a backstage dressing table, scrutinizing herself in the mirror as she applies her makeup.

Fade Up Music: Connie Francis Singing "Follow the Boys":

> *I'll follow the boys, wherever they go,*
> *I'll follow the boys, because in my heart I know,*
> *I know that somewhere, somewhere along the way,*
> *I'll find my love, my own true love someday. . . .*

(over CLOVIS's face)

TITLE: A MAN'S WOMAN

TITLE:
"IT IS DIFFICULT TO UNDERSTAND THE LAWS OF MOTION
FROM THE POINT OF VIEW OF A TENNIS BALL"
                                                    —BRECHT

2. An Auditorium   Night/Int

CLOVIS KINGSLEY is at the podium: impassioned, gesticulating, exhorting the audience. She's midfortyish, blond bouffant, primly dressed, and very feminine, but a demagogue in pearls, an Evita from the suburbs. There is a large banner behind her proclaiming: "CLOVIS KINGSLEY: MORAL FORUM WOMAN OF THE YEAR."

CLOVIS: There are basic biological differences between men and women that can't be denied, differences that are the work of the Divine Architect of the human race!

3. Outside the Auditorium   Night/Exterior

A gaggle of FEMINIST PROTESTERS are marching and chanting on the street outside the hall. They carry protest signs reading, "KINGSLEY BETRAYS ALL WOMEN," "STOP CLOVIS NOW," "SEND MRS. KINGSLEY BACK TO HER KITCHEN," "DEPOSE KINGSLEY."

4. Auditorium

CLOVIS: What do feminists want? They want a gender-free, unisex society!

5. Outside Auditorium

PROTESTERS: Stop Kingsley now!

6. Auditorium

CLOVIS: They want bigger government, more federal spending—

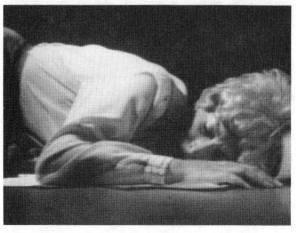

higher taxes! They want to turn the government into a giant baby-sitting service for mothers and they want you the taxpayer to pay!

7. Outside Auditorium

PROTESTERS: Stop Kingsley now!

8. Auditorium   Night/Int

CLOVIS: It is the so-called "feminists" who are against women—bitter, militant, straggly-haired, disappointed women who want the rest of us to give up the rights and privileges we've worked long and hard for, the right to raise our families and be supported by our husbands! The right of a wife to her husband's support is not only a matter of United States law but of compliance with divine command! "Thy desire shall be unto thy husband and he shall rule over thee." "Wives, submit yourself unto your own husbands as unto the Lord."

CLOSE-UP: A hand holding a gun creeps over the balcony railing.

Suddenly there is a CRACK of gunfire.

In slow motion, CLOVIS grasps her chest and falls to the ground, the pages of her speech scattering around her.

The ASSASSIN, a stocky woman in a suit and pearls, flees through an exit.

FREEZE FRAME of CLOVIS lying on the floor, dead.

9. Outside the Auditorium   Night/Ext

The ASSASSIN pushes her way through protesters into a black getaway car.
The SQUEAL of tires as it pulls away from curb, fast.

FADE UP MUSIC: "FOLLOW THE BOYS," CONNIE FRANCIS
singing:

> *And there'll be no place too far,*
> *No ocean too wide . . .*

10. TV News Set

MALE TV NEWSCASTER: And this just in. Clovis Kingsley, the right-
wing antifeminist activist, largely credited with the defeat of the
women's movement in this country, has been shot dead while speaking in Washington, D.C.

A box insert photo of CLOVIS appears with the dates: 1944–1988.

Mrs. Kingsley, mother of four, began her public career as a Republican organizer and fundraiser. She was a strong proponent of military
escalation, and a hard-line anti-Communist who attracted notoriety
by publicly accusing Henry Kissinger of being a Communist agent.
After running unsuccessfully for Congress twice, she turned her attention to the private sphere and founded the popular Total Submission course for women. Police are seeking the identity of a stocky
woman seen fleeing the scene.

We've just received word that a communiqué has been issued by a
group calling itself the "Women's Defense League" claiming responsibility for the assassination.

Clovis Kingsley, dead at age forty-four.

11. Inside the Getaway Car   Night/Int

The ASSASSIN pulls off her wig and earrings, and we see that she's actually
a MAN—a clean-shaven young Republican type.

CONNIE FRANCIS singing:

> *Wherever he goes, I'll be right by his side,*
> *I'll follow the boys . . .*

12. Producer's Office—A Metropolitan TV Station
Day/Int

CLOSE-UP: Young Asian female TV REPORTER

NARRATOR: *(voice-over)* This is a career woman.

CLOSE-UP: Middle-aged white male PRODUCER

NARRATOR: *(voice-over)* This is yet another male in a position of institutional power.

PRODUCER: Okay, this Kingsley assassination. Dig up the dirt on her. John Birch Society . . . the fundraising . . . get the angle on the husband. . . . Was he threatened by her career? What was she after? What were her last words? It isn't enough to tell us what she did— you have to tell us who she was. Talk to the people who knew her, who loved her, who hated her guts. Don't go through the phone directory.

REPORTER: So what if there's no dirt?

PRODUCER: Be creative.

13. Reporter's Office   Night/Int

A tight shot of CLOVIS. As the CAMERA dollies back we see we're watching news footage on a television monitor, and as we continue dollying back we see the REPORTER is studying the footage on the monitor.

On the monitor:

A talk-show set.

CLOVIS: *(to host)* Now if Gloria Steinem and Betty Friedan and other marital misfits want to call themselves Ms. to conceal the fact that they can't get a man it's fine by me. But the rest of us worked hard

for the *R* in our names and we don't want a title that conveys nothing but *misery* and *feminist ideology!*

WIPE to CLOVIS being interviewed in her office.

CLOVIS: If your house is on fire, do you want to be carried down the ladder by a man or a woman? Are you satisfied with the knowledge that a *person* will respond to your fire alarm? Well, I'm not either.

WIPE to CLOVIS on her radio call-in show.

CLOVIS: Now we believe in granting husbands and wives certain rights that are not given to those choosing *immoral* lifestyles. We call for tax breaks for families, and a tax on homosexuality. Tax the homosexuals! If the Lord can't make them see the error of their ways, maybe the IRS can!

WIPE to CLOVIS lecturing to a group of students in a classroom. Behind her is a blackboard with this message: Lack of hygeine — loss of self-esteem — loss of chastity — AIDS.

CLOVIS: Chastity is not only a great personal virtue but is vital to a disciplined and creative society. To think that the Lord had to visit a plague upon us before he could convince some of us of the error of our ways! Just say no to sin!

WIPE to CLOVIS on her radio show.

CLOVIS: Do you want your children forced to read textbooks in which men wear aprons and clear the dining-room table and use hairspray? In which mothers do heavy construction? In which no pronouns are allowed? In which men and women are forced to use the same bathrooms?

CUT to the REPORTER's office.

REPORTER: *(directly to camera)* I make thirty-eight thousand a year. I want to get ahead in my profession. I don't think being a woman is really a drawback anymore, it's not like it used to be. That's all changed. I don't mind competing with men, but I think you can get ahead without threatening them. If some woman comes in who's a ball-

buster, it just makes it harder for the rest of us. Sure, I've had to fight my way into a male-dominated profession. I think I probably make a bit less than male reporters, but they say that's because women have less presence on camera. Men are more credible, more reassuring. It's not management's fault, it's the viewers. They trust men with the facts. It's all done scientifically, by measuring galvanic skin response. You can't argue with the ratings.

TITLE: POSTFEMINISM

14. News Footage Clips: The Real Phyllis Schlafly

SCHLAFLY: Comparable worth is a notion that's not compatible with private enterprise, and it is the free system in this county that has brought the highest wages for the most people of any system in the history of the world.

15. Reporter's News Story

The story begins with a MONTAGE of clips from CLOVIS's life:

   CLOVIS in various political activities:

   On the phone to Washington

   Storming into City Hall

   Typing the Clovis Kingsley Newsletter

   Addressing women's groups

   Dictating to her secretary

   Greeting her staff

The montage is shown in a box over a freeze frame of her dead body lying on the auditorium floor following her assassination.

REPORTER: *(voice-over)* This was Clovis Kingsley, the notorious enemy of women's liberation. She traveled the country insisting that a woman's place is in the home, and she didn't even see the contradiction. Clovis was the author of a self-help book for women called *The Power of Total Submission*. It told how her own marriage had been saved and renewed by accepting the Lord into her heart, and by recognizing that her husband was the Lord's representative in the

home. The book was an instant best-seller. Clovis founded the Total Submission Course. Millions of women signed up. Clovis became a leading political force on the right, and a heroine of dissatisfied housewives everywhere, who learned to cure their unhappiness through obedience to their husbands and submission to their biology. There seemed to be a need, and Clovis Kingsley seemed to fill it.

CUT TO:

16. A Classroom   Day/Int

A number of suburban HOUSEWIVES. ALL of them wear pink T-shirts with CLOVIS's picture emblazoned on their chests.

GROUP LEADER: Because of their procreative capabilities women are . . .

GROUP: *(in unison)* Nurturing, intuitive, self-effacing, and in harmony with nature.

GROUP LEADER: And men are . . .

GROUP: *(in unison)* Aggressive, logical, and good in a crisis.

REPORTER: *(voice-over)* Women in desperate unhappy marriages flocked to the Total Submission courses. Clovis was an instant celebrity — and the most controversial woman of the decade. She testified before Congress, she had a weekly radio show — and still did all her own housework.

CUT TO:

17. Radio Station   Day/Int

TALK-SHOW CALLER: *(over phone)* But Clovis, I really think that men and women are more alike than they are different. My boyfriend —

CLOVIS: *(into mike)* How can anyone say that men and women are alike? Now in my experience, if you say to a man, "Where did you get that steak?" he'll say, "At the corner market." But if you say to a woman, "Where did you get that steak?" she'll say, "Why, what's wrong with it?"

REPORTER: *(voice-over)* Clovis's book opened with the same question that feminists were asking: "How are women to achieve power in the world?" But Clovis was a pragmatist: her philosophy was that in a man's world, you had to be a either a man, or a man's woman. She instructed women on how to make themselves more acceptable to men.

CUT TO:

18. Total Submission Classroom

GROUP LEADER: So that even when they are cold, abstract, and self-absorbed we are . . .

GROUP: *(in unison)* Understanding and supportive.

REPORTER: *(voice-over)* She lectured women on how to merge kinky sex and traditional Christian values: greet your husband at the door wearing nothing but Saran Wrap, then pray together.

19. A Suburban Home   Ext/Evening

A middle-aged WOMAN dressed entirely in Saran Wrap greets her startled HUSBAND at the front door.

WIFE: Unwrap me, darling.

CLOSE-UP of the HUSBAND's startled reaction.

20. A Church, Stained-Glass Window
of the Saints   Day/Int

Swelling organ MUSIC.

REPORTER: *(voice-over)* Clovis's claim to speak for women came directly from an Almighty God who voted Republican and gave America nuclear superiority to protect the American family against anything that threatened it—namely feminists, homosexuals, the Kremlin, or secular humanism.

This is Connie Yu for Channel 2 News.

21. Reporter's Kitchen   Night/Int

EXTREME CLOSE-UP of pasta extruding from a pasta maker directly at camera.

The REPORTER enters the kitchen and pours herself a drink.

BOYFRIEND: Hi. I'm making pasta. How was your day?

REPORTER: Well, I'm on the Clovis Kingsley story, for starters.

BOYFRIEND: God, that pathetic woman.

TITLE: A LEFT LIBERAL ACADEMIC

BOYFRIEND: She was like some sort of suburban Ayatollah, with all those idiotic women goose-stepping behind her — right back into the nineteenth century.

REPORTER: *(offhanded)* Well, they couldn't have all been brainwashed. She must have offered them something, she must have made some sense to them.

BOYFRIEND: *(distracted by pasta making)* Oh, for god's sake, don't be so wishy-washy. The woman was a menace to society. That's what's wrong with television news — no one takes a stand. I still can't understand why you turned down that public television job. Dinner's almost ready.

REPORTER: Sorry, I'm not very hungry, I stopped on the way home.

A BRIEF FLASH of the REPORTER surreptitiously eating cookies out of a package in a grocery store as she pushes her cart through the aisles.

BOYFRIEND: Suit yourself.

The REPORTER exits.

BOYFRIEND: *(directly to camera, passive-aggressive, waving his spatula)* I don't mind that I make less money than she does. All my girlfriends have been successful women in their fields. I admire successful women. I'm not the kind of guy who's threatened by powerful women. I try to be supportive, I don't expect her to always put my needs first, or even let me know if she's not eating at home. I can be flexible.

(He slaps the spatula against his hand.)

TITLE: WOMAN: THE DARK CONTINENT

SOUND EFFECT: JUNGLE NOISE

22. News Footage: The Real Phyllis Schlafly

SCHLAFLY: I think the gender gap is a myth. It's a hoax that is exaggerated by media flap. Everything indicates that the president is getting high marks from a big majority of the American people. The people who are flapping around about women's rights and the gender gap did not support Ronald Reagan in 1980, and he won in a landslide.

23. Montage

A MAN and a WOMAN sit across a long dining-room table from each other in silent hostility.
TEXT ROLLS OVER THEM:

During the great colonial war, the 5,000-year-war — also known as the battle between the sexes — the tactics favored were covert and ruthless.

TITLE: PETTY SABOTAGE

CLOSE-UP of burning toast. A female hand with wedding ring grabs it out of a smoking toaster, carries it to a table, and slaps it in front of a suited male figure.

TITLE: CRIMES AGAINST CAPITAL

CLOSE-UP of a WOMAN slipping a steak under her coat in a grocery store.
A WOMAN slipping Sweet'n Low into her purse at a restaurant.

A WOMAN slipping money out of her husband's wallet.

TITLE: DISINFORMATION

A WOMAN on an exercycle reading book titled How to Fake an Orgasm.

TITLE: MALINGERING

A public health poster on the symptoms of depression.

TITLE: RIDICULE

A stand-up COMEDIENNE — JOAN WATERS (who closely resembles Joan Rivers) — does her routine.

Can we talk here? My husband is not what you'd call well-equipped. The other day he came home from the office and I said, "Is that a pencil stub in your pocket or are you just happy to see me?" You know why women are no good at math? It's because all our lives we've been told that this —

> *(she holds up her index finger)*

equals twelve inches.

TITLE: TAKING HOSTAGES

A wedding video: the bride marches the groom down the aisle.

TITLE: FEMININITY

A woman shaving her legs.

TEXT ROLLS OVER THE WOMAN:

There are many forms of subversion and resistance in everyday life. Strategies against power may often take a covert form — a necessary tactic in response to a system of power that militates against direct action.

As Frantz Fanon noted, colonial war is singular in the pathology it gives rise to. As with the case of the "laziness of the native," are these symptoms — or strategies of the oppressed? Femininity — is it a

pathology, a sum of all the degradation inflicted upon the native by the colonial situation?

Or is it a response, a strategy? For its defenders, its practitioners: is it a strategy of subversion?

These apologists for the system: are they collaborators in their own oppression, or is it they who recognize the system of power for what it is and devise the strategic response?

24. Reporter's Office   Day/Int

The REPORTER watches footage of CLOVIS on the monitor.

CLOVIS: It's not those straggly-haired women on talk shows who have liberated women—it was men like Thomas Edison and other remarkable inventors. The real liberator of women in America is the free enterprise system, which has lifted the drudgery of housekeeping from women's shoulders. It wasn't militant, bitter women's libbers who invented automatic washers and driers, or vacuum cleaners, or dishwashers, it was good old American free enterprise.

A FEMALE COLLEAGUE enters the office, and regards CLOVIS on the monitor.

COLLEAGUE: Clovis Kingsley, what a cow!

REPORTER: So then tell me, why she was so popular?

COLLEAGUE: Women are sheep.

REPORTER: I think I have to find out why all those women were so drawn to her if I'm going to do this report on her life.

COLLEAGUE: Didn't you get the feeling that there was some ventriloquist somewhere who was really the one making her say that stuff? Total Submission!

The COLLEAGUE turns and addresses the camera.

COLLEAGUE: I'm single. I'm over thirty. Statistically speaking, it's all over for me. Married or gay, married or gay. Sometimes I want to just give up. Men are such pigs. Sometimes I think, why bother to

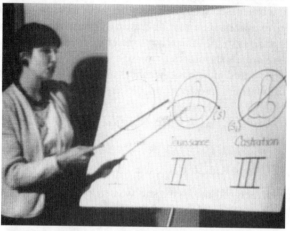

get up at 6:00 A.M. and go to aerobics class four times a week? Who cares if my thighs rub together when I walk?

25. In Reporter's Car   Day/Int

She compulsively eats cookies out of a package on the seat next to her.

REPORTER: *(voice-over)* A famous French psychoanalyst who'd written a book all about women and power was lecturing at a local university. I thought maybe I could get some background for a psychological profile of Clovis from her.

26. A Classroom   Day/Int

The PROFESSOR, chic in a Chanel knockoff, gestures toward a chart full of obscure Lacanian symbols.

PROFESSOR: *(in heavy French accent)* Now what we can see is zat zere is no indifference to ze phallus. Women's relation to ze phallus is one of deformation, of lack, in zat zey lack ze phallus, zerefore zey are denied access to power, and zerefore take up ze various positions of deformations. Ze lights, please.

The lights go off and the PROFESSOR begins showing slides of various women.

Slide of a very fat woman.

We see some women, zey grow progressively larger, zey want to increase zeir size in the world, zey want to be large like a man so zey too can possess ze phallus.

Slide of Nancy Reagan looking emaciated.

We see some women, zey grow progressively smaller, what you call anorexic. Zey feel zey do not deserve to take up space, because zey are not men, and lack ze phallus.

Slide of a career woman.

We see some women, zey go into ze career where zey dress like men. We see zey don ze necktie, which substitutes for ze missing phallus,

but in women it is tied in a bow, obviously zis signifying zeir ambivalence.

Slide of Donna Rice in a teddy.

We see some women, zey become childlike, put on ze baby doll act—zis is obviously a substitute, a displacement of ze desire for ze baby, which is truly a desire to possess ze phallus inside ze body.

Slides of Gloria Steinem, Angela Davis, and Betty Friedan.

Now some women, zey become feminists, zey want to annihilate ze phallus. But feminism, like all ze philosophies of liberation, invites its own annihilation—after all, if zere is feminism ten years from now, feminism will have been a failure, as it tries to bring about ze conditions for its own destruction—zat is, ze liberation of women.

AFTER THE LECTURE:

REPORTER: *(to professor)* Professor, Clovis Kingsley described herself as "a man's woman." Can you tell me what that means?

PROFESSOR: Well, you see, we would have to say zat all women are men's women. Women are women by virtue of not being men. Zere is no escape from ze other term. All women are men's women.

REPORTER: So you're saying that that's normal.

PROFESSOR: *(indignant)* Normal? I don't know what zis means. I simply describe ze social order, I do not prescribe it.

27. DA's Office   Day/Int

FADE UP MUSIC: Film-noirish walking bass.

REPORTER: *(voice-over)* I was in the neighborhood and thought I'd check the DA's office to see if they had any leads.

A FEMALE DA slaps a folder onto the desk. On the cover is a black-and-white photo of a large militant-looking woman—ANDROPHONOS JONES. ZOOM IN on PHOTO.

DA: Androphonos Jones, well-known radical feminist. Author of books ranging from *Heterosexuality Is Rape*, *Western Civilization as Gang Bang*, and *Woman as Victim*. Founder of the radical organization called Women Against Sex. Off the record, our office is investigating her in regard to the Kingsley assassination. They were deadly political rivals, they both claimed to speak for women, so who knows? Those extremists will do anything to put their point across.

28. Producer's Office   Night/Int

REPORTER: And the DA's office has a lead. This Androphonos Jones woman. Androphonos Jones: on record as saying that penetration is central to women's oppression. She compares the erect penis to a battering ram, a nuclear warhead, and various other weapons of destruction. Her view seems to be that if men didn't have penises, women would be a lot better off.

(She looks up at producer.)

One of the problems with this politically is that it just isn't very popular with a lot of women, particularly the ones who imagine that they like sex with men.

PRODUCER: Sounds like another fringe radical.

REPORTER: Well, I'd like to get some tape on her.

PRODUCER: Wait and see if they actually pin anything on her first.

REPORTER: It occurs to me that Androphonos and Clovis really have a lot in common. Both of them saw that the basic problem for women is men, and both of them constructed a politics out of regulating men: Androphonos wants to abolish pornography, Clovis wanted to use the weapon of the family to regulate male behavior. I think both of them wanted more power for women. I think I could make something out of it.

PRODUCER: No. It's too theoretical, too abstract. Look, I told you I want you to get out there and interview the people who knew her. Give us the human interest angle. Get on the stick!

75. Backstage   Night/Int

REPORTER: *(voice-over)* Joan wanted to see me. She had something to tell me.

JOAN: *(to reporter)* That same-sex bathroom line was mine. So was the drafting pregnant women line. Oh! I loved that joke! But then Clovis asked if she could use it. She wanted to make people hysterical about gender, you know, stir up their fears—she thought it would work for her. So I started writing more material for her. Everything was going great until she starting getting those phone calls in the middle of the night—

(delivered like a punch line)

death threats!

DISSOLVE TO:

76. Joan's Flashback: Clovis's Kitchen   Night/Int

CLOVIS is on the phone.

MALE VOICE: *(over phone)* We made you what you are and we can take it all away.

CLOVIS: I made it on my own, you little thug!

MALE VOICE: *(over phone)* That's not what we like to hear, baby.

77. Underground Parking Garage   Night/Int

The REPORTER talks to REPUBLICAN 2/THE ASSASSIN. He blows smoke in her face and jabs her shoulder.

REPUBLICAN/ASSASSIN: The Right channeled political funds to Kingsley because she could say things that we couldn't get away with saying in public, sort of hysterical things, you know, like that the Equal Rights Amendment would mean same-sex bathrooms, drafting pregnant women, all that. She stirred up resentment and fear and that served our purposes. So we used her. She was a tool. But then she wouldn't give up her computer lists, you know—mailing lists—

which were crucial to fundraising. We wanted those lists. She claimed it was out of loyalty to her women, but we think she wanted power on her own. She thought *she* could use *us*. *We* were the secret of her success. We made her, but she got too big for her britches, she wasn't a team player. So we took her down. Nobody likes a pushy broad. And we figured a dead martyr was better for us than a live pain in the ass. Just remember you can't prove a thing. Everyone knows a feminist did it.

78. Producer's Office   Night/Int

REPORTER: They killed her. They wanted her as a martyr instead of a pushy broad.

PRODUCER: You can't put that on the air. We'll get sued.

REPORTER: The irony is that she was so pathologically unable to hold men responsible for anything, she'd probably thank them for it — or find some way to blame a woman.

PRODUCER: Maybe she planned it herself. Made herself a martyr. After all, you say she dedicated herself to disempowering women.

REPORTER: That's right, blame the victim.

PRODUCER: *(disgusted)* You're starting to sound like a feminist.

REPORTER: She wanted to be part of the establishment and instead she was destroyed by it. She refused to see male power as a system that was against her. She thought they'd share their power with her if only she was better than other women — she thought she could be the one woman who transcended her gender.

79. A Cemetery — Clovis's Funeral   Day/Ext

The REPORTER is doing an on-camera stand-up with CLOVIS's MOURNERS gathered graveside behind her.

REPORTER: The police still report no leads in the Kingsley assassination. Clovis Kingsley's story remains, in death as in life, a mystery.

Connie Yu, for Channel 2 News.

VERY SLOW DISSOLVE TO:

80. Backstage Auditorium — from the Opening Scene
Night/Int

CLOVIS is at the dressing-table mirror putting on her makeup.

CUT TO:

The empty stage. The "Moral Forum Woman of the Year" banner is being hoisted up by a stagehand.

CUT TO:

The ASSASSIN/REPUBLICAN pulling up in a black car with smoked windows.

CUT TO:

CLOVIS contemplating herself at the mirror.

The ASSASSIN exits from the Ladies' Room.

CLOVIS at mirror. She watches herself.

CLOVIS: *(slowly, as if a new thought)* I want to — affect history. I want to be part of something greater than myself. . . . I want to . . . I want to . . .

> *(she pauses, a moment of recognition)*

make things better for women.

FADE TO BLACK

FADE UP MUSIC:

> *I'll follow the boys, wherever they go . . .*

CHAPTER 6

"The Phantom Twitchings of an Amputated Limb"

Colonialism as a Female Disease

I ONCE CAME ACROSS a cartoon in *Harper's* (reprinted from something called *American Atheist*) depicting a man and a woman sitting at a bar, over cocktails. The man is protesting, "Well gosh . . . gee whiz . . . sure I'd talk to you if you didn't have a vagina . . . of course I would . . . uh . . . you DO have one, don't you?" A decade of feminist film theory of a psychoanalytic inflection suggests that while men may consent to talk to women who don't have vaginas, they certainly wouldn't make movies about them, as it's been a well-circulated premise that female sexuality and its repression are central elements in dominant cinema. Female sexuality, in this analysis, functions as a disruption to the linear process of the classical narrative, and insofar as these menacing aspects of the figure of the woman pose the threat of castration and disruption to the patriarchial order, the work of narrative is to reduce the threatening image of female sexuality through the work of fetishization. As Jacqueline Rose puts it, "Woman gets set up, not simply as a certain *image*, something which can be criticized historically or sociologically, but as a *guarantee* against the difficulties of the cinematic system itself" — as the system is constituted only as a function of that which it attempts to evade.[1]

Feminist considerations of the function of spectacle tend to pay homage to the early conjunctions of film theory and psychoanalysis, which probed the ways in which women are figured within a system of voyeuristic-scopophilic looks. As Judith Mayne writes in summary of what has become, in her words, the commonplace position on spectacle, "However diverse the manifestations of spectacle in the cinema, they are all — sooner or later — about men looking at women. . . . Or put another way, it is through the terms of spectacle that the cinema puts forth its version of sexual difference."[2]

But if classical feminist film theory tells us that female sexuality is implicated in a structure of sexual difference whereby it poses the threat of castration, we might also keep in mind that the structuring principle of this set of social meanings, phallocentrism, also describes a range of social consequences *beyond* the register of sexual difference. What I want to do in this essay is bring back the historical and sociological dimensions that Rose forecloses. It may just be that in rigorously reading the most variegated cinematic emplotments of female sexuality according to the terms of a master code — the psychoanalytic emplotment of female sexuality — we're closing off the possibility that femininity, or woman-as-signifier, carries a different discursive sense and force in different ideological formations. We may be passing over discursive *shifts* in these sign systems in favor of a focus on fixed elements (the Oedipal scenario, etc.) and fixed meanings. We may be missing the way that female sexuality in *postmodern* cinematic signification, as a sign formed within a previous system—classical narrative cinema—may now play a different and enlarged role in what Barthes would call a second-order semiological system.[3] What I'm suggesting is that female sexuality, as a current cinematic signifier, a signifier "itself formed by a sum of signs," may have undergone a transformation. Perhaps it has now become an *acceptable* sign for castration or psychic wounds occurring in *other* spheres and, as a second-order signifier, functions as a sort of screen allegory, condensing and displacing these sorts of disturbances—and so is not repressed or contained within the narrative at all, but is instead insistently visible, on full display in all its horror and monstrousness.

In her introduction to a collection of the work of the Subaltern Studies group, Gayatri Spivak makes a related point.[4] In the group's work, she writes, social transformation is "signaled or marked by a functional change in sign-systems." Working against theories of change that locate the agency of change outside the subaltern or insurgent (specifically, against classical Marxism, which privileges the determining weight of modes of production over subaltern agency), the group theorizes change, instead, in terms of the "displacement of function between sign-systems." These discursive displacements, charging political signifiers with new functions, are brought about by "the force of a crisis." Spivak's elaboration upon the Subaltern Studies group's work is to see that *the figure of woman* "is pervasively instrumental in the shifting of the function of discursive systems," so that, for example, in colonial India, "when cow protection becomes a volatile signified . . . the cow is turned into a female figure of one kind or another." Spivak goes on to say that "a functional change in a sign system is a violent event." I'd like to partially revise this to say that a functional change in a sign system is an *epic* event, and suggest that the cinematic epic is just such a vehicle to marshal the combined forces of spectacle and capital in order to forcibly wrench the text of history—and its latest crisis to the first-world sovereign ego—into more ego-palliating configurations. The decline of empire and accompanying shifts in geopolitical spheres of influence, for example, may now be, in the first-world political unconscious, just such a volatile signified as to summon the figure of the woman as a discursive displacement—a political signifier charged with a new function, and one most effectively disseminated in an *epic* form. This further suggests that the relation between phallocentrism and colonialism is such that a disturbance to the colonial order is in a certain analogous relation to a disturbance in the phallic order, such that the cinematic figure of woman—the sum of all those previously encoded implications of castration—can function as the most immediate synecdoche of this more global, and exopsychic, disturbance—that is, decolonization.[5]

In two recent, expensively lavish epic revisions of the British colonial experience, one an American production, Out of Africa, and the other British, Passage to India, we will indeed find this volatile signified rendered as a furtive displacement onto the feminine—but a femininity rendered abnormal and pathological. Both films rely on the vehicle of not simply female sexuality, but the spectacle of diseased or deformed female sexuality—syphilis in Out of Africa, hysteria in Passage to India—to stand in for and bear the historical brunt of a renounced colonial past. E. M. Forster's novel and Isak Dinesen's writings (along with her heavily revised biography) are the raw materials reworked and recoded into representations of the past that make sense only as an attitude or necessity of the present: the necessity to produce a first-world discourse of postcolonialism.

That the politics of the revival can only be understood in terms of a present historical necessity is made manifestly clear by these films. But the question of what exactly is under revision has been a subject of contention. Critics on the left have read the necessity of both films as a nostalgic return to a golden age: both have been ritually denounced as Reaganesque or Thatcheresque rehabilitations of a vanished or fading vision of empire in all its splendor. But I'd argue that more is going on here. What we're seeing is the cinematic production of a postcolonial revision of history that rehabilitates, through disavowal, the male experience of colonialism by coding colonialism as female. The filmic spectacle performs the work of disavowal by gendering colonialism and by displacing its scandal onto the female. This is a semiotic shift from the more familiar convention whereby the colony or colonial subject is coded female to a new kind of formation in which the historical adventure of colonialism itself is represented in retrospect, and falsely, as a female enterprise—a "female disease."

In a peculiarly American narrative convention that Nina Baym has identified as the "melodrama of beset manhood," social critique is enacted through precisely this representation of the social as female.[6] Society is envisioned as a corruption of a natural order, and played out as a sort of good mother/bad mother fantasy, with the romantic promise of the frontier held up against the corruption of social convention. The "entrammeling society," encroaching on, constricting, and destroying the male hero, is "represented with particular urgency in the figure of one or more women." Women are hypersocial entrappers and domesticators, while the wilderness offers to the male "the medium on which he may inscribe his own destiny and his own nature."

Now if we undertake to analyze the image of the woman in the first-world postcolonial cinema (and I'm arguing that it's only through an analysis of the way the figure of the woman functions within the space of the narrative that we can read these films' postcolonialism at all), what these films tell us is that colonialism "was" not only immoral, rapacious, and racist, but a fundamental historical error. But if, in addition, we see the way these qualities are generated in the narrative only to be displaced onto and condemned in the figure of a central female character, we would have to concede that this is a very different ideological project than a simple rehabilitation of empire. The first point that should be emphasized is that these films' liberal sentiments are completely dependent on their misogyny. The second is that *if* these films have been read as merely the "trumpeting of imperial triumph" or "imperial chic," it is because, in neglecting the sexual politics of the films, these (primarily male) critics have completely missed the moments of critique and revision, which are, in both films, inscribed across the body of the woman. (On the other hand, a liberal feminist critic, Molly Haskell, writing in *Ms.*, will see in *Out of Africa* only the image of the strong woman, and in not seeing the politics of colonialism under revision, will not see that the woman is constantly undercut, ridiculed, instructed, and put in her place by a white male anachronistic fount of postcolonial enlightenment.) The sexual politics of this representation of woman-as-colonist *is*, at least inadvertently, brought home by one left male critic, Salman Rushdie. Writing of the Raj revival—*Jewel in the Crown, Gandhi, Mountbatten*, and *Passage to India*—Rushdie does see in these films the "refurbishment of the Empire's tarnished image," and Britons turning their eyes "nostalgically to the lost hour of their precedence." Britain, he goes on, "is in danger of entering a condition of cultural psychosis, in which it begins once again to strut and to posture like a great power while in fact its power diminishes every year," putting one in mind, he writes, "of the phantom twitchings of an amputated limb."[7] Rushdie doesn't identify which amputated limb it is that's doing the twitching, but, given the psychic interchangeability of detachable body parts, perhaps we can infer from his apt castration metaphor, and a certain knowledge of how the figure of woman has been encoded in cinematic representation, that an anxiety around female sexuality will constitute an essential element in this ideological formation.

In the two accounts of empire under discussion, we are given two versions of female sexuality as pathology: two scenes of aversion, anxiety, and disavowal. First there is the woman of sexual experience, Karen Blixen in *Out of Africa*, diseased and demanding, whose desire the narrative explicitly identifies with the bourgeois drive for acquisition and will-to-power of European colonialism. Secondly, there is the

sexually repressed virgin, Adela Quested of *Passage to India*, who im-
agines an attempted rape — a charge that the narrative puts into analogy
with colonialism as a sort of failure of cross-cultural understanding.
There is an emblematic moment in *Out of Africa* in which female pathology literally propels the woman into the frame, as in a shock cut Karen
actually and emblematically falls to the ground and *into* the frame.
Struck down by her disease, it is the disease, launching her into the
frame, which is made the very condition of her representability.

For Adela Quested, in *Passage to India*, the conditions of representability are more convoluted. The figure of Adela in Forster's novel is a
woman whose unattractiveness is continually remarked upon. She is an
object of speculation and inquiry to all, her visage is a form of distortion
and monstrousness, a veritable slap in the face to expectations of the
feminine. The rape charge is, in fact, *derived* from her unattractiveness,
according to her victim Dr. Aziz, who has previously himself remarked
on her homeliness, as well as the fact that "she has practically no
breasts." He later refers to her as a "treacherous hideous harridan" and
is offended to have his name linked with hers sexually. After Adela
breaks down in court and admits there *was* no rape attempt, Aziz wants
to elicit from her the admission that "Dear Dr. Aziz, I wish you had
come into the cave; I am an awful old hag, and it is my last chance."
The monetary damages Aziz decides to sue her for (but is then talked
out of) correspond to the colonial expropriation of the wealth of
India — it is money rightfully belonging to an Indian that is allowed to
escape overseas, money that Adela will, Aziz speculates, use to buy herself a husband. In other words, Adela is such a distortion of femininity
that it will take all the wealth of India to insert her into the realm of
normal sexuality.

What becomes of all this female hideousness in the movie makes for
a strange tension around the figure of Adela. David Lean, the auteur behind the movie, says of the novel, "Miss Quested . . . well, she's a bit
of a prig and a bore in the book, you know. I've changed her, made her
more sympathetic. Forster wasn't always very good with women."[8]
What Lean means is that as a director, he has made of Adela an accepta-
bly attractive woman: he has directed and filmed the character within
all the conventions of cinematic desire. Yet at the same time, Lean the
writer has allowed to migrate from the novel into the script a number
of lines about just how unattractive and undesirable Adela is, creating
a certain disjuncture around the character: while visually a conventional figure of desire, her character is also subject to the sound track's
speculation and ridicule about her undesirability and unattractiveness.

So there is a certain problem around the figure of the woman, and
thus an intensification of vision. She must be examined with an eye to

this problem, a problem located in her sexuality. The heart of the movie is, of course, the rape charge against the Indian doctor Aziz (turned into a hapless subcomic—and strangely feminized—figure by the film), revealed as a rape *fantasy* that is the product of an overheated imagination —overheated by the sexual promise of India itself.

Adela, who "wants to get to know the real India," develops, on the two occasions she is confronted with the "real India," hysteria. The first bout (and this is a scene not in the novel) comes when she happens upon some erotic statuary on a solo bicycle trip in the countryside—statuary that suddenly springs alive with violent screeching *monkeys*. Geoffrey Nowell-Smith has written of the way in which in what he calls "the hysterical text," the repressed sexual content of a film's narrative, often bursts forth as excess and incoherence in the film's mise-en-scène.[9] Perhaps Nowell-Smith's point functions similarly in relation to repressed political contents. *Monkeys*?? This scene is a moment of pure epic semiosis that manages to congeal and reconform the elements of pathological sexuality, the landscape, and the *unheimlich*-ness of the Orient, as these strange simians, humanlike but not quite human, transform the bucolic moment of Adela's burgeoning sexual awakening into a scene of screeching animality. It's a vivid analogy of the fear and desire attached to the woman's "letting go" (one reminiscent of Paul Schrader's *Cat People*), as well as to the Western stereotype of the sexual threat and promise of the East.

Adela's second hysterical episode comes in the scene in the Marabar Caves with their famous echoes, where the imagined rape attempt happens. The excess of Adela's sexual imaginings come to stand in for the injustice of colonial administration through the juridical mechanism that her charge sets in motion. This sexual excess culminates in the rape trial, which will be the scene of her humiliation and her exposure. It is also a scene of vindication for Fielding, the white male conscience and moral center of the narrative: he who understands Indians and knows the real India, who sees through the sham of the Raj and embodies the postcolonial future. Once Aziz is acquitted, the full weight of epic spectacle is marshaled—the thousands of extras taking to the streets, the vividness of the festivals and celebrations after Aziz's acquittal—all of this would almost convince us that India achieved independence immediately after Adela recanted.

It's interesting to note the contradiction between the director's stated intentions and what appears on the screen. "Forster was a bit anti-English," Lean has been quoted as saying, "anti-Raj and so on. I suppose it's a tricky thing to say but I'm not so much. I intend to keep the balance more. I don't believe all the English were a lot of idiots. Forster rather made them so. He came down hard against them."[10] Yet what

Lean *has* retained of Forster's anti-Raj sentiments is their displacement onto the female — it is women who make the best (or worst) colonists. Forster's novel revels in myriad misogynistic ruminations on how much more vile the colonial female is in every regard than the colonial male, and the movie seizes the novel's preoccupation to parade before us a veritable henhouse of repellently racist and utterly ridiculous older women.

But the main show is Adela's sexuality, made visible through her "illness." Hysteria, "a malady through representation," is a sexual theater, a staging, and it is this insistence on sexual visibility that the film relies on to perform its ideological work. How can a post-Freudian audience think repression without thinking sex? The hermeneutical question posed around Adela's sexuality means that narrative resolution will necessitate exposing Adela's sexuality to full public view, full visibility, but visibility as illness, as repression, as pathology. The trial is clearly Adela's trial rather than Aziz's, and the stakes are made out to be enormous, not merely the fate of one repressed English virgin. Uncovering the truth of Adela's sexuality will mean the undoing of the colonial juridical system itself. As the rape charge is unraveled as a fabrication, so will colonial administration come undone — both are revealed as elaborate injustices, which it is the project of the film to disavow and renounce.

Whereas the epic elements of *Passage to India* (in other words, dollars on the screen) represent India as something the British were well rid of — the landscape teeming with dead and half-dead, impoverished, dirt-encrusted bodies, "a muddle" — *Out of Africa* is decidedly more elegiac in its representation of a colonial paradise. The cinematography spells out rapture in every shot. (And in this American movie, the Kenyan landscape will be explicitly compared to the American frontier.) The movie plays out the complicated sexual ballet of Karen Blixen, who later wrote as Isak Dinesen, and Denys Finch-Hatten, one of the last of the "great white hunters." The film was widely received as a strong-woman picture about an "adult relationship." But in reading the film's politics of colonialism against its sexual politics, this impression quickly falls through. The film is a series of running jokes at the woman's expense. Blixen, the aristocratic settler-colonist who tries to civilize her black house servants by making them wear white gloves, is acquisitive, overladen with baggage and overconcerned with "things," possessive, imperious, European, and diseased; she is played by Meryl Streep, the master of accents. Finch-Hatten, as played by Robert Redford, delivers epigrammatic pearls of perfectly enlightened knowledge: he is the movie's subject-supposed-to-know. He is at one with the land, the animals, the "natives"; he understands the Masai, who are wild, truculent, and unpredictable ("We think we'll tame them but we won't"). He is the existential hero: "I'm willing to be lonely, to die alone if I have to." He is also the perfect male feminist (this from the director of *Tootsie*), even criticizing Karen for mending his shirt — in this movie she is always on the moral low ground. Over the course of the film, he gives her three gifts: he gives her a pen — enabling her writing; he gives her a compass — her direction; and he gives her a gramophone to play Mozart on — joy, rapture, sex. He creates her, allows her her writing, while performing the film's ideological work of producing woman-as-colonizer.

The real Blixen was, apparently, for her time, something of an enlightened reformer. She opened a school to teach the Kikuyu, who lived on what became her land, to read, and fought the taxation imposed by the British, which impoverished the indigenous populace and drove them into wage labor. Here is the film's imagining of a debate on the politics of literacy between Blixen and Finch-Hatten, played as a seduction scene — this takes place while they are dancing:

HIM: When they said they'd like to read, how did they put that exactly? I mean, did they know they'd like Dickens?

HER: You don't think they should learn to read?

HIM: I think you might have asked them.

HER: Did you ask to learn when you were a child? How can stories possibly harm them?

HIM: They have their own stories, they're just not written down.

HER: And what stake do you have in keeping them ignorant?

HIM: They're not ignorant. I just don't think they should be turned into little Englishmen. (pause) You do like to change things, don't you?

HER: For the better, I hope. I want my Kikuyu to learn to read.

HIM: *My* Kikuyu, *my* Limoges, *my* farm — it's an awful lot to own, isn't it?

HER: I have paid a price for everything I own.

HIM: And what is it exactly that's yours? We're not owners here, we're just passing through.

(One gets the feeling the movie thinks she's dating Jomo Kenyatta, played in whiteface by Robert Redford.)

Her reformism will later be explicitly identified with her syphilis by Denys, who theorizes that the school is her compensation for her inability to have children due to her disease. (According to the Dinesen biography, Karen did actually become pregnant by Denys and he encouraged an abortion.)

Karen's desire for a romantic commitment, ever thwarted by the Redford character, is equated by the narrative with her desire to tame and control the land and its inhabitants. Her desire is continually problematized as an excess, something that disturbs a natural order. In a scene where she demands a display of commitment from him, his line is, "You confuse need with want, you always have" — this delivered like a Lacanian *Übermensch*. When she tries to impose her will on him, the result is their breakup. Her desire is constricting, encroaching, and bourgeois; like syphilis, the condition of her sexuality is such that if not checked it will spread, and in fact, Denys does become fatally contaminated by her desire, to his ruin. When they reconcile (after she has lost everything and gone bankrupt), his conciliation to her will spell out his destruction.

HIM: I was beginning to like your things.

HER: I was beginning to like living without them.

HIM: You've ruined being alone for me.

HER: You were right, the farm never really belonged to me.

HIM: I may have been wrong.

Then he dies, himself struck to the ground (as she had been earlier, by her disease) in a plane crash.

Both *Out of Africa* and *Passage to India* also produce strangely similar moments between European women and their native counterparts, in which the narratives are interrupted to display European women as oppressors with respect to female colonial subjects — scenes for which, of course, there are no equivalents for male colonists. In *Out of Africa*, Denys's friend Berkeley becomes ill with "black water fever," a diagnosis that achieves a racially coded irony when he is found out to have been secretly living for a number of years with Mariammo, an African woman. At Berkeley's funeral, Mariammo, exiled to an observation place outside the cemetery gates, exchanges a prolonged glance with Karen — a clear rebuke to the European woman usurping the place that rightfully belongs to the dignified and stately Mariammo. The colonial usurpation of rights is reduced to a moment of friction between two women over a man and, again, a moment in which the weight of colonial injustice is brought to bear on the female colonist, in which men are strangely innocent. And *Passage to India* gives us a single encounter between native women and European women in which Mrs. Moore, Adela's future mother-in-law, trying to communicate with a chattering and colorful group of Indian women at a colonial social gathering engineered to "meet the natives," asks for a translator. "Perhaps *we* speak *your* language," offers one of the women, another rebuke, and one that will later be repeated in the film's displacement to women — personified by Adela — of the injustice of colonial misunderstanding.

In both these films white female sexuality is emplotted as a form of regulation — a strategy of domination. In *Passage* it's Adela's sexuality that ensnares the colonial subject in the mechanism of colonial subjugation; in *Out of Africa* it's represented as the pathological female desire for control: colonialism is revealed as female megalomania. In both films it is the white male moral center of the film, possessing anachronistically enlightened consciousness, who *resists* these positions of mastery. This, I believe, is the ideological project of these films, to disavow the moral culpability for a tainted history and to sanitize that history (for the male) by conferring it onto the female, reenacting colonialism as a female disease. Sexual disease or pathology here works to double the impact of female sexuality as a scene of castration. The disavowal of castration is said to be the prototype — perhaps even the origin — of other types of disavowal of reality. But in these two films, I believe what we see is a recognition and *insistence* on female sexuality as a site of contamination and loss: here that threat is not contained through fetishization or various devices of closure or regulation — in neither film is the female character ultimately recouped into the realm of "normal" sexuality through some form of closure around cure or heterosexual union, or even annihilated through punishment. Instead, the *avowal* of one sort of castration threat is put to ideological work through the vehicle of the epic, in order to disavow the global and pressing first-world psychopolitical wound of decolonization. Here, in the postcolonial epic, female sexuality must be fully visible — as a second-order signifier — to function as a screen allegory of colonialism as political scene of castration. "*Myth hides nothing*: its function is to distort, not to make disappear," and its structure is, Barthes writes, that of the *alibi*: "I am not where you think I am, I am where you think I am not."[11] And this is precisely what is enacted in these two films — a historical alibi. By deflecting the position of mastery onto the female, while at the same time *affirming* the female embodiment of castration, the historical wound of decolonization is acknowledged and assimilated. But it is not where you think it is, and it is where you think it is not: by conferring it onto female sexuality, a sign already in circulation as a scene of castration, these narratives work to disavow the consequences and meaning of the political loss. What we can see is that in both these films, the dialectic of colonialism—that is, the historical *certainty* of anticolonialist and nationalist movements and revolutions—is put into analogy with the dialectic of having and not having the phallus. Insofar as these two positions mirror each other, they both involve a repressed knowledge continually threatening consciousness, which is that the position of mastery is always implicated in the eventuality of loss. In that sense, both films portend the political, social, and perhaps even sexual transformations to come.

CHAPTER 7

Aesthetics and Foreign Policy

This essay was first written in 1985 for a conference panel on "Aesthetics and Hermeneutics" in which panelists were posed the question, "What would it mean to understand the arts from the point of view of hermeneutics rather than aesthetics?" The essay posits a relation between the then quite current Reagan-era anti-Communist Cold War rhetoric and the production of first-world aesthetic ideology. As I revise these essays for republication, the political landscape is shifting, and the superpower binary seems to wield a bit less sovereignty in the first-world imagination (although Cuba clearly remains inscribed in that residual paradigm). But the tactics of political demonization have hardly waned, though the demons may vary. As the United States blithely "bombs Baghdad back to the Stone Age," destroying not only the lives and civilization of its inhabitants, but also a few millennia of its culture—or at least those remnants that haven't already somehow found their way to the British Museum—it seems clear that emerging binary stratifications of power and new world orders will produce companion aesthetic ideologies, as well, and that those dominant aesthetics will serve the interests of first-world power rather than its upheaval.

During the summer of 1985 I went to Cuba for two weeks with a group whose mission was to investigate culture and cultural institutions as they've developed within tropical socialism. The origin of this essay was my surprise and dismay at comments made to me upon my return from this voyage by various friends, family, colleagues, and certain "left intellectuals" of my acquaintance—all right, just about everyone—suggesting that the term "culture in Cuba" was oxymoronic: Cuban culture, being state sponsored, has the status of propaganda rather than culture, they said; I was also frequently and somewhat tautologically assured that "they only showed us what they wanted us to see." I want to try to outline some of the cultural paradigms that allow us to refuse the status of Culture to culture in Cuba.

Foremost is the Romantic legacy of the artist; it says that the free expression of the self is the sine qua non of culture. The whole notion of free expression, like that of a free press, is, of course, somewhat ideological in that it manages to ignore minor details like economic necessity, the market, and other hard questions about who really gets to express what. It's also somewhat ahistorical in that it has little to say about the way that the celebration of "creative expression" and the fact that only certain people get to do it directly relates to a particular, historically specific organization of work and the workplace—in part the legacy of Fordism—in which creativity, planning, and decision making are segmented off into separate job categories and then valorized as the sole province of a "creative" few.[1] (Not to say that Fordism hasn't had its admirers in "actually existing socialisms," as well.)

The second might be referred to as our modernist inheritance: it says that official culture or even affirmative culture is not Culture, because authentic Culture (ours) is necessarily negative. The legacy of the avant-garde (or perhaps an index of what is often referred to as its institutionalization) is the pervasive belief that authentic high culture's underlying principle is revolt and rebellion—for example, Susan Sontag: "The task of the writer is to promote dissidence." Whether this dissidence and rebellion are meant to take place against society or only against previous art depends on the degree of autonomy culture is thought to have from the rest of social life—typically, in liberal society culture is its own sovereign sphere. It's precisely this separation that would allow a generation of New York postwar Abstract Expressionists, for example, to have zealously fulfilled all the criteria of rebellion and dissidence, and would simultaneously allow their work to be circulated abroad by the State Department as PR for American freedom and as an ideological tool in Cold War foreign policy. Coloring this second paradigm is a slippage of the signifiers of revolt and rebellion from the work of art to the figure of the artist as rebel-hero, arguably a subject-effect of this negation paradigm. A variant on the rebellion criterion is a position like that of George Steiner's, that "great art" is only possible under conditions of adversity and persecution: this position would, of course, tend, a priori, to valorize émigré and dissident culture over the culture of the Cuban revolution.

These positions are all premised in one way or another on the notion of a self that expresses. A third paradigm, which ostensibly abandons that criterion, holds that culture, avant-gardiste or not, is a mode of ideological reproduction, and the Artist, a mere structural effect. But it's still possible (as my post-trip-to-Cuba conversations made clear) to view culture as an ideological apparatus, to have a sophisticated analysis of "free expression" *and* the subject who expresses as the exact loci of ideological reproduction in bourgeois society, and to simultaneously denigrate the cultural products of "actually existing socialism" *on* free expression grounds, to believe in one's heart of hearts in an aesthetics beyond politics, a state beyond ideology, and to decry the constraints on cultural production "there."

Upon examination, these paradigms of cultural production—from across the political spectrum—all hold that it's possible to specify, in advance of its production *or* its reception, the conditions of possibility for "good art," and, not coincidentally, all of them would dictate against finding "good art" emerging from within the Cuban revolution. I'd like to propose that aesthetic reception is produced discursively: it's a subject-effect opened up within discourse. This array of positions on artistic production, which constitute an aesthetic *discourse* (one in which Cuban culture is inscribed as an absence), work to establish a perceptual field in which Cuban culture doesn't *look* like culture and is unassimilable as culture. The aesthetic discourse conditions vision, producing a form of seeing we could label "first-world perception." So the aesthetic discourse becomes both a strategic political instrument and a site on which foreign policy — *and* the discourse on nation and the constitution of "nationals" — becomes assimilated to subjectivity: foreign policy becomes a lived relation of perception and knowledge that is exercised in the practice of the aesthetic judgment.

The modern aesthetic discourse — the post-Cartesian aesthetic discourse — is central to the constitution of subject positions from which first-world domination is effected and reproduced. The aesthetic judgment, from its Kantian formulation to its current exercise in art-world glossies, works as a crucial site of political dissemination. In certain instances it labors in the service of colonial ideologies. A case can be made that it is structured precisely by this political necessity.

An example of the aesthetic judgment as political weapon is one passed by the historian Hugh Thomas in a 1985 book, collectively written under his auspices, entitled *The Cuban Revolution: Twenty-Five Years Later.*[2] It summarizes and negates the entirety of Cuban culture in a single sentence: "Tragically, the Cuban revolution cannot offer a single notable novelist, a famous poet, a penetrating essayist, nor even a fresh contribution to Marxist analysis." Cuban film and mass culture fare no better with Sir Hugh: "Along with the fine arts, popular culture in Cuba, that is the music, literature, art, dance, theater, and film enjoyed by the broad sections of the population, has lost its creative zeal under a regime that restricts artistic freedom and individualism." (p. 42)

Rather than undertake to refute Thomas's claims point by point by offering counterexamples, an abundance of which are available — Cuban film, for example, having attracted world attention for its "creative zeal" — I want to present these claims simply as a demonstration of the strategic use of the aesthetic judgment. This book is politically placed in such a way that it *has* to hate Cuban culture. Although Sir Hugh Thomas was an adviser to the Thatcher government, although the book is put out by a think tank partially funded by a Cuban émigré organization and is written by a collection of émigré scholars and men from places like the Rand Corporation, the Hoover Institution, Freedom House, and offices of the U.S. government, its political interest is unacknowledged in the text, which assumes what Hannah Arendt called the "myth of Archimedian knowledge": that fabled land of objectivity outside politics, history, or self-interest that so typically characterizes the aesthetic judgment.

By way of contrast, decoding the foreign policy of the aesthetic judgment is the concern of Cuban poet and literary critic Roberto Fernández Retamar in this passage from his essay "Caliban: Notes toward a Discussion of Culture in Our America."[3] He reports a conversation with a European journalist, a leftist, who asked him, "Does a Latin American culture exist?" For Retamar, the question is a way of asking, "Do *you* exist?" "For to question our culture, is to question our very existence, our human reality itself, and thus to be willing to take a stand in favor of our irremediable colonial condition, since it suggests that we would be but a distorted echo of what occurs elsewhere." (p. 7)

Retamar is politically placed in such a way that he has to refute the first-world aesthetic judgment as a matter of survival: for a Cuban culturalist, Thomas's position is the cultural equivalent of the invasions of Grenada or the Falklands. To misunderstand a culture is the groundwork necessary to dominate it. That Thomas's position is an aesthetics of foreign policy is clear. But the fact is, its complacent self-certainty has typified and constituted the aesthetic discourse from its inception. Modern aesthetics has always functioned as a discursive screen for the political aims of the bourgeoisie, and its global will to power has never been very far beneath the surface of the aesthetic discourse. Maybe returning to some of the specific historical determinations around the modern aesthetic discourse's inception will help to make clearer some of that buried political necessity.

The types of economic, political, and discursive transformations that occur in what we might call the Descartes-Kant axis have been well documented as the social and institutional ground for the formation of modern (bourgeois) subjectivity and subjection.[4] These are contemporaneous with a series of transformations in the economics of artistic production, as well: from patronage system to market system, including not only concomitant formal and stylistic developments in art, and transformations in the content of art — from religious subject matter to documentations of property and prestige — but also the production of an entirely different social function of the artist.[5] It's also worth noting that Jacques Lacan has called attention to the development of optics as contemporaneous with the inauguration of the Cartesian subject, and points to the historical dimension of the scopic domain, or the gaze, with reference to this same time frame.[6]

The term "aesthetics" was first employed by Baumgarten in 1750, making modern aesthetics essentially a post-Cartesian phenomenon, which is to say that this is a discourse centrally concerned with the self and its centrality in the world: modern aesthetics is essentially an episode of the bourgeois ego. The political reverberations of the sorts of discussions that constituted early aesthetic discourse and their relation to emerging bourgeois political forms are hard to ignore. Early aestheticians were centrally concerned with the problem of relativism: the

seventeenth-century quest for the method from which to derive in-
dubitable and universal truths, and the concomitant production of the
"rational" man who is the subject of these universal truths, devolves
into the eighteenth-century project of mining this kind of certainty
from the terrain of aesthetics. For example, Mary Louise Pratt, discussing a related discourse, early travel writing, finds that its disinterested
descriptions of landscape resonate with fantasies of dominance, that the
European encounter with the Other in its pre-Imperial forays off the
Continent produces a surfeit of descriptive language that masks an
ideological task: to present the subject as fixed and unchangeable, establishing credibility and authority in the face of its loss to a system of
difference where the European confronts "not only an unfamiliar Other, but unfamiliar selves."[7]

The aesthetic discourse, too, is crucially concerned with the dilem-
mas of the subject-object relation. (And as is made clear in Pratt's essay,
there is little distinction between object and Other in the European
mind of the period.) How are the lines of power drawn, why do certain
objects so unsettle subjects, how does one effect and preserve dominion
over the object-world, how does one avoid being overwhelmed or tak-
en in by, or losing one's mastery to, recalcitrant, seductive, or exotic
objects? In the aesthetic New World, a succession of aesthetic subjects
(Baumgarten, Hume, Kant, Lessing, Schiller, Diderot) battle a succession of aesthetic objects (nature, beauty, art) for mastery: first one tri-
umphs, then the other, in a progression of aesthetic theories that describe an array of contentious relations of subject to object. Do qualities
inhere in objects independent of subjects? Is there a basis for taste that
can claim some authority other than individual feeling? Does beauty
exist independent of the mind of a contemplating subject? Aesthetics
provides for philosophy both a heightened subject and a valorized object with which to enact the Parnassian encounter of the two without
reference to the political-allegorical ramifications of the project of
dominion over the Object world. "Art seeks to obliterate the gap between subject and object," says Ernst Cassirer.[8] Obliterating the gap
seems to entail constructing a scaffold of certainty, centrality, and self-
possession on which to mount the bourgeois subject and give it effectivity in the world. This is a problem that does not, despite the protests
of Cassirer and other neo-Kantians, seem confined to "an independent
universe of discourse"; rather it has clear political and economic implications. The "man of reason, good sense, and intelligibility," the
eighteenth-century aesthetic subject, is a political actor in the drama of
an emerging class struggling for cultural hegemony, and in the imperial
project of the coming century — of conquering and dominating newly
discovered territories and their inhabitants.

Modern aesthetics further distinguished itself from classical aesthetics in its attention to the issue of value. The aesthetic object is that which is approached evaluatively — it is through the act of appraisal that it qualifies for aesthetic objecthood, and aesthetics, in directing itself to this evaluative moment, is a discursive production of value. Value is, at root, a representation: it only exists or comes into existence within the process of exchange. Thus the aesthetic discourse (and its current manifestation, art-critical discourse) works, through its evaluative endeavors, to mediate value in art, value being a precondition for the existence of an art market. (And note that Raymond Williams has pointed out that the very idea of taste is inseparable from the existence of the consumer.)[9] As aesthetic value becomes exchange value, every activity of aesthetic evaluation is inextricably bound up in economic relations. It should be clear, then, that Hugh Thomas's aesthetic judgment of the entirety of Cuban culture as *valueless* is an aesthetic judgment firmly wedded to U.S. foreign policy on Cuba — Thomas's aesthetic judgment is the U.S. trade embargo writ aesthetic: denying value to Cuban culture is simple cultural obedience to the U.S. law prohibiting export of hard currency, goods, or services — of any value whatsoever — to Cuba.

Of course, I wouldn't want to reduce either the embargo or Thomas's aesthetic judgment *entirely* to their economic moments. The embargo, our response to the economic and political insult of Cuban self-determination, isn't particularly in U.S. economic interests — its determining moments are on various other "rational" grounds. And so with Thomas's aesthetic judgment: it's overdetermined. Within the terms of our dominant aesthetic discourse, the Cuban project of reinventing the notion of culture is read as the *absence* of Culture, and it's an absence that risks provoking the kind of instrumentalization or disregard typically reserved for what is nonculture: the object world, the animal world, nature — it's the dialectic of the Enlightenment. This Cuban absence, however, is also a continual presence: I'd argue that Communist culture, or our representation of it, was a *necessary* figure in the American ideology of culture in the postwar years, making the real referent of the signifiers circulating around the free-expression paradigm the ongoing hysteria over the Communist Other. So there's a dialectical relation between Communist culture and culture of the so-called free world, such that culture, for us, has been wholly inscribed in that biggest binary opposition of them all, the division of the world into the rival domains of the two superpowers.

Thomas wields his aesthetic judgment as a contemporary Cold War political club, but precedents for this move can be found, not only in the aesthetic judgment's inception, but in every instance of it since. Kant himself delineates the aesthetic judgment precisely by its a priori claim to universal validity: the aesthetic judgment necessarily demands that *all* feel the same form of pleasure as the particular aesthetic subject making his particular subjective aesthetic judgment.[10] This claim for universality, however, does not appeal to logic for its rationale, according to Kant, because it is not logical; it does not appeal to concepts, because, actually, to offer grounds for the judgment would be wrong, given that the aesthetic judgment is not a cognitive judgment and is not based on concepts, or deduction or induction. *The claim for universal consent is made a priori and is an essential feature of the judgment,* according to Kant, and indeed he writes, "We may now see that in the judgment of taste nothing is postulated but such a *universal voice*" (p. 50).

The sole grounds offered for the demand for universal agreement is the presumption of universal communicability of such feelings, that is, a universal subjectivity. The claim to universality is thus made and the assent of everyone demanded, Kant says, just *as if* the subjective judgment *were* objective. Kant provides, under the rubric of the "aesthetic judgment," the legitimation for subjectivity that acts in the world as objectivity: subject and object get tentatively reunited within the aesthetic field. The aesthetic judgment borrows the authority of logical argumentation while finessing the evidence-conclusion structure: grounds for an aesthetic judgment must *not* be offered, and argumentation is unnecessary, because claims for universal assent are made "just as if it were an objective judgment," according to Kant—this is an intrinsic, a priori feature of the aesthetic judgment.

The Kantian aesthetic license runs a straight course to Thomas: not only is no justification offered for his sweeping aesthetic condemnation of Cuban culture, there is no evidence that either he or his writers had even been to Cuba or seen any examples of Cuban culture. The judgment rests entirely on subjectivity that acts *as if* it were objective and that demands, a priori, universal consent. Kant's formulation of the aesthetic judgment, reproduced by Thomas, propagates the myth that the aesthetic observer, the self who judges, is purely and totally "disinterested": the Cartesian self-knowable subject reappears to claim Kantian aesthetic certainty. The fiction of the disinterested aesthetic gaze, maintained by Thomas, is the ballast for the fiction of the subject outside history, politics, economics, or power, and the aesthetic judgment reconfirms, as an ongoing project, that myth of the self. If, as Kant postulates, the aesthetic judgment always "refers the representation, by which an object is given, to the subject, and brings to our notice no characteristic of the object" (p. 64), then every aesthetic judgment reinstates the myth of the universal subject, which is, in turn, elaborated by and dependent on all the various discourses and institutions that permit, uphold, and legitimate the aesthetic judgment.

The political mission of this aesthetic self-certainty can be seen in Hugh Thomas's unproblematic assumption that Cuban culture exists as an object for his disinterested aesthetic gaze and assessment, that this gaze has no relation to power and surveillance, and that he can so easily arrogate a culture that aspires to be revolutionary to the terms of the aesthetic discourse. The presumption that the truth of art is transhistorical and eternal and that objective evaluations can be made of it by disinterested aestheticians such as Thomas and his cronies is a presumption intrinsic to the reproduction of the first-world power-knowledge complex. As Kant writes: "In all judgements by which we describe anything as beautiful we allow no one to be of another opinion . . . [E]veryone *ought* to agree.[p. 76] . . . And so it is not the pleasure, but the *universal validity of this pleasure*, perceived as mentally bound up with the mere judgment upon an object, which is represented a priori in a judgment of taste as a universal rule for the judgment and valid for everyone" (p. 131).

These first-world judgments by first-world subjects take the rest of the world as their body, extension, periphery. Kant's assertion of the universality of the aesthetic judgment is an early register of the universalizing first-world-white-male "we": the mastering discourse of the self-knowable subject who is captain of his ship and the rest of the seas as well, the "we" that so unproblematically assimilates the rest of the world as its object and dominion.

A question remains. *Can* "we" interpret culture in Cuba, and on what grounds?

If culture is seen as central to social reproduction, it seems to follow that in a society in which reproduction occurs, in the first instance, economically, as ours, artists are subjected to the terrors and rigors of the marketplace, whereas in a society that reproduces itself, in the first instance, politically, as Cuba, artists are subjected to the terrors and rigors of current political policies. It would follow that in an economically reproducing society, the ultimate social meaning of a work of art is thoroughly mediated and contained through the economic institutions of art — the market — whereas in Cuba, where art institutions are by definition political and politicized, the political meanings of works emerge unmediated, with more genuine potential to be subversive to reproduction.[11] What this seems to mean is that the concept of counterrevolutionary culture, a phrase that tends to provoke knowing smirks here, *does* have a reality in a social formation like Cuba's, whereas the possibility of a truly political art or a counterhegemonic art is to a large degree absorbed by art markets and institutions here.

This has been a lengthy preamble to my answer to the question, "What would it mean to understand the arts from the point of view of hermeneutics rather than aesthetics?" This formulation brings to my mind its famous obverse, Susan Sontag's 1964 call, in *Against Interpretation*, to substitute an "erotics" of art for a hermeneutics of art.[12] Sontag, who in 1982 gave great glee to the American Right by proclaiming, at a pro-Solidarity rally, that "communism is fascism," was in 1968 a self-proclaimed radical who visited Cuba and wrote about it in an essay entitled "Some Thoughts on the Right Way (for Us) to Love the Cuban Revolution."[13] Although Sontag felt favorably toward Cuba, it didn't meet her standards *aesthetically*:

> The reaction of Americans visiting Cuba brings home how profound a part of American radicalism is the revulsion against native vulgarity. Finding the Cubans not very sensitive to questions of taste, many Americans are surprised. . . . The remarkable thing is that they have done as much as they have, not that one still finds such expressions of spic taste as the ubiquitous girls on the street wearing their hair in pink plastic rollers or the relics of Miami rhinestone chic like the Tropicana nightclub.

If there was irony here, its reception hinged on the mediation provided by Sontag's identity as a Leftist, a mediation that the current Sontag, as a political figure, no longer guarantees. Sontag's shift to the right unfastens the rhetoric from its appeal to irony to reveal its imbrication in the colonizing operation of the aesthetic judgment, whose raw materials are the appeal to a transcendent sensibility and the vigilant enforcement of "good taste."

While the essay generously pardons the Cubans for not living up to her standards of taste, given the "degraded" elements with which they have had to work ("Spanish, Yoruba, and American" elements), this is less an attempt on Sontag's part to historicize or problematize such taste ("An integral part of the adversary culture developed by American radicals is the cultivation of good taste") than to snitch on deviations from it. These tend to be the social markers of lower classness, or what Sontag daringly refers to as "spic taste," or the social signifiers of middle classness: "For us," she writes, "it is self-evident that the *Reader's Digest* and Lawrence Welk and Hilton hotels are organically connected with the special forces napalming villages in Guatemala." Parenthetically, *Reader's Digest* gets recuperated in the 1982 Solidarity speech when Sontag uncharacteristically goes middlebrow, proclaiming that people who read the *Reader's Digest* were better informed about the realities of Communism than were those who read the *Nation* or the *New Statesman*.[14]

So *this* is the triumph of "erotics" over "hermeneutics": an unfettered subjectivity that utilizes aesthetics for class snobbism and imperial pronouncements, and that, as is true of all aesthetic judgments, asserts an a priori demand for universal assent. The structural similarity between the aesthetic judgment and ideological interpellation as described by Althusser and Laclau should be noted. What is Sontag's "erotics" but the desire for the self-certainty of a subjectivity outside history, a desire for the immediacy of the unmediated relation, not only to the work of art, but to all the rest of political and social life, as well? This attempt to objectify taste, to stake out an ahistorical role for the subject; this assertion of a perception that refuses any spatiotemporal location for the knower in the world; this demand for feeling over interpretation are all very alluring when repackaged as "erotics," yet when Sontag, who is, in fact, fond of quoting Benjamin, proclaims that "communism is fascism," simply because it *looks* that way to her, there truly is the aestheticization of politics. As with Ronald Reagan's somewhat more metaphysical but no less ahistorical bon mot that "the Soviet Union is the root of all evil in the world," it is an aesthetic judgment masquerading as knowledge and dancing on the world stage: it is political interest dressed in an aesthetic guise—like the aesthetic, universally valid, demanding universal assent. "All efforts to render politics aesthetic culminate on one thing: war," wrote Benjamin, and Sontag's rejection of hermeneutics for a subjective "erotics" puts her in the company of a strange bedfellow: the Reagan presidency Cold War machine, along with its surgical strikes and swelling military.

The primacy of sight in bourgeois perception dictates the resistance of the visual to historicization and critical evaluation: bourgeois perception is exactly that belief in the possibility of an ahistorical, unmediated *visual* relation to the world. This point, made by Donald Lowe in *The History of Bourgeois Perception*,[15] is reiterated in Lacan's ruminations on the domain of the visual and its relation to the institution of the Cartesian subject. Lacan's interrogation of the gaze, as well as the "*belong-to-me* aspect of representations, so reminiscent of property," provides a further gloss, in the register of the psychoanalytic, on the aesthetic judgment. As Lacan notes, "The level of reciprocity between the gaze and the gazed at is, for the subject, more open than any other to alibi."[16]

Aesthetics has always been political; it has always been about the exercise of power. It's time to stop making alibis.

CHAPTER 8

(Male) Desire and (Female) Disgust

Reading Hustler

Lᴇᴛ's ʙᴇɢɪɴ ᴡɪᴛʜ ᴛᴡᴏ ɪᴍᴀɢᴇs. The first is of feminist author-poet Robin Morgan as she appears in the anti-pornography documentary *Not a Love Story*. Posed in her large book-lined living room, poet-husband Kenneth Pitchford at her side, she inveighs against a number of sexualities and sexual practices: masturbation — on the grounds that it promotes political quietism — as well as "superficial sex, kinky sex, appurtenances and [sex] toys" for benumbing "normal human sensuality." She then breaks into tears as she describes the experience of living in a society where pornographic media thrive.[1] The second image is the one conjured by a recent letter to *Hustler* magazine from E. C., a reader who introduces an account of an erotic experience involving a cruel-eyed, high-heeled dominatrix with this vivid vocational self-description: "One night, trudging home from work — I gut chickens, put their guts in a plastic bag and stuff them back in the chicken's asshole — I varied my routine by stopping at a small pub."[2] Let's say that these two images, however hyperbolically (the insistent tears, the insistent vulgarity), however inadvertently, offer an approach route toward a consideration of the relation between discourses on sexuality and the social division of labor, between sexual representation and class. On one side we have Morgan, laboring for the filmmakers and the audience as a feminist intellectual, who constructs, from a particular social locus, a normative theory of sexuality. And while "feminist intellectual" is not necessarily the highest-paying job category, it's a markedly different class location — and one definitively up the social hierarchy — from that of E. C., whose work is of a character that tends to be relegated to the lower rungs within a social division of labor that categorizes jobs dealing with things that smell, or that for other reasons we prefer to hide from view — garbage, sewage, dirt, animal corpses — as of low status, both monetarily and socially. E. C.'s letter, carefully (certainly more carefully than Morgan) framing his sexuality in relation to his material circumstances and to actual conditions of production, is fairly typical of the discourse of *Hustler* — in its vulgarity, in its explicitness about "kinky" sex, and in its imbrication of sexuality and class. So as opposed to the set of norms Morgan attempts to put into circulation (a "normal human sensuality" far removed from E. C.'s night of bliss with his Mistress, who incidentally, "mans" herself with just the kind of appurtenances Morgan seems to be referring to), *Hustler* also offers a theory of sexuality — a "low theory." Like Morgan's radical feminism, it too offers an explicitly political and counterhegemonic analysis of power and the body; unlike Morgan it is also explicit about its own class location.

The feminist antiporn movement has achieved at least temporary hegemony over the terms in which debates on pornography take place:

current discourses on porn on the left and within feminism are faced with the task of framing themselves in relation to a set of arguments now firmly established as discursive landmarks: pornography is defined as a discourse about male domination, is theorized as the determining instance in gender oppression—if not a direct cause of rape—and its pleasures, to the extent that pleasure is not simply conflated with misogyny, are confined to the male sphere of activity. "Prosex" feminists have developed arguments against these positions on a number of grounds, but invariably in response to the terms set by their opponents: those classed by the discourse as sexual deviants (or worse, as "not feminists")—S/M lesbians, women who enjoy porn—have countered on the basis of experience, often in first person, both asserting that women *do* "look" and arguing the compatibility of feminism and alternative sexual practices, while condemning antiporn forces for their universalizing abandon in claiming to speak for all women. There have been numerous arguments about the use and misuse of data from media-effects research by the antiporn movement and charges of misinterpretation and misrepresentation of data made by proporn feminists (as well as some of the researchers). On the gendered pleasure front, psychoanalytic feminists have argued that fantasy, identification, and pleasure don't necessarily immediately follow assigned gender: for instance, straight women may get turned on by gay male porn or may identify with the male in a heterosexual coupling. Others have protested the abrogation of hard-won sexual liberties implicit in any restrictions on sexual expression, further questioning the politics of the alliance of the antiporn movement and the radical Right.[3] Gayle Rubin has come closest to undermining the terms of the antiporn discourse itself: she points out, heretically, that feminism, a discourse whose object is the organization of gendered oppression, may in fact not be the most appropriate or adequate discourse to analyze sexuality, in relation to which it becomes "irrelevant and often misleading."[4] Rubin paves the way for a reexamination of received truths about porn: is pornography, in fact, so obviously and so simply a discourse about gender? Has feminism, in arrogating porn as its own privileged object, foreclosed on other questions? If feminism, as Rubin goes on, "lacks angles of vision which can encompass the social organization of sexuality," it seems clear that at least one of these angles of vision is a theory of class, which has been routinely undertheorized and underdetermined within the antiporn movement in favor of a totalizing theory of misogyny. While class stratification and the economic and profit motives of those in the porn industry have been exhaustively covered, we have no theory of how class plays itself out in nuances of representation.

The extent of misogyny is so monumental as to be not only tragic, but banal in its omnipresence. It may appear as superficially more evident in the heightened and exaggerated realms of fantasy, pleasure, and projection—the world of pornography—but this is only a localized appearance, and one that may be operating under other codes than those of gender alone. So if the question of misogyny is momentarily displaced here to allow a consideration of questions of class, it isn't because one supersedes the other but because bringing issues of class into the porn debates may offer a way of breaking down the theoretical monolith of misogyny—and in a manner that doesn't involve jumping on the reassuring bandwagon of repression and policing the image world or the false catharsis of taking symptoms for causes. The recent tradition of cultural studies work on the body might pose some difficult questions for feminism (and thus might contribute to the kind of revamped critical discourse on sexuality that Rubin calls for): questions such as whether antiporn feminists, in abjuring questions of class in analyzing representation, are constructing (and attempting to enforce) a theory and politics of the body on the wrong side of struggles against bourgeois hegemony and are thus ultimately complicit in its enforcement. But at the same time, in taking on porn as an object, U.S. cultural studies—or at least that tendency to locate resistance, agency, and micropolitical struggle just about everywhere in mass cultural reception—might have difficulty finding good news as it takes on the fixity of sexuality and power.

Hustler is probably the most reviled instance of mass-circulation porn, and at the same time one of the most explicitly class-antagonistic mass-circulation periodicals of any genre. Although it's been the tendency among writers on porn to lump it together into an unholy triad with *Penthouse* and *Playboy*, the other two top-circulating men's magazines, *Hustler* is a different beast in any number of respects, even in conventional men's magazine terms. *Hustler* set itself apart from its inception through its explicitness and its crusade *for* explicitness, accusing *Playboy* and *Penthouse* of hypocrisy, veiling the body, and basically not delivering the goods. The strategy paid off—*Hustler* captured a third of the men's market with its entrée into the field in 1974 by being the first to reveal pubic hair—with *Penthouse* swiftly following suit (in response to which a *Hustler* pictorial presented its model shaved),[5] then upping the explicitness ante and creating a publishing scandal by displaying a glimpse of pubic hair on its cover in July 1976 (this a typically *Hustler* commemoration of the Bicentennial: the model wore stars and stripes, although not enough of them). Throughout these early years *Hustler's* pictorials persisted in showing more and more of the forbidden zone (the "pink" in *Hustler*-speak), with *Penthouse* struggling to keep up and *Playboy*—whose focus was always above the waist, anyway—keeping a discreet distance. *Hustler* then introduced penises, first limp ones, currently hefty erect-appearing ones, a sight verboten in traditional men's magazines, where the strict prohibition on the erect male sexual organ impels the question of what traumas it might provoke in the male viewer. *Hustler*, from its inception, made it its mission to disturb and unsettle its readers, both psychosexually and sociosexually, interrogating, as it were, the typical men's magazine codes and conventions of sexual representation: *Hustler*'s early pictorials included pregnant women, middle-aged women (horrified news commentaries referred to "geriatric pictorials"), overweight women, hermaphrodites, amputees, and, in a moment of true frisson for your typical heterosexual male, a photo spread of a preoperative transsexual, doubly well endowed. *Hustler* continued to provoke reader outrage with a 1975 interracial pictorial (black male, white female), which according to *Hustler* was protested by both the KKK and the NAACP. It's been known to picture explicit photo spreads on the consequences of venereal disease, the most graphic war carnage — none of these your typical, unproblematic turn-on.

Even more so than in its explicitness, *Hustler*'s difference from *Playboy* and *Penthouse* is in the sort of body it produces. Its pictorials, far more than other magazines, emphasize gaping orifices, as well as a consistent sharp focus on *other* orifices. *Hustler* sexuality is far from normative. It speaks openly of sexual preferences as "fetishes," and its letters and columns are full of the most specific and wide-ranging practices and sexualities, which don't appear to be hierarchized and many of which have little to do with the standard heterosexual telos of penetration. (Male-male sexuality is sometimes raised as a possibility, as well, along with the men's magazine standard woman-woman scenario.) The *Hustler* body is an unromanticized body — no Vaselined lenses or soft focus: this is neither the airbrushed top-heavy fantasy body of *Playboy* nor the ersatz opulence, the lingeried and sensitive crotch shots of *Penthouse*, transforming female genitals into objets d'art. It's a body, not a surface or a suntan: insistently material, defiantly vulgar, corporeal. In fact, the *Hustler* body is often a gaseous, fluid-emitting, *embarrassing* body, one continually defying the strictures of bourgeois manners and mores and instead governed by its lower intestinal tract — a body threatening to erupt at any moment. *Hustler*'s favorite joke is someone accidentally defecating in church.

Particularly in its cartoons, but also in its editorials and political humor, *Hustler* devotes itself to what tends to be called "grossness": an obsessive focus on the lower stratum, humor animated by a downward movement, representational techniques of exaggeration and inversion. *Hustler*'s bodily topography is straight out of Rabelais, as even a partial inventory of the subjects it finds of interest indicates: fat women, assholes, monstrous and gigantic sexual organs, body odors (the notorious Scratch 'n Sniff centerfold, which, due to "the limits of the technology," publisher Larry Flynt apologized, smelled definitively of lilacs), and anything that exudes from the body: piss, shit, semen, menstrual blood (particularly when it sullies a sanitary or public site), and, most especially, farts: farting in public, farting loudly, Barbara Bush farting, priests and nuns farting, politicians farting, the professional classes farting, the rich farting. . . . [6] Certainly a far remove from your sleek, overlaminated *Playboy/Penthouse* body. As *Newsweek* complained, "The contents of an average issue read like something Krafft-Ebing might have whispered to the Marquis de Sade. . . . *Hustler* is into erotic fantasies involving excrement, dismemberment, and the sexual longings of rodents. . . . [W]here other skin slicks are merely kinky, *Hustler* can be downright frightful. . . . The net effect is to transform the erotic into the emetic."[7]

It's not clear if what sets *Newsweek* to crabbing is that *Hustler* transgresses bourgeois mores of the proper or that *Hustler* violates men's magazine conventions of sexuality. On both fronts its discourse is transgressive — in fact on *every* front *Hustler* devotes itself to producing generalized transgression. Given that control over the body has long been associated with the bourgeois political project, with both the "ability and the right to control and dominate others,"[8] *Hustler*'s insistent and repetitious return to the iconography of the body out of control, rampantly transgressing bourgeois norms and sullying bourgeois property and proprieties, raises certain political questions. On the politics of such social transgressions, for example, Peter Stallybrass and Allon White, following Bakhtin, write of a transcoding between bodily and social topography, setting up a homology between the lower bodily stratum and the lower social classes — the reference to the body invariably being a reference to the social.[9]

Here perhaps is a clue to *Newsweek*'s pique, as well as a way to think about why it is that the repressive apparatuses of the dominant social order return so invariably to the body and to somatic symbols. (And I should say that I write this during the Cincinnati Mapplethorpe obscenity trial, so this tactic is excessively visible at this particular conjuncture.) It's not only because these bodily symbols "are the ultimate elements of social classification itself" but also because the transcoding between the body and the social sets up the aesthetic mechanisms through which the body is a privileged political trope of lower social classes, and through which bodily grossness operates as a critique of dominant ideology. The power of grossness is predicated on its opposition from *and to* high discourses, themselves prophylactic against the debasements of the low (the lower classes, vernacular discourses, low culture, shit . . .). And it is dominant ideology itself that works to enforce and reproduce this opposition—whether in producing class differences, somatic symbols, or culture. The very highness of high culture is structured through the obsessive banishment of the low, and through the labor of suppressing the grotesque body (which is, in fact, simply the material body, gross as that can be) in favor of what Bakhtin calls "the classical body." This classical body—a refined, orifice-less, laminated surface—is homologous to the forms of official high culture that legitimate their authority by reference to the values—the highness —inherent in this classical body. According to low-theoretician Larry Flynt, "Tastelessness is a necessary tool in challenging preconceived notions in an uptight world where people are afraid to discuss their attitudes, prejudices and misconceptions." This is not so far from Bakhtin on Rabelais: "Things are tested and reevaluated in the dimensions of laughter, which has defeated fear and all gloomy seriousness. This is why the material bodily lower stratum is needed, for it gaily and simultaneously materializes and unburdens. It liberates objects from the snares of false seriousness, from illusions and sublimations inspired by fear."[10]

So in mapping social topography against bodily topography, it becomes apparent how the unsettling effects of grossness and erupting bodies condense all the unsettling effects (to those in power) of a class hierarchy tenuously held in place through symbolic (and less symbolic) policing of the threats posed by bodies, by lower classes, by angry mobs.

Bakhtin and others have noted that the invention of the classical body and the formation of this new bodily canon have their inception in the sixteenth-century rise of individualism and the attendant formation and consolidation of bourgeois subjectivity and bourgeois political hegemony, setting off, at the representational level, the struggle of grotesque and classical concepts.[11] A similar historical argument is made by Norbert Elias in his study *The Civilizing Process*, which traces the effects of this social process on the structure of individual affect. The invention of Bakhtin's classical body entails and is part of a social transformation within which thresholds of sensitivity and refinement in the individual psyche become heightened.[12] Initially this reform of affect takes place in the upper classes, within whom increasingly refined manners and habits—initially a mechanism of class distinction—are progressively restructuring standards of privacy, disgust, shame, and embarrassment. These affect-reforms are gradually, although incompletely, disseminated downward through the social hierarchy (and finally to other nations whose lack of "civilization" might reasonably necessitate colonial etiquette lessons). These new standards of delicacy and refinement become the very substance of bourgeois subjectivity: constraints that were originally socially generated gradually become reproduced in individuals as habits, reflexes, as the structure of the modern psyche. And as Elias reminds us, the foundational Freudian distinction between id and ego corresponds to historically specific demands placed on public behavior in which certain instinctual behaviors and impulses—primarily bodily ones like sex and elimination—are relegated to the private sphere, behind closed doors, or in the case of the most shameful and most socially prohibited drives and desires, warehoused as the contents of the unconscious.

So we can see, returning to our two opening images, how Morgan's tears, her sentiment, might be constructed *against* E. C.'s vulgarity, how her desire to distance herself from and if possible banish from existence the cause of her distress—the sexual expression of people unlike herself—has a sort of structural imperative: as Stallybrass and White put it, the bourgeois subject has "continuously defined and redefined itself through the exclusion of what it marked out as low—as dirty, repulsive, noisy, contaminating. . . . [The] very act of exclusion was constitutive of its identity."[13] So disgust has a long and complicated history, the context within which should be placed the increasingly strong tendency of the bourgeois to want to remove the distasteful from the sight of society (including, of course, dead animals, which might interest E. C.—as "people in the course of the civilizing process seek to suppress in themselves every characteristic they feel to be animal").[14] These gestures of disgust are crucial in the production of the bourgeois body, now so rigidly split into higher and lower stratum that tears will become the only publicly permissible display of bodily fluid. So the bodies and bodily effluences start to stack up into neat oppositions: on the one side upper bodily productions, a heightened sense of delicacy, and the project of removing the distasteful from sight (and sight, of course, is at the top of the hierarchization of the senses central to bourgeois identity and rationality); and on the other hand, the lower body and *its* productions, the insistence on vulgarity and violations of the bourgeois body. To the extent that in Morgan's project, discourse and tears are devoted to concealing the counterbourgeois body from view by regulating its representation and reforming its pleasures into ones more consequent with refined sensibilities, they can be understood, at least in part, as the product of a centuries-long sociohistorical process, a process that has been a primary mechanism of class distinction, and one that has played an important role as an ongoing tool in class hegemony. So perhaps it becomes a bit more difficult to see feminist disgust in isolation, and disgust at pornography as strictly a gender issue, for any gesture of disgust is not without a history and not without a class character. And whatever else we may say about feminist arguments about the proper or improper representation of women's bodies—and I don't intend to imply that my discussion is exhaustive of the issue—bourgeois disgust, even as mobilized against a sense of violation and violence to the female body, is not without a function in relation to class hegemony, and is more than problematic in the context of what purports to be a radical social movement.

Perhaps this is the moment to say that a large part of what impels me to write this essay is my own disgust in reading *Hustler*. In fact, I have wanted to write this essay for several years, but every time I trudge out and buy the latest issue, open it, and begin to try to bring analytical powers to bear upon it, I'm just so disgusted that I give up, never quite sure whether this almost automatic response is one of feminist disgust or bourgeois disgust. Of course, whether as feminist, bourgeois, or academic, I and most likely you are what could be called *Hustler*'s implied target, rather than its implied reader. The discourse of *Hustler* is quite specifically *constructed against* not only the classical body, a bourgeois holdover of the aristocracy, but all the paraphernalia of petite-bourgeoisiehood, as well. At the most manifest level *Hustler* is simply against any form of social or intellectual pretension: it is against the pretensions (and the social power) of the professional classes—doctors, optometrists, dentists are favored targets—it is against liberals, and it is particularly cruel to academics who are invariably prissy and uptight. (An academic to his wife: "Eat your pussy? You forget, Gladys, I have a Ph.D.") It is against the power of government—which is by definition corrupt, as are elected officials, the permanent government, even foreign governments. Of course it is against the rich, particularly rich women; it is down on the Chicago Cubs; and it devotes many pages to the hypocrisy of organized religion—with a multiplication of jokes on the sexual instincts of the clergy, the sexual possibilities of the crucifixion, and the scam of the virgin birth, and as mentioned previously, the plethora of jokes involving farting/shitting/fucking in church and the bodily functions of nuns, priests, and ministers. In *Hustler* most forms of social power are fundamentally crooked and illegitimate.

These are just *Hustler*'s more manifest targets. Reading a bit deeper, its offenses provide a detailed road map of a cultural psyche. Its favored tactic is to zero in on a subject, an issue, that the bourgeois imagination prefers to be unknowing about, that a culture has founded itself upon suppressing and prohibits irreverent speech about—things we would call "tasteless" at best, or might even become physically revulsed by: the materiality of aborted fetuses,[15] where homeless people go to the bathroom, cancer, the proximity of sexual organs to those of elimination—

any aspect of the material body, in fact. A case in point, one that again subjected *Hustler* to national outrage: its two cartoons about Betty Ford's mastectomy. If one can distance oneself from one's automatic indignation for a moment, *Hustler* might be seen as posing, through the strategy of transgression, an interesting metadiscursive question: which are the subjects that are taboo ones for even sick humor? Consider for a moment that while, for example, it was not uncommon, following the Challenger explosion, to hear the sickest jokes about scattered body parts, while jokes about amputees and paraplegics are not entirely unknown even on broadcast TV (and of course abound on the pages of *Hustler*), while jokes about blindness are considered so benign that one involving Ray Charles features in a current "blind taste test" soda pop commercial, mastectomy is one subject that appears to be completely off limits as a humorous topic. But back to amputees for a moment, perhaps a better comparison: apparently a man without a limb is considered less tragic by the culture at large, less mutilated, and less of a cultural problem than a woman without a breast; a mastectomy more of a tragedy than the deaths of the seven astronauts. This, as I say, provides some clues into the deep structure of a cultural psyche—as does our outrage. After all, what *is* a woman without a breast in a culture that measures breasts as the measure of the woman? Not a fit subject for comment. It's a subject so veiled that it's not even available to the "working through" of the joke. (It is again a case where *Hustler* seems to be deconstructing the codes of the men's magazine: where *Playboy* creates a fetish of the breast—its raison d'être is, in fact, very much the cultural obsession with them—*Hustler* perversely points out that they are, after all, materially, merely tissue—another limb.)[16]

Hustler's uncanny knack for finding and attacking the jugular of a culture's sensitivity might more aptly be regarded as intellectual work on the order of the classic anthropological studies that translate a culture into a set of structural oppositions (obsession with the breast/prohibition of mastectomy jokes), laying bare the structure of its taboos and arcane superstitions. (Or do only "primitive" cultures have irrational taboos?) *Hustler*, in fact, performs a cultural mapping similar to that of anthropologist Mary Douglas, whose study *Purity and Danger* produces a very similar social blueprint.[17] The vast majority of *Hustler* humor seems to be animated by the desire to violate what Douglas describes as "pollution" taboos and rituals—these being a society's set of beliefs, rituals, and practices having to with dirt, order, and hygiene (and by extension, the pornographic). As to the pleasure produced by such cultural violations as *Hustler*'s, Douglas cheerily informs us, "It is not always an unpleasant experience to confront ambiguity," and while it is clearly more tolerable in some areas than in others, "there is a whole gradient on which laughter, revulsion and shock belong at different points and intensities."[18]

The sense of both pleasure and danger that violation of pollution taboos can invoke is clearly dependent on the existence of symbolic codes, codes that are for the most part only semiconscious. Defilement can't be an isolated event, it can only engage our interest or provoke our anxiety to the extent that our ideas about such things are systematically ordered and that this ordering matters deeply — in our culture, in our subjectivity. As Freud notes, "Only jokes that have a purpose run the risk of meeting with people who do not want to listen to them."

Of course, a confrontation with ambiguity and violation can be profoundly displeasurable as well, as the many opponents of *Hustler* might attest. And for Freud this displeasure has to do with both gender and class. One of the most interesting things about Freud's discussion of jokes is the theory of humor and gender he elaborates in the course of his discussion of them, with class almost inadvertently intervening as a third term.[19] He first endeavors to produce a typology of jokes according to their gender effects. For example, in regard to excremental jokes (a staple of *Hustler* humor), Freud tells us that this is material *common to both sexes*, as both experience a common sense of shame surrounding bodily functions. And it's true that *Hustler*'s numerous jokes on the proximity of the sexual organs to elimination functions, the confusion of assholes and vaginas, turds and penises, shit and sex — for example, a couple fucking in a hospital room while someone in the next bed is getting an enema, and all get covered with shit — can't really be said to have a gender basis or target (unless, that is, we women put ourselves, more so than men, in the position of upholders of "good taste").

But obscene humor, whose purpose is to verbally expose sexual facts and relations, is, for Freud, a consequence of male and female sexual incommensurability, and the dirty joke is something like a seduction gone awry. The motive for (men's) dirty jokes is "in reality nothing more than women's incapacity to tolerate undisguised sexuality, an incapacity correspondingly increased with a rise in the educational and social level" (p. 101). Whereas both men and women are subject to sexual inhibition or repression, apparently upper-class women are the more seriously afflicted in the Freudian world, and dirty jokes thus function as a sign for both sexual difference ("smut is like an exposure of the sexually different person to whom it is directed. . . . [I]t compels the person who is assailed to imagine the part of the body or the procedure in question" [p. 98]) and class difference. So apparently, if it weren't for women's lack of sexual willingness and class refinement the joke would be not a joke, but a proposition: "If the woman's readiness emerges quickly the obscene speech has a short life; it yields at once to a sexual action," hypothesizes Freud (p. 99). While there are some fairly crude gender and class stereotypes in circulation here—the figure of the lusty barmaid standing in for the lower-class woman—it's also true that obscene jokes and pornographic images *are* only perceived by *some* women as an act of aggression against women. But these images and jokes are aggressive only insofar as they're capable of causing the woman discomfort, and they're capable of causing discomfort *only* insofar as there *are* differing levels of sexual inhibition between at least some men and some women. So Freud's view would seem to hold out: the obscene joke is directed originally toward women; it not only presupposes the presence of a woman, but presupposes also that women are sexually constituted differently from men, and upper classness or upper-class identification—as Morgan's discourse also indicates— exacerbates this difference.

But if there are differing levels of inhibition, displeasure, or interest between some men and some women (although *Hustler*'s readership is primarily male, it's not exclusively male), the origins of this pleasure/displeasure disjunction are also a site of controversy in the porn debates. For Freud it's part of the process of *differentiation* between the sexes, not originative—little girls are just as "interested" as little boys. Antiporn forces tend to reject a constructionist argument such as Freud's in favor of a description of female sexuality as inborn and biologically based—something akin to the "normal human sensuality" Morgan refers to.[20] Women's discomfiture at the dirty joke, from this vantage point, would appear to be twofold. There is the discomfort at the intended violation—at being assailed "with the part of the body or the procedure in question." But there is the further discomfort of being addressed as a subject of repression—as a subject with a history—and the rejection of porn can be seen as a defense erected against representations that mean to unsettle her in her subjectivity. In other words, there is, in pornography, a violation of the very *premise* of the "naturalness" of female sexuality and subjectivity, exacerbated by the social fact that not all women *do* experience male pornography in the same way. That "prosex" feminists, who tend to follow some version of a constructionist position on female sexuality, seem to feel less violated by porn is some indication that these questions of subjectivity are central to porn's address, misaddress, and violations. To the extent that pornography's discourse engages in setting up disturbances around questions of subjectivity and sexual difference—after all, what does *Hustler*- variety porn consist of but the male fantasy of women whose sexual desires are in concert with men's?—and that this fantasy of female compliance is perceived as doing violence to female subjectivity by some women but not others, the perception of this violence is, to a large degree, an issue of difference among women.[21] But the violence here is that of misaddress, of having one's desire misfigured as the male's desire. It is the violence of being absent from the scene. The differences between female spectators as to how this address or misaddress is perceived appears to be bound up with the degree to which a certain version of female sexuality is hypostatized as natural, versus a sense of mobility of sexuality (at least at the level of fantasy). But hypostatizing female sexuality and assigning it to all women involves universalizing a historically specific class position as well, not as something acquired and constructed through difference, privilege, and hierarchy, but as somehow inborn. Insisting that all women are violated by pornography insists that class or class identification doesn't figure as a difference among women, that "normal human sensuality" erases all difference between women.

For Freud, even the form of the joke is classed, with a focus on joke technique associated with higher social classes and education levels. In this light it's interesting to note how little *Hustler* actually engages in the technique of the joke — even to find a pun is rare. But then as far as obscene humor, we're subject to glaring errors of judgment about the "goodness" of jokes insofar as we judge them on formal terms, according to Freud — the technique of these jokes is often "quite wretched, but they have immense success in provoking laughter." Particularly in regard to obscene jokes, we aren't "in a position to distinguish by our feelings what part of the pleasure arises from the sources of their technique and what part from those of their purpose. Thus, strictly speaking, we do not know what we are laughing at."[22] And so, too, with displeasure — it would seem we can't be entirely sure what we're *not* laughing at either, and this would be particularly true of both the bourgeois and the antipornography feminist, to the extent that both seem likely to displace or disavow pleasure or interest in smut, one in favor of technique — like disgust, a mechanism of class distinction — and the other against perceived violations against female subjectivity. So for both, the act of rejection takes on far more significance than the terrains of pleasure; for both, the nuances and micrologics of *displeasure* are defining practices.

Yet at the same time, there does seem to be an awful lot of interest in porn among both, albeit a negative sort of interest. It's something of a Freudian cliché that shame, disgust, and morality are reaction-formations to an original interest in what is not "clean." One defining characteristic of a classic reaction-formation is that the subject actually comes close to "satisfying the demands of the opposing instinct while actually engaged in the pursuit of the virtue which he affects," the classic example being the housewife obsessed with cleanliness who ends up "concentrating her whole existence on dust and dirt."[23] And it does seem to be the case that a crusader against porn will end up making pornography the center of her existence. Theorizing it as central to women's oppression means, in practical terms, devoting one's time to reading it, thinking about it, and talking about it. It also means simultaneously conferring this *interest*, this subject-effect, onto others—predicting tragic consequences arising from such dirty pursuits, unvaryingly dire and uniform effects, as if the will and individuality of consumers of porn are suddenly seized by some (projected) all-controlling force, a force that becomes—or already is—the substance of a monotonic male sexuality. Thusly summing up male sexuality, Andrea Dworkin writes: "Any violation of a woman's body can become sex for men; this is the essential truth of pornography."[24]

The belief in these sorts of essential truths seems close to what Mary Douglas calls "danger-beliefs"—"a strong language of mutual exhortation":

> At this level the laws of nature are dragged in to sanction the moral code: this kind of disease is caused by adultery, that by incest. . . .
> [T]he whole universe is harnessed to men's [sic] attempts to force one another into good citizenship. Thus we find that certain moral values are upheld and certain social rules defined by beliefs in dangerous contagion.[25]

And Douglas, like Freud, also speaks directly about the relation of gender to the "gradient" where laughter, revulsion, and shock collide: her discussion of danger beliefs opens onto questions of class and hierarchy, as well. For her, gender is something of a trope in the realm of purity rituals and pollution violations: it functions as a displacement from issues of social hierarchy.

> I believe that some pollutions are used as analogies for expressing a general view of the social order. For example, there are beliefs that each sex is a danger to the other through contact with sexual fluids. . . .
> Such patterns of sexual danger can be seen to express symmetry or hierarchy. It is implausible to interpret them as expressing something about the actual relation of the sexes. I suggest that many ideas about sexual dangers are better interpreted as symbols of the relation between parts of society, as mirroring designs of hierarchy or symmetry which apply in the larger social system.[26]

While men certainly do pose sexual danger to women, the content of pollution beliefs expresses that danger symbolically at best: it would be implausible to take the content of these beliefs literally. So while, for Douglas, gender is a trope for social hierarchy, a feminist might interpret the above passage to mean that *danger* is a trope for gender hierarchy. Douglas's observations on the series of displacements between defilement, danger, gender, and class puts an interesting cast on female displeasure in pornography in relation to class hierarchies and "the larger social system." It also sheds light on the relation between *Hustler*'s low-class tendentiousness and its production of bourgeois displeasure, and on how the feminist response to pornography might end up reinscribing the feminist into the position of enforcer of class distinctions.

Historically, female reformism aimed at bettering the position of women has often had an unfortunately conservative social thrust, as in, for example, the case of the temperance movement. The local interests of women in reforming male behavior can easily dovetail with the interests of capital in producing and reproducing an orderly, obedient, and sober workforce. In social history terms we might note that *Hustler* galumphs onto the social stage at the height of the feminist second wave, and while the usual way to phrase this relation would be the term "backlash," it can also be seen as a retort — even a political response — to feminist calls for reform of the male imagination. There's no doubt that *Hustler* sees itself as doing battle with feminists: ur-feminist Gloria Steinem makes frequent appearances in the pages of the magazine as an uptight and, predictably, upper-class bitch. It's fairly clear that from *Hustler*'s point of view, feminism is a class-based discourse. *Hustler*'s production of sexual differences are also the production of a form of class consciousness — to accede to feminist reforms would be to identify upward on the social hierarchy.

But any automatic assumptions about *Hustler*-variety porn aiding and abetting the entrenchment of male power might be put into question by actually reading the magazine. Whereas Freud's observations on dirty jokes are phallocentric in the precise sense of the word — phallic sexuality is made central — *Hustler* itself seems much less certain about the place of the phallus, much more wry and often troubled about male and female sexual incommensurability. On the one hand it offers the standard men's magazine fantasy babe — always ready, always horny, willing to do anything, and inexplicably attracted to the *Hustler* male. But just as often there is her flip side: the woman who is disgusted by the *Hustler* male's desires and sexuality, a superior, rejecting, often upper-class woman. It becomes clear how class resentment is modulated through resentment of what is seen as the power of women to humiliate and reject: "Beauty isn't everything, except to the bitch who's got it. You see her stalking the aisles of Cartier, stuffing her perfect face at exorbitant cuisineries, tooling her Jag along private-access coastline roads. . . . " This reeks of a sense of disenfranchisement rather than any sort of certainty about male power over women. The fantasy life here is animated by cultural disempowerment in relation to a sexual caste system and a social class system. The magazine is tinged with frustrated desire and rejection: *Hustler* gives vent to a vision of sex in which sex is an arena for failure and humiliation rather than domination and power. There are numerous ads addressed to male anxieties and sense of inadequacy: various sorts of penis enlargers ("Here is your chance to overcome the problems and insecurities of a penis that is too small. Gain self-confidence and your ability to satisfy women will skyrocket," reads a typical ad), penis extenders, and erection aids (Stay-Up, Sta-Hard).[27] One of the problems with most porn from even a pro-porn feminist point of view is that men seize the power and privilege to have public fantasies about women's bodies, to imagine and represent women's bodies without any risk, without any concomitant problematization of the male body—which is invariably produced as powerful and inviolable. But *Hustler* does put the male body at risk, representing and never completely alleviating male anxiety (and for what it's worth, there is a surprising amount of castration humor in *Hustler*, as well). Rejecting the sort of compensatory fantasy life mobilized by *Playboy* and *Penthouse*, in which all women are willing and all men are studs—as long as its readers fantasize and identify upward, with money, power, good looks, and consumer durables—*Hustler* pulls the window dressing off the market/exchange nature of sexual romance: the market in attractiveness, the exchange basis of male-female relations in capitalist patriarchy. Sexual exchange is a frequent subject of humor: women students are coerced into having sex with professors for grades; women are fooled into having sex by various ruses, lies, or barters, usually engineered by males in power positions—bosses, doctors, and the like. All this is probably truer than not true, but problematic from the standpoint of male fantasy: power, money, and prestige are represented as essential to sexual success, but the magazine works to disparage and counter identification with these sorts of class attributes on every other front. The intersections of sex, gender, class, and power here are complex, contradictory, and political.

Much of *Hustler*'s humor *is*, in fact, manifestly political, and much of it would even get a warm welcome in Left-leaning circles, although its strategies of conveying those sentiments might give some pause. A 1989 satirical photo feature titled "Farewell to Reagan: Ronnie's Last Bash" demonstrates how the magazine's standard repertoire of aesthetic techniques—nudity, grossness, and offensiveness—can be directly translated into scathingly effective political language. It further shows how the pornographic idiom can work as a form of political speech that refuses to buy into the pompously serious and high-minded language

in which official culture conducts its political discourse: *Hustler* refuses
the language of high culture along with its political forms. The photo
spread, laid out like a series of black-and-white surveillance photos, begins with this no-words-minced introduction:

> It's been a great eight years—for the power elite, that is. You can bet
> Nancy planned long and hard how to celebrate Ron Reagan's successful
> term of filling special-interest coffers while fucking John Q. Citizen
> right up the yazoo. A radical tax plan that more than halved taxes for
> the rich while doubling the working man's load; detaxation of indus-
> tries, who trickled down their windfalls into mergers, takeovers, and in-
> vestments in foreign lands; crooked deals with enemies of U.S. allies in
> return for dirty money for right wing killers to reclaim former U.S.
> business territories overseas; more than 100 appointees who resigned in
> disgrace over ethics or outright criminal charges . . . are all the legacies
> of the Reagan years . . . and we'll still get whiffs of bullyboy Ed
> Meese's sexual intimidation policies for years to come, particularly with
> conservative whores posing as Supreme Court justices.[28]

The photos that follow are of an elaborately staged orgiastic White
House farewell party as imagined by the *Hustler* editors, with the appropriate motley faces of the political elite photomontaged onto naked
and seminaked bodies doing fairly obscene and polymorphously perverse things to each other. (The warning "Parody: Not to be taken seriously. Celebrity heads stripped onto our model's bodies" accompanies
each and every photo—more about *Hustler*'s legal travails further on.)
That more of the naked bodies are female and that many are in what
could be described as a service relation to male bodies clearly opens up
the possibility of a reading limited to its misogynistic tendencies. But
what becomes problematic for such a singular reading is that within
these parodic representations, this staging of the rituals of male hegemony also works in favor of an overtly counterhegemonic political
treatise.

The style is something like a *Mad* magazine cartoon come to life with
a multiplication of detail in every shot (the Ted Kennedy dartboard in
one corner; in another, stickers that exhort "Invest in South Africa"; the
plaque over Reagan's bed announcing "Joseph McCarthy slept here").
In the main room of the party, various half-naked women cavort, and
Edwin Meese is glimpsed filching a candelabra. Reagan greets a hooded
Ku Klux Klanner at the door, and a helpful caption translates the action:
"Ron tells an embarrassed Jesse Helms it wasn't a come-as-you-are party," while in the background the corpse of Bill Casey watches benignly
over the proceedings (his gaping mouth doubles as an ashtray), as does
former press secretary James Brady—the victim of John Hinckley's at-

tempted assassination and Reagan's no-gun-control policy—who, propped in a wheelchair, wears a sign bluntly announcing "Vegetable Dip" around his neck. In the next room Ollie North as a well-built male stripper gyrates on top of a table while a fawning Poindexter, Secord, and Weinberger gathered at his feet stuff dollar bills into his G-string holster in homoerotic reverie. In the next room Jerry Falwell is masturbating to a copy of *Hustler* concealed in the Bible, a bottle of Campari at his bedside and an "I love Mom" button pinned to his jacket (this a triumphant *Hustler* pouring salt on the wound—more on the Falwell Supreme Court case later on). In another room "former Democrat and supreme skagbait Jeane Kirkpatrick demonstrates why she switched to the Republican Party," as, grinning and topless, we find her on the verge of anally penetrating a bespectacled George Bush with the dildo attached to her ammunition belt. A whiny Elliott Abrams, pants around his ankles and dick in hand, tries unsuccessfully to pay off a prostitute who won't have him; and a naked Pat Robertson, doggie style on the bed, is being disciplined by a naked angel with a cat-o'-nine-tails. And on the last page the invoice to the American citizens: $283,000,000.

While the antiestablishment politics of the photo spread are fairly clear, *Hustler* can also be maddeningly incoherent, all over what we usually think of as the political spectrum. Its incoherence, as well as its low-rent tendentiousness, can be laid at the door of publisher Larry Flynt as much as anywhere, as Flynt, in the early days of the magazine, maintained such iron control over the day-to-day operations that he had to approve even the pull quotes. Flynt is a man apparently both determined and destined to play out the content of his obsessions as psychodrama on our public stage; if he weren't so widely considered such a disgusting pariah, his life could probably supply the material for many epic dramas. The very public nature of Flynt's blazing trail through the civil and criminal justice system and his one-man campaign for the first amendment justify a brief descent into the murkiness of the biographical—not to make a case for singular authorship, but because Flynt himself has had a decisive historical and political impact in the realpolitik of state power. In the end it has been porn king Larry Flynt—not the left, not the avant garde—who has decisively expanded the perimeters of political speech.

Larry Flynt is very much of the class he appears to address; his story is that of a pornographic Horatio Alger. He was born in Magoffin County, Kentucky, in the Appalachias, the poorest county in America. The son of a pipe welder, he quit school in the eighth grade, joined the navy at fourteen with a forged birth certificate, got out, worked in a General Motors auto assembly plant, and turned $1,500 in savings into a chain of go-go bars in Ohio named the Hustler Clubs. The magazine originated as a two-page newsletter for the bars, and the rest was rags to riches: Flynt's income was as high as thirty million dollars a year when *Hustler* was at its peak circulation of over two million. (He then built himself a scale replica of the cabin he grew up in, in the basement of his mansion to remind him, he says, where he came from. The model is complete with chickenwire and hay and a three-foot lifelike statue of the chicken he claims to have lost his virginity to at age eight.)

Since the magazine's inception Flynt has spent much of his time in and out of the nation's courtrooms on various obscenity and libel charges, as well as an array of contempt charges and other bizarre legal entanglements—notably his somehow becoming entangled in the government's prosecution of automaker John DeLorean. All proceeded as normal (for Flynt) until his well-publicized 1978 conversion to evangelical Christianity at the hands of presidential sister Ruth Carter Stapleton. The two were pictured chastely hand in hand as Flynt announced plans to turn *Hustler* into a *religious* skin magazine and told a Pentecostal congregation in Houston (where he was attending the National Women's Conference), "I owe every woman in America an apology." Ironically, it was this religious conversion that led to the notorious *Hustler* cover of a woman being ground up in a meat grinder, which was, in fact, another sheepish and flat-footed attempt at apologia by Flynt. "We will no longer hang women up as pieces of meat" was actually the widely ignored caption to the photo. (Recall here Freud's observation on the sophistication of the joke form as a class trait.)[29]

In 1978, shortly after the religious conversion, during another of his obscenity trials in Lawrenceville, Georgia, Flynt was shot three times by an unknown person with a .44 Magnum. His spinal nerves were severed, leaving him paralyzed from the waist down and in constant pain. He became a recluse, barricading himself in his Bel Air mansion, surrounded by bodyguards. His wife, Althea, then twenty-seven, a former go-go dancer in the Hustler clubs, took over control of the corporation and the magazine, and returned the magazine to its former focus. Flynt became addicted to morphine and Dilaudid, finally detoxing to methadone. (He repudiated the religious conversion after the shooting.) Now confined to a wheelchair, he continued to be hauled into court by the government for obscenity and in various civil suits. He was sued by *Penthouse* publisher Bob Guccione and a female *Penthouse* executive who claimed *Hustler* had libeled her by printing that she had contracted VD from Guccione. He was sued by author Jackie Collins after the magazine published nude photos it incorrectly identified as the nude author. He was fined ten thousand dollars a day—increased to twenty thousand dollars a day—when he refused to turn over to the feds tapes he claimed he possessed documenting a government frame of DeLorean. Flynt's public behavior was becoming increasingly bizarre. He appeared in court wearing an American flag as a diaper and was arrested. At another 1984 Los Angeles trial, described by a local paper as "legal surrealism," his own attorney asked for permission to gag his client and after an "obscene outburst," Flynt, like Black Panther Bobby Seale, was bound and gagged at his own trial.

The same year the FCC was forced to issue an opinion on Flynt's threat to force television stations to show his X-rated presidential campaign commercials. Flynt, whose compulsion it was to find loopholes in the nation's obscenity laws, vowed to use his presidential campaign to test those laws by insisting that TV stations show his campaign commercials featuring hard-core sex acts. (The equal time provision of Federal Communications Act prohibits censorship of any ad in which a candidate's voice or picture appears, while the U.S. Criminal Code prohibits dissemination of obscene material.) He had begun to make it his one-man mission to exploit every loophole in the first amendment, as well. In 1986 a federal judge ruled that the U.S. Postal Service could not constitutionally prohibit *Hustler* and Flynt from sending free copies of the magazine to members of Congress, a ruling stemming from Flynt's decision to mail them the magazine so they could be "well informed on all social issues and trends." Flynt's next appearance, ensconced in a gold-plated wheelchair, was at the $45 million federal libel suit brought by the Reverend Jerry Falwell over the notorious Campari ad parody, in which the head of the Moral Majority describes his "first time" as having occurred with his mother behind an outhouse. A Virginia jury dismissed the libel charge but awarded Falwell two hundred thousand dollars for intentional infliction of emotional distress. A federal district court upheld the verdict, but when it landed in the Rehnquist Supreme Court, the judgment was reversed by a unanimous Rehnquist-written decision that the Falwell parody was not reasonably believable, and thus fell into category of satire—an art form often "slashing and one-sided." This Supreme Court decision significantly extended the freedom of the press won in the 1964 *New York Times v. Sullivan* ruling (which mandated that libel could only be founded in cases of "reckless disregard"). It "handed the press one of its most significant legal triumphs in recent years," was "an endorsement of robust political debate," and ended the influx of "pseudolibel suits" by celebrities with hurt feelings, crowed the grateful national press, amid stories generally concluding that the existence of excrescences like *Hustler* is the price of freedom of the press.

Flynt and wife Althea had over the years elaborated various charges and conspiracy theories about the shooting, including charges of a

CIA-sponsored plot (Flynt claimed to have been about to publish the names of JFK's assassins—conspiracy theories being another repeating feature of the *Hustler mentalité*). Further speculation about the shooting focused on the mob, magazine distribution wars, and even various disgruntled family members. The shooting was finally acknowledged by white supremacist Joseph Paul Franklin, currently serving two life sentences for racially motivated killings. No charges were ever brought in the Flynt shooting. That Flynt, who has been regularly accused of racism, should be shot by a white supremacist is only one of the many ironies of his story. In another—one that would seem absurd in the most hackneyed morality tale—this man who made millions on the fantasy of endlessly available fucking is now left impotent. And in 1982, after four years of constant and reportedly unbearable pain, the nerves leading to his legs were cauterized to stop all sensation—Flynt, who built an empire on offending bourgeois sensibilities with their horror of errant bodily functions, is now left with no bowel or urinary control.

Flynt, in his obsessional one-man war against state power's viselike grip on the body of its citizenry, seized as his matériel the very pornographic idioms from which he had constructed his *Hustler* empire. The exhibitionism, the desire to shock, the deployment of the body—these are the affronts that have made him the personification of evil to both the state and antiporn feminists. Yet willingly or not, Flynt's own body has been very much on the line, as well—the pornographer's body has borne the violence of the public and private enforcement of the norms of the bourgeois body. If *Hustler*'s development of the pornographic idiom as a political form seems—as with other new cultural political forms—incoherent to traditional readings based on traditional alliances and oppositions—right-left, misogynist-feminist—then it is those very political meanings that *Hustler* throws into question. It is *Hustler*'s political incoherence—in conventional terms—that makes it so available to counterhegemonic readings, to opening up new political alliances and strategies. And this is where I want to return to the issue of *Hustler*'s misogyny, another political category *Hustler* puts into question. Do I feel assaulted and affronted by *Hustler*'s images, as do so many other women? Yes. Is that a necessary and sufficient condition on which to base the charge of its misogyny? Given my own gender and class status, I'm not sure that I'm exactly in a position to trust my immediate response.

Take, for example, *Hustler*'s clearly strategic use of nudity. It is unmistakable from the "Reagan's Farewell Party" photo spread that *Hustler* uses nudity as a leveling device, a deflating technique following in a long tradition of political satire. And perhaps this is the subversive force behind another of *Hustler*'s scandals (or publishing coups, from its point of view), its notorious nude photo spread of Jackie Onassis, captured sunbathing on her Greek island, Skorpios. Was this simply another case of misogyny? The strategic uses of nudity we've seen elsewhere in the magazine might provoke a conceptual transition in thinking through the Onassis photos: from Onassis as unwilling sexual object to Onassis as political target. Given that nudity is used throughout the magazine as an offensive against the rich and powerful—Reagan, North, Falwell, Abrams, as well as Kirkpatrick and, in another feature, Thatcher, all, unfortunately for the squeamish, through the magic of photomontage, nude—it would be difficult to argue that the nudity of Onassis functions strictly in relation to her sex, exploiting women's vulnerability as a class, or that its message can be reduced to a genericizing one like "you may be rich but you're just a cunt like any other cunt." Onassis's appearance on the pages of *Hustler* does raise questions of sex and gender insofar as we're willing to recognize what might be referred to as a sexual caste system, and the ways in which the imbrication of sex and caste makes it difficult to come to any easy moral conclusions about *Hustler*'s violation of Onassis and her right to control and restrict how her body is portrayed. As recent pulp biographies inform us, the Bouvier sisters, Jacqueline and Princess Lee, were more or less bred to take up positions as consorts of rich and powerful men, to, one could put it bluntly, professionally deploy their femininity. This is not so entirely dissimilar from *Hustler*'s quotidian and consenting models, who, while engaged in a similar activity, are confined to very different social sites—such sites as those pictured in a regular *Hustler* feature, "The Beaver Hunt," a gallery of snapshots of nonprofessional models sent in by readers.[30] Posed in paneled rec rooms, on plaid Sears sofas or chenille bedspreads, amid the kind of matching bedroom suites seen on late-night, easy-credit furniture ads, nude or in polyester lingerie, they are identified as secretaries, waitresses, housewives, nurses, bank tellers, cosmetology students, cashiers, factory workers, saleswomen, data processors, nurse's aides. Without generalizing from this insufficiency of data about any kind of *typical* class-based notions about the body and its appropriate display, we can simply ask, where are the doctors, lawyers, corporate executives, and college professors?[31] Or moving up the hierarchy, where are the socialites, the jet-setters, the wives of the chairmen of the board? Absent because of their fervent feminism? Or merely because they've struck a better deal? Simply placing the snapshots of Onassis in the place of the cashier, the secretary, and the waitress violates the rigid social distinctions of place and the hardened spatial boundaries (boundaries most often purchased precisely as protection from the hordes) intrinsic to class hierarchy. These are precisely the distinctions that would make us code differently the deployment of femininity that achieves marriage to a billionaire shipping magnate and one that lands you a spot in this month's "Beaver Hunt." The political implications of the Onassis photo spread call for a more nuanced theory of misogyny than those currently in circulation. If *any* symbolic exposure or violation of *any* woman's body is automatically aggregated to the transhistorical misogyny machine that is the male imagination, it overlooks the fact that *all* women, simply by virtue of being women, are not necessarily political allies, that women can both symbolize and exercise class power and privilege, not to mention oppressive political power.

Feminist antipornography arguments attempt to reify the feminine as an inviolate moral high ground against pornographic male desires. While apotropaic against the reality of male violence, their reification of femininity also demonizes any position that dares to suggest that femininity is not an inherent virtue, an inborn condition, or in itself a moral position from which to speak—positions such as those held by prosex feminists, psychoanalytic theory, and the discourse of pornography itself. But foremost among the myriad political problems that the reification of femininity gives rise to is the contradiction of utilizing class disgust as its agent.[32] And a theory of representation that automatically conflates bodily representations with real women's bodies, and symbolic or staged sex or violence as equivalent to real sex or violence, clearly acts to restrict political expression and narrow the forms of political struggle by ignoring both differences between women and the class nature of feminist reformism. The fact that real violence against women is so pervasive as to be almost unlocalizable may lead us to want to localize it within something so easily at hand as representation, but the political consequences for feminism—to reduce it to another variety of bourgeois reformism—make this an insufficient tactic.

However, having said this, I must add that *Hustler* is certainly not politically unproblematic. If *Hustler* is counterhegemonic in its refusal of bourgeois proprieties, its transgressiveness has real limits. It is often only incoherent and banal where it means to be alarming and confrontational. Its banality can be seen in its politics of race, an area where its refusal of polite speech seems to have little countercultural force. *Hustler* has been frequently accused of racism, but *Hustler* basically just wants to offend—anyone, of any race, any ethnic group. Not content merely to offend the Right, it makes doubly sure to offend liberal and left sensibilities, too; not content merely to taunt whites, it hectors blacks. Its favored tactic in regard to race is to simply reproduce the stupidest stereotype it can think of—the subject of any *Hustler* cartoon featuring blacks will invariably be huge sexual organs that every women lusts after, or alternately, black watermelon-eating lawbreakers.

CHAPTER 9

Marx: The Video
A Politics of Revolting Bodies
(1990)

A Note on the Production

The tape was produced using a blue-screen process called Ultimatte, which allows you to matte or layer images on top of one another, creating a different sort of space than a conventional photographic realism. Characters can be forced into a visual juxtaposition with history and the social by being composited into other images (like film projections or stills). In the script I've used the term "A Historical Tableau" to designate scenes where characters exist in a space meant to indicate the effects and determinations of the social.

There is a sort of "Greek Chorus" of three drag queens. They periodically pop in and out of the frame, commenting on the action.

As for the sound track, there's very little sync sound in the tape. The voices are primarily voice-overs, often accented. The Doctor-Biographer's voice is British upper class. The Worker's voice is British working class. The Psychoanalytic voice is French. Marx and Helene Demuth are American. The audio is also heavily layered with sound effects, which were produced using the Audiofile digital audio system.

The letters Marx reads are excerpts from his actual letters.

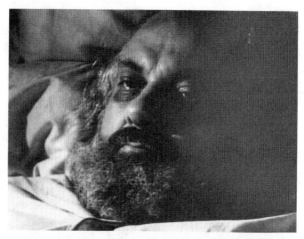

FADE UP:

Karl Marx's Bedroom

Haunting music. The room is dim. CLOSE-UP on MARX, who is lying in his bed, ill and in pain.

ROLLING TEXT OVER:

Karl Marx was born in Germany in 1818, and died in London in 1883, having been deported from numerous European countries for revolutionary activity. Throughout his life he suffered from chronic and painful outbreaks of carbuncles — agonizing skin eruptions — particularly during the years he was at work on his magnum opus, *Capital.* His thirty-year correspondence with Frederick Engels, his friend and collaborator, deals regularly and in great detail with the state of his own body.

FADE TO BLACK

A Nineteenth-Century Examining Room

MARX's DOCTOR keyed over a sepia-tinted still of a nineteenth-century examining room. He addresses the camera.

DOCTOR: His body just erupted. It became like a battleground. The only cure at the time was arsenic. Terribly painful, like a body trying to turn itself into another body. I think it started shortly after his mother died. It continued throughout his life.

Three DRAG QUEENS suddenly pop into the frame over the doctor.

DRAG QUEEN CHORUS: His body just erupted!

TITLE (keyed over MARX'S FACE):
    MARX: THE VIDEO
    A POLITICS OF ERUPTING BODIES

The 1848 Revolution—Engraving

WORKER: In 1848, Tocqueville warned: "We are sleeping on a volcano. A wind of revolution blows, the storm is on the horizon." That year Marx and Engels completed *The Communist Manifesto*. Jean-Martin Charcot, who would later devote himself to the study of hysteria, entered medical school. The same year, revolution swept Europe. Students and workers united, but three years later the revolution was toppled.

SNEAK UP MUSIC: "La Marseillaise."

Marx's Bedroom, 1863

MARX sits in his bed, his head down. There is a sense of despair about him. As he lies down, black-and-white IMAGES briefly loom on his white nightshirt and then disappear. The voice of MARX's DOCTOR continues as the voice of the BIOGRAPHER.

DOCTOR-BIOGRAPHER: Looking back, fifteen years later, to the failed revolution.

MARX: *(voice-over)* Dear Engels: One thing is sure, the era of revolution is now once more fairly opened in Europe. And the general state of things is good. But the comfortable delusions and the almost childish enthusiasms with which we greeted the era of revolution before February 1848 are gone to the devil. Old comrades are gone . . .

An image of Trotsky briefly, dreamily appears on MARX's nightshirt and fades off.

others have fallen away or decayed, and a new generation is not yet in sight.

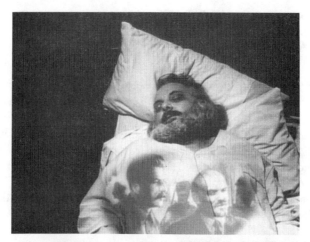

A Newspaper headline — "Millions Demand Trotsky's Death" — over MARX's nightshirt.

In addition, we now know what role stupidity plays in revolutions . . .

A painting of Stalin and Lenin in the heroic Socialist Realism style.

and how they are exploited by scoundrels.

Another image of Stalin over the nightshirt.

Let us hope that this time the lava pours from East to West and not vice versa.

A poster of Mao being carried aloft by a crowd of Chinese workers.

DOCTOR-BIOGRAPHER: He writes with nostalgia and longing for something thwarted. For something that didn't happen.

Paris, May 1968 — Black-and-White Photo

A FRENCHWOMAN: France, May '68. Students and workers united in a three-week general strike, demanding radical democratic reforms. Momentarily, revolution seemed possible, but once again that possibility was soon dispelled. [*SFX — glass crashing*] In the decades following '68, like the aftermath of 1848, the defeat of forces of change left traces, absences, an unfilled place where something is wanting.

Marx's Study — Day

FADE UP on MARX, wearing a suit, and sitting at his desk writing. A suitcase is at his feet.

MARX: Dear Frederick: Two hours ago I received a telegram that my mother is dead. Fate claimed one of my family. I must go to Trier to settle my inheritance. I myself stood with one foot in the grave. . . .

A Historical Tableau

MARX is lying in his bed. In the background is a film clip of a smoking factory, workers toiling, sweating. A din of factory sound effects.

DOCTOR-BIOGRAPHER: Writing *Capital*, his account of the conditions of the English proletariat, his body broke out with "a proletarian disease." Marx was desperate to finish his work, but unable to. Instead of writing, he was being written. The revolution he anticipated, the thwarted revolution, was displaced onto his own skin.

Marx's Bedroom — A Darkened Sickroom

MARX lies in bed, writing as the camera circles around him relentlessly, examining, probing.

MARX: Dear Fred: It is clear that on the whole I know more about the carbuncle disease than most doctors. Here and there I have the beginnings of new carbuncles, which keep on disappearing, but they force me to keep my working hours within limits. I consider it my vocation to remain in Europe to complete the work in which I have been engaged for so many years, but I cannot work productively more than a very few hours daily without feeling the effect physically. I think this work I am doing is much more important for the working class than anything I could do personally at a Congress of any kind. I would consider myself impractical if I had dropped dead without having finished my book, at least in manuscript.

One of the DRAG QUEENS, in red spangles with a red-feathered neckline, pops on over the scene.

DRAG QUEEN 2 (Dale Ray): His body just erupted!

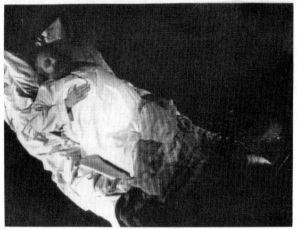

A Historical Tableau

MARX is writing at his desk, a blanket over his shoulders. In the background, the Russian Revolution rages.

MARX: Dear Kugelmann: Cut, lanced, etc., in short treated in every respect. In spite of this the thing is continually breaking out anew. I hope it will end this week, but who can guarantee me against another eruption?

WORKER: Marx, writing *Capital*, imagining Capital's overthrow. His body living out its split identifications —

All three of the DRAG QUEENS pop on over the scene, snorting with laughter.

Marx's Room — Night

A high overhead angle on MARX lying in bed.

MARX: Dear Frederick: You see I am still here and I will tell you more, I am incapable of moving about. This is a perfidious Christian illness.

WORKER: Marx took up the task of exhaustively analyzing the historical moment in which he found himself: the rise of industrialization and the inception of the working-class movement.

Images of grinding gears and industrial machinery superimposed onto MARX's nightshirt.

MARX: In the meantime, I can neither walk nor stand nor sit, and even lying down is damned hard. You see how the wisdom of nature has afflicted me.

WORKER: He stripped the facade off capital to reveal what was concealed: the labor in the commodity, the alienation of the worker, naked exploitation by the capitalist. He looked to the material foundations of the moment, he looked to the body.

Workers exiting a mine, superimposed onto MARX.

MARX: Would it not have been more sensible if instead of me it had been consigned to try the patience of a good Christian?

WORKER: His analysis of capital relies on a language of the body: "production," "consumption," "reproduction," and "circulation." For Marx, the collective wealth of the state is the body — the labor — of the workers. Capital amputates the worker from his own body; he has phantom pain for his missing limbs.

Images of various modern workers superimposed on MARX's body.

MARX: Like a true Lazarus, I am scourged on all sides.

WORKER: But for Marx, which bodies were absent, unspoken, unacknowledged?

Slow-motion images of old beauty queens — women's bodies — displace the image of MARX. As they do, one of the DRAG QUEENS pops on.

DRAG QUEEN 2 (Dale Ray): What's a real body, a natural body? It doesn't exist, there's only the social body, the body as theater, the body that speaks. But in whose language?

A CLOSE-UP of a pensive MARX dissolves into images of the BEAUTY QUEENS — as if they are Marx's fantasy, his reverie.

Marx's Study — Night

MARX writes.

DOCTOR-BIOGRAPHER: As he nears completion of the first volume, his carbuncles, mobile, sardonic, and insistent, break out in ever new vicinities —

A DRAG QUEEN pops on over the scene, interrupting.

DRAG QUEEN 3 (Kathleen): His body became sarcastic —

DOCTOR-BIOGRAPHER: —seizing the flesh, sculpting it into a body bulging, protuberant, not closed and finished, not refined.

She pops back on.

DRAG QUEEN 3 (Kathleen): This wasn't a body you could take into the drawing room. This was an ill-mannered body.

Marx's Study — Day

MARX writes, his arms bandaged.

MARX: You have too low an opinion of the English doctors if you think that they cannot diagnose carbuncles, particularly here in England — the land of carbuncles, which is actually a proletarian illness. It is only in the last few years that I have been persecuted by the thing. Before that, it was entirely unknown to me.

A Historical Tableau

MARX lies stretched out in bed, in pain. Scenes of LABOR RIOTS of the thirties are superimposed onto his body. He twists and turns, the rioters run from police, throw stones, shout. There is the crack of GUNFIRE and an explosion in the area of his crotch.

DOCTOR-BIOGRAPHER: Marx, who would disavow the opposition between the social and the psychic as mere bourgeois psychology, was possessed of a body whose symptoms mocked the social order; it had become grotesque: open, protruding, extended, secreting; in process, taking on new forms, shapes; his body the figure of the new soci-

ety that had failed to emerge. He was producing more and more body—too much body for a social order dedicated to its concealment.

Marx's Study

MARX lies on the couch, writing.

Marx: Dear Engels: It was good you did not come on Saturday. My story—now fourteen days old—had reached the crisis point. I could talk a little, and it hurt even to laugh on account of the big abscess between nose and mouth, which this morning has been reduced at least to reasonable proportions. Also the violently swollen lips are becoming reduced closer to their previous dimensions. May the head of the devil go through such fourteen days. All this stops being a joke.

A DRAG QUEEN pops on.

Drag Queen 1 (Felicia): What a problem the body is.

TITLE (keyed over FELICIA):
1. KEEPING IT CONFINED TO ITS BOUNDARIES (LIKE THE LOWER CLASSES).
2. CONCEALING ANYTHING THAT COMES OUT OF IT, OR PROTRUDES FROM IT.

Drag Queen 1 (Felicia): The creation of a meek, submissive, hygienic public body.

Hygiene Products Float through the Sky

Worker: Capital produces a disgusting body, so it can create new regimes, new products, to police it and make it acceptable. Capital has achieved historical advances in the threshold of delicacy, it produces new varieties of bourgeois disgust, then markets a new and improved body without by-products, without smells, to exist in a public sphere that is increasingly phobic about the collective body, the lower-class body—the mob—a body that might not mind its manners.

College Girls' Dorm Room—Documentary Footage

(Note: This is a transcript of an unscripted—although edited—conversation.)

Three COLLEGE GIRLS are sitting around gabbing. The conversation is fragmentary, as if overheard. The CAMERA roves around them, fragmenting their bodies.

TITLE (over the GIRLS): REVOLTING BODIES

—and I figure that's the best bet I have cause I hate my legs—
—I would just never expose my stomach ever, I could never wear a half shirt—
—I'll take this pair of size fourteen shorts with the size five belt because my hips are rather large—
—I have a really big problem with, like, the roll—
—the over-the-bathing-suit roll—
—You wouldn't think you have fat back here but you really do—
—the over-the-bathing-suit roll—
—and you can't see the string on me cause my fat covers up the string—
—but I think white fat stomachs are uglier than tan fat stomachs—
—I'm always conscious of the way I sit, I think, I'm sitting like this—
—That's why I hate summer clothes, I hate exposing my body for some reason, and I'm always conscious of, like, how am I sitting, can you see my stomach?
—Tell me, how do you exercise this part of your body, what do you do to get this out of there *[indicating the area on the underside of her upper arm]*?
—cut it off or something—
—I refuse to, like, I let him order first—
—I pretend I'm dieting—
—I've done every single diet—
—Really? Have you done Slimfast?
—I've done Slimfast, Weight Watchers, Weightloss clinic—
—But don't you know there's like no way the diets work?
—I feel so uncomfortable eating in front of my boyfriend, in front of any guy—
—You feel so much better, you're so full—
—I have a friend who used to do it, you eat huge salads and you gob on all the dressing and stuff, and that's easy to, you know . . . regurgitate—
—What's the word?

(laughter)

—Regurgitate!

Two DRAG QUEENS pop on over the scene.

DRAG QUEEN 2 (Dale Ray): Women's bodies, as tablets of social meaning, as sites of regulation . . .

DISSOLVE TO:

A Bathroom

A GIRL is retching into the toilet.

TITLE (over the TOILET): THE AGE OF CONSUMPTION

A Map of the United States

Little toilets with girls kneeling down at each one appear at each of the nation's
large cities.

FRENCHWOMAN: Anorexia, bulimia—epidemic in abundant Western
societies, post-1968. Ten to 20 percent of American women now
have eating disorders. Let's wrest this out of secrecy, out of the private sphere and view it for a moment as a social collective act.

TITLE (over the MAP): ELIMINATING THE BODY

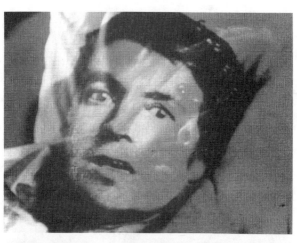

Diet Pills and Laxatives Float By over Blue Sky

WORKER: With our increasingly phobic relation to the collective body, the working-class body, with our creation of an ideal public body without fat, without snot or B.O., with a yearning for refinement, we will the disappearance of the body, the containment of the mass, the body politic, the threat.

Marx's Bedroom

DOCTOR-BIOGRAPHER: Marx, writing history from below, a history of wealth as labor, a history of the body, a history of the mass, his own body acting out.

FRENCH PSYCHIATRIC VOICE: Stories told by the body — after the failed revolutions of 1848 this comes to be known as "hysteria" and sweeps Europe.

A CLOSE-UP of MARX's face dissolves into a CLOSE-UP of a FEMALE HYSTERIC. They merge, then back to MARX's face alone.

TITLE: THE HYSTERIC IS SUBJECT TO MULTIPLE IDENTIFI-CATIONS

A Historical Tableau

MARX is sitting at his desk, dressed, writing, smoking a cigar. In the background a miner rides out of the mine, looming closer and closer toward MARX.

MARX: Dear Frederick: I would have written you sooner, but for approximately the last twelve days all reading, writing, and smoking have been strictly forbidden. I had a sort of eye inflammation tied up with very unpleasant effects on the nervous system. The thing is now so far under control that I can again dare to write. In the meantime I had all kinds of psychological reveries . . .

At the word "reveries," the miner dissolves into the old bathing-beauty footage; they float in slow motion through the space.

like a person going blind or crazy.

The Psychiatrist Charcot's Clinic—*Leçon clinique de Charcot*

The camera moves around the painting and comes to rest on the figure of a fainting, presumably hysterical, WOMAN.

FRENCH PSYCHIATRIC VOICE: Marx's symptoms make their appearance around the time that Freud's future teacher, Charcot, is beginning to recognize and treat a new disease, "traumatic hysteria." Charcot began to recognize that what is novel about traumatic hysteria is that in these cases what lay behind the symptoms were not physical disorders, and not just nerves, but ideas.

A Still of Charcot

As CHARCOT speaks, we dissolve to footage of MARX in the midst of what looks like a hysterical attack—sweating, heart pounding, breathing heavily.

CHARCOT: *(heavy French accent)* Male hysteria is not all that rare, and just among us, gentlemen, if I can judge from what I see each day, these cases are often unrecognized even by distinguished doctors. One will concede that a young and effeminate man might develop hysterical findings after experiencing significant stress, or deep emotions. But that a strong and vital worker, for instance, a railway engineer never prone to emotional instability before, should become hysteric—just as a woman might—this seems to us beyond imagination. And yet it is a fact—one which we must get used to.

The British Museum

MARX, walking with some difficulty, makes his way through the building.

MARX: Dear Fred: I wanted to write you yesterday from the British Museum, but I suddenly became so unwell that I had to close the very interesting book—

A paperback copy of Mary Wollstonecraft's Vindication of the Rights of Woman *falls to the ground with a CRASH.*

that I held in my hand. A dark veil fell over my eyes. Then a frightful headache and a pain in the chest. I strolled home. Air and light helped, and when I got home I slept for some time. My condition is such that I really should give up all working and thinking for some time to come; but that would be difficult, even if I could afford it.

Marx's Study

MARX lies on the couch, unwell. The CAMERA unsteadily moves toward him in an examining fashion.

MARX: Dear Frederick: In recent weeks it has been positively impossible for me to write even two hours a day. Apart from pressure from without, there are the household headaches which always affect my liver. I have become sleepless again, and have had the pleasure of seeing two carbuncles bloom near the penis. Fortunately they faded away. My illness always comes from the head.

Industrial Smokestacks

FRENCH PSYCHIATRIC VOICE: Charcot related male hysteria to trauma. As the industrial era progressed, the number of unexplained work-related illnesses increased enormously. Charcot worked to demonstrate how these could be understood as hysterical.

DISSOLVE TO:

A Historical Tableau

The smoke-stacks now appear behind MARX as he writes at his desk. They then DISSOLVE into pages from CAPITAL *which loom behind him.*

MARX: Dear Frederick: The doctor is quite right: the excessive night work was the main cause of the relapse —

A DRAG QUEEN pops on. She is posed against the Delacroix painting "Liberty Leading the Masses" and dressed as the figure of Liberty. Like Liberty, she has one breast bared.

DRAG QUEEN 2 (Dale Ray): It was an infection by ideas.

DISSOLVE back to MARX's STUDY: A section of Capital, "The Workday," looms behind him, coming in and out of focus.

MARX: The most disgusting thing for me was the interruption of my work. But I have drudged on, lying down, even if only at short intervals during the day. I could not proceed with the purely theoretical part, the brain was too weak for that. Hence I have enlarged the historical part on the workday, which lay outside the original plan.

A European Spa

The background is the exterior of a country spa retreat. MARX is in a wheelchair, dressed in a robe. A DRAG QUEEN, garbed as a NURSE, is in the foreground. BIRDS CHIRP.

DRAG QUEEN 3 (Kathleen as a nurse): Like other symptomatics of the day, he took the cure.

She exits frame.

DOCTOR-BIOGRAPHER: The medical world had devised various techniques for palliating an irritated and erupting human nervous system. Popular techniques included warm milk and bed rest, hydrotherapy and sojourns at peaceful pastoral spas. Doctors intuitively offered patients physical and psychological means to flee psychocultural stress — sending patients to the country, the sea, the mountains. Marx tried all of these. On doctor's orders, he fled his work.

The Baths

MARX, in bathing suit, takes the waters.
RUSHING WATER SFX.

Marx: Dear Frederick: So far I have had two sulfur baths, tomorrow the third. From the bath one steps on a raised board, in the altogether; the bath attendant alternately bombards all parts of the corpus except the head for three minutes, first strongly, then weakly, up to the legs and feet, an always advancing crescendo. You can see how little desire a man has to write here.

A DRAG QUEEN appears in the foreground.

Drag Queen 1 (Felicia as a nurse): Removing himself from his work brought *some* relief.

The Spa

MARX sits on a bench. He examines his pocket watch. It TICKS loudly. A pile of books sits unopened next to him. BIRDS CHIRP.

Marx: Dear Frederick: From the delayed appearance of this letter you can see how professionally I use my time here. I read nothing, write nothing. Because of the arsenic three times daily, one has time only for meals and strolling along the coast and the neighboring hills, there is no time left for other things. Evenings one is too tired to do anything but sleep.

Drag Queen: 2 (Dale Ray): His symptoms began to speak him!

The Spa

MARX, now dressed, strolls the grounds, leaning heavily on a cane.

Marx: My dear daughter: I am afflicted with an inflammation of the eye, not that there is much to be seen of it. . . . The eye has taken to the vicious habit of shedding tears on its own account, without the least regard to the feelings of his master.

Marx's Bedroom

MARX sits at the edge of the bed, head down, despairing.

DOCTOR-BIOGRAPHER: The carbuncles continued to erupt, stalling the writing of *Capital*, inscribing themselves into the text. Marx focused doggedly on the laboring body (while his own body exploded into new and ever-changing configurations) as if fearful of the effect of introducing the unregimented body into the realm of the political.

MARX glances off, at a print on the wall of "Liberty Leading the Masses."

FELICIA, dressed as Liberty, one fake breast revealed, pops on in front of the painting.

DRAG QUEEN 1 (Felicia): But then, this brings other bodies into the picture — the desiring body, the woman's body, the undisciplined body.

DISSOLVE TO:

TITLE: HELENE *(keyed over)*

Marx's Study

DOCTOR-BIOGRAPHER: Marx, even in the most dire poverty, did what he could to maintain a bourgeois household. It was Helene Demuth, the servant, who marked his own separation from the working class. She, more than Marx, straddles two worlds, belonging to both the bourgeois family and the working class: she was certainly the member of that world that Marx knew best.

HELENE DEMUTH enters, dressed as a maid, carrying a bucket of coal, which she lugs to the furnace. MARX sits at his desk and continues writing, ignoring her.

A Historical Tableau

MARX is at his desk writing. In the rear, projections of riots and revolutions (from Eisenstein's October*) roll. HELENE enters and serves MARX's tea.*

MARX: Dear Laura: Some recent Russian publications, printed in Holy

Russia, not abroad, show the great run of my theories in that country. Nowhere is my success more delightful to me; it gives me the satisfaction that I damage a power, which besides England, is the true bulwark of the old society.

Helene Scrubbing a Floor

A very high overhead shot. HELENE scrubs the black-and-white-tiled floor.

HELENE DEMUTH: For the nineteenth-century bourgeois male, the servant provokes social anxiety. She was ten years younger than Marx's wife Jenny. Lenchen, as she was called, ran the Marx household. Often Marx was too poor to pay her but she cast her lot with the Marx family. She did the cooking, housecleaning, laundering, dressmaking, nursing, and everything else, including taking the bedsheets to the pawnshop when eviction was threatened. In 1851, at age twenty-eight . . .

MARX trods across the frame.

she gave birth to Marx's son, secretly.

Marx's Study — Day

MARX writes, HELENE enters, serves tea. As she turns it becomes clear she's very pregnant.

DOCTOR-BIOGRAPHER: Marx wrote to Engels of a "very tangled family situation," hinting at a "mystery," a "tragicomic" mystery, in which he, Engels, also played a role. Marx traveled to Manchester to see Engels, where the two negotiated Lenchen's fate.

A DRAG QUEEN pops on over the scene—also very pregnant and in a white wedding dress.

DRAG QUEEN: 2 (Dale Ray): As men are accustomed to negotiating the fate of women's bodies!

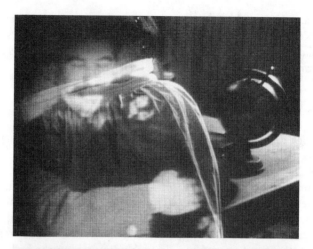

Close-Up—Helene's Pregnant Stomach

Archival footage of a Soviet woman hugging and kissing Josef Stalin is projected onto HELENE's stomach.

DOCTOR-BIOGRAPHER: Marx persuaded Engels to accept paternity for Lenchen's child, who was named Frederick, after him, in the custom of patrilineage. Engels accepted responsibility for the child, binding the two men together over Helene's mute body, over the body of the working-class woman.

TITLE (over HELENE): THE SECRET

HELEN DEMUTH: *(directly to camera—sync sound)* I never betrayed the secret; I let my baby be brought up by a working-class family. Engels occasionally sent money. Marx never acknowledged Freddy as his son. He chose not to acknowledge paternity.

Two DRAG QUEENS appear over HELENE's face.

DRAG QUEEN: 3 (Kathleen): As men are accustomed to negotiating the fate of women's bodies.

HELENE: After Marx's death, I moved into Engels's home as *his* housekeeper. My son Freddy visited regularly once a week: however, as an ordinary working man, he entered through the kitchen. He was Marx's only living son. He had grown up to be a poorly educated proletarian, his wife had left him and run away with his few possessions. His life was one of trouble, worry, and hardship.

TITLE: THE FATE OF WOMEN'S BODIES *(keyed over)*

College Girls' Dorm Room—Documentary Footage

—He says, "It looks like you gained a little weight" and he's just kidding—
—Oh, he's not kidding, it's his way of dropping a subtle hint—

—oh, great—

—and I know he's looking at me like maybe you should start dieting—

—he says, "I think I need to lose a few," and you're like, "Lose a few?"

—and you're walking down the street thinking look at her legs compared to mine—

—but think about, they're looking at you at the same time—

—Have you ever done the naked thing where you jump in front of a mirror, and you see how much is still jumping when you stop?

—WHAT?

—You're supposed to do it—I do it all the time.

—That seems like self-torture to me.

—(looking at a magazine) First of all I would never ever sit like that, with your legs up—

—I wouldn't be able to—

—once the legs go up the stomach goes out—

—if anything I guess I would do my stomach—

—Really? My legs is what I'd do—

—I'm OK from here up, anything below—

TITLE: THINKING THROUGH THE BODY

Marx's Study—Day

He writes at his desk. HELENE appears over the scene.

HELENE: *(sync sound, addressing camera)* He simply chose not to acknowledge paternity. I didn't have that choice.

Montage: A State Supreme Courtroom

JUDGE: *(threateningly)* You want a continuance so you can murder your baby—is that it?

Abortion Rights Rally Footage

The ACT UP contingent demonstrates in front of the Supreme Court.

DEMONSTRATORS: Get your laws off our bodies! Get your laws off our bodies!

Courtroom

JUDGE: *(severely)* I can't define it but I know it when I see it.

A Porn Still of a Woman in Bondage

FELICIA is posed in front in leopard skin and leather.

DRAG QUEEN 1 (Felicia): They want to ban pornography because it tells the truth.

Abortion Rights Rally Footage

DEMONSTRATORS: Get your laws off our bodies! Get your laws off our bodies!

Fast Zoom into Porn Still—Woman in Bondage

DRAG QUEEN 2 (Dale Ray): Get your laws off my body!

A Woman Bent over a Toilet

TEXT ROLLS OVER:

DESIRING A BODY THAT DOESN'T SPEAK,
DESIRING A BODY THAT HAS THE RIGHT DESIRES,
DESIRING A DIFFERENT SOCIAL BEING, A DIFFERENT
SOCIAL BODY . . .

END OF MONTAGE

Marx's Bedroom—Night

MARX lies in bed, writhing in pain.

MARX: *(sync sound)* How can I live in my body? Where could I live in my body?

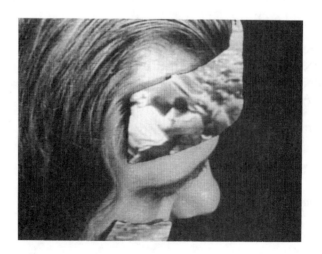

Marx's Bedroom

MARX lies in bed. TEXT from Capital is keyed over his body so that one seems to be emerging from the other.

MARX: Dear Engels: I had decided not to write you until I could announce the completion of the book, which is now the case. Also I did not want to bore you with the reasons for the frequent delays, namely carbuncles on my posterior and in the vicinity of the penis, the remains of which are now fading and which permit me to assume a sitting (that is, writing) position only at great pain. I do not take arsenic, because it makes me too stupid and at least for the little time that I have when writing is possible, I want to have a clear head.

DOCTOR-BIOGRAPHER: Finishing the book left his body racked and scarred. He was subject to increasing outbursts with each new translation of the book. He continued to search for a cure.

Marx's Study

MARX is writing. HELENE is cleaning around him.

MARX: My dear Jenny: I am sending you today the proofs of the French translation of *Das Kapital*. Today is the first day that I have been able to do anything at all. That is also the reason why I am postponing my return, because it is absolutely necessary to return in a condition for work.

DOCTOR-BIOGRAPHER: The eruptions of his body were not matched by the social eruptions he anticipated.

Marx's Study

MARX sits at his desk writing. His face is covered in bandages. Footage of LABOR RIOTS is keyed onto his bandages, so that they appear to be emerging from his carbuncles.

MARX: Dear Sorge: How did it happen that in the U.S. where, relatively, that is—compared with civilized Europe—land was accessible to the great masses of the people and to a certain degree (again relatively) still is, the capitalist economy and the corresponding enslavement of the working class have developed more rapidly and more shamelessly than in any country?

A DRAG QUEEN appears over the scene.

D<small>RAG</small> Q<small>UEEN</small> 1 (Felicia): His body continued its parody. Marx came to regard the carbuncles as having a life of their own. His affliction had a theory and a practice.

Marx's Bedroom

MARX lies in bed as HELENE fluffs his pillows.

M<small>ARX</small>: Dear Frederick: The doctor has opened up the pleasant prospect that I will have to deal with this loathsome disease until late in January. Still this second Frankenstein on my hump is by far not so fierce as was the first in London. You can see this from the fact that I am able to write. If one wants to vomit politics out of nausea, one must take it daily in the form of telegraphic pills, such as are delivered by the newspapers.

TITLE: IF ONE WANTS TO VOMIT POLITICS OUT OF NAU-SEA *(keyed over)*

A Woman Bending over a Toilet

W<small>OMAN</small>: How can I live in my body? Where can I live in my body?

A DRAG QUEEN appears.

D<small>RAG</small> Q<small>UEEN</small> 2 (Dale Ray): Where is the history of the body written?

Another DRAG QUEEN pops on over footage of police beating a man against a car.

D<small>RAG</small> Q<small>UEEN</small> 1 (Felicia): In your symptoms!

The police brutality footage freezes and TEXT rolls over.

TEXT:
LIKE THE REVOLUTIONARY, THE ERUPTING SYMPTO-MATIC BODY DISPLAYS MONSTROUS AND UNREADABLE FORMS TO A HORRIFIED SOCIETY.

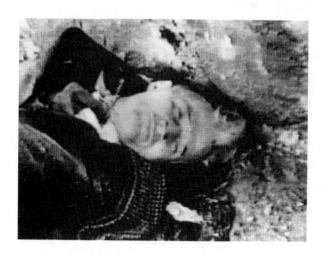

DISSOLVE TO:

TITLE: 1789 *(keyed over)*

Film Clip—*LA MARSEILLAISE*

WORKER: Once, power resided in the person of the king. The people's task was clear. Get rid of the king.

Dialogue from the film:

KING: What is it?

MINISTER: Sire, the Parisians have taken the Bastille.

KING: So, is it a revolt?

MINISTER: No sire, it is revolution.

FREEZE on KING

TITLE: 1989 *(keyed over)*

Film Clip: Riots in Rumania

WORKER: Once power resided in repressive state bureaucracies. The people's task was clear. Smash the state.

Still: Nicolae Ceausescu Lying Dead on the Ground

WORKER: At certain moments in history power is centralized and visible, the sites of repression are clear and identifiable; resistance movements arise out of those relations of subordination and antagonism.

Postmodern Urban Landscapes

WORKER: At other moments the task is less clear. Power is entrenched, but dispersed. Where does power reside? Who are the agents of change?

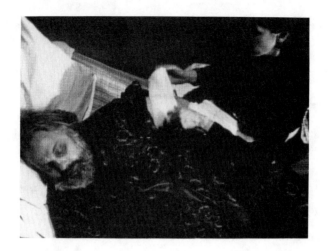

Marx's Bedroom —Night

MARX is in bed. HELENE is slowly unwrapping his bandages. As she does the camera zooms into the carbuncles, which become scenes from riots and revolts throughout the twentieth century—labor riots, race riots, abortion rights and AIDS protests; they appear to emerge out of the carbuncles.

MARX: Dear Frederick: I hope that with this, I will have paid my debt to nature. In my state of ill health, I can do little writing, and then only by fits and starts. At any rate, I hope the bourgeoisie will remember my carbuncles all the rest of their lives.

The RIOTS continue for some time.

FADE TO BLACK

Notes

Foreword

1. Hal Foster, *Recodings* (Port Townsend, Wash.: Bay Press, 1985); Pauline Rosenau, *Post-Modernism and the Social Sciences* (Princeton, N.J.: Princeton University Press, 1991); Meaghan Morris, "The Banality of Cultural Studies," in *Logics of Television,* ed. P. Mellencamp (Bloomington: Indiana University Press, 1990), pp. 14–43; Christopher Norris, *What's Wrong with Postmodernism? Critical Theory and the Ends of Philosophy* (Baltimore, Md.: Johns Hopkins University Press, 1990); and *Universal Abandon? The Politics of Postmodernism,* ed. Andrew Ross (Minneapolis: University of Minnesota Press, 1988).

2. See Perry Anderson, *Considerations on Western Marxism* (London: Verso, 1976).

3. For an account of some of the ways American intellectuals have played out this antagonism at the expense of popular culture, see Andrew Ross, *No Respect: Intellectuals and Popular Culture* (New York: Routledge, 1989).

4. Fredric Jameson, interview by Anders Stephanson, *Flash Art,* no. 131 (December 1986/January 1987), pp. 71–72.

5. Tania Modleski, in *Feminism without Women* (New York: Routledge, 1991), rejects the discourses that have come to constitute "postfeminism" and argues the need for a return to the solidarity amongst women that she says characterized the kind of feminism Kipnis criticizes.

6. Kristeva's position as avant-gardist and vanguardist intellectual was consolidated in autumn 1991 by her becoming the hostess for French television's attempt to revive the tradition of literary "salons."

7. Morris, "Banality of Cultural Studies," p. 25.

8. One place where I have tried to argue this point, rather than just suggest it, is "The Secret Agent of Laclau and Mouffe," in *Community at Loose Ends,* ed. Miami Theory Collective (Minneapolis: University of Minnesota Press, 1991), pp. 99–110.

1. Introduction: Crossing the Theory/Practice Rubicon

1. Mary Douglas, *Purity and Danger: An Analysis of the Concepts of Pollution and Taboo* (London: Routledge, 1966), p. viii.

2. Laura Mulvey, "Visual Pleasure and Narrative Cinema," *Screen* 16, no. 3 (Fall 1975): 6–18.

3. Gaylyn Studlar, "Masochism and the Perverse Pleasures of the Cinema," in *Movies and Methods,* vol. 2, ed. Bill Nichols (Berkeley: University of California Press, 1985), pp. 602–21.

4. Janet Wolff, *Feminine Sentences* (Berkeley: University of California Press, 1990), pp. 121–41.

5. See Wolff, *Feminine Sentences*, p. 128; also Mary Russo, "Female Grotesques: Carnival and Theory," *Center for Twentieth Century Studies Working Papers* (Milwaukee, 1985), no. 1, pp. 1–13.

6. Rebecca Piirto, "Beyond Mind Games," *American Demographics* 13, no. 12 (December 1991): 52. I'm grateful to Rick Maxwell for the reference.

2. Repossessing Popular Culture

1. Andy Grundberg, "As It Must to All, Death Comes to Post-Modernism," *New York Times*, September 16, 1990, p. 47.

2. Walter Benjamin, *Understanding Brecht* (London: New Left Books, 1973), pp. 93–94.

3. Louis Althusser, "Ideology and Ideological State Apparatuses," in *Lenin and Philosophy and Other Essays* (New York: Monthly Review Press, 1971), pp. 127–86.

4. Reported by CBS News from the 1984 Republican convention.

5. Ernesto Laclau, *Politics and Ideology in Marxist Theory* (London: New Left Books, 1977). See also Chantal Mouffe, "Hegemony and Ideology in Gramsci," in her *Gramsci and Marxist Theory* (London: Routledge and Kegan Paul, 1979), pp. 168–204.

6. Raymond Williams, *Keywords* (New York: Oxford University Press, 1976), pp. 158–63.

7. Peter Burger, *Theory of the Avant-Garde* (Minneapolis: University of Minnesota Press, 1984).

8. Michael Taussig, *The Devil and Commodity Fetishism in South America* (Chapel Hill: University of North Carolina Press, 1980).

9. See Ernest Mandel, *Late Capitalism* (London: New Left Books, 1975), p. 191 and passim.

10. Guy Debord, *Society of the Spectacle* (Detroit, Mich.: Black and Red, 1977).

11. Clement Greenberg, "Avant-Garde and Kitsch," in *Art and Culture: Critical Essays* (Boston: Beacon Press, 1964), pp. 3–21; "The Necessity of Formalism," *Lugano Review* (October 1972), pp. 105–6; and "The Recentness of Sculpture," in *American Sculpture of the Sixties* (Los Angeles County Museum of Art, 1967), pp. 24–26.

12. Mary Kelly, "Re-Viewing Modernist Criticism," *Screen* 22, no. 3 (1981): 41–62.

13. Ben Yagoda, "Don't Squeeze the Ionesco," *Village Voice*, December 4, 1978, p. 66.

14. Colin MacCabe, "Coming Down: Elements of an Intellectual Autobiography," in *Tracking the Signifier* (Minneapolis: University of Minnesota Press, 1985), p. 11.

15. Nat Hentoff, "If It's Not a Human Being, What's the Crime?" *Village Voice*, March 6, 1984, p. 6.

16. Laclau, "Toward a Theory of Populism," pp. 143–98.

4. Looks Good on Paper: Marxism and Feminism in a Postmodern World

1. Jane Gallop, *Reading Lacan* (Ithaca, N.Y.: Cornell University Press, 1985).

2. Russell Jacoby, *Dialectic of Defeat: Contours of Western Marxism* (New York: Cambridge University Press, 1981).

3. Ernesto Laclau and Chantal Mouffe, *Hegemony and Socialist Strategy: Toward a Radical Democratic Politics* (London: Verso, 1985), p. 48. Laclau and Mouffe adapt the psychoanalytic theory of suture to theoretical discourse, their discussion of which has influenced my thinking on the relationship between psychoanalysis and aesthetics.

4. Ellen Willis, "Radical Feminism and Feminist Radicalism," in *The 60s without Apology*, ed. Sohnya Sayres et al. (Minneapolis: University of Minnesota Press, 1984), p. 97.

5. The term "cultural feminism" refers to a position within American feminism based on a belief in an immutable male and female sexual essence, or nature, most often held

on Postmodern Culture, ed. Hal Foster (Port Townsend, Wash.: Bay Press, 1983), pp. 57–82; and Huyssen's "Mass Culture as Woman."

20. Quoted in Alice Echols, "The Radical Feminist Movement in the United States, 1967–75" (Ph. D. diss., University of Michigan, 1986), p. 32, revised and published as *Daring to Be Bad: Radical Feminism in America, 1967–1975* (Minneapolis: University of Minnesota Press, 1989).

21. Phyllis Schlafly, *The Power of the Positive Woman* (New York: Jove, 1977).

6. "The Phantom Twitchings of an Amputated Limb"

1. Jacqueline Rose, "Woman as Symptom," in *Sexuality in the Field of Vision* (London: Verso, 1986), p. 220.

2. Judith Mayne, "The Limits of Spectacle," *Wide Angle* 6, no. 3 (1984): 4.

3. Roland Barthes, "Myth Today," in *Mythologies*, trans. Annette Lavers (New York: Hill and Wang, 1976), pp. 115–16.

4. Gayatri Chakravorty Spivak, "Subaltern Studies: Deconstructing Historiography," in *Selected Subaltern Studies*, ed. Ranajit Guha and Gayatri Chakravorty Spivak (New York: Oxford University Press, 1988), pp. 26–31.

5. Neil Hertz's essay "Medusa's Head: Male Hysteria under Political Pressure," *Representations* 4 (Fall 1983): 27–54, should also be cited here. Hertz discusses a number of instances in which what would seem to be political threats are represented as if they were sexual threats—although his examples are primarily drawn from the 1848 revolution in France.

6. Nina Baym, "Melodramas of Beset Manhood," in *The New Feminist Criticism*, ed. Elaine Showalter (New York: Pantheon Books, 1985), pp. 62–80.

7. Salman Rushdie, "Outside the Whale," *American Film*, January-February, 1985, pp. 16–18. I should mention that this essay was written long before Rushdie's run-in with the Ayatollah.

8. David Lean, in Derek Malcolm, "Interview with David Lean," *Guardian*, Jan. 23, 1984; quoted in Rushdie, "Outside the Whale."

9. Geoffrey Nowell-Smith, "Minnelli and Melodrama," *Movies and Methods*, vol. 2, ed. Bill Nichols (Berkeley: University of California Press, 1985), pp. 190–94.

10. Lean, quoted in Rushdie, "Outside the Whale."

11. Barthes, "Myth Today," p. 121.

7. Aesthetics and Foreign Policy

1. See Harry Braverman, *Labor and Monopoly Capital: The Degradation of Work in the Twentieth Century* (New York: Monthly Review Press, 1974).

2. Hugh S. Thomas, Georges A. Fauriol, and Juan Carlos Weiss, eds., *The Cuban Revolution: Twenty-Five Years Later* (Boulder, Colo.: Westview Press, 1984), p. 43.

3. Roberto Fernández Retamar, "Caliban: Notes toward a Discussion of Culture in Our America," *Massachusetts Review* 15, nos. 1 and 2: 7–72.

4. See, for example, Francis Barker, *The Tremulous Private Body: Essays on Subjection* (New York: Methuen, 1984).

5. Arnold Hauser, *The Social History of Art* (New York: Vintage Press, 1957), vols. 2 and 3; and John Berger, *Ways of Seeing* (London: Penguin Books, 1972).

6. Jacques Lacan, *The Four Fundamental Concepts of Psychoanalysis* (New York: Norton, 1981), p. 85.

7. One connection between the two is that both are deeply concerned with the language with which to describe nature. Mary Louise Pratt, "Scratches on the Face of the Country; or, What Mr. Barrow Saw in the Land of the Bushmen," in *"Race," Writing and*

to be biologically determined rather that culturally constructed. It equates w
liberation with the establishment and practice of a female counterculture based
male values" such as reciprocity, intimacy, nurturance, and nonviolence. This te
probably now the dominant one in mainstream feminism, is the backbone of the
antipornography movement, among the leaders of which are some of the leading
ticians of cultural feminism. See Alice Echols, "The New Feminism of Yin anc
in *Powers of Desire: The Politics of Sexuality*, ed. Ann Snitow, Christine Stansell, anc
Thompson (New York: Monthly Review Press, 1983), pp. 439–59.

6. See, for example, Christine Froula, "The Daughter's Seduction: Sexual
and Literary History," *Signs* 11, no. 4 (Summer 1986): 621–44.

7. Edward Said, *Beginnings* (New York: Columbia University Press, 19
169–73.

8. Dominick LaCapra, "History and Psychoanalysis," *Critical Inquiry* 13, no
ter 1987): 245.

9. See Alice Jardine's *Gynesis: Configurations of Woman and Modernity* (Itha
Cornell University Press, 1985), a well-detailed report from the front lines of th
"feminine." Jardine tends to use the term "modernity" rather than "moderni
classes writers as postmodernist that I would see as modernist; I think this is be
doesn't theorize modernism through its antinomy to the popular, and also ass
correlation of poststructuralism and postmodernism.

10. Perry Anderson, *Considerations on Western Marxism* (London: Verso, 1
chap. 3, "Formal Shifts."

11. See Andreas Huyssen, "Mapping the Postmodern," *New German Critiqu*
1984): 5–52.

12. This point is raised by both Tania Modleski, in "The Terror of Pleasure:
temporary Horror Film and Postmodern Theory," and Andreas Huyssen, in "I
ture as Woman: Modernism's Other," both in *Studies in Entertainment: Critical*
to Mass Culture, ed. Modleski (Bloomington: Indiana University Press, 1986)

13. Theodor Adorno, *Aesthetic Theory* (New York: Routledge and Kegan P;
pp. 16–17.

14. See Paul Smith, *Discerning the Subject* (Minneapolis: University of Minne
1988), for a thorough exploration of the term and its deployment. In revising
it occurs to me that the current rubric of "identity" may have somewhat repla
the subject lately.

15. Terry Eagleton, "The End of English," paper delivered at the School
Institute of Chicago, April 1986.

16. See Hélène Cixous, "The Laugh of the Medusa," in *New French Fen*
Elaine Marks and Isabelle de Courtivron (New York: Schocken Books,
245–64; and Luce Irigaray, *Speculum of the Other Woman* and *This Sex Which*
(Ithaca, N.Y.: Cornell University Press, 1985). See Toril Moi's *Sexual/Tex*
(New York: Methuen, 1985) for a comparison of the Anglo-American and G
traditions.

17. Fredric Jameson, *The Prison House of Language* (Princeton, N.J.: Princet
sity Press, 1972), p. 182. Jameson is writing about *Tel Quel* here (including K1
about Derrida, who has invented a new transcendental signified, "namely th
itself."

18. On dependency theory see André Gunder Frank, *Capitalism and Unde*
in Latin America (New York: Monthly Review Press, 1969).

19. Two examples of how this narrative occurs in aesthetic theory are Cra
"The Discourse of Others: Feminists and Postmodernism," in *The Anti-Aes*

Difference, ed. Henry Louis Gates, Jr. (Chicago: University of Chicago Press, 1986), p. 140.

8. Ernst Cassirer, *Philosophy of the Enlightenment* (Boston: Beacon Press, 1951), p. 102.

9. Raymond Williams, *Keywords* (New York: Oxford University Press, 1976), p. 266.

10. Immanuel Kant, *Critique of Judgment*, trans. J. H. Bernard (New York: Haffner Press, 1951). See particularly the sections "Analytic of the Beautiful" and "Dialectic of the Aesthetical Judgment."

11. This point follows Peter Burger's argument in *Theory of the Avant-Garde* that cultural works derive their meaning more ultimately from their institutional relations than from their content. The point about reproduction was suggested to me by James Kavanagh.

12. Susan Sontag, *Against Interpretation* (New York: Dell, 1966), p. 14.

13. Susan Sontag, "Some Thoughts on the Right Way (for Us) to Love the Cuban Revolution," *Ramparts*, April 1969, pp. 6–19.

14. The text of Sontag's address was reprinted in *Nation*, February 20, 1982.

15. Donald Lowe, *The History of Bourgeois Perception* (Chicago: University of Chicago Press, 1982).

16. Lacan, *Four Fundamental Concepts*, pp. 77–81.

8. (Male) Desire, (Female) Disgust: Reading Hustler

1. For an interesting and far more extensive analysis of the politics of *Not a Love Story*, see B. Ruby Rich, "Anti-Porn: Soft Issue, Hard World," in *Films for Women*, ed. Charlotte Brunsdon (London: British Film Institute, 1986), pp. 31–43.

2. Several writers who have visited the *Hustler* offices testify that to their surprise these letters *are* sent by actual readers, and *Hustler* receives well over a thousand letters a month. As to whether this particular letter is genuine in its authorship I have no way of knowing, so I'm simply considering it as part of the overall discourse of *Hustler*.

3. Central anti-antiporn texts are *Pleasure and Danger*, ed. Carole S. Vance (Boston: Routledge and Kegan Paul, 1984); *Caught Looking: Feminism, Pornography and Censorship*, ed. Kate Ellis et al. (Seattle: Real Comet Press, 1988); *Powers of Desire: The Politics of Sexuality*, ed. Ann Snitow, Christine Stansell, and Sharon Thompson (New York: Monthly Review Press), especially section 6 on,"Current Controversies." Also see Linda Williams, *Hard Core: Power, Pleasure and the Frenzy of the Visible* (Berkeley: University of California Press, 1989); and Andrew Ross, " The Popularity of Pornography," in *No Respect: Intellectuals and Popular Culture* (New York: Routledge, 1989), pp. 171–208, for a thorough summation of antipornography arguments.

4. Gayle Rubin, " Thinking Sex: Notes for a Radical Theory of the Politics of Sexuality," in *Pleasure and Danger*, ed. Vance, pp. 267–319.

5. This corresponds to Linda Williams's analysis of pornography as a "machine of the visible" devoted to intensifying the visibility of all aspects of sexuality, but most particularly to conducting detailed investigations of female bodies (Williams, *Hard Core*, pp. 34–57).

6. See Mikhail Bakhtin, *Rabelais and His World* (Bloomington: University of Indiana Press, 1984).

7. *Newsweek*, February 16, 1976, p. 69.

8. Leonore Davidoff, "Class and Gender in Victorian England," *Feminist Studies* 5 (Spring 1979): 97.

9. Peter Stallybrass and Allon White, *The Politics and Poetics of Transgression* (Ithaca, N.Y.: Cornell University Press, 1986).

10. Bakhtin, *Rabelais*, p . 376.

11. Ibid., p. 320. See also Francis Barker, *The Tremulous Private Body* (New York: Methuen, 1984).

12. Norbert Elias, *The History of Manners* (New York: Urizen Books, 1978).

13. Stallybrass and White, *Politics and Poetics of Transgression*, p. 191.

14. Elias, *History of Manners*, p. 120.

15. And there are ongoing attempts to regulate this sort of imagery. In the current NEA controversies, a Republican representative plans to introduce amendments that would prohibit funding of art that depicts aborted fetuses, the *New York Times* reports (October 10, 1990, p. 6). This would seem to be something of a short-sighted strategy, as the aborted fetus has been the favored incendiary image of antiabortion forces, including antiabortion artists. See pp. 27–29.

16. Of course, the counterargument could be made that such a cartoon really indicates the murderous male desire to see a woman mutilated, and that the cartoon thus stands in for the actual male desire to do violence to women. This was the widespread interpretation of the infamous *Hustler* "woman in the meat grinder" cover, about which more later. This sort of interpretation would hinge on essentializing the male imagination and male sexuality as, a priori, violent and murderous, and on a fairly literal view of humor and representation, one that envisions a straight leap from the image to the social practice rather than the series of mediations between the two I'm describing here.

17. Mary Douglas, *Purity and Danger: An Analysis of the Concepts of Pollution and Taboo* (London: Routledge, 1966).

18. Ibid., p. 37.

19. Sigmund Freud, *Jokes and Their Relation to the Unconscious* (New York: Norton, 1963), p. 90. Freud's observations on jokes, particularly on obscene humor, might be extended to the entirety of *Hustler*, as so much of its discourse, even aside from its cartoons and humor, is couched in the joke form.

20. For an interesting deconstruction of the essentialism/antiessentialism debate, see Diana Fuss, *Essentially Speaking: Feminism, Nature and Difference* (New York: Routledge, 1989).

21. By violence here I mean specifically violence to subjectivity—the perception of violation. The vast majority of porn represents sex, not physical violence. The continual conflation of sexual pornography and nonconsensual physical violence is a roadblock to thinking through issues of porn—only abetted by a theorist like Andrea Dworkin, for whom *all* heterosexuality is violence. It's akin to trying to understand popular culture by starting from the premise that all popular culture is violence and ignoring all examples that don't fit the model.

22. Freud, *Jokes*, p. 102.

23. J. Laplanche and J. B. Pontalis, *The Language of Psychoanalysis* (New York: Norton, 1973), pp. 376–78.

24. Andrea Dworkin, *Intercourse* (New York: Macmillan, 1987), p. 138.

25. Douglas, *Purity and Danger*, p. 3.

26. Ibid., p. 3. Compare Douglas's comments on danger beliefs around sexual fluids to this passage by Andrea Dworkin: "[I]n literary pornography, to ejaculate is to *pollute* the woman" (her emphasis). Dworkin goes on to discuss, in a lengthy excursus on semen, the collaboration of women-hating women's magazines, which "sometimes recommend spreading semen on the face to enhance the complexion," and pornography, where ejaculation often occurs on the woman's body or face (see Linda Williams, pp. 93–119, on another reading of the "money shot") to accept semen and eroticize it. Her point seems to

be that men prefer that semen be a violation of the woman by the man, as the only way they can get sexual pleasure is through violation. Thus semen is "driven into [the woman] to dirty her or make her more dirty or make her dirty by him." But at the same time semen has to be eroticized to get the woman to comply in her own violation (Andrea Dworkin, *Intercourse*, p. 187). In any case, that Dworkin sees contact with male "sexual fluids" as harmful to women seems clear, as does the relation of this pollution (Dworkin's word) danger to Douglas's analysis.

27. *Hustler*'s advertising consists almost entirely of ads for sex toys, sex aids, porn movies, and phone sex services, as the automobile makers, liquor companies, and manufacturers of other upscale items that constitute the financial backbone of *Playboy* and *Penthouse* refuse to hawk their wares in the pages of *Hustler*. In order to survive financially, *Hustler* began, among other enterprises, a successful and extensive magazine distribution company that includes among its periodicals the *New York Review of Books*.

28. "Farewell to Reagan: Ronnie's Last Bash," *Hustler*, February 1989, pp. 66–74.

29. The story of the cover was related by Paul Krassner, who worked for *Hustler* in 1978, in "Is This the Real Message of Pornography?" *Harper's*, November 1984, p. 35. Recall also that this cover was instrumental in the founding the following year of Women Against Pornography. The meat-grinder joke seems to encapsulate many of the aforementioned issues of class, humor, vulgarity, and gender.

30. Recently *Hustler*, after yet another legal entanglement, began threatening in its model release form to prosecute anyone who sent in a photo without the model's release. They now demand photocopies of two forms of ID for both age and identity purposes; they also stopped paying the photographer and began paying only the model (currently $250 and the promise of consideration for higher-paying photo spreads).

31. Throughout this essay, my intent has not been to associate a particular class with particular or typical standards of the body, but rather to discuss how *Hustler* opposes hegemonic, historically bourgeois conceptions of the body. Whether the *Hustler* bodily idiom represents a particular class or class fraction is not readily ascertainable without extensive audience studies of the sort difficult to carry out with a privatized form like porn magazines. The demographics that are available aren't current (since the magazine doesn't subsist on advertising, its demographics aren't made public, and *Hustler* is notoriously unwilling to release even circulation figures). The only readership demographics I've been able to find were published in *Mother Jones* magazine in 1976, and were made available to them because publisher Larry Flynt desired, for some reason, to add *Mother Jones* to his distribution roster. Jeffrey Klein writes: "Originally it was thought that *Hustler* appealed to a blue collar audience yet . . . demographics indicate that except for their gender (85 percent male), *Hustler* readers can't be so easily categorized. About 40 percent attended college; 23 percent are professionals; 59 percent have household incomes of $15,000 or more a year [about $29,000 in 1989 dollars], which is above the national mean, given the median reader age of 30." His analysis of these figures is that "probably it's more accurate to say that *Hustler* appeals to what people would like to label a blue-collar urge, an urge most American men seem to share" (Jeffrey Klein, "Born Again Porn," *Mother Jones*, February/March 1978, p. 18).

32. For an analysis of the structuring contradictions in the discourse of Catharine MacKinnon, who, along with Dworkin, is the leading theorist of the antipornography movement, see William Beatty Warner, "Treating Me like an Object: Reading Catharine MacKinnon's Feminism," in *Feminism and Institutions: Dialogues on Feminist Theory*, ed. Linda Kauffman (Cambridge: Basil Blackwell, 1989), pp. 90–125.

33. For a critique of this tendency, see Mike Budd, Robert M. Entman, and Clay Steinman, "The Affirmative Character of U.S. Cultural Studies," *Critical Studies in Mass Communication* 7 (1990): 169–84.

Index

Laura Kipnis is a video artist and theorist whose tapes have been shown widely in the United States and Europe. Her latest tape is *Marx: The Video*. She teaches in the Department of Radio/TV/Film at Northwestern University, and has written extensively on the politics and aesthetics of postmodernism, feminism, and popular culture.

Paul Smith is associate professor of Literary and Cultural Studies at Carnegie Mellon. He is the author of *Pound Revised, Discerning the Subject,* and *Clint Eastwood: A Cultural Production*, and a coeditor, with Alice Jardine, of *Men in Feminism*.

He identifies the stages as Demoralization, Destabilization, Crisis and Normalization.

"Demoralization takes from fifteen to twenty years. This is the minimum number of years required to educate one generation of students in the Marxist-Leninist ideology ... without being challenged, or counter-balanced by the basic values of Americanism (American patriotism).

"Most of the people who graduated in the sixties (drop-outs or half-baked intellectuals) are now occupying positions of power in the government, civil service, business, mass media, and the educational system. You are stuck with them. You cannot get rid of them. They are programmed to think and react to certain stimuli in a certain pattern. You cannot change their minds, even if you expose them to authentic information. Even if you prove that white is white and black is black, you still cannot change the basic perception and the logic of behavior. The process of demoralization is complete and irreversible. To rid society of these people, you need another fifteen to twenty years to educate a new generation of patriotic-minded and common sense people.

"Here [in the USA] you can get popular like Daniel Ellsberg and filthy rich like Jane Fonda for being dissidents, for criticizing your Pentagon. [In the Marxist-Leninist system] nobody is going to pay them for their beautiful, noble ideas of equality.

"The demoralization process in the United States is basically completed already. Actually, it's over-fulfilled because demoralization now reaches areas ... of such a tremendous success. Most of it is done by Americans to Americans, thanks to a lack of moral standards.

"As I mentioned before, exposure to true information does not matter anymore. A person who was demoralized is unable to assess true information. The facts tell nothing to him. That's the tragedy of the situation of demoralization.

"In this psychological warfare, the next stage of the Marxist-Leninist strategy is destabilization. It takes only from two to five years to [subvert] economic, foreign and defense issues. The next stage is crisis.

It may take only up to six weeks to bring a country to the verge of crisis. And, after crisis, with a violent change of power, structure, and economy, you have [the so-called] period of normalization. It may last indefinitely. Normalization is a cynical expression borrowed from Soviet propaganda.

"If this process is not turned around and such an ideology comes about, the promise of goodies and the destabilization of our economy will lead to the elimination of a free market economy and the institution of a Big Brother welfare government in Washington, D.C...."

TOWARD A NEW WORLD ORDER

A new world order will be instituted and controlled by an elitist group for the coming kingdom of the Antichrist. It takes the miracle working power of the Holy Spirit to penetrate the darkness of such deceived and demoralized hearts and minds.

The reality is that we are now in a period of total war between the forces of good and evil; between Satan, who is the god of this world, and the one and only true God, creator of heaven and earth. Soon there will be nowhere to hide, and those who have fallen away from the truth of God's inerrant Word will be like the five foolish virgins described in Matthew chapter 25 who had no oil when the Bridegroom appeared.

The apostle Paul prophesied,

"This know also, that in the last days perilous times shall come, for men shall be lovers of their own selves, covetous, boasters, proud, blasphemers, disobedient to parents, unthankful, unholy, without natural affection, trucebreakers, false accusers, incontinent, fierce, despisers of those that are good, traitors, heady, highminded, lovers of pleasures more than lovers of God; having a form of godliness, but denying the power thereof: from such turn away" (2 Timothy 3:1-5).

In these perilous times, professing Christians will deliberately reject revealed truth concerning the deity of Christ and redemption through His atoning and redeeming sacrifice. The apostle Paul speaks of apostates who deliberately turn away from the truth of God's inerrant Word:

"For the time will come when they will not endure sound doctrine; but after their own lusts shall they heap to themselves teachers, having itching ears; and they shall turn away their ears from the truth, and shall be turned unto fables" (2 Timothy 4:3-4).

Can we learn from history? It really depends upon whose history you choose to believe.

CHAPTER ONE FOOTNOTES

1 Billy Graham, <u>Religious News Service</u> (New York, NY, June 11, 1976).

2 Francis A. Schaeffer, *The God Who Is There* (Downers Grove, IL: Inter Varsity Press,1968).

3 Francis A. Schaeffer, *The Great Evangelical Disaster* (Westchester, IL: Crossway Books, 1984), p. 37.

4 E. Michael and Sharon Rusten, *The One Year Book of Christian History* (Carol Stream, IL: Tyndale House Publishers, Inc., 2003).

5 Ibid.

6 Yuri Bezmenov, Several of his talks are posted on www.youtube.com. Type in search box: "*Bezmenov on Demoralization in America.*"

TWO KINDS OF HISTORY

You ask, "How can there be two kinds of history? Aren't facts unchangeable? Isn't history a study of past factual events?" But man is so influenced by his philosophical view of life that he interprets facts to suit his preconceived view of the universe. There is the humanist view of history, and there is the biblical view of history. The biblical view is accurate and trustworthy so long as we believe that God's Word is inerrant.

WHAT VALUE IS HISTORY?

Automaker Henry Ford was heard to observe that history is bunk! Joseph J. Spengler, an American historian on economic theory, taught that history was superb aimlessness. Historian Mircea Eliade saw history as being cyclical. He believed history continues to repeat itself. This view fits into the Eastern religious idea of reincarnation with a hope that things will become better in our new life, which depends on how we live our present life. Edward Gibbon was primarily known for his book titled, *The History of the Decline and Fall of the Roman Empire*, where he viewed history as a way to interpret the passing of various civilizations. An exception to his view was the rebirth of Israel in 1948, after about 2,000 years of being dispersed throughout the world.

Our entire Western civilization is concerned with history. Unlike other civilizations, ours has always been extremely attentive to its past. Evangelical Christian philosopher, Gordon H. Clark, underscored the scholarly importance of how history is written with integrity.[1] Christianity is a religion of historians. The sacred Bible of the Christian faith is the accurate, historical revelation of God, describing His work in creation and redemption.

After the close of the New Testament era, since most of the early church fathers were educated in the classics, they entered religious service with a classical Greek bias. Once they were introduced to the Jewish origin of their faith found in the Old Testament, they naturally became aware of the deficiencies of the Grecian historical view of man and its origin of the world.

The children of Abraham were the first to recognize a real grandeur in history. They viewed it as a divine epic stretching back before the creation of man. The central figure was the personal infinite Creator God who has spoken to man through the Holy Scriptures and who will ultimately bring the conflict between light and darkness to a cataclysmic and final end. [See the Appendix for an analysis of the conflict between the kingdoms of light and darkness.] So it was not unusual for someone to write a history of the world from a biblical viewpoint, and integrate it with classical Greek and Roman history.

The Bible is historical in a deeper sense. It teaches us that the destiny of mankind is located between the fall of man and the coming judgment. Biblical history tells us that life is a long adventure and every life is an individual pilgrimage. It is in time and history that the great drama of sin and redemption unfolds as the central axis of all biblical thought.

Whenever our exacting Western society, in the continuing crisis of growth, begins to doubt itself, then that society needs to ask itself whether it has done well in trying to learn from the past, and whether it has correctly learned. It was philosopher and poet, George Santayana, who observed that "those who cannot remember the past are condemned to repeat it."[2] Certainly that observation comes to life when we read the historical account of the nation of Israel as recorded in the Old Testament book of Judges. Israel's past revealed that each generation needed to learn to begin with God, the Author of order and design.

God acts in history starting with the supernatural. The secular mind thinks only in terms of the natural, and thus excludes God from the historical process. When the supernatural is omitted, then events like the virgin birth, the substitutionary atonement of Jesus Christ, His bodily resurrection from the dead, and His second coming are discarded as historical non-events or labeled as religious superstition.

The biblical Christian view of history begins with the presupposition that God is sovereign over all history, be it called sacred or secular. In the secular sense, history can be probed and written about. But behind so-called secular history, God is at work and in control of the levers of history.

As the Lord of history, God has His own plan in operation, which is unknown to those who disregard the Bible. Yet God's ultimate purpose is being carried out unchangingly because God is sovereign. The hidden things of God can only be known to man when God chooses to disclose them. Moses recorded it succinctly when he said,

> "The secret things belong unto the Lord our God: but those things which are revealed belong unto us and to our children forever, that we may do all the words of this law" (Deuteronomy 29:29).

So why examine history? Man has an unquenchable and universal fascination with events from the past. A thinking person, eager to penetrate into hidden causes, would want to write with integrity and truthfulness.

The very best any historian can do will fall short of those men who were inspired by God to write the inerrant Word of God under the influence of the Holy Spirit.

> "All Scripture is given by inspiration of God, and is profitable for doctrine, for reproof, for correction, for instruction in righteousness" (2 Timothy 3:16).

The apostle Peter said,

> "So we have the prophetic word made more sure, to which you do well to pay attention as to a lamp shining in a dark place, until the day dawns and the morning star arises in your hearts. But know this first of all, that no prophecy of Scripture is a matter of one's own interpretation, for no prophecy was ever made by an act of human will, but men moved by the Holy Spirit spoke from God" (2 Peter 1:19-21 NASB).

> "That the man of God may be perfect, thoroughly furnished unto all good works" (2 Timothy 3:17).

ROBERT DICK WILSON'S SCHOLARLY TESTIMONY

Princeton Theological Seminary's Professor Dr. Robert Dick Wilson commented on the validity and reliability of the Old Testament manuscripts. Dr. Wilson joined with other scholars to form Westminster Theological Seminary when Princeton departed from believing in the inerrancy of the Bible in 1929. He was fluent in over forty Semitic languages and has been regarded as one of the greatest ancient Middle East language scholars of all times.

Dr. Wilson said:

"For forty-five years continuously … I have devoted myself to the one great study of the Old Testament, in all its languages, in all its archaeology, in all its translations…. The critics of the Bible, who go to it to find fault, claim for themselves all knowledge and all virtue and all love for truth. One of their favorite phrases is, 'All scholars agree.' When a man says that, I wish to know who the scholars are and why they agree. Where do they get their evidence? I defy any man to make an attack upon the Old Testament on the ground of evidence that I cannot investigate.

"After I learned the necessary languages, I set myself about the investigation of every consonant in the Hebrew Old Testament. There are about a million and a-quarter of these, and it took me years to achieve my task. I had to observe the variations of the text in the manuscripts, or in the notes of the Massoretes, or in the various versions, or in the parallel conjectural emendations of critics; and then I had to classify the results, to reduce the Old Testament criticism to an absolute objective science; something which is based on evidence and not on opinion.

"The result of those forty-five years of study which I have given to the text has been this: I can affirm that there is not one page of the Old Testament concerning which we need have any doubt. For example, to illustrate its accuracy: there are twenty-nine kings whose names are mentioned, not only in the Bible but also on monuments of their own time. There are 195 consonants in these twenty-nine proper names. Yet we find that in the documents of the Hebrew Old Testament there are only two or three out of the entire 195 about which there can be any question of there being written in exactly the same way as they were inscribed on their own monuments (which archaeologists have to this date discovered). Some of these go back 4,000 years and are so written that every letter is clear and correct.

"Compare this accuracy with the greatest scholar of his age, the librarian at Alexandria in 200 BC. He compiled a catalogue of the kings of Egypt, thirty-eight in all. Of the entire number, only three or four are recognizable. He also made a list of the kings of Assyria, in only one

31

case can we tell who is meant; and that one is not spelled correctly. Or take Ptolemy, who drew up a register of eighteen kings of Babylon. Not one of them is properly spelled; you could not make them out at all if you did not know from other sources to what he was referring.

"If anyone talks about the Bible, ask them about the kings mentioned in it. There are twenty-nine, all of whom are included in the Bible and on monuments. Every one of these is given in his right name in the Bible, his right country, and placed in correct chronological order. Think what that means!"[3]

CHRISTIAN PHILOSOPHY OF BIBLICAL HISTORY

The biblical text is concerned with the concrete events of history and the activities of the Creator God dealing with mankind. Many view the Bible as just a compilation of moralistic fables and optional good ideas about living. Biblical archaeology has, however, unearthed hard facts of actual historical happenings. Twentieth century Middle East archaeological discoveries have abundantly validated the veracity of biblical texts that nineteenth century skeptics began to question and doubt, and present-day skeptics choose to ignore and dismiss. Secular and religious humanists are biased. Because of their commitment to evolution, they reject the Creator who supernaturally works and communicates in space, time, and history.

We live in a poor, sinful world which stands upon the threshold of God's end-time judgment. Our pride in technological accomplishments will prove fruitless as we ignore the lessons of the past. Hundreds of biblical prophecies have been fulfilled moving the earthly human experience in a linear direction toward a cataclysmic and final climax.

Postmodern humanists have lost sight of the value of knowing history. Yet a future meaningful life would be incomplete without a clear understanding of the recorded events of history. The knowledge of history can direct our actions for today. The debating platform of exchanged existential ideas has replaced the discussion platform of researched historical facts that starts with the Creator personal God—the God who has supernaturally communicated and acted in history. This paradigm shift was done to justify, in advance, humanists' ignorance or simple rejection of historical facts.

When you begin with, "In the beginning God…" (Genesis 1:1), you find God's order and design. His Word has been, and continues to be, the real measure of all true and reliable history.

HUMANISTIC PHILOSOPHY OF HISTORY

Humanism produces men who are convinced that they know what's best for all mankind. This blindness comes from humanism's limited view which tries to explain the miracle of life and the universe apart from God and His inerrant revelation. The humanistic view of life motivates men who think they are the rightful rulers over the common people. They promote themselves as the knowledgeable elite—with all the right answers for a new world order necessary for the survival of humanity.

From the end of the nineteenth century into the twentieth century, society was mesmerized by advancements in the physical and social sciences. With the dawn of this modern era, men educated in these sciences were expected to discover and implement solutions to all of life's problems. Humanists announced that the world is now modern.

Today the intellectual humanist community has issued a new announcement. Modern is out; it is over. Postmodern now describes the current reality and paradigm. New ways of thinking and doing things are now required.

Many believed it was possible to establish a science of human evolution that would develop into a pan-scientific ideal. They were willing to abandon, as outside of true science, a great many human realities which appeared to them to be outside human comprehension.

They proposed that certain religious beliefs were construed as upper story matters and beyond our five human senses to understand. They construed the lower story of reality to be where space, time, and history exist; we know it solely through our five human senses. Therefore, they view Jesus Christ's virgin birth, miracles, resurrection from the dead, and second coming as only matters of upper story, unverifiable beliefs. In their paradigm these major events surrounding Jesus Christ are not historical and verifiable truths in their construed lower story of space, time, and history. Therefore, they require people to take an existential leap of faith into the unverifiable and unknowable second story. This view in both the modern and postmodern paradigms really represents a troubling sameness. Christians accept as fact that God revealed His truths and promises in space, time, and history.

The real failure of the physical and social sciences to yield a successful paradigm for solving life's problems has exhausted many intellectuals. They've collapsed into a heap of hopelessness, doubt, and cynicism. To now trust and believe in the reliable truth of God's inerrant Word would do harm to their intellectual pride and jeopardize their profession. So they continue the charade, like the emperor with no clothes!

RELIABLE REVELATION FROM THE CREATOR IS INDISPENSABLE

Regardless of where the physical and social sciences take us, we can't ignore where we've been. That's what history is all about. Apart from God's revelation, history is like a boat tossed on the overwhelming sea of facts without a rudder. The humanists are at a terrible disadvantage when they reject absolutes that come from the God of the Bible. As they reject truth, they play the "fool who says in his heart, 'There is no God'" (Psalm 14:1). Their methodology for historical inquiry is crippled by their unwillingness and inability, apart from

God's special grace, to view reality from the Creator's perspective. The Creator has authenticated Himself in His own supernatural revelatory self-disclosure to His creatures: mankind. The Holy Scriptures are the deposit of that special revelation.

The historic Christian faith starts with the one and only true God who has always been in existence. He is personal. God communicated with our first parents, Adam and Eve, in an understandable language; and continues to communicate with all mankind through His inerrant Word as revealed by the Holy Spirit. God's Word has always been reliable, trustworthy, and sufficient; simply because God has always been reliable, trustworthy, and sufficient.

The Holy Spirit supernaturally used the temperament and personalities of the human authors to write the Word of God. His message of salvation, through grace alone, has been communicated across language barriers. Jesus Christ commissioned His followers to make disciples of all nations, baptizing them in the triune name of the Father, and of the Son, and of the Holy Spirit:

> "… teaching them to observe all things whatsoever I have commanded you: and, lo, I am with you always, even unto the end of the world" (Matthew 28:19-20).

Thankfully when Jesus uttered these words 2,000 years ago, He followed up over the following sixty-plus years providing the reliable, trustworthy, sufficient, and error-free written Word. This New Testament we can read and study. Our generation needs to rediscover and embrace these twin sufficiencies: First, God's inerrant Word; and second, the power and ministry of the Holy Spirit to open our understanding of His Holy Word, the Old and New Testaments.

This is why we confront those who are dumbing down our children with modern reading techniques that avoid the use of words and a vocabulary through which truth can be communicated. Many Christian universities and seminaries have lost their way. Their once sound biblical worldview has been eroded by accommodation to the spirit of this age. The lights have gone off at the guard posts and the remaining watchmen on the wall are being ignored as men fail to see the detrimental effects of humanism, the new evangelicalism, and the denial of biblical inerrancy.

Before we examine some key historical figures surrounding three theological seminary case studies that clearly illustrate the twentieth century battle for the Bible, I will address the central issue: Did God communicate error in His written Word, the Bible?

Was the communication from the Creator God of the Bible reliable or unreliable? Does the Bible teach inerrancy?

CHAPTER TWO FOOTNOTES

1 Gordon H. Clark, *Historiography: Secular and Religious* (Nutley, NJ: The Craig Press, 1971).

2 George Santayana, *The Life of Reason*, Volume 1, 1905. http://www.quotationspage.com/quotes/George_Santayana.

3 Robert D. Wilson, *Bible League Quarterly*, (1955), pp. 39-48.

DOES THE BIBLE TEACH INERRANCY?

Some have suggested the battle for the Bible was the wrong war. The church must avoid any cleavage in the ranks of American evangelicals when our forces must be united against liberalism, humanism, and Marxism. However, I believe that objective authority demands an infallible Scripture. Most sane men believe there is a difference between right and wrong, between the noble and the base, between justice and tyranny.

We are driven to the conclusion that there must be such a thing as accountability before the moral order underlying the created universe. But apart from divine revelation, we can never attain certainty as to the meaning and purpose of our existence. The Bible presents itself as that kind of "Thus saith the Lord" revelation. Listen to the distinction the Bible makes:

> "When you received the word of God which you heard from us, you did not receive it as the word of men, but as it is in truth, the word of God" (1 Thessalonians 2:13).

The Holy Spirit played an indispensable role in divine communication.

> "For prophecy came not in old time by the will of man; but holy men of God spoke as they were moved by the Holy Spirit" (2 Peter 1:21).

The apostle Paul states in language that is totally unambiguous that this communication is error free when he says,

> "All Scripture is given by inspiration of God, and is profitable for doctrine, for reproof, for correction, for instruction in righteousness; that the man of God may be perfect, thoroughly furnished unto all good works" (2 Timothy 3:16-17).

In this passage, the word "inspiration" is translated from the Greek word *theopneustos*, which is a compound word literally meaning "God-breathed." This specific word, given to Paul by the Holy Spirit, begs the monumental question: Does God breathe error? Does God communicate error? There is only one correct answer. No. God does not breathe nor communicate error! This text is, of course, referring to the entire Old Testament canon.

The entire Bible commences with the words, "In the beginning God created the heaven and the earth" (Genesis 1:1). Consider this: If God is capable enough to supernaturally create everything, is He not also capable to supernaturally communicate? And do so without error? Yes, He is so infinitely capable, and did so without error. A god who breathes error is not worthy of our respect and worship. A god who communicates error must be crafty, deceptive, and untrustworthy. A god who breathes and communicates error has been created in our own sinful and finite image.

Now in the face of overwhelming manuscript evidence, are we to conclude that the Old Testament is without error, but not the New Testament? This would amount to an incredulous indictment against God's capability and sovereignty. The presuppositional starting point is with the one and only true God who can both supernaturally create and communicate. The Old and New Testaments in the autographs, as originally given in Hebrew, Aramaic, and Greek are without error.

The Holy Spirit gave us the Bible through human instrumentality, which exhibits personal human writing styles. Yet it presents us with a message that purports to be the very word of God. It is a message incapable of human invention; moreover, it is altogether repugnant to the wisdom of fallen man apart from the special enablement of the Holy Spirit.

If there were so much as a single mistake in Scripture, it would inevitably follow that the Bible is capable of mistakes. Then it would require infallible human verification to certify it as valid. But humans are not infallible. We would be left at the mercy of man's mere opinion or conjecture, resulting in no genuine certainty as to the great issues of life and death. Only an infallible Bible can truly accomplish any redemptive purpose as the reliable Word of God to man.

There are two major views of the Bible popular in evangelical circles. The first view claims that the Bible is infallible, meaning it does not deceive. It means the Bible will never deceive us in matters of faith. In spiritual matters it is trustworthy. It has absolute authority and will never lead us astray.

The word "infallible" is an excellent word to describe the Bible, and we ought to continue to use it. However, we should always remember that the word "infallible," as currently used, neglects to tell us something about the Bible. Is the Bible historically accurate? Did the events of the Bible really happen? Just the word "infallible" leaves us with a broad range of choices here.

The second view of the Bible states that the Bible is inerrant. This word means that the Bible does not make a statement contrary to fact, not only in matters of faith, but also in all other matters. Some of these matters under attack are the historical and scientific accuracy of the Bible. Every part of Holy Scripture is true, not just those parts which speak about matters of faith. Therefore, the term "plenary inspiration" (from the Latin *plenus*, meaning "full") is utilized. Not just some parts of Scripture are inspired by God and completely true, but all parts are fully true.

The clear statements of the Bible teach inerrancy. The inerrant character of God revealed in Scripture makes inerrant divine communication necessary. The phenomena of the supposed errors reflect more on our finite limitations rather than cause us to abandon our confidence in inerrancy. Making a distinction between faith issues and historical facts is a false presupposition imposed on the Bible. It can only lead to more serious problems.

The apostle Paul assumed the historical factualness of the exodus when he wrote:

> "Now all these things happened unto them as examples: and they are written for our admonition, upon whom the ends of the world have come" (1 Corinthians 10:11).

Paul says that they both happened and were written down for our admonition. The Bible teaches us that historical facts and matters of faith are inseparably linked together.

In 1 Corinthians 10:1-10, we see facts enumerated: the cloud, the crossing of the Red Sea, the manna from heaven, the water from the rock, the plague at Shittim, the serpents, the sitting down to eat and drink, and the rising up to dance. These events historically happened. Paul considers the Old Testament inerrant.

Similarly in Romans, Paul justifies the use of Old Testament quotations that pertain to Christ by claiming: "For whatsoever things were written before were written for our learning" (Romans 15:4). The fact that Paul is referring to the Old Testament is clear because in verse 4 he specifically names "the Scriptures" in the same context. Orthodox Jewish scholars contemporary to Paul accepted a complete and finalized canon of Holy Scriptures which we know as the Old Testament. Paul refers to these same Scriptures as "whatsoever things were written before."

This inclusion does not presumptively exclude historical facts while only embracing matters that pertain to moral lessons about faith. It was all written for our instruction. This is the doctrine of plenary inspiration (the full inspiration of Scripture). To Paul, a concept like "non-revelational" Scripture would have been absurd. And Paul was not alone in this view.

Responding to the Devil, Jesus answered and said,

> "It is written, 'Man shall not live by bread alone, but by every word that proceeds out of the mouth of God'" (Matthew 4:4).

Jesus quoted Deuteronomy 8:3. Does Jesus Christ, the God-man in the flesh, want us to assume there are errors in those words that were written, having proceeded from the very mouth of God? Did Jesus believe or assume that God breathed error?

No. Jesus said, "Till heaven and earth pass, one jot or one tittle shall in no way pass from the law, till all be fulfilled" (Matthew 5:18). The law, as used here, refers at least to the Pentateuch and the Prophets because of Jesus' inclusion of prophetic Scripture in the phrase, "till all be fulfilled." But it also refers to the whole Old Testament, because in John 10:34 ("Jesus answered them, Is it not written in your law, I said, You are gods?"), Jesus uses the word "law" to refer to this quote in Psalm 82:6. So, in Matthew 5:18, Jesus says that *all* the Scripture is firmly fixed and will not change.

Jesus was brought up on what the Jews referred to as the Hebrew acronym, The *Tanakh*, equivalent to our Old Testament consisting of the Masoretic Text's three traditional subdivisions: The Law (Teaching), The Prophets, and The Writings. The *Tanakh* teaches, "Forever, O Lord, Your Word is settled in heaven" (Psalm 119:89).

"Every word of God is pure" (Proverbs 30:5).

"Thy Word is true from the beginning: and every one of Thy righteous judgments endures forever" (Psalm 119:160).

Here are a few examples of how Jesus used the historical facts of the Old Testament:

- The Queen of Sheba came to hear Solomon (Matthew 12:42 and 1 Kings 10:2).

- God made man (Matthew 19:4 and Genesis 1:27).

- Elijah visited the widow, and no rain fell for three-and-a-half years (Luke 4:25-26 and 1 Kings 17).

- Noah entered the ark, and the flood waters destroyed all humankind except those in the ark (Luke 17:27 and Genesis 7:23).

- Fire and brimstone rained on Sodom (Luke 17:29 and Genesis 19:24).

Clearly Jesus believed in an inerrant *Tanakh* or Old Testament.

The real point is whether we are going to adopt the view of Christ and His apostles concerning the inerrant trustworthiness of the Holy Scriptures, or we are going to settle for some lower estimate of the reliability of the Bible. The difficulties of understanding certain Scripture passages are diminishing in the face of the mounting archaeological evidence that supports biblical historical facts.

No major doctrine of the Christian faith rests solely upon a questionable difficult text in the Bible. Sincere inquiries into understanding seemingly perplexing texts can be amply assisted by such academic work as the *Encyclopedia of Bible Difficulties* by Gleason L. Archer Jr. (1916-2004) who earned a Harvard PhD degree and was a highly respected scholarly advocate of biblical inerrancy.[1]

The advantages of settling the issue for infallibility only—without inerrancy—suffers from three serious difficulties. First, the Bible does not appear to be aware of any such distinction between theological and non-theological truth. The second difficulty proceeds from the first. The New Testament affirms that Jesus Christ is God in human flesh, the second Person of the Trinity. If Jesus was mistaken about the historicity of Adam and Eve, or if He believed incorrectly that Jonah was swallowed and preserved in the stomach of a great fish, or the flood destroyed the entire human race except the eight passengers on the ark, then it follows that God was mistaken.

What is at stake is God's integrity. The third difficulty of subscribing to infallibility without inerrancy is that it assumes a logical impossibility. It presumes that even though the Bible may err in factual matters of history and science; nevertheless, it is to be believed as a whole with respect to its so-called moral and theological lessons. And that somehow these lessons are without error. Such a contradiction lacks power to maintain itself with credibility.

The doctrine of the objective authority of the Holy Scriptures is the most crucial issue we have to face in our lifetime. To deny the inerrancy of God's Word produces evil consequences down the road. The church is in the midst of its greatest confusion, which will result in the loss of missionary outreach. The missionary passion to see individuals become born again will be quenched. An accommodating and diminishing view of the Bible inevitably produces church growth strategies that are in the flesh and not in the Spirit.

Departure from inerrancy also lulls congregations to sleep and undermines their belief in the complete truth of God's Word. It produces spiritual deadness and decay. It will finally lead to apostasy.

Next let's examine the battle between modernism and fundamentalism.

CHAPTER THREE FOOTNOTE

1 Gleason L. Archer Jr., *Encyclopedia of Biblical Difficulties* (Grand Rapids, MI: Zondervan, 1982).

THE BATTLE BETWEEN MODERNISM AND FUNDAMENTALISM

The beginnings of theological modernism, also called "liberalism," had its roots in Europe. Germany was the birthplace of higher criticism, which was nineteenth-century skeptical humanistic thinking applied to the Bible. With the dawn of the scientific era, many thought we were on the verge of discovering the secrets of the universe and unlocking the ability to understand and solve every problem of mankind.

Anti-Christian thinkers such as Darwin, Hegel, Marx, and Lenin began leading movements to dethrone God and replace Him with scientific humanism.

Christian biblical fundamentalism responded to this liberalism, and by the 1920s found itself under full-scale attack. Liberalism was spreading through many of America's historic seminaries, mainline church denominations, and into our pulpits. In 1924, H.L. Mencken remarked, "Christendom may be defined briefly as that part of the world in which, if any man stands up in public and solemnly swears that he is a Christian, all his auditors will laugh."[1]

Walter Lippmann, who helped organize the anti-Christian Intercollegiate Socialist Society in 1905, became the Society's president of the Harvard chapter and later wrote weekly articles for *Time Magazine*. He was also director of the Council on Foreign Relations. [For more details on this Council see chapter 11.]

In his book, *Preface to Morals*, he wrote, "… irreligion of the modern world is radical to the degree for which there is, I think, no counterpart."[2] Joseph Krutch, in referring to the death of religion, said, "Both our practical morality and our emotional lives are adjusted to a world that no longer exists."[3]

PRINCETON SEMINARY'S SOLID BEGINNING

At Princeton Theological Seminary in 1857, Charles Hodge observed:

> "Some interpreters suggested that 'inspiration' applied to the thoughts of sacred writers, but not to their exact words. The purpose of inspiration was to communicate a 'record of truth.' For such a 'record of truth,' the accuracy of a statement and an 'infallible correctness of the report were essential.' This could not be assured if the selection of words were left to humans, whose memories were faulty. It was necessary for the Holy Spirit to guarantee the accuracy of the reports by inspiring the authors to select correct words."[4]

The apostle Paul confirmed this in 2 Timothy 3:16, "All scripture is given by inspiration of God, and is profitable for doctrine, for reproof, for correction, for instruction in righteousness."

This high view of Scripture had been taught by Archibald Alexander since Princeton's inception in 1812. It received its classic expression in 1881 when A.A. Hodge and B.B. Warfield wrote their famous article, "Inspiration," which set forth and defended the inerrancy of Holy Scripture. They reminded us that this cardinal doctrine was built upon the great theological contributions of men like Luther, Calvin, Knox, Wesley, Whitefield, and Chalmers. That article pointed to "a supernatural origin for the Scriptures; of genuineness and authenticity for its books; and of absolute freedom from error of its statements."[5]

This was the universal doctrine of biblical inspiration—that the Scriptures not only contain, but they are the very Word of God. Hence, in all elements and affirmations, the original Hebrew, Aramaic, and Greek manuscripts of the Holy Scriptures are absolutely errorless; therefore requiring the faith and obedience of men. Following the elder Hodge, they insisted that inspiration must extend to the words. Infallible thought must be definite thought, and definite thought implies words.[6]

Prior to the 1920s, Princeton Seminary continued to hold the firm position that Scripture be accepted without error, including its historical details. They held that the objective statements of inspired Scripture were without error. The essence of theological modernism was an assault on the infallible authority of the Bible. These old-school Presbyterians had preserved a distinctive view of truth. They held the view that truth in its purest form is precisely stated in biblical propositions and in the promises of God.

Truth was a stable entity best expressed in written language that conveyed one message relevant for all time and in every place. At Princeton, as well as in many nineteenth-century Protestant American churches, the idea was held that persons of simple common sense could rightly understand Scripture. They also held the view that a genuine religious experience grew out of right ideas, and right ideas could only be expressed in written words.

At Princeton it was an article of faith that God would provide nothing less than wholly accurate facts, whether large or small. Common sense assured that throughout the ages people could discover the same truths in the unchanging storehouse of the Holy Scriptures.

This view that the past could be known directly through reliable testimony meant that the Bible was not regarded as presenting points of view of its authors regarding the past, but it was an infallible representation of that past itself.

Back then the demand at Princeton was that the Bible be accepted without error in all its historical details. There was no confusion caused by humanistic postmodern deconstructionism. They believed, as the Bible taught, that the gospel would spread worldwide—that people of every language group would accept the fact of their sinfulness resulting in a need to personally repent and receive forgiveness through the atoning death of Christ alone.

During the 1890s, there was a growing Presbyterian battle over the inerrancy of Scripture, especially when moderate liberals attempted to revise the Confession of Faith. That attempt was defeated in 1893. Between 1900 and 1920 a truce prevailed. The defenders of the Bible continued to strengthen their position. It was this defense preparation that had a positive effect upon the growing fundamentalist movement.[7]

In 1910 the Presbyterian General Assembly, the highest court of appeal, adopted a five-point declaration of essential doctrines in response to some questions raised about the orthodoxy of some of the Union Theological Seminary graduates. These declarations included:

1. The inerrancy of Scripture.

2. The virgin birth of Christ.

3. Christ's substitutionary atonement.

4. Christ's bodily resurrection.

5. The authenticity of the miracles.[8]

In the 1920s these became the famous five points that were the academically tested rallying position of the conservative party before a modern liberal program took over the seminaries. As the division broadened, many Presbyterians were willing to cooperate with others who had a strict view of Scripture and stood fast against any compromise of the essential supernatural elements in the Christian faith.

This opened the door for the Keswick teachers, who were dispensationalists, to appear more attractive to the theologically reformminded Presbyterians who were anti-modernist. The conservative Presbyterians already included some prominent leaders with a more evangelical-oriented ministry. These Presbyterians were attracted to a closer relationship with the Bible-centered interdenominational teachers' movement. A broad alliance was forged of pastors and leaders who had a core commitment to the non-negotiable fundamental truths of the Bible.

THE RISE OF FUNDAMENTALISM

The first laymen reaction to unbelieving modernism came from the founders of the Union Oil Company of California. The founders were two brothers, Lyman and Milton Stewart. Between 1910 and 1915 they compiled and published twelve paperback volumes consisting of ninety articles, sermons, and testimonials covering a wide range of subjects on Bible doctrines, apologetics, cult groups, and more. Lyman Stewart described the authors as the best and most loyal Bible teachers in the world.

A.C. Dixon was hired as the first editor. Dixon was a well-known evangelist, author, and pastor of Moody Memorial Church in Chicago. Dixon was followed by Reuben A. Torrey, and they gathered articles from conservative Christian authors in America and Great Britain.

Titled *The Fundamentals*, they were distributed freely to Christian workers in the United States and twenty-one foreign countries. They were available to every pastor, missionary, theological professor, seminary student, YMCA and YWCA secretary, college professor, Sunday school superintendent, and religious publication editor in the English-speaking world. This amounted to some three million copies. Later, R.A. Torrey edited the papers into a four-volume hard cover set, and another 300,000 copies were distributed; and in 1998, Baker Books reprinted them.

The articles defended the infallible inspiration of the Bible, justification by faith, the new birth, the deity of Jesus Christ, His virgin birth, miracles, and resurrection. Not only did *The Fundamentals* address the heresy of modernism, but also of Mormonism, Romanism, Socialism, and other cult groups. Some of the contributors included: W.B. Riley, James Grey, G. Campbell Morgan, H.C.G. Moule, James Orr, A.T. Pierson, Thomas Spurgeon, J.C. Ryle, Philip Mauro, W.H. Griffith Thomas, B.B. Warfield, R.A. Torrey, and others.

At the turn of the twentieth century, numerous groups holding firm to biblical fundamentals organized. Some had separated from the modernist movement holding fast to biblical inerrancy.

Many others continued to enjoy the gifts of the Holy Spirit and were launching revivals in the United States, Wales, and soon, around the world. The movement included Pentecostals, Holiness groups, independent fundamentalists, and many of the Black churches. The Assemblies of God began revivals in Topeka, Kansas and were rapidly growing throughout the U.S. and Canada. The Church of the Nazarene encouraged unity among the Holiness groups and a number of independent Holiness churches merged into a single fellowship in Chicago. The Nazarenes and Wesleyan Methodists drew together many of the Holiness Movement's independent churches.

By 1908, there were newly established fundamentalist groups in Canada, India, Cape Verde, and Japan; soon followed by works in Africa, Mexico, and China. By 1915, mergers added congregations in the British Isles, Cuba, Central and South America. There were also congregations in Syria and Palestine by 1922. In the 1920s, the International Church of the Foursquare Gospel became established in Los Angeles, about the time of the Azusa Street outpouring of the Holy Spirit.[9]

The World Conference on Christian Fundamentals, a gathering of over 6,000 attendees in Philadelphia in 1919, further advanced the cause of fundamentalism. Forty-two of the forty-eight states were represented, including the six Canadian provinces. Speakers included Lewis Sperry Chafer, R.A. Torrey, Paul Rader, C.I. Scofield, W.H. Griffith Thomas, and James Grey, resulting in a published book titled, *God Hath Spoken.*

The preface states,

> "We believe in the Scriptures of the Old and New Testaments as verbally inspired of God, and inerrant in the original writings, and that they are of supreme and final authority in faith and life."[10]

PRINCETON SEMINARY GOES MODERN

Westminster Theological Seminary documented the theological shift to modernism that occurred at Princeton in the 1920s. Westminster's catalogue states,

> "When formal theological seminaries were organized, one of the first was the Theological Seminary of the Presbyterian Church at Princeton, New Jersey, where instruction began in 1812. Founded by the General Assembly of the Presbyterian Church of the United States of America, the seminary held to the Westminster Confession of Faith and Catechism as its doctrinal standards.

> "Princeton excelled under the leadership of distinguished teachers who devoted themselves vigorously and effectively to the development,

propagation, and maintenance of the Reformed faith. Princeton was of immense symbolic significance in the fundamentalist community. When all the other northern educational institutions had turned away from evangelicalism, Princeton Seminary was left as the last bastion of orthodoxy with any prestige. Among those best known as teachers of the great scriptural system of theology set forth by Princeton's first professor, Archibald Alexander, were Charles Hodge; J.A. Alexander; B.B. Warfield; Robert Dick Wilson; and J. Gresham Machen. But eventually a movement surfaced to end Princeton's adherence to scriptural theology, and in 1929 Princeton Theological Seminary was reorganized under modernist influences."[11]

Seriously objecting to Princeton's modern reorganization, Wilson, Machen, Oswald T. Allis and Cornelius Van Til founded Westminster Theological Seminary in Philadelphia.

George Marsden gave this background information in his book, *Fundamentalism and American Culture*:

"Fundamentalism, while fading from the reputed centers of American life since 1925, was in fact taking solid hold in other less conspicuous areas. The movement had entered into a distinct new phase. The effort to purge the leading denominations having failed, the leadership now re-emphasized working through local congregations and independent agencies, such as Bible schools and mission organizations.

"Local pastors, often independent from major denominations, either formally or simply in practice, built fundamentalist empires, both large and small. Bible schools flourished, with twenty-six new schools founded during the depression years of the 1930s. Other important new institutions of learning, such as Dallas Theological Seminary and Bob Jones University, became significant centers for branches of the movement. Wheaton College was for several years during the 1930s the fastest growing liberal arts college in the nation. Fundamentalist publications increased in circulation; summer Bible conferences and other youth movements attracted the young; mission agencies continued to grow.

"The movement took three principal forms. The fundamentalist within major denominations had now abandoned all hope of excluding the modernist advances within their churches. Second, strong fundamentalist influences outside of the traditional denominational structures of American culture, but within denominations, were not purely fundamental. Finally, some of the most extreme fundamentalists separated into their own denominations or into independent churches."[12]

In the first half of the twentieth century, the term "evangelical" in the U.S. was nearly synonymous with "fundamentalism" and the words were often interchangeable. The eroding morality of the roaring twenties and growing restlessness among the youth had produced concern within the Christian community. A growing number of interchurch groups joined together to reach out to the youth more effectively. In a spirit of cooperation they were motivated to evangelize the lost with the good news, the evangel, about a new life in Jesus Christ.

When the National Association of Evangelicals (NAE) was formed in 1942, some strong fundamentalist leaders, such as Bob Jones Sr., John R. Rice, Harry Ironside, and David Otis Fuller (unrelated to Charles and Daniel Fuller) became part of the movement. It was during and after the World War II period that the NAE grew rapidly as a variety of church groups worked together.

Some of these groups included Youth for Christ, InterVarsity Christian Fellowship, Young Life Campaign, Campus Crusade for Christ, Fellowship of Christian Athletes, World Vision, Christian Service Brigade, Pioneer Girls, Christian Camping, Word of Life, Youth with a Mission, and Missionary Assist. Church historian Garth M. Rosell documents well this mid-twentieth century period in his book titled, *The Surprising Work of God*.[13]

WESTMINSTER SEMINARY HOLDS FAST TO INERRANCY IN 2008

A historical pattern begins to appear as Christian men, churches, denominations, educational institutions and movements start to drift away from a commitment to believing in the inerrancy of the Bible. This pattern needs to be firmly grasped and understood. Note well that Westminster Seminary had to terminate Professor Peter Enns in 2008, after fourteen years, for drifting away from the reliability of God's inerrant Word.

The historical pattern is clearly described by Carl R. Trueman, the seminary's vice president for Academic Affairs and professor of Church History and Historical Theology.

"As a historian, the one thing I always try to avoid is making definitive statements about recent events: while eyewitness and participant accounts of historical happenings can make very exciting reading, they often lack the more dispassionate perspective which time and emotional distance bring in their wake. Thus, they are frequently less satisfying as historical interpretations than they are what English schoolboys of yesteryear might have called 'ripping yarns.' Nevertheless, it seems apposite at this point, even as an eyewitness and participant in recent events at Westminster, to offer a few simple thoughts for the lay observer on the historical context and significance of our struggles.

"It has become something of a proverb in evangelical circles that most conservative or confessional theological institutions have about seventy-five years of life in them before they evidence significant changes in theological direction. One might add to that another oft-repeated observation that such a change does not occur slowly by a kind of gradual evolution, rather such change tends to take place almost overnight. A third comment, perhaps just as frequently heard in such circles, is that theological institutions always become broader theologically, and the clock can never be turned back in a more orthodox direction.

"Where do these ideas originate? And why is it that they do not seem to many, at least at the level of a gut reaction, to be true? Well, the answer, of course, is that there is plenty of historical evidence to suggest that they do in fact reflect reality, even if the generalized time-line is somewhat negotiable. Think of Princeton Theology Seminary. It was founded in 1812, enjoyed a heyday of orthodoxy, and then in 1929 was reorganized and the old theology of the Westminster Standards vanished from its lecture theatres almost overnight.

"Think of Fuller Seminary, founded after World War II to spearhead the development of an evangelical scholarship which was both ortho-dox and academically rigorous. It boasted a stellar evangelical faculty; yet its commitment to inerrancy vanished within two generations. In both cases, the change happened swiftly and, up until this point anyway, there appears to have been no significant return within these institutions to anything resembling the older theological paths.

"There are good reasons why these kinds of things can happen. Don Carson, author of the book, *Becoming Conversant with the Emerging Church* (2005), once commented that the first generation fights for orthodoxy, the second generation assumes orthodoxy, and the third generation abandons orthodoxy. That, of course, gives you roughly seventy-five years before problems start to become evident.

"We might flesh that out a little. In the case of institutions founded out of times of crisis, members of the first generation were often bound together by common struggles, perhaps within a denomina-tion or within a specific institution. Thus, they knew who they were and what they believed; they had made a clear stand on points of prin-ciple, and some had even made huge personal sacrifices to so do. The second generation lived in the intellectual and cultural space carved out for them by the first generation but lacked the controversial con-text which bound their fathers together. The third generation has little or no contact with the struggles of the first and, in almost Freudian fashion, can actually find the behavior of their institutional founding fathers to be somewhat embarrassing."[14]

I believe these insights by Carl Trueman are helpful in under-standing the amazing growth and miraculous work of God in the Calvary Chapel Movement. Calvary Chapel can be best under-stood as a marvelous work of God. Its success can only be grasped through acknowledging the sufficiency of God's Word and the sufficiency of the Holy Spirit to apply God's Word through men who believe in the inerrancy of God's Word. These pastors simply teach the whole counsel of God verse by verse, simply, from Genesis to Revelation. The best training for effective pastors appears to come from schools of ministry planted on the campus of a local church and Bible colleges that hold fast to the inerrant Word of God. By God's grace, Pastor Chuck Smith has modeled it at Calvary Chapel, Costa Mesa, California.

THE BEGINNING OF THE NATIONAL ASSOCIATION OF EVANGELICALS

While associations of evangelicals had organized in New England as early as 1889, for our focus, we'll note the movement that was afoot in the 1940s. Evangelicals banded together for strength, fellowship, and as much of a united witness as could be mustered. Harold Ockenga and Carl McIntire, friends and classmates from Westminster Seminary days, were among sixteen leaders who were tasked with exploring ways to expand the influence of the evangelical New England Fellowship (NEF).

Weeks earlier, McIntire and other colleagues met in New York City and founded the American Council of Christian Churches (ACCC). The Council's purpose was to promote and defend biblical orthodoxy in contrast to the liberally infected Federal Council of Churches (FCC), which was the precursor to the current, extremely liberal National Council of Churches (NCC), the American arm of the highly ecumenical and liberal World Council of Churches (WCC). Sadly, the ACCC and the NEF were unable to unite forces over three issues.

The first issue related to membership. The ACCC and McIntire wanted a limited membership open only to denominational entities. The NEF wanted the membership to be open to all denominations, missionary organizations, associations, congregations, and individuals who shared a common mission and were able to sign a common statement of faith.

The second issue related to opening the door to the rapidly growing Pentecostal groups. McIntire's group was wary of Pentecostalism, considering it obnoxious and likely to develop into a hybrid fundamentalist movement. They were not alone, for as recently as 1928, the World Christian Fundamentals Association (WCFA) had gone on record as unreservedly opposed to modern Pentecostalism, including speaking in unknown tongues, divine healing, and miracles.

The third issue was the McIntire faction's insistence on the biblical principle of separation. Only those denominations willing to renounce modernism, as a denomination, and separate themselves from the Federal Council of Churches were welcome to join the ACCC. Separation had a problematic dimension for a number of fundamentalists who were accused of emphasizing too strongly the big five sins of smoking, dancing, drinking, card playing, and attending movies to the exclusion of the fruit of the Spirit.

This attitude would soon cast the term "fundamentalism" into a negative image that conjured up notions of behavior rather than its original principles of truth to embrace. For many, the term "fundamentalism" was beginning to morph into a label to be avoided. Well-meaning and earnest Bible-believing men were bogged down in differences. Liberals delighted in using the term as a pejorative that dismissed all fundamentalists as naïve, puritanical, and anti-intellectual.

Another attempt to structurally associate together was launched in April 1942 in St. Louis, Missouri. At a national conference for United Action Among Evangelicals, Harold Ockenga electrified the delegates with a keynote appeal. He began,

"Gentlemen, we are gathered here today to consider momentous questions and perhaps to even arrive at decisions [that] affect the whole future course of evangelical Christianity in America.

"Evangelical Christianity has suffered nothing but a series of defeats for decades. In virtually every arena of culture, evangelical Christianity has been placed on the defensive. The terrible octopus of liberalism, which spreads itself throughout our Protestant Church, has dominated innumerable organizations, pulpits, and publications, as well as seminaries and other schools."[15]

This was the birth of the National Association of Evangelicals (NAE).

Historian George M. Marsden writes,

"The emergence of the 'new fundamentalism,' as distinct from fundamentalism, was a gradual process. In retrospect, we can see it clearly taking shape between 1942, when the (NAE) was founded, and 1957, when the break between Billy Graham and his former separatist fundamentalist mentors was complete, and 'neo-evangelicalism' became a current term."[16]

Marsden connects the dots. In 1942, the NAE attempted to consolidate fundamentalists who were now calling themselves evangelicals. Bible-believing pastors and teachers joined to declare their faith in God's inerrant Word. It was believed that if God could supernaturally create, then surely God could supernaturally communicate His Word without error.

In California, prominent American radio evangelist, Dr. Charles Fuller, envisioned a new theological seminary. His heart for the gospel of Jesus Christ and personal commitment to the inerrancy of the Bible was a promising foundation for his pastoral training school. Fuller Seminary quickly attracted professors, money, and endorsements. There was a strong beginning.

But by about 1957, something quite different began to emerge. Appearing on the scene was something neo or new; it would ultimately become known as new evangelicalism. The process appeared gradual but was deceptively fast, as the definitional content of the word "evangelicalism" would drastically change. The battle continued as the borders expanded. The term "fundamentalism," with its original doctrinal meaning, was already disappearing into the shadows.

Let's examine how the story unfolds.

CHAPTER FOUR FOOTNOTES

1 George M. Marsden, *Fundamentalism and American Culture* (New York, NY: Oxford, 2006), p. 3.

2 Ibid. p.3.

3 Ibid. p.3.

4 Ibid. pp. 112-113.

5 "Inspiration," *The Presbyterian Review 6*, April 1881, pp. 225-260. www.bible-researcher.com/warfield4.html.

6, Ernest Sandeen, *The Roots of Fundamentalism: British and American Millenarianism, 1800-1930* (Chicago, IL: University of Chicago Press, 1970), pp. 103-131.

7 George M. Marsden, *Fundamentalism and American Culture* (New York, NY: Oxford, 2006), p. 177.

8 Ibid. p. 117.

9 Stanley Frodsham, *With Signs Following. The Story of the Pentecostal Revival in the Twentieth Century* (Springfield, MO: Gospel House, 1941).

10 *God Hath Spoken: Twenty-five addresses delivered at the World Conference of Christian Fundamentals* (Philadelphia, 1919), pp. 7-9.

11 The Westminster Seminary Catalogue 2009, Philadelphia.

12 George M. Marsden, *Fundamentalism and American Culture* (New York, NY: Oxford, 2006), pp. 193-195.

13 Garth M. Rosell, *The Surprising Work of God* (Grand Rapids, MI: Baker Academic, 2008).

14 Westminster Theological Seminary, "A Message From the President," "Knowing the Times: Recent Controversies in Context," www.wts.edu.

15 Garth M. Rosell, *The Surprising Work of God* (Grand Rapids, MI: Baker Academic, 2008), p. 97.

16 George M. Marsden, *Reforming Fundamentalism: Fuller Seminary and the New Evangelicalism* (Grand Rapids, MI: Eerdmans, 1987), pp. 165-171.

BEGINNINGS AT FULLER SEMINARY

CHARLES FULLER—THE FUNDAMENTALIST PREACHER

Dr. Charles Edward Fuller was born in Los Angeles, California. After graduating from Pomona College in 1910, he worked in the citrus packing business in Southern California until 1918. He then studied at the Bible Institute of Los Angeles (BIOLA).

Two controversial episodes in Charles Fuller's early career in the 1920s illustrate the dynamics of fundamentalism that centered on two unresolved issues. The first was the inerrancy of God's Word and the second was independence from denominationalism. These two issues permanently marked Charles Fuller's independent reputation among loyal denominationalists. When Charles Fuller became a member of the board at BIOLA, he believed that alleged apostasy needed to be purged from the school. His activity closely paralleled the doctrinal campaign of J. Gresham Machen in Princeton at about the same time period, although with a different result.

In the 1920s, Charles Fuller was as original a fundamentalist as any could be found. His views of Christianity had been shaped by his studies at BIOLA, especially from the Bible classes taught by the famed dispensationalist teacher and BIOLA president, Reuben A. Torrey. Torrey was a New Englander, Yale graduate, and a scholarly fundamentalist with links to Congregationalism.

Fresh from his BIOLA studies, Charles Fuller started an adult Sunday school class at the Presbyterian Church located in Placentia, California. By 1925, the class had grown so large as it focused on fundamentalism that it caused a serious rift with the pastor of the church. Fuller led his class out of the Presbyterian Church and reorganized it as the Calvary Church of Placentia.

Divisions were becoming increasingly frequent among the dispensationalists/fundamentalists and the modernists/humanists. Prior to the 1920s, fundamentalists had usually taken for granted their traditional denominational affiliations. But they began breaking off into independent congregations, which often named themselves Calvary churches. Many Bible-believing pastors and laymen were convinced that their local congregation must separate from an organizational relationship with apostate congregations and denominations.

A vigorous branch of evangelicals was forming outside the major mainline denominations. Charles Fuller did not seem to care much about denominationalism. Having separated from the Presbyterians, he secured his ordination through the Baptist Bible Union, an organization with strict dispensational/fundamentalist views and separatist tendencies.

In 1927, young Fuller was elected to the BIOLA board of trustees. This position placed him in the middle of a classic intra-fundamentalist struggle. It revealed the tensions within the movement that he would have to contend with in his latter, more moderate years.

Charles Fuller saw the vast possibilities in the growing invention called radio broadcasting. As a visionary he could see spreading the gospel of the saving grace of Jesus Christ via this new medium. He founded and became the radio preacher of "The Old-Fashioned Revival Hour," which aired from 1937 to 1968. ABC Radio Network carried his voice on more than 650 stations. When he and his popular musicians traveled throughout North America holding citywide rallies, they were often broadcast live.

THE OPENING OF FULLER THEOLOGICAL SEMINARY

Evangelist Fuller wanted to do far more than preach weekly on the radio. Compelled by a sense of urgency, he wanted to train young men to go forth with the gospel. He envisioned a seminary that would be a scholarly theological Caltech in the evangelical world. He believed this new seminary could become the dominant source of twentieth-century fundamentalism with a healthy dose of nineteenth-century holiness tradition, which emphasized a personal walk with God and the leading of the Holy Spirit.

In their daily walk with the Lord, such fundamentalists might look for verses of Scripture that were given to them by the Holy Spirit, or verses that would suddenly illuminate an issue. In the early days at Fuller Seminary, it was a common practice to put out a fleece to find the will of God and discern God's opening and closing of doors. It was the difference between being God-led or man-led.

By June of 1947, a group of fundamentalist scholars gathered in support of Dr. Fuller's vision and plan to establish an evangelical seminary of outstanding academic excellence. Harold J. Ockenga, Everett F. Harrison, Harold Lindsell, Wilbur M. Smith, and Carl F.H. Henry comprised the founding faculty in establishing Fuller Theological Seminary in Pasadena, California in the expanding and budding culture of the Western United States.

Fuller Seminary's first president, Harold Ockenga, gave a convocation address on October 1, 1947 titled, "The Challenge of the Christian Culture of the West." He asked,

> "Why should the West forever look to the East for its preachers? Why should it be, as it has been in part at least, a theological vacuum? Why has it not to date entered its maturity of Christian leadership so that it will in turn send forth those who may blaze the trail of theological, ecclesiastical, and religious thinking in our own day? The hour for the West to enter its maturity theologically is come."[1]

It was the dawn of a new age when 2,500 people crowded the Pasadena Civic Auditorium. World War II had raised serious questions about whether Western civilization could survive. The destructive power of the atomic bomb and the sudden appearance of a massive Russian-Marxist empire presented a bleak future for Christianity turned modern. The ideas of freedom and democracy had been grounded in Christianity, but humanistic pragmatism allowed little or no room for absolutes.

Both Harold Ockenga and Francis A. Schaeffer were students of Dr. J. Gresham Machen at Westminster Seminary, right after Princeton adopted a modernist program in 1929. Westminster Seminary had been in the middle of the whole fundamentalist-modernist battle over the place of the inerrant Bible in contemporary life.

Dr. Ockenga believed the task of meeting the challenge of the age was not going to be accomplished by ordinary Christians. It would be done by those who could redefine Christian thinking and evangelical theology as the only adequate theology and hope remaining for Western culture. American conservative evangelicals were the heirs of Reformation culture, which was the key to the amazing rise of power in the West. A greater danger was to return to heathenism, rationalism, and the authority of the human mind above all else. This had already happened in Germany, which had crumbled into moral relativism and humanism.

Dr. Fuller stated,

> "I keep asking myself what is the greatest need and how best to meet that need. And the answer came back, the greatest need is to send out Holy Spirit-empowered men, men in whom the Word of God dwells richly."[2]

The radio preacher preferred to stay in the background at the seminary. But when he spoke in chapel for the first time, his message rang with the fundamentalist tones of his thirty-two years experience in the ministry,

> "We are no doubt in the closing hours of the church age. The greatest need of the hour is to send out trained men, but not those with just head knowledge … the key is to be sanctified, consecrated, and cleansed; to be a Spirit-filled, controlled, empowered true witness for Christ."[3]

An all-important theme in the holiness tradition that had contributed much to fundamentalism was spiritual cleansing. Dr. Fuller devoted the bulk of his address to an exposition of Leviticus 14, which describes Old Testament regulations for cleansing infectious diseases.

HAROLD LINDSELL—A FAITHFUL ADVOCATE FOR INERRANCY

Harold Lindsell (1913-1998) played a key role in founding Fuller Seminary, advocating for the doctrine of inerrancy and carefully documenting the subsequent controversy. His doctorate was in history from the University of New York. He later departed from Fuller Seminary over the issue of inerrancy. Lindsell went on to write books, become editor of *Christianity Today* magazine, serve on the faculty of Wheaton College, and help establish Trinity Law School in Anaheim, California.

With the opening of Fuller Seminary, Lindsell began teaching a course on missions. During his first year at Fuller, he wrote a book titled, *A Christian Philosophy of Missions*.[4] He taught that without

Jesus Christ, every person will suffer eternal punishment in hell. This doctrine made missions the supreme effort of compassion. This consuming vision of the urgency to reach the lost uniquely shaped American evangelicalism and its doctrine of the church. He believed the function of the church was to evangelize the world, and it was to be completed before the return of the Lord. The secondary task of the church was for its members to build each other up in the faith. Many churches that supported the early Fuller Seminary fed on this message.

Lindsell's call for the consecration of a life to missions was much like that repeatedly heard at young people meetings, summer camps, and missionary rallies. It was first a call to a victorious life and yield-edness to God. All Christians were called to this higher order and walk with the Lord. Those who were distracted by the flesh, Lindsell taught, were carnal Christians still living in the flesh. This was essen-tially standard 1930s Keswick holiness teaching. It was a central theme in the fundamentalist tradition of holy living and evangeli-cal service. It could be found in places like Moody Bible Institute, Wheaton College, Columbia Bible College, and Dallas Theological Seminary, all of which were sources for Fuller Seminary's original faculty.

FULLER SEMINARY BEGINS TO ERODE ON INERRANCY

The seminary began on a solid footing with the faculty and adminis-tration committed, in a written Statement of Faith, to biblical iner-rancy. However, in a few short years there was a sad retreat from that position. The controversy grew and impacted the greater evangeli-cal community. This prompted Fuller professor and vice president, Harold Lindsell, to write a letter to Harold Ockenga on Christmas day, 1962.

"Dear Harold:

This is a tragic day. Instead of joy and peace there are fightings with-out and fears within. The very Spirit of God seems to have departed

66

from our midst. In place of prayer and the infilling of the Holy Spirit, there is bickering, deception, and antagonism. I ask myself the questions: Where did we go wrong? What did we fail to do? What did we do that we shouldn't have done? We need divine help for deliverance, yet my very tongue cleaves to my mouth and the words do not form. God have mercy on us ... even yet.

"The problem of David Hubbard [candidate for president of the seminary] is ancillary. The larger problem takes precedence. Were he to come, he would be indebted to those who no longer entertain the view of inerrancy as we have long understood it. His hands would be tied from the start, whatever his own views might be. He would come with a divided board and a divided faculty. He would come having already compromised himself in the Laurin affair. He would come in the backwash of what seems to be some complicated backstage jockeying. I think he would be insane to come, in the first place; and unable to stabilize and save the situation, in the second place.

"If the report I heard is true that Mr. Weyerhaeuser [board member] has written to Ed Johnson [board member] and stated that he has never signed our Statement of Faith without mental reservation, then the situation is grim indeed. We should forget Hubbard or anyone else until this problem is clarified. Moreover, we should await the results of the Hutchinson survey before taking any steps of any kind. To solidify a situation before the survey is completed and the reports circulated is unsound procedure. I do not wish to be quoted in my remarks, but here they are for what they are worth to you. Maybe the only solution is for you to come out yourself and under a board of different composition than we now have it. But I fear that Dr. Fuller has been alienated from you on top of all this.

"God help you and the others when you meet soon and make what will be historic decisions that will determine the future of this institution to which we have given the best years of our lives.

Faithfully yours, Harold Lindsell"[5]

Dr. Lindsell wrote a book titled, *The Battle for the Bible*, published in 1976.[6] The book includes a chapter titled, "The Strange Case of

Fuller Theological Seminary." Lindsell also wrote a sequel to the *Battle* book titled, *The Bible in the Balance*, published in 1979.[7] This second book answers questions created by Lindsell's position concerning the inerrancy of Scriptures, after he published his *Battle for the Bible* book. The *Balance* book gives extended insight into Fuller Seminary.

By 1979, during David Hubbard's tenure as president of Fuller Seminary, he told his board that the history of the seminary should "make a contribution to the larger evangelical history with which the seminary was 'so interwoven'."[8]

Dr. Hubbard wanted to commission a scholar, who had no previous connections with the seminary, to write a favorable history of that institution. George M. Marsden was selected to research and write the book which in 1987 he titled, *Reforming Fundamentalism: Fuller Seminary and the New Evangelicalism*.[9] The book was carefully researched and documented. A later paperback edition was published in 1995, which included a nine-page preface titled, "The Contested History of Fuller Seminary." The seminary had unhappily contested the critical findings of Marsden.

The happenings at Fuller in the more recent past, and how they repeated the errors that led Princeton Seminary to forsake its biblical roots in 1929, offer serious lessons we must study. This distressing process occurred over a period of approximately forty-eight years at Princeton and approximately thirty-one years at Fuller.

In addition to the published research on Fuller Seminary by Marsden and Lindsell, there are over forty boxes of files and records collected by Lindsell that are archived at the Billy Graham Center in Wheaton, Illinois. This research data covers Lindsell's days as professor and vice president at Fuller Seminary, and his becoming associate editor and then editor of *Christianity Today* magazine. Most of the material concerns the issues surrounding the inerrancy of the Holy Scriptures which came about in the 1960s and 70s at Fuller Seminary.

Fifty of these folders were *restricted* from research until January 15, 2008. Six additional folders are presently *restricted* from research until after the death of Dr. Billy Graham; another three folders are *restricted* from research until January 15, 2019. I have only scanned six folders of the former fifty restricted folders. Those six folders include correspondence between Dr. Lindsell and Dr. Charles Fuller, and many other related documents. The six folders contain about 700 documents.

Lindsell's doctoral training in history prepared him for his pursuit of facts and truth. Some of the documents I have read include the changing of Fuller Seminary's Statement of Faith, letters that indicate choices Dr. Fuller was encouraged to make before his death, and many papers and letters of important note that changed the course and focus of the seminary. Both the original and the revised Statement of Faith were required to be signed each semester by faculty members and members of the seminary's board of directors.

I believe it is important for more scholars to research the Lindsell files in order for us to fully understand what is at stake in the battle for the Bible. A high price has been paid because Christian seminaries and professing Christians have departed from believing in the inerrancy of God's Holy Word. It is not a surprising consequence that the term "evangelical" has become meaningless in its usage today. The term has been totally discredited, as far as truly and accurately describing Christianity.

This will be more clearly understood as we examine how historical drift happens.

CHAPTER FIVE FOOTNOTES

1 George M. Marsden, *Reforming Fundamentalism : Fuller Seminary and the New Evangelicalism* (Grand Rapids, MI: Eerdmans, 1987), p. 53.

2 Ibid. p. 83.

3 Ibid. p. 83.

4 Harold Lindsell, *A Christian Philosophy of Missions* (Wheaton, IL: Van Kampen Press, 1949).

5 Billy Graham Center Archives, Wheaton, IL. Harold Lindsell Collection 192, Folder 7-27A, Item 5.

6 Harold Lindsell, *The Battle for the Bible* (Grand Rapids, MI: Zondervan, 1976).

7 Harold Lindsell, *The Bible in the Balance* (Grand Rapids, MI: Zondervan, 1979).

8 George M. Marsden, *Reforming Fundamentalism : Fuller Seminary and the New Evangelicalism* (Grand Rapids, MI: Eerdmans, 1987).

9 Ibid.

HOW HISTORICAL DRIFT HAPPENS

In this chapter I discuss modern secular humanism. Then I want to examine some men very closely associated with Fuller Seminary. These men had to depart from Fuller because they believed the seminary had tragically lost its moorings. I pray that as you review this historical drift you will be encouraged to hold fast to your belief that the Word of God is inerrant.

NO ABSOLUTES IN MODERN SECULAR HUMANISM—POSTMODERNISM

For modern secular humanists, truth is relative. There are no absolutes. Man is the center of all things and the measure of all things. However, the average person does not realize that this conclusion is based on the philosophical proposition that there is no personal infinite God and man can determine truth within himself.

This is the 2000-year-old Alexandrian Greek philosophical view that gradually brought about the infusion of secular humanism into every fabric of our society over the last eight centuries.

Secular humanism is the offspring of pagan Greek Platonism and Gnosticism that views man's mind as the center of reality rather than God. The problem is that the Gnostics and humanists cannot know what reality or truth is, because man has no means of determining truth. Only God knows what the truth is:

"Sanctify them by Your truth: Your word is truth" (John 17:17).

I've limited the scope of this current topic to new evangelicalism. Therefore, I'm not developing the problematic contributions of ancient humanistic philosophy. Certainly much from the ancients until now could be historically examined.

The Christian view of reality is that God created man in His image with five senses that perceive the real world as it truly is because God does not deceive.

"God is not a man, that He should lie; neither the son of man, that He should repent: or has He said, and shall He not do it? Or has He spoken, and shall He not make it good?" (Numbers 23:19; see also 1 Samuel 15:29; Titus 1:2; Hebrews 6:18).

The humanist is left with no way to know what his five senses tell him about the reality of the world he inhabits. He cannot explain love, beauty, music, or attach any meaning to life's experiences. Man is only a biological machine. This is what leads to the despair of humanism and all its derivatives: hedonism, drugs, and suicide.

The Christian needs to understand the humanistic worldview by which Satan deceives the world and how it differs from God's view.

"And you has He made alive, who were dead in trespasses and sins; wherein in time past you walked according to the course of this world, according to the prince of the power of the air, the spirit that now works in the children of disobedience: among whom also we had our conversation in times past in the lusts of our flesh, fulfilling the desires of the flesh and of the mind; and were by nature the children of wrath, even as others" (Ephesians 2:1-3).

Satan knows that to bring about his plan for the world, he must capture man's mind by influencing what man believes to be true. The Bible teaches that what we think determines what we are. "As a man thinks in his heart, so he is" (Proverbs 23:7). How we look at life determines how we live our life. People's views about truth also determines how they interpret the Bible. Social scientists think that if you can control a person's concept of truth, then you can control that person.

Jesus made one of the most radical and divisive statements in history when He said, "I am the way, the truth and the life: no man comes to the Father, but by Me" (John 14:6). Ever since He uttered those words they have been challenged. Pilate asked Jesus a very postmodern question when he asked, "What is truth?" The Gnostics came along in the second and third centuries, as the precursors of the New Age movement, and questioned the existence of absolute truth. They turned truth into a secret, mystical concept.

Today postmodernists dismiss the idea of absolute truth; epistemology, the study of knowledge, is still a hot button issue. Why do some postmodernists stand in the pulpits of Christian churches as ministers of our Lord Jesus Christ? They are pretenders with invisible garments; they are as naked as the proverbial emperor!

GOD REVEALED HIMSELF IN PROPOSITIONAL TRUTH

Truth is timeless; it never changes! (Psalm 119:43, 89; John 14:6). "Your word is true from the beginning: and every one of Your righteous judgments endures forever" (Psalm 119:160). Francis Schaeffer emphasized that biblical truth is stated in propositional form; in words that can be understood by all mankind. The basic problem with philosophy, sociology, and anthropology in academia is that it begins with man; and man has no inherent capacity to discern truth because he is in a spiritually fallen state.

The apostle Paul underscored this when he said,

> "But the natural man receives not the things of the Spirit of God: for they are foolishness unto him: neither can he know them, because they are spiritually discerned" (1 Corinthians 2:14).

God and His Word, in essence or essential nature, is truth (Deuteronomy 32:4; Psalms 5:5; 33:4; 105:5; 119:151, 160; John 1:17; 14:6; 16:13). Many Christians consider all truth as God's truth, yet they will look to other sources beyond the Bible. However, the only reliable source of truth is God's inerrant Word, the Bible (Psalm 18:30; John 8:31-32; 2 Timothy 3:16-17). All other sources are fallible and cannot be used as the measure for truth.

Apart from God's revealed Word, we cannot be sure about other sources. Man has no inherent capacity to know what is absolute and what is not. The sovereign Creator God alone knows what is absolute truth. He is its source. God is incomprehensible and limitless. Yet according to His gracious good pleasure, He has supernaturally communicated in His Holy Word, the Bible, that which He wants man to comprehend (Deuteronomy 32:4; Daniel 10:21; Hebrews 1:1-2). Hence, the only way mankind can know the truth is to read or hear God's Word with the accompanying work and ministry of the Holy Spirit of truth (John 16:13; 1 Corinthians 2:13).

The Triune God created man in His image as a dependent, moral, reasoning entity and holds him accountable (Genesis 1:27-30; 2:17; 3:16-19; Luke 16:23; Hebrews 9:27-28). In every generation, each person must decide what to believe, either God's Word (John 3:33) or Satan's lies (John 8:44).

MEN WHO HELD FAST TO BIBLICAL INERRANCY

This section contains statements from men who had close connections with Fuller Seminary and the reasons they could no longer support the direction the school had taken. These men believed it was important to hold fast to the authority and the inerrancy of God's Word. Their statements should encourage all of us to hold fast to a high view of God's revelation to man. When Fuller Seminary changed its Statement of Faith, it headed down the slippery slope that spawned new evangelicalism, humanistic church growth programs, and practices that have caused churches to neglect the work of the Holy Spirit as revealer of God's truth.

Harold Lindsell had this to say about what happens when inerrancy is abandoned:

> "It is my opinion that once that step is taken, it is next to impossible to stop the process of theological deterioration. I have said that it is a theological watershed just as the Continental Divide is the watershed for the United States and Canada. The water that flows on one side of the divide ends up in the Atlantic Ocean. The water that flows on the other side of the divide ends up in the Pacific Ocean. But once the water starts down one side or the other, it continues until it reaches its oceanic destination."[1]

Errancy and inerrancy of Scripture constitute two mutually exclusive principles. A choice once made will determine where one ends up. Schaeffer said it so well,

> "The generation of those who first give up biblical inerrancy may have a warm evangelical background and real personal relationship with Jesus Christ so that they can live theologically on the basis of their limited-inerrancy viewpoint. But what happens when the next generation tries to build on that foundation? I am saying that whether it takes five or fifty years, any denomination or parachurch group that forsakes inerrancy will end up shipwrecked. It is impossible to prevent the surrender of other important doctrinal teachings of the Word of God when inerrancy is gone."[2]

Schaeffer further underscored the point by saying, "Holding to a strong view of the Scripture or not holding to it is the watershed of the evangelical world."[3]

Wayne Grudem was a student at Fuller, and on March 25, 1971, he made a one-minute speech before the seminary faculty and trustees. He said,

"While I was still an undergraduate at Harvard, I had heard warnings that Fuller Seminary was seriously compromising the truth of God's Word. Even though these warnings came from such respected sources as Francis Schaeffer, John Montgomery, and *Christianity Today*, I didn't believe them. Now I do.

"Not one of my courses here has strengthened my confidence in the Bible. Even more distressing is an intellectual narrow-mindedness: I have not had one professor who teaches biblical inerrancy as a possible option. Students that I talk to are completely unacquainted with the great defenses of inerrancy made recently by men like E.J. Young, Ned Stonehouse, and Cornelius Van Til.

"I am concerned for Fuller Seminary, but I don't have any proposed solutions. The cards are all stacked in the direction of further concessions and compromise. Faculty members seem to think they are holding the only possible solution; those who thought otherwise have left the school. But as for myself, I want a seminary to make me a minister of God's Word, not its critic. I have no choice but to leave."[4]

Earlier that year in the school's paper, *The Opinion*, student Grudem wrote an article titled, "God Loves You and Has a Plan for Your Theological Education." He began with this question:

"I want to ask a very simple question: Is the Bible really the basis for everything we study at Fuller Seminary? Let me explain what I mean. I don't want to say that every class period should be a topical Bible study. But I would like a biblical approach to each course. It seems to me that the fundamental question underlying a course should be, 'What does the Bible say about this subject?' Only after that question has been answered can we ask, 'What have various men said about this subject?' I have been disappointed to find that this is not the approach at Fuller.

"Look, for instance, at the first three courses for Juniors. In prolegomena, the basic question should have been, 'What does the Bible say about theology?' We could have discovered what biblical guidelines there are for how we do our theology and why we do theology. After that, we could have read various theologians and evaluated them according to a biblical standard. From this statement, Hermeneutics was much the same: we were restricted to the opinions of men. The basic question in this course was, 'What do smart men (neo-orthodox), Adler (Jewish) and Dr. Daniel Fuller (whose position was to read it like any other book) say about how to interpret the Bible?' Although we dealt with God's Word on other questions, we never used it to answer the most important question, 'What does the Bible say about how to interpret the Bible?'

"Evangelism was more biblically-oriented, but it still suffered from imbalance. The question, 'What does the Bible say about evangelism?' was certainly asked, but in our readings and discussions it was always far subordinate to the question, 'What seems to be working in churches today?' The second is a vital question, but the first question must have the priority.

"Have we forgotten that God has established the basis for theological education? 'All scripture is inspired by God and profitable for teaching, for reproof, for correction, and for training in righteousness, in order that (*hina*) the man of God may be exactly fitted to do his job (*artis*), completely furnished (*ekesertismenos*) for every good work' (2 Timothy 3:16-17). Give me less of men's opinions and more of God's Word."[5]

Wayne A. Grudem transferred to Westminster Seminary and earned a Master of Divinity degree, and then earned a PhD from Cambridge University, England. Today he is a prominent author and research professor of Theology and Biblical Studies at Phoenix Seminary, Arizona. He is a dedicated inerrancy scholar and member of the Evangelical Theological Society.

Edward L. Johnson resigned from the Fuller board after the seminary changed its Statement of Faith concerning inerrancy. Responding to

Professor William Sanford LaSor's article in the student publication, *Theology News and Notes*, dated December 29, 1976, Mr. Johnson wrote,

> "In an effort to correct your understanding as to why I resigned as a trustee of Fuller Seminary, you should know that my concern was totally related to the desire on the part of others to change the original Statement of Faith. Being a trustee is a sacred position of dealing with something not my own. I felt in this role I shared in the responsibility of directing the policy of the Seminary for the benefit of others. This included a fiduciary responsibility different from something of my own....

> "Another view which I also recognized in this fiduciary capacity was the responsibility to the founders, to the donors, to the alumni, to the parents of the seminarians, to the students, to the employees, and to the faculty. I view the tendency for so many seminaries to deteriorate from their initial high standards, and I sought to be alert to any sign that would suggest a variation from the original position at Fuller. When the question of changing the Statement of Faith appeared, I asked the simple question, 'Why was it necessary?' I never received an answer acceptable to me.

> "I believed then and believe now that the Seminary could have continued and prospered with the original Statement of Faith and took the position that this was one of my obligations to maintain that standard which had been acceptable initially in the creation of the school with the full knowledge of all the faculty ... The issue really was not to be contrary to change, but to suggest that the change should be made by individuals who were displeased with the original concept, especially a subject as important as believing in an inerrant Scripture ... I used the term 'benchmark' to warn of the dangers in tampering with the 'starting point.' Actually, I had a strong conviction that if the Statement of Faith was tampered with, it would cause a lack of confidence which apparently is the case today, as evidenced in articles such as yours..."[6]

Dr. Harold Ockenga, Fuller's founding president and later founding president of Gordon-Conwell Theological Seminary in South Hamilton, Massachusetts, wrote the foreword in Harold Lindsell's book, *The Battle for the Bible*. Ockenga said,

> "There is a pressing need for Dr. Lindsell's book in the growing evangelical branch of Protestantism. If evangelicalism bids to take over the historic mainline leadership of nineteenth-century Protestantism, as Dr. Martin Marty suggests, this question of biblical inerrancy must be settled. It is time for an evangelical historian to set forth the problem … Dr. Lindsell has done the church, and especially the evangelical cause, a great service in writing this book."[7]

Dr. John F. Walvoord, president of Dallas Theological Seminary, made the following statement about Lindsell's book:

> "I think this will be one of the most strategic books to be published by evangelicals for some time to come. It is a mine of information on the whole battle between fundamentalists and liberals with which our current generation of evangelicals are only partially aware."[8]

As stated earlier, Billy Graham endorsed the book saying,

> "*The Battle for the Bible* is one of the most important and controversial books of our generation. The battle over the veracity of God's Word has been in progress since the garden of Eden. It is still raging and Dr. Lindsell expertly diagnoses the battle in our generation."[9]

So this historical drift from inerrancy, as corrupt seed, was sown into the soil of evangelicalism. New evangelicalism sprouted. Sadly, Fuller Seminary models this drift process. We will continue to examine the liberalization process in this case history.

CHAPTER SIX FOOTNOTES

1 Harold Lindsell, *The Battle for the Bible* (Grand Rapids, MI: Zondervan, 1976), p. 142.

2 Ibid. pp. 142-143.

3 Ibid. See front inside jacket cover. Also see Harold Lindsell, *The Bible in the Balance* (Grand Rapids, MI: Zondervan, 1979), pp. 46 and 356.

4 Billy Graham Center Archives, Wheaton, IL. Harold Lindsell Collection 192, Folder 6-20FF, Item 3.

5 Ibid. Folder 6-20FF, Item 5.

6 Ibid. Folder 1-12J, Item 9. (Letter dated Dec. 29, 1976).

7 Harold Lindsell, *The Battle for the Bible*, Foreword.

8 Ibid. Front inside jacket cover.

9 Billy Graham, Religious News Service (New York, NY: June 11, 1976).

LIBERALIZING FULLER SEMINARY

In order to clearly see the image of new evangelicalism on the fabric of Christianity, we will examine many threads. These threads represent numerous persons, events, and dates. The threads have been sown into this fabric at different times. In this whole discussion we will unavoidably do some jumping around in time; so that as the threads are better understood there will be greater visual clarity as we view the fabric. Let's examine the threads.

DANIEL FULLER STUDIES UNDER KARL BARTH

Daniel P. Fuller, the only child of Charles and Grace Fuller, emerged as a major player in the liberalizing shift at his father's seminary. At age nineteen, he graduated from the University of California, Berkeley. Following a Bachelor of Divinity degree from his father's seminary, he earned two doctorate degrees: one from Northern Baptist Seminary and the other from the University of Basel, Switzerland. The latter contributed a major influence upon him under the neo-orthodox teaching of Basel's celebrated Professor Karl Barth. Along the way he studied at Princeton Theological Seminary and briefly served on Dr. Harold Ockenga's pastoral staff at Boston's Park Street Church. Daniel Fuller's tenure at Fuller Seminary was from 1953 to 1993, where he retired as professor of Hermeneutics.

In 1959 Daniel was on leave from the seminary faculty and studying under Barth in Switzerland. At this time Edward J. Carnell, who strongly opposed fundamentalism, was acting president of Fuller Seminary. Because of Carnell's own emotional health struggles, it fell upon Harold Lindsell to administrate the day-to-day operations of the seminary. Already party lines were forming within the faculty and the board that would ultimately bring the seminary to a fork in the road. The central issue: inerrancy. Dr. Charles Fuller's own health was declining. The energy to back his old fundamentalist preaching convictions just wasn't there. As confusion emerged, he struggled with whose counsel to trust.

In a nutshell, Harold Lindsell found himself walking on eggs. The seminary was growing. Daniel Fuller, the only heir to the founder, was on the faculty. Young Fuller was on leave and abroad studying corrupted theology that denigrated the view of biblical inerrancy. The acting seminary president, Edward Carnell, was unable to act due to health. Negative tension was growing between Ockenga, the founding president, and Charles Fuller, founder of the seminary. Charles Fuller, of course, loved his son and grandchildren. Charles Fuller was conflicted over whom he could lean on for advice. And, as he was growing old, his health and energy were significantly decreasing.

So by 1960, irreparable changes were in the making at Fuller Seminary, just thirteen years after its beginning. Early that year Harold Lindsell and Charles Fuller exchanged correspondence concerning the thrust and outreach of the seminary. Dr. Lindsell wrote Dr. Fuller on February 15, 1960:

"Dear Charles:

From time to time in our discussions concerning the seminary and its thrust and outreach, you have indicated that you would like to see the policies established by Dr. Carnell continued. In chatting with some of the faculty members at different times, this same idea has been elaborated.

"I think a most useful purpose would be served if you would put down on paper what you think this thrust is. It will serve as a useful guide now and in the future, for we would like to have such an expression from the founder. And who is better equipped than our founder to do this?

"It seems to me that it would be well to ask, at the same time, whether the thrust you have in mind is the same as that enunciated by Dr. Ockenga when first the school was founded. If it differs from Dr. Ockenga's thrust, in what do these differences consist?

"Some years ago, when Dr. Carnell first assumed the presidency, I urged upon him the necessity of having a faculty committee examine the question of what we were trying to do, and spell it out on paper. A committee was appointed and later dismissed. Nothing ever came from it. This task still remains to be done and in this critical stage of the institution's development it would be wholesome and helpful to see it come to fruition.

Sincerely yours, Harold Lindsell"[1]

The following month on March 16, 1960, Charles E. Fuller responded with this letter:

"Dear Dr. Lindsell:

Regarding your letter of some time ago with the suggestion that I should seek to express in writing what I believe the future thrust of Fuller Theological Seminary should be, as I told you before, I thought this was a good suggestion and I would take time to think about it. Now I am ready to give you my thoughts.

"As to denominations, I do feel that Fuller Seminary ought to be dedicated to the cause of providing well-trained consecrated ministers and Christian workers for the major and smaller denominations. I do not want our seminary to become divisive, negative, and critical in its attitude toward the organized Protestant Church. In this respect, I think both Doctors Ockenga and Carnell have given the seminary the right kind of leadership. By stressing this point I do not mean, of course, that we should have no fellowship with those who in good conscience are serving the Lord in independent churches or in smaller groups which have cut themselves off from some larger denominational group. It seems to me that the implication of Christian love is that we should acknowledge our brethren in the Lord and work with them in the advancement of the gospel of Christ wherever they are. I hope, therefore, that Fuller Seminary will always be willing that students from all backgrounds denominationally shall be encouraged to take our degree and that the faculty will give them a positive approach to the truth in the classroom and show them how to be real leaders in the Christian Church which is the household of faith.

"Regarding the doctrinal position of the school, I want to make it very clear that it is my sincere hope that Fuller Seminary will always be solidly based in its teachings upon the Scriptures as being the inspired Word of God. As I have often said of the 'Old-Fashioned Revival Hour,' I have sought to be true to the Book, and I think this is the key to understanding God's blessing upon my radio ministry. Again let me say that I believe the implication of Christian love is that we should be able to recognize differences of opinion in secondary matters of doctrine and such differences should be no impediment to anyone's having a teaching post on the faculty of Fuller Seminary. It is, in my judgment, a healthy and wholesome situation when different points of view in doctrine are held in love, providing these matters are not essential to the evangelical, orthodox, Protestant faith. There certainly is a core of truth which, if a man does not believe and preach, he has another gospel.

"In correspondence with my son, Daniel, he has helped me appreciate the fact that there are difficulties with the dispensational interpretation of prophecy and that we should not be dogmatic about details of eschatology (when the rapture will take place; whether there is a millennium or not) which has unhappily divided Christians in our day. Of course we know that God's Word plainly teaches that the Lord Jesus is coming in person and power to establish His glorious kingdom. Dan has given me a respect for Calvinism and I hope that in our theology department this point of view will always have a fair representation. In other words, I want our school to be true to the great Protestant, orthodox, and evangelical tradition with no limitations that would prevent our having the finest faculty that it is possible to get, of men committed to the Word of God and the gospel of grace in these latter days.

"Finally, may I say a word about personal zeal and soul winning. As you know, these matters are very dear to my heart. I have always loved the souls of men and I want our seminary to inculcate a desire in our students and graduates to win men to Christ, to be evangelists and missionaries. I hope, therefore, that Fuller Seminary will always combine with its scholarship in theology a dedication to the task of giving men experience in the practical work of witnessing that they may go forth with a vision of the fields white unto harvest to serve the Lord wherever He shall call them. Finally, 'Go ye into all the world and preach the gospel to every creature,' this is the goal—my heart's desire for this seminary.

Most sincerely yours, Charles E. Fuller"[2]

On March 18, 1960, Dr. Lindsell wrote back to Dr. Fuller:

"Dear Dr. Fuller:

Thank you for your good letter of March 16. I am pleased indeed to have these words which express your own heartbeat regarding the perspective and outreach of our institution. I believe this will better enable us to keep before us those things which are dear to your heart. I trust that we always will be characterized by breadth of theology within the basic historical fundamentals of the Christian faith. I would like to talk with you further and in person about one phase of your letter relative to the details of eschatology. I trust that when you have fully regained your strength, we will have opportunity to do this. I believe that it has been a wonderful thing that you and Dan have been able to discuss theological matters in an objective way. I trust that our school will ever remain within the Calvinistic tradition and I feel that it will. Let me thank you for taking the time to give thought and consideration to this subject which we had under advisement. With every good wish,

I am faithfully yours, Harold Lindsell"[3]

During that time Lindsell persisted in pressing the matter of the inerrancy of the Bible at the seminary. Behind Lindsell's back, another faculty member was busy—Donald Weber, who happened to be Carnell's brother-in-law. Weber sent panicky pleas to young Fuller in Switzerland fearfully alleging that Lindsell would take over and end the faculty's academic freedom of speech with an insistent return to the old Princeton inerrancy party line on the Bible.

DANIEL FULLER RETURNED—
WITH BARTH'S LOW VIEW OF THE BIBLE

Daniel Fuller later returned from Switzerland indoctrinated with Karl Barth's view that the Bible contains both revelational and non-revelational Scripture. Barth taught that the Bible contains the Word of God and that the Bible is not, in totality, equivalent to the very Word of God. This begs the question, what part of the Bible contains the Word of God, or is revelational, and what part does not?

Charles Fuller's vigorous and energetic launching of a seminary for the Lord Jesus Christ and His glorious gospel, rooted solidly in His Word, is sadly bumped out of orbit on the very issue of the authority of the Bible. George Marsden reports an account about Charles and Grace Fuller's concern about the succession of their God-blessed ministry. Their fondest dream was that their son, Daniel, their only child, would succeed his father.[4]

No one watched for apostasy in American evangelicalism more closely than conservative scholar, Wilbur M. Smith. Years before Dr. Fuller had invited Smith to become part of the seminary's founding faculty, Smith had become a friend and encourager to J. Gresham Machen. Smith watched closely as Machen departed liberal Princeton Seminary to start Westminster Seminary. Old Princeton was in a theological nosedive.

Wilbur M. Smith wrote Charles Fuller saying,

> "When the entire faculty at Princeton approves of extending an invitation to one like Dr. Bowman who denies the great fundamentals of our faith … then I can no longer recommend Princeton to young men."[5]

Daniel Fuller surprised his parents by going off to Princeton to study. Grace Fuller forwarded Wilbur M. Smith's correspondence to her son and added a classic statement of her conservative misgivings about him studying at an institution that had lost its moorings. She wrote to Daniel saying:

> "We are praying earnestly for you that God will give you a crystal-clear vision to detect the error and also to see and cling to the truth. Satan is a liar from the beginning, deceptive and so subtle! He is wily, and so extremely clever and would deceive the very elect.

> "May none of these heresies find any lodgment in your heart, and I pray the same for the other students. I pray that you may be able to help other men there who may be taken in by these subtle lies. Do you feel that you should leave Princeton? Do you feel that by being there that you are endorsing the college for other young men …?

> "Dad feels that you would have his vision and carry on in his way to mold the school, possibly to teach there, and keep it in the middle of the road, though we did not say all this to Smith."[6]

In Grace Fuller's letter, she also reiterated the hope that Dan would eventually play a leading role at his father's new seminary.

Grace Fuller also observed that Charles was very disturbed by divisions among conservative Christians and that she believed he had been wise in keeping clear of many entanglements. During Daniel's studies at Princeton, Charles Fuller wrote to another friend that his son was learning a good deal about the subtle teachings of Barth and liberalism.

When Harold Lindsell became the editor of *Christianity Today* magazine, he wrote the following letter to Daniel Fuller, dated September 23, 1964:

"Dear Dan:

Last weekend I covered the Billy Graham Crusade in Boston.... During my three-day stay in Boston, I spent more than an hour with Dr. Ockenga in his office at the Park Street Church. During the course of the conversation, certain questions were directed to me which occasioned the writing of this letter. I indicated to Dr. Ockenga that in conversation with Dr. Schoonhoven [Calvin Schoonhoven, a Fuller graduate, friend of Daniel Fuller, also studied in Switzerland, and had admitted he did not believe in an inerrant Bible when he was hired by Fuller Seminary.] some time ago, he had at no time affirmed his belief in a Bible which in the autographs is wholly without theological, scientific, historical, factual, or other errors of any kind. I also told Dr. Ockenga that as a result of conversations with you, at no time had you ever affirmed that you believe that the Bible in the autographs is without factual, historical, scientific, or theological errors of any kind. Dr. Ockenga asked whether he had my permission to quote me at this point.

"I told Dr. Ockenga that he could quote me, but on second thought I concluded that I would write to you about this matter first. This would give you an opportunity to correct any misunderstanding which I have on that subject, indeed to assure me that I am wrong if such be the case. Am I, in point of fact, misquoting your theological position when I say that you cannot affirm that the Bible in the autographs is wholly without factual, historical, scientific, or theological errors of any kind? An answer to this inquiry will be greatly appreciated, for I have no wish whatever to misrepresent you before Dr. Ockenga....

I am sincerely yours, Harold Lindsell"[7]

Daniel Fuller responded to Harold Lindsell on October 9, 1964:

"Dear Harold:

First, let me tell you how much I thank you for your sense of fair play in telling me of your conversation with Dr. Ockenga. In telling me of this you were certainly doing unto others as you would be done by. I realize, too, that in speaking with Dr. Ockenga your purpose was not to discuss this matter, but that it just came up in the course of the conversation.

"The summary of my views (and of Calvin's) as you give it in the letter is not accurate. Neither Calvin nor I recognize ourselves in this summary. Possibly the reason for this is that we were never able to discuss inspiration with you in a relaxed manner. This was certainly not your fault, but it was just the way things were. I think it would be better, until we can discuss this in a relaxed, leisurely context, not to go into the matter further. This is especially true since the only way I can talk with you, now that you are in Washington, D.C., is by letter, and letters are a poor substitute for a discussion.

Sincerely, your friend, Dan"[8]

OCKENGA—NEW EVANGELICALISM—A PARADIGM SHIFT

Changes accelerated at Fuller Seminary when Edward Carnell succeeded Harold Ockenga as president. On that occasion, Ockenga labeled the new paradigm shift calling it neo- or new evangelicalism which he said "embraces the full orthodoxy of fundamentalism in doctrine but manifests a social consciousness and responsibility which was strangely absent from fundamentalism."[9]

Strangely absent from this initial label was any alluding to the ongoing central issue—the inerrancy of the Bible. Ockenga knew better, if for no other reason than he had studied under one of the century's most capable inerrancy scholars, Machen, at Westminster Seminary. So confusion is apparently sown into the initial fabric of this newly coined term called "new evangelicalism" by Ockenga.

From the birthing platform of the National Association of Evangelicals through the establishment of Fuller Seminary, Ockenga was fleeing from the term "fundamentalist." To him it seemed to be an embarrassment instead of a badge of honor. He envisioned a new generation of non-militant conservatives who were pursuing intellectualism, non-judgmentalism, and appeasement; applying the gospel to the sociological, political, and economic areas. From the inception of the seminary, Ockenga had remained bi-coastal—assuming responsibilities as Fuller's president in absentia and maintaining his position as senior pastor of Boston's prestigious Park Street Church.

The inerrancy advocates on Fuller's faculty were not confused as they began to react to this paradigm shift with the ascendancy of Dr. Carnell. They knew what was involved and it was definitely quite more than a new movement with a heightened social consciousness. The conservatives included: Wilbur M. Smith, Charles J. Woodbridge, Everett Harrison, Carl F.H. Henry, and Harold Lindsell. Dr. Carnell even pleaded for a sweet, forgiving appeasement toward heretics. But these fundamentalist professors began making plans to relocate elsewhere.

PRESIDENT EDWARD CARNELL BELIEVED THE BIBLE HAS ERRORS

Carnell's drift away from inerrancy began during his educational journey. At Wheaton College his philosophy mentor was the respected apologist, author, and inerrancy advocate, Gordon H. Clark.[10] Carnell's grounding in a high view of Scripture continued during his studies at Westminster Seminary. His doctoral studies at both Harvard and Boston University certainly took him in the wrong direction. Carnell's doctoral theological dissertation was on the world-renowned liberal theologian, Reinhold Niebuhr; his philosophical dissertation was on existentialist, Søren Kierkegaard, who will be examined more later. Carnell's negative reaction to fundamentalism, which he perceived as anti-intellectualism plus the intense liberal and neo-orthodox influence from his graduate school studies, eroded his personal confidence in the doctrine of inerrancy.

Karl Barth's heretical influence upon new evangelicalism became even more apparent when years later, in 1962, the internationally-known

Swiss theologian addressed a scholarly audience at the University of Chicago. Carnell and Richard J. Mouw, current president of Fuller Seminary, were both in the audience. Sitting next to Mouw was Gordon H. Clark.

During the Q & A session, Carnell submitted a written question inquiring how does Barth "harmonize his appeal to Scripture as the objective Word of God with his admission that Scripture is indeed sullied by errors, theological as well as historical or factual?" Carnell, seeming to fear that he would look like an unthinking fundamentalist, added this candid parenthetical observation, "This is a problem for me, too, I cheerfully confess."

Barth answered that the Bible was a true and fitting instrument to point man to God, who alone is infallible. The Bible contains errors in its time-bound human statements. To this latter remark Barth wryly added, "Is that enough to encourage you to continue to cheerfully confess that here is a problem for you?"[11]

FULLER SEMINARY MOVED AWAY FROM FUNDAMENTALISM

Carnell's actions contributed to moving the seminary away from the fundamentalist camp. Fuller's growing faculty included George Eldon Ladd and Paul K. Jewett. Ladd was critical of dispensationalism. Jewett defended the ordination of women, accepted human evolution, was pro-abortion and opposed capital punishment. It wasn't long until Carnell, Ladd, and Jewett teamed up with Daniel Fuller in an effort to remove the view of premillennialism from the seminary's Statement of Faith.

After hosting a dinner, Jewett and Daniel Fuller attempted to persuade Charles Fuller to remove the premillennial view from the Statement of Faith. They were unable to make headway with the old fundamentalist. However, they succeeded at convincing the elderly Fuller to sign a statement declaring that after his death, that eschatological view would be removed from the statement signed by all faculty and board members. Today that document is in the seminary's vault.

Grace Fuller remained consistently loyal to her son and fell in line with Jewett. Charles Fuller remained a premillennialist with deep conviction and continued to reassure his radio audience that every professor at Fuller Seminary was a premillennialist. But they were not!

BILLY GRAHAM—SEPARATIST CONTROVERSY— CHRISTIANITY TODAY

The divisiveness between fundamentalist separatists and non-separatists continued to complicate the American scene. Billy Graham had decided that most churches in a city had to be united in their invitation to him to come and conduct an evangelistic crusade before he would go to that city and preach. So now representative clergy from nearly the full spectrum of Protestantism would sit behind the evangelist on the crusade platform. Some clergy would be members of the National and World Council of Churches denominations. Not infrequently some clergy would be present who did not believe in inerrancy, the virgin birth of Christ, and other core historic fundamentalist views.

As early as January 1955, Harold Lindsell wrote to Billy Graham and Graham's father-in-law, L. Nelson Bell. Bell was a retired medical missionary doctor to China. Lindsell suggested that Carl F.H. Henry would make an excellent editor for the new monthly magazine, *Christianity Today*. The periodical was Wilbur M. Smith's idea and was funded by J. Howard Pew of Sun Oil. Graham responded by indicating that the new magazine should "plant the evangelical flag in the middle of the road, taking a conservative theological position but a definite liberal approach to social problems. It would combine the best in liberalism and the best in fundamentalism without compromising theologically."[12]

Graham was apprehensive that Carl F.H. Henry would be too conservative for the image that he, the evangelist, wanted reflected in the new magazine. Following his crusade in England, Graham believed he could make great inroads into major denominations in the U.S. but only if he could be free from fundamentalism's perceived image of separatism, anti-intellectualism, and contentiousness. In responding to Lindsell about Carl F.H. Henry, Graham candidly asked, "Would he [Carl F.H. Henry] be willing to recognize that fundamentalism is in need of an entirely new approach and that this magazine would be useless if it had the old fundamentalist stamp on it?"[13]

Finally Graham launched *Christianity Today* magazine in 1956 with Carl F.H. Henry as the editor-in-chief, a position he held until 1968. Henry sought a more balanced fundamentalism with a return to the 1910-15 era published work of *The Fundamentals* that would reignite scholarship with evangelistic fervor.

While the fundamentalists were sorting themselves out from the new evangelicals, many remained confused. During 1957 and 1958, when the crisis was particularly intense, Billy Graham and Fuller Seminary were thrown into each other's arms. Both agreed that they had to somehow disconnect themselves from the counterproductive negative image of extreme fundamentalism. They had to be open to those believers who had remained in the old mainline denominations; even if the leadership of those old denominations had come under liberal control. Soon after, Charles Fuller invited Graham to join the Fuller Seminary board, and he did. Ockenga had taken this opportunity to give the emerging alliance a distinct identity as the "new evangelicals."

While Billy Graham always preached, "The Bible says …" and would later fully endorse Lindsell's book, *The Battle for the Bible*, he was conflicted in his predicament. Alluding to strong, well-known individuals in the separatist movement, Billy Graham expressed his frustration to Wilbur M. Smith on April 9, 1958, saying,

> "As you know, Dr. John Rice, Dr. Bob Jones, and Dr. Carl McIntire have kept a running attack on me for the last two years. The things they are telling border on the ridiculous…. As the psalmist said in Psalm 56, 'They mark my steps.' Again the psalmist said, 'They wrest my words.' Every move I make is now under careful scrutiny by these men. They never print but one side of every story. Thus far I have refused to answer them. I have tried to avoid any controversy for the fear of being deterred from my God-called mission of soul winning."[14]

FULLER SEMINARY CONTROVERSY CONTINUED UNRESOLVED

Charles Fuller announced that he had selected David Allan Hubbard to be the next seminary president. Thirty-two-year-old Hubbard held that position for thirty years until his death. Hubbard was a Fuller graduate, stayed on for a master's degree, and earned a doctorate degree from Scotland's St. Andrews University, which consisted of a faculty that had been highly influenced by Karl Barth.

Responding to the idea of Hubbard being the next president, Daniel Fuller indicated to his father that Hubbard would be satisfactory if he was truly dedicated to taking the seminary in the direction Carnell had pointed out. In a letter, Daniel opened his heart to his parents saying,

> "If the Bible were indeed God's book, superior to all merely human writings, then the Bible should be capable of defense in the open market of ideas according to intellectual standards on which all candid inquirers could agree. If Christians were faithful to this principle, then only the lack of grace, and hence, fallen humanity's perverse love of untruth, not the lack of good arguments for Christianity, could explain unbelief.

> "To maintain this high ideal, however, evangelicals would have to face up to one colossal error in the way they typically defended the faith,

by insisting that the 'Bible is without error in whole and in part,' and at the same time paying lip service to their openness to the latest archaeological findings. Fundamentalists had made a joke of their claims that Scripture met the highest intellectual standards. Unbelief laughs and I see no reason why I should not laugh with them.

"Some of the chronologies in Scripture were simply wrong, and, although the errors were innocent bookkeeping errors, it was an apologetic disaster to act as though such errors in detail did not exist. It made a sham of evangelical claims to take history seriously on such vitally important matters as the fact of the resurrection. So the Fuller Seminary creed should be revised to say the infallibility of the Bible had to do with its statements on faith and practice, not its precision of historical detail."[15]

Daniel Fuller apparently had not read the scholarly research of Robert Dick Wilson or chose to disregard it.

By now the seminary faculty was roughly divided into progressive and conservative camps over the choice of a president, and a full-scale power struggle began. Donald Weber was intensely devoted to his brother-in-law, Carnell, and they both wanted a definitive break with fundamentalism. Weber, also a faculty member, was in a power gap conflict with Lindsell.

Charles Fuller continued to be conflicted about his seminary. While he felt Dr. Carnell was taking the seminary in the right direction, President Carnell had to resign because of pressures and health. Ockenga reappeared as interim president but physically remained in his Boston church. Daniel Fuller was in Switzerland studying under Karl Barth. The elderly Fuller was relying more on son, Daniel, for opinions about the seminary. Daniel Fuller wanted the Carnell direction to be followed, departing from a commitment to inerrancy. Complications continued as Lindsell filled in much of the power vacuum by taking over many of the daily executive functions at the seminary. And Charles Fuller's radio listener giving to the seminary was way down!

With finances down, Weber and Carnell secured two non-fundamentalist board members. One was Gerrit P. Groen, a highly respected patent lawyer and member of the Christian Reformed Church, a denomination known to be doctrinally opposed to dispensationalism. The second new member of the board was C. Davis Weyerhaeuser, a wealthy timber company owner from Tacoma, Washington. The lumber executive was in the midst of a break with fundamentalism. He had recently left the board of Moody Bible Institute.

Daniel Fuller was still abroad studying and Weber urgently appealed to him to take over the seminary deanship, lest Lindsell consolidate more power and control. Young Fuller agreed to accept the position when he returned from his studies.

Between 1960 and 1962 the school was busy publishing its Statement of Faith, assuring its constituents that the faculty and board were signing it annually. In 1962, the public relations department distributed 20,000 brochures and 15,000 scrolls containing these signatures attached to the Statement of Faith.

When Daniel Fuller returned to the seminary, he was appointed dean of the faculty and Lindsell was moved to vice president. Ockenga again became president in absentia. It was soon publicly known that young Fuller's views did not embrace the inerrancy of the Bible.

Calvin Schoonhoven was a graduate of the seminary and a close friend of young Fuller. The hiring of David Hubbard as president left no more room on the faculty so Schoonhoven was hired to fill a vacant library directorship so that he could actively teach. When examined, Schoonhoven admitted he did not believe in the inerrancy of the Bible.

Charles Fuller's support of Hubbard for president of the seminary was now backed by Daniel Fuller and board member, C. Davis Weyerhaeuser. Hubbard maintained that his own views on the Bible were orthodox. The theological core issue came to a head right at this time.

BLACK SATURDAY—INERRANCY ABANDONED BY FULLER SEMINARY

In December 1962, a faculty-board retreat was held at the Huntington Sheraton Hotel in Pasadena. The issue of biblical infallibility surfaced. A definitive decision was called for with regard to the seminary's Statement of Faith advocating that the Bible is "free from all error in the whole and in part." Stenographers were present taking down every word in shorthand. Board member Edward Johnson focused the issue when he spoke of the need to have a benchmark. Once the benchmark was changed, the institution would lose its bearing and depart from orthodoxy. The failure of the board to stand firm on its original inerrancy commitment led to Johnson's resignation within a month. That dismal outcome labeled the retreat Black Saturday in the seminary's inerrancy controversy.

Lindsell received a letter from Charles Fuller saying,

> "I think it is best to take the written record of the discussion concerning inspiration and keep them under my supervision for a time since the president at the end of the discussion expressed a desire that the discussion be kept within the seminary family. If copies of the discussion fall into many hands, the chances of realizing the president's purpose would not be carried out. Moreover, it might be misunderstood and could hurt the school."[16]

The stenographer's notebooks and those parts that had been transcribed were placed into the possession of Charles Fuller. Lindsell observed, "I doubt that anyone has seen them from that day to this."[17]

An article about Fuller Seminary's internal conflict appeared in the liberal *Union Theological Seminary Quarterly Review* saying,

"The paradox that Barth, Brunner, Cullmann, and Eichrodt provide more attractive models at Fuller for an evangelical approach to Scripture than do the fundamentalists, and they are at the same time major representatives of neo-orthodoxy, helps us to understand more clearly what has happened at Fuller today that has made them a comfortable 'nesting place' for so many confusing religious views that have resulted from what former board member, Edward Johnson, said was removing their 'benchmark.' The action has rendered the term 'evangelical' meaningless in defining Christianity today.

"Only by restoring the biblical definition of the word 'evangel' can its older, more accurate meaning be recovered. Only by clearly defining the term 'evangelical' as 'neo-orthodoxy' or 'neo-evangelical,' which has become the position of liberal seminaries, could Fuller's President Hubbard protect their uniquely 'marketable' status of being 'evangelical' and sell it to the public. The obscurity of making a distinction between the terms 'inerrancy' and 'infallibility,' coupled with the uncertainty over whether scholars like Karl Barth are evangelical or neo-orthodox, suggests that many of the clear theological differences between Fuller and the modernist seminaries were already seriously in question. The fundamentalists were clearly on their way out at Fuller."[18]

The 1963-64 seminary catalogue retained the usual statement about the creed of the school. It said in part:

"The Seminary has formulated a Statement of Faith as expressed in the following propositions, to which each member of the faculty subscribes at the beginning of each academic year. This concurrence is without mental reservation, and any member who cannot assent agrees to withdraw from the institution."[19]

Every member of the faculty and board signed the Statement.

When the 1965-66 catalogue appeared, the Statement of Faith deleted this sentence:

> "This concurrence is without mental reservation, and any member who cannot assent agrees to withdraw from the institution."

It was replaced with,

> "every member of the faculty subscribes at the beginning of each academic year."[20]

The 1975-76 catalogue reflects a further change from the 1965-66 catalogue. No longer appeared the following: "at the beginning of each academic year..."[21]

As time went by, a dark cloud hung over the institution. Faculty and board members were signing the Statement of Faith, one important part of which some of them did not believe or agree with. They were signing with mental reservation at a time when the promotional literature of the seminary kept assuring its constituency that all was well and nothing had changed.

Faculty resignations followed on the heels of this change of direction. Charles Woodbridge was the first to leave. His departure preceded the Black Saturday episode. Wilbur M. Smith was next to resign when the 1962-63 school year ended. Lindsell left the following school year, and Gleason Archer departed several years later. All four departures were directly related to the question of biblical inerrancy. Others on the faculty who held to a view of inerrancy chose to remain, as did some members on the board.[22]

FIFTY-ONE EVANGELICAL SCHOLARS MET ON INERRANCY

This was followed by a reconciliation attempt by Ockenga to put together the new evangelical coalition. He was especially distressed by its threatened breakup over the inerrancy conflict. He had cultivated cordial contacts on both sides. The result was a scholars' conference; initiated substantially by Fuller people and privately funded by C. Davis Weyerhaeuser, J. Howard Pew, Billy Graham, and Charles Fuller. Even the arrangement caused controversy in Pasadena. Charles Fuller's longtime friend, James Henry Hutchins, pastor of Pasadena's Lake Avenue Church, resigned from his long-held position on the board. The inerrancy issue was Hutchins' main concern.

In this atmosphere of ongoing tension that divided long-standing friends, fifty-one evangelical scholars from ten countries gathered for discussions at Wenham, Massachusetts in June 1966. There for ten days, they had it out on the doctrine of Scripture. Though hoping for peace, the issues became too hot to keep at a dispassionate level. Some of the key people in the Fuller controversy were not there, including Lindsell, Henry, and Jewett. Daniel Fuller attended, and his views invited very strong criticism from inerrancy advocates in the group.

Kenneth Kantzer, Gleason Archer, John Warwick Montgomery, and D.A. Carson attended. Carson authored an important analysis, *Becoming Conversant with the Emerging Church: Understanding a Movement and Its Implications*.[23] He currently teaches at Trinity Evangelical Divinity School. The inerrancy advocates made it clear they were not going to give an inch on this central belief. Though the discussions were largely cordial, occasional blowups dashed all hopes of issuing a meaningful collective statement and the conflict continued to smolder.[24]

After the Fuller Seminary Black Saturday, Weyerhaeuser wrote Edward Johnson attempting to explain how he could honestly sign Fuller's Statement of Faith and yet be uncomfortable with its inerrancy clause. An exchange of letters between Lindsell and Weyerhaeuser is housed in the Billy Graham Archives.[25] After examining these documents, in my opinion, there appears to be a full lack of candor on Weyerhaeuser's part when he signed the Fuller Seminary Statement of Faith.

EVANGELICALISM MORPHED INTO NEW EVANGELICALISM

All these issues led to a broader definition of evangelicalism, which morphed into what became more commonly known as "new evangelicalism." Now there was a new movement; it was self defined as Christian, but it fully endorsed inclusiveness and accommodation because it had opened the door to many who no longer believed in the inerrancy of the Bible. Sadly, deception and a full lack of candor were involved.

Above all, Fuller Seminary wished to retain the label "evangelical." Dr. Lindsell wrote,

"Basically I made three observations about the seminary. The first two were factual, and their rightness or wrongness can be appraised from the evidences given. The third was prophetic. The first allegation had to do with the changing of the doctrinal statement of the school. I charged that Fuller Seminary has been infiltrated by an aberrant view of Scripture. It had started as an institution committed to biblical inerrancy ... Drs. Wilbur M. Smith, Carl F.H. Henry, Harold J. Ockenga, and myself can bear and have born testimony to that fact.... Article 2 said that the Bible is 'free from error in the whole and in the part.' The statement made clear this was true in the autographs for it said 'as originally given.' This allowed for the possibility of copyists' errors, few though they may be.

"In the new statement, Fuller Seminary no longer says that the Bible 'is the infallible Word of God, the only infallible rule of faith and practice.' It simply says the Bible is the word (lower-cased) of God, and then adds that infallibility is limited to matters of faith and practice. Fuller Seminary has given up on its cherished belief in an inerrant or infallible Scripture....

"Second, I charged that Fuller Seminary has taken the second step. It has gone beyond a denial of infallibility in matters of history, science, and the cosmos to a place where members of the faculty now deny the truth of Scripture in matters of faith and practice....

"The third point I made about Fuller Seminary was in the form of prophecy. I asserted that once an institution surrenders biblical 'inerrancy' it will sooner or later scrap other basic doctrines of the Christian faith."[26]

More recently Fuller has issued a four-page online catalogue under the heading, What We Believe and Teach. A careful reading makes clear how far removed from the 1910 era of fundamental Christian beliefs Fuller has gone. They are now organized into three degree granting schools: the School of Theology, the School of Psychology, and the School of Intercultural Studies (no longer called the School of World Mission). Some classes teach Christian workers are to accommodate those in other cultures where they differ in the moral values taught in the Bible.

The Fuller Seminary catalogue says:

"At times some Christians have become unduly attached to the precise wording of doctrine—whether of events in the last days, the meaning of baptism, or the use of a catchphrase like the inerrancy of Scripture. But it is well to remember that all our formulations of Christian truth must ultimately conform not to some preset statement but to the Scriptures, all parts of which are divinely inspired. Thus, sloganeering can never be a substitute for the careful, patient analysis of what God's Word teaches, including what it teaches about itself. This being true, when it comes to a loyalty to the trustworthiness, the authority and the power of Scripture, we at Fuller are convinced that our commitment matches anything to be found in contemporary evangelical Christianity."[27]

Sadly, a definitive movement away from the central doctrine of inerrancy in the battle for the Bible engulfed Fuller Seminary and spilled over into the American church scene. With the battle for inerrancy lost in the fight over the seminary's revised Statement of Faith, the door was opened wide so that the seminary became a strange nest for unbiblical practice in preparing men for the ministry in the church of Jesus Christ.

Labels for clarification and identification began to blur. There was confusion because many new evangelicals, with their abandonment of inerrancy, simply continued to consider themselves and refer to themselves as evangelicals. This led many to conclude that we should abandon the use of the term "evangelical" as a label because it no longer tells the world what historic evangelicals believe. What term or label should take its place?

Some inerrancy-believing evangelicals decided to go back to the use of the term "fundamentalism." Unfortunately, this term was loaded with attitudinal and behavioral connotations. The true genius of the term "fundamentalism" has always resided in its power-packed definitional content associated with its usage as early as 1910. Therefore, liberals despised it. Secularists misunderstood it. Academia disdained it—even to this day. Today the average church member is completely unaware of its historical roots. Rick Warren contributed to the ambiguity by calling fundamentalism "a very legalistic, narrow view of Christianity."[28]

But there are inerrancy advocates who are attracted to the term "fundamentalism" because its core meaning includes intense opposition to syncretism, universalism, and the notion that non-Christian religions are roads that also lead to paradise. The Christian community feels conflicted regarding the term's usage.

Fuller Seminary's compromise and accommodation were the twigs and brushwood that became the nest for aberrant practice, where workers are prepared for the twenty-first century postmodern Emerging church.

CHAPTER SEVEN FOOTNOTES

1 Billy Graham Center Archives, Wheaton, IL. Harold Lindsell Collection 192, Folder 3-17A, Item 9.

2 Ibid. Folder 3-17B, Item 2.

3 Ibid. Folder 3-17B, Item 1.

4 George M. Marsden, *Reforming Fundamentalism: Fuller Seminary and the New Evangelicalism* (Grand Rapids, MI: Eerdmans, 1987), p. 20.

5 Ibid. p. 22.

6 Ibid. p. 23.

7 Billy Graham Center Archives, Wheaton, IL. Harold Lindsell Collection 192, Folder 6-20 HH, Item 4.

8 Ibid. Folder 6-20HH, Item 5.

9 George M. Marsden, *Reforming Fundamentalism: Fuller Seminary and the New Evangelicalism* (Grand Rapids, MI: Eerdmans, 1987), p. 146.

10 Gordon H. Clark, *Historiography: Secular and Religious* (Unicoi, TN: Trinity Foundation, 1994).

11 George M. Marsden, *Reforming Fundamentalism: Fuller Seminary and the New Evangelicalism* (Grand Rapids, MI: Eerdmans, 1987), p. 194-195.

12 Ibid. p.158.

13 Ibid. p.160.

14 Ibid. p.153.

15 Ibid p. 201.

16 Harold Lindsell, *The Battle for the Bible* (Grand Rapids, MI: Zondervan, 1976), pp. 110-111
17 Ibid. p. 111.

18 Gerald T. Sheppard, "Biblical Hermeneutics: The Academic Language of Evangelical Identity," *Union Seminary Quarterly Review*, Vol. 32, No. 2, (Winter 1977), pp. 89-90.

19 Harold Lindsell, *The Battle for the Bible* (Grand Rapids, MI: Zondervan, 1976), p. 111.

20 Ibid. p.111.

21 Ibid. p. 111.

22 Ibid. pp. 111-112.

23 D.A. Carson, *Becoming Conversant with the Emerging Church: Understanding a Movement and Its Implications* (Grand Rapids, MI: Zondervan, 2005).

24 George M. Marsden, *Reforming Fundamentalism: Fuller Seminary and the New Evangelicalism* (Grand Rapids, MI: Eerdmans, 1987), pp. 228-229.

25 Billy Graham Center Archives, Wheaton, IL. Harold Lindsell Collection 192, 1-12ii, Item 4, Sam Reeves to Lindsell; Item 3, Lindsell to Sam Reeves; 1-12i, Item 6, C. Davis Weyerhaeuser to Lindsell; 1-12ii, Item 1, Lindsell to Weyerhaeuser.

26 Harold Lindsell, *The Bible in the Balance* (Grand Rapids, MI: Zondervan, 1979), p. 183.

27 Fuller Seminary, What We Believe and Teach, Home Online Catalogue, 5 pages, 2009.

28 Rick Warren, interview held during the Biannual Faith Angle Conference on Religion, Politics, and Public Life, Key West, Florida, May 2005.

A NEST FOR ABERRANT PRACTICE

The great deception began in the garden of Eden when Satan asked Eve, "Has God said...?" (Genesis 3:1). Those who have been in Christian ministry for any length of time recognize the continual battle "against principalities, powers, and the rulers of the darkness of this world" (Ephesians 6:12). The apostle John warned, "For we know that we are of God, and the whole world lies in wickedness" (1 John 5:19). Thankfully we can "be strong in the Lord, and in the power of His might. Put on the whole armor of God, that you may be able to stand against the wiles of the devil" (Ephesians 6:10-11).

The "wiles of the devil" means that the Devil works by a planned method and strategy in an orderly and detailed manner. The Greek word is *methodeias*. The *King James* translates that same word as "wiles" in Ephesians 6:11 and "craftiness" in Ephesians 4:14; where we are admonished to "be no more children, tossed to and fro, and carried about with every wind of doctrine, by the sleight of men, and cunning craftiness, whereby they lie in wait to deceive." It appears obvious that the humanistic methods to grow churches are being orchestrated by Satan, the ruler of the darkness in this world. Fuller Seminary no longer affirms belief in an inerrant Bible; plus humanistic sociology, psychology, and cultural studies are accommodatingly sown into the fabric of church growth methodologies.

In the early days at Fuller Seminary, the graduating classes of 1950 to 1952 came with a 75 percent belief in inerrancy. By the time they left, about 48 percent of them remained firm in that view. By 1982 it was reported that the commitment to inerrancy had dropped to 15 percent of the graduates. Compromise and accommodation produced tragic results.[1] Whatever happened to the seminary envisioned by Charles Fuller?

Accommodation sounds like a commendable attitude. The dictionary defines it: (1) to make fit, suitable, or congruous; (2) to bring into agreement or concord; (3) to furnish with something desired, needed, or suited; (4) to make room for, to hold without crowding or inconvenience; (5) to give consideration to allow, for example, the special interests of various groups to adapt themselves.

Accommodation is the very essence of hospitality. It is the core characteristic of civility. How has such an honorable concept become such a dangerous and deplorable process in turning one's faith away from the authority of the Word of God? The answer comes from the two sides of accommodation. It is about conforming, which is an essential element in communication.

However, it also has a dangerous side when we conform to the wrong pattern. God predestined us to "be conformed to the image of His Son" (Romans 8:29). "Conformed" brings us to the strong challenge: "And be not conformed to this world: but be transformed by the renewing of your mind, that you may prove what is that good, and acceptable, and perfect, will of God" (Romans 12:2). This can only happen when we hold to the absolute authority of Scripture.

THE FULLER SEMINARY CHURCH GROWTH MOVEMENT

The Fuller School of World Missions' founding dean, Donald McGavran, introduced a new theory. The term describing the idea of missionary endeavor was replaced with the word "missional" endeavor. McGavran taught that because individuals are always found in homogeneous ethnic or people groups, therefore "missional" methods that appeal to the unbelieving people groups should be used. He advocated that missionaries should not make a gospel appeal for a response from an individual, but elicit responses from groups of people. The nomenclature change from mission to missional and missiology packaged new content into the meaning.

This new missional theory appealed to unbelieving homogeneous people groups to collectively:

1. Agree to abandon their old religion.

2. Identify with Christ.

3. Claim the Bible as their authority.

4. Claim the church as their religious institution.

It made the mission strategies of the past obsolete. Contrary to this, Jesus said personally and individually to Nicodemus, "You must be born again" (John 3:7). Our Lord was appealing to an individual, not a people group. Jesus was anticipating an individual response, not a group response.

The new theory sounds familiar. It is similar to the unintended consequences that followed the early fourth century AD Roman Emperor Constantine's adoption of the Christian faith for the entire Roman Empire. In effect, Constantine implied that with the stroke of a brush the empire would be colored Christian. But history has taught us that vital spiritual fruit from a group being Christianized cannot be equated with individuals, one by one, being born again. After Constantine's edict, Christianity became entangled and interwoven with the empire's existing secular and occultic beliefs and holidays spawning confusion which remains with us to this day.

Arnold L. Cook earned a doctor of missiology degree from Fuller Seminary studying under McGavran. Cook sums up McGavran by saying, "Men like to become Christians without crossing racial, linguistic, or class barriers."[2]

Unfortunate changes continued at Fuller when C. Peter Wagner became a professor of Church Growth in 1971. During his thirty-year tenure at the Fuller School of World Mission, which ended in 2001, he had the opportunity to teach students from many countries of the world. The school continued to become multi-denominational with students from seventy countries and more than 100 denominations, which required a lot of accommodation.

Interest in the social sciences exploded. What had been helpful in assisting missionaries to understand their target culture now became primary. The way for many pastors to grow their churches was by using social programs. For over three decades C. Peter Wagner has served as an advisor to mission-oriented ministries, committees, organizations, and global Holy Spirit movements. Teaching the immensely popular Signs and Wonders class with John Wimber catapulted Wagner as an outspoken advocate of praying for the sick, spiritual mapping, identification repentance, the role of apostles and prophets in the church today, spiritual warfare, demonic deliverance, and sinless perfection.

Wagner said his mentor in church growth research was McGavran. He said,

> "For years I have had the singular privilege of carrying the title, Donald A. McGavran, Professor of Church Growth. One of the most basic lessons I learned from McGavran was that the best way to discover what makes a church grow is to study growing churches. I

noticed that the churches that seemed to grow most rapidly were, for the most part, those that outwardly featured the immediate present-day supernatural ministry of the Holy Spirit."[3]

However, Wimber was his mentor for helping him make a paradigm shift into what he called spiritual principles of church growth.

> "This began my second season of research, focusing first of all on the relationship between supernatural signs and wonders, church growth, and then prayer and spiritual warfare."[4]

In his book, *Historical Drift*, Dr. Arnold Cook encouraged his readers to return to biblical essentials. He spoke of a weakened commitment to the authority of Scripture, which fails to follow a five-point test of a high view of clearly teaching the Word. Those points were:

1. "Go with the clarity of Scripture, not with obscure passages.

2. Listen for the Spirit of Scripture on any given issue.

3. Let Scripture interpret Scripture to find consensus and harmony.

4. Follow Christ's handling of Scripture, e.g., referencing issues back to the Old Testament, especially Genesis.

5. Hold tenaciously to a literal interpretation of Scripture wherever possible."[5]

It is a weakened view of Scripture that opened the door to the present humanistic Emergent Movement that has weakened the faith of many today.

FROM WORLD MISSION TO INTERCULTURAL STUDIES

As Fuller Seminary continued its drift, it increasingly became the nurturing place of the postmodern church growth and Emerging Movements. World mission became missiology. The School of World Mission became the School of Intercultural Studies. The new paradigm morphed from World Mission (singular) to the studies (plural) of culture, anthropology, sociology, and psychology; with the objective of becoming postmodern and seeker friendly in order to better communicate with the postmodern homogeneous groups. Accommodation became the oil that lubricated the process.

It is important to note that Jesus gave a singular mission to His church. It is not the great commissions. It is not plural. It is the Great Commission. In the Matthew 28:19-20 passage, the imperative verb is the Greek word *matheteusate* which is translated "make disciples." That imperative is supported by three participles: going, baptizing, and teaching. The Great Commission is to make disciples of Jesus by going, baptizing, and teaching the new disciples all that Jesus redemptively accomplished and taught.

So by contrast to the new paradigm, the old traditional paradigm for world mission is the Bible's Great Commission which heralded the simple message: "For all have sinned and come short of the glory of God" (Romans 3:23). "For the wages of sin is death; but the gift of God is eternal life through Jesus Christ our Lord" (Romans 6:23). "That if you confess with your mouth the Lord Jesus, and believe in your heart that God has raised Him from the dead, you will be saved. For with the heart one believes unto righteousness; and with the mouth confession is made unto salvation" (Romans 10:9-10 NKJV). "You must be born again" (John 3:7). From the beginning, the oil that lubricated this process was, is, and always will be the Holy Spirit. The twin sufficiencies are the inerrant Word and the Holy Spirit.

Otto Helwig had the opportunity to see the results of those who had minimized the effectiveness of mission evangelism by teaching that the Bible contains truth, instead of teaching that the Bible is inerrant truth. Helwig served as a missionary in Iran. When he shared Christ with students and emphasized the importance of reading the Bible so they could understand the doctrines of sin and grace; students asked, "How do you know the verses are true since our teacher says the Bible has mistakes?"[6]

To students already seeking to discredit Christianity, the "so called" errors in historical matters and science were all that many students needed to keep them from searching the Bible for truth. Why learn from a source book that is unreliable?

The new evangelical concept of evangelism has placed man's social needs first and above spiritual needs. This has replaced the primary need for sinners to hear the good news of the saving grace of Jesus Christ. The primacy of social reformation rather than spiritual reformation is the postmodern Emerging church missiology. The humanistic grand and noble presumption is that man's basic need is material and secular rather than spiritual and eternal.

The theology of this philosophy rejects the sinfulness of man in favor of the corporate physical needs of society. The Purpose Driven model ushers in a new reformation based on behavior rather than beliefs; deeds rather than creeds; and what the church does rather than what the church believes.

No one denies the need for social reforms. But to suggest that the church replace the gospel message of salvation through Christ alone with social, economic, and political reform is a shameful departure from the clear teaching of the Word of God. To suggest that all Evangelicals, mainline Protestant liberals, Catholics, Muslims, Hindus, Confucians, and people of all faiths be joined together to solve our world's social problems would leave a world populated with unredeemed sinners.

The great social reformations of the past have come through spiritual awakenings where the gospel of God's redeeming grace, through Jesus Christ, was the central theme. Evangelism which centers on social reforms is not true to the Great Commission of our Lord when He said,

> "Go therefore, and teach all nations, baptizing them in the name of the Father, and of the Son, and of the Holy Ghost: teaching them to observe all things whatsoever I have commanded you: and, lo, I am with you always, even unto the end of the world" (Matthew 28:19-20).

Evangelism that ignores the fact of sin in every individual life, while decrying the corporate sins of society, is an exercise in sociology and not the proclamation of the gospel. Humanitarian concerns are compatible with the thinking of an unregenerate world. The preaching of the cross, with all its implications, is utter foolishness to all but those who believe. Lose sight of man's spiritual need and all is lost. The need of all humanity is acutely personal and the gospel tells man where his need can be met. Omit this and a man remains "dead in trespasses and sins" (Ephesians 2:1) and without hope in a godless world.

C. Peter Wagner disclosed errors in his church growth thinking at a meeting of the Evangelical Theological Society. That interdenominational organization was founded in 1949 as a professional society of scholars, educators, and pastors with the stated purpose of serving Jesus and His church by advancing evangelical scholarship. Belief in the inerrancy of the Scriptures has been foundational in the ETS from its inception.

At a society meeting held at Fuller Seminary on November 9, 1974, Wagner's comments were transcribed from a recording in a panel discussion saying,

> "I would like to come back, if I could, to the question of methodology... I think that it is the really crucial issue for the Evangelical Theological Society. I recall the days when the ETS was first formed, and as I recall, the statement of faith consisted of one line—the Bible is the infallible Word of God. Is that not right?"

At this moment, Amaya [another ETS member] corrected Wagner saying, "the inerrant Word of God."

Then Wagner continued,

"And it seems to me that at that time, two decades ago, this question of methodology never even could have come up in the ETS."[7]

Wagner continued,

"However, that even the question of methodology is now able to be raised in this room is because of the very success in recent years, quite recent years, of the Christian world mission and the emergence of full-blooded Christian people, born again by the Spirit of God, but who look at the Scriptures from a completely different worldview from the worldview of us in the West and of those who formed the ETS, who were almost virtually monoculture, and who assumed that Christian theology was the Western expression of theology … and I think that most of us, at least in our generation, were trained through seminary to think in these categories, so that Western theology became the touchstone against which everything else was measured. And we missionaries at that time engaged in a little bit of theological imperialism.

"Well, I think that we evangelicals need to be aware that we are actually living in the 1970s, in a fantastically changing age, an age in which there are fantastic changes in a perspective on theology, that by the time the 1970s are over, if anyone talks of theology in the singular —he might just as well not talk about theology, because we need to see, we need to learn to see theology in a plural sense….

"Theology, seems to me, is an effect, now that we see it in a contemporary world, nothing more or less, than an attempt to give answers from the basis of God's revelation to questions that people are asking. The point is that different people ask different kinds of questions. And for every different kind of people, theology has to take different forms. Not only that, but there are a certain set of questions that were asked in the New Testament times, in the first century, in which the revelation of God itself had to take certain forms.

"And to apply the revelation of God—which I can even sign the ETS statement that the Bible is infallible, or inerrant Word of God, and I buy all those adjectives because—because when it was contextualized in the first century situations that's exactly what the revelation of God was.

"But if we don't realize that the Bible was … is contextualized in the Greek or Roman civilization, or the Hebrew before that, and understand that it must be de-contextualized in order to answer contemporary questions, and go back to that from the point of view of the contemporary questions, I don't— I don't think that we as evangelicals are going to be exactly what Richard Quebedeaux [religious cultural writer] said we are going to be. Again, we are just going to be taking up the rear and moving where people lead us rather than being avantgarde in this thing. There is no reason why evangelicals have to bring up the rear."[8]

Fuller Seminary has adopted a more mystical approach, influenced by Wagner and his prodigy, in church growth programs. There has been a leaning towards signs and wonders and the "touchy feely" rather than simply teaching the Word as central and essential to evangelism. New courses train students in the practice of these signs and wonders and other altered state-of-mind practices, coming from what is called ancient-modern, which was influenced by ancient Hinduism and earliest ascetic Christian mystics. New terms are being used such as the supernatural doctrines of the Manifested Sons of God, sinless perfection, third wave of spiritual power, restoration of the offices of apostles and prophets, and dominionism. In some schools these teachings are replacing the simple teaching of the Word of God.

Fuller Seminary became a sad case study of what happens when an institution not only resists, but refuses to embrace the inerrancy of the written Word of God. It opened the door for a radical paradigm shift away from evangelicalism. It destroyed the initial vision of Charles Fuller for his seminary which, on this slippery slope, became the nesting place of the new evangelicalism movement that is accommodating the new world order of the coming Antichrist. It is indeed aberrant!

On August 31, 1977, Harold Lindsell wrote to Chris Crossan, whose father was a close friend of Dan Fuller, saying,

> "I remember your father very well. I know of his friendship with Dan Fuller. I think your situation at the seminary is most unfortunate. I do not know that anything can be done about it without radical surgery taking place. If the seminary were to return to its former position, it would have to remove from its faculty a substantial number of people. It would be a traumatic experience and it would require some drastic reorganization starting with the office of the president and going down to the last faculty member."[9]

While Fuller Seminary was liberalizing and on the new evangelical slippery slope downward away from a belief in inerrancy of the Bible, a wide variety of historic rooted evangelicals were mounting a summit to make a public and monumental statement affirming belief in the one and only Creator God who supernaturally communicated, without error, to mankind.

THE CHICAGO STATEMENT ON BIBLICAL INERRANCY— BELIEVING IN IT

The "Chicago Statement on Biblical Inerrancy" was produced at an international summit conference of evangelical leaders sponsored by the International Council on Biblical Inerrancy and held at the Hyatt Regency O'Hare in Chicago in the fall of 1978. Detailed articles of affirmation and denial were agreed upon in addition to a preface and the following, referred to as, "A Short Statement."

> "1. God, who is Himself truth and speaks truth only, has inspired Holy Scripture in order thereby to reveal Himself to lost mankind through Jesus Christ as Creator and Lord, Redeemer, and Judge. Holy Scripture is God's witness to Himself.

"2. Holy Scripture, being God's own Word, written by men prepared and superintended by His Spirit, is of infallible divine authority in all matters upon which it touches: it is to be believed, as God's instruction, in all that it affirms: obeyed, as God's command, in all that it requires; embraced, as God's pledge, in all that it promises.

"3. The Holy Spirit, Scripture's divine Author, both authenticates it to us by His inward witness and opens our minds to understand its meaning.

"4. Being wholly and verbally God-given, Scripture is without error or fault in all its teaching, no less in what it states about God's acts in creation, about the events of world history, and about its own literary origins under God, than in its witness to God's saving grace in individual lives.

"5. The authority of Scripture is inescapably impaired if this total divine inerrancy is in any way limited or disregarded, or made relative to a view of truth contrary to the Bible's own; and such lapses bring serious loss to both the individual and the Church."[10]

The content of The Chicago Statement was published by Carl F.H. Henry.

The Chicago Statement was signed by nearly 300 noted evangelical scholars, including James Boice, Norman L. Geisler, John Gerstner, Carl F.H. Henry, Kenneth Kantzer, Harold Lindsell, John Warwick Montgomery, Roger Nicole, J.I. Packer, Robert Preus, Earl Radmacher, Francis A. Schaeffer, R.C. Sproul, and John Wenham.

EMERGING CHURCH MOVEMENT IN FULLER SEMINARY

Edmund (Eddie) Gibbs was appointed to the Fuller faculty in 1984 and is senior professor of Church Growth in the School of Intercultural Studies. Previously he had worked on six Billy Graham Crusades in the United Kingdom, and he has authored over a dozen books. Gibbs is a strong advocate for the positive study of postmodernism and Emerging churches which is expressed in the Brehm

Center for Worship, Theology, and Arts located on the seminary campus. The Brehm Center boasts of hosting Brian McLaren and other prominent leaders of the postmodern Emerging Church Movement.

Ryan K. Bolger, a Fuller associate professor of Church in Contemporary Culture, has collaborated with Gibbs in a book titled, *Emerging Churches*. The authors offer this definition:

> "Emerging churches are communities that practice the way of Jesus within postmodern cultures."[11]

The word "culture" appears to be the key word in their vocabulary. For these leaders, the word "culture" is a driving force to make the gospel acceptable in the postmodern twenty-first century. However, whenever culture shapes the gospel, truth inevitably diminishes with the culture's strong embrace.

Gibbs and Bolger continue,

> "It is not that postmodern people do not want truth per se, but whose truth?"[12]

In their view, the experience of community determines truth. It is a collective consensus that starts with man rather than with the Bible.

These authors tell us,

> "Emerging churches became increasingly dissatisfied with using the Bible in a modern way … Emerging church leaders are under no compulsion to stand up and fight for truth … Standing up for the fight or fighting the culture wars has no appeal to Emerging church leaders."[13]

The apostle Paul sees it differently when he says, "The church of the living God, the pillar and ground of the truth" (1 Timothy 3:15). The root problem is that Emerging church practitioners deny the reality of God-ordained absolute truth that is uniformly sovereign over all cultures.

POSTMODERNISM AND THE HERMENEUTICS OF DECONSTRUCTION

Dan Kimball, another Emergent church author, writes,

> "Since language is constantly shifting according to postmodern thought, there can be many interpretations of a [Bible] word or text, not just one meaning ... biblical terms like 'gospel' and 'Armageddon' need to be deconstructed and redefined."[14]

Deconstruction is a postmodern philosophical literary approach that utilizes the hermeneutics of suspicion. This approach hunts down tensions and inconsistencies in the text; postmodernists believe all literary texts, as well as Bible texts, have them. The purpose is to deconstruct or dismantle the text. This generates new insights that probably will contradict the actual text.

This concept is built upon the triadic dialectic of nineteenth-century German philosopher, Georg Wilhelm Friedrich Hegel. In his dialectic he started with a thesis. In opposition to the thesis was antithesis. It was resolved with a synthesis. Contradictions are most acceptable. Karl Marx and Communism gained much traction from this.

Gibbs and Bolger continue,

> "One must dismantle the old, clear the way, before one builds something new ... is what the apostle Paul really meant after being deconstructed and reconstructed ... If we state the agenda of Paul's mission in modern terms, it seems clear that he was building an international, anti-imperial, alternative society embodied in local communities."[15]

The authors do not show us precisely where in the New Testament Paul the apostle was deconstructed and reconstructed.

Gibbs and Bolger said,

> "The Bible presents a fascinating collection of stories that together make up a big story that stretches from before creation to beyond

the end of time … God communicates with humanity, not primarily through the form of propositions but through a story illustrated by parables, riddles, sayings, and folk songs. It is a story that is still unfolding and in which we have a part of time."[16]

This viewpoint is a complete undermining of the authority and inerrancy of Scripture by two Fuller Seminary church growth professors. They do not believe propositional truth is a primary form of God's communication and they do not include predictive prophecy as a way in which God communicates with humanity.

Gibbs and Bolger said,

"How did Emerging churches come to emphasize the gospel of the kingdom? It began as a change of focus from the Epistles to the Gospels as a way to understand Jesus more profoundly."[17]

"Emerging churches, in their attempt to resemble the kingdom, avoid all types of control in their leadership formation. The church needs to operate as a consensual process in which all have a say in influencing outcomes … Emerging churches share the conviction that leadership must not be invested in one person … What do we mean by 'the way of Jesus'? Simply the life of Jesus and His engagement with culture, as embodied in community and given verbal expression in the Sermon on the Mount, is prescriptive for Christians…. We don't dismiss the cross; it is a central part. But the good news is not that He died but that the kingdom has come … The idea of a kingdom focus instead of a church focus is a huge paradigm shift, one that does not come easy."[18]

Jesus promised His disciples, "I will build My church" (Matthew 16:18). Nowhere in the four Gospels do we see Jesus make a huge paradigm shift from His church to either the kingdom of heaven or the kingdom of God. The kingdom and the church are not interchangeable entities in the New Testament. The good news is not that the kingdom has come but that Jesus died on the cross for our sins and rose from the dead on the third day. "The Son of man came not to be ministered unto, but to minister, and to give His life a ransom for many" (Mark 10:45). Without the full redemptive work of Jesus there is no kingdom good news! Jesus did not engage culture, He engaged sinners who needed to be ransomed. The Sermon on the Mount without the full and completed redemptive work of Jesus is empty.

The New Testament is not a smorgasbord wherein the reader can simply choose to shift emphasis from the Epistles to the Gospels. When inerrancy is abandoned, we end up with a smorgasbord. The New Testament pattern follows the life, death, resurrection, ascension, and second coming of Jesus; and His teachings in the Gospels. This is followed by the recorded practice of the early church in the book of Acts, followed by what was taught in the Epistles.

The New Testament practice and teaching were under the direction of the Holy Spirit. There is unity and harmony. This is not the Gospels equaling a thesis; the Epistles equaling antithesis; and then, lo and behold, a new synthesis, namely, the postmodern Emergent church focusing only on the kingdom and the Sermon on the Mount.

Gibbs and Bolger said,

> "The focus of the Emerging churches on the gospel of the kingdom as distinct from a gospel of salvation has produced a new ecclesiology."[19]

Again we see the outworking of the Hegelian triadic dialectic. Did Jesus really want His Jewish listeners to conclude that there is no gospel of salvation in His teaching on the kingdom of God and the kingdom of heaven? One can really play fast and loose with the Bible when one believes that God can breathe error in His communication to man. It is a terrible indictment against God.

HUMANIST PETER DRUCKER—MENTOR FOR CHURCHES

Fuller Seminary Professor Gibbs has been numbered among a growing company of church leaders who have been highly influenced by

Peter Drucker, who in his latter years liked to refer to himself as a social ecologist. Drucker has led religious leaders into a cooperative relationship between the private (corporate) sector, the governmental sector, and what is called the social sector. Drucker does not start with the Bible; nor does he even attempt to bring the Bible into his model.

Peter Drucker (1909-2005) was born in Vienna, Austria. In 1933 he immigrated to England, and the following year was impacted by the legendary Cambridge liberal economist, John Maynard Keynes. Harvard economist, Joseph Schumpeter, influenced Drucker's thinking on innovation and entrepreneurship.

Drucker wrote philosophical essays about the nature of man and society, which demonstrated he was a social philosopher as well as a management authority. He believed that, unlike the physical universe, the social universe has no natural laws. This included religions. Therefore, religions were subject to continuous change in his systems theory. Drucker believed this meant that man and society are continuously evolving and man can harness or accomplish a direct change in order to speed up his evolution.

In his book, *The Future of Industrial Man,*[20] Drucker announced the most important insight that many people are not aware of yet. It is the inevitable failure of not only absolutism, but also rationalism. Hence, Drucker's view of the basic nature of man is derived not from absolute truth, but rather from the ever-changing social sciences.

Paul warns Timothy,

> "Keep that which is committed to your trust, avoiding profane and vain babblings, and oppositions of science falsely so called: which some professing have erred concerning the faith" (1 Timothy 6:20-21).

Drucker's chief accomplishment has been to blend social sciences with economic theory. He created a new view of the nature of man, namely, a postmodern economic man, which is incomplete without community. He originally conceived of the corporation as an organism to meet man's need for community.

In Drucker's General Systems Theory, man is thought to be evolving to the collective state of organism. Fifty years ago he thought that the large business enterprise would serve as the community for the individual. He envisioned the corporation as the social institution, far superior to government in providing a retirement income, health care, education, childcare, and other fringe benefits—corporate welfare would replace government welfare.

But it did not work. So he found another system which is "a separate and new social order." He envisioned that the mission of the social sector was to change lives. It was to accomplish this mission by addressing the needs of the spirit, mind, and body of individuals, the community, and society. The social sector would also provide a significant sphere for individuals and corporations to practice effective and responsible citizenship.

This is the language description of humanistic sociology. It is not redemptive language that is God-centered. Drucker is pragmatically horizontal; man and society. There is no vertical where the gracious holy Creator redemptively reaches down to His sinful rebellious creatures. Drucker is man-centered.

The social sector has been Drucker's main interest, especially the megachurches. These three sectors of society—corporate, governmental, and religious—have been identified by Drucker as a three-legged stool. The religious sector was pragmatically needed to bring stability to the other two sectors because a two-legged stool is unstable.

In the first half of the twentieth century, Peter Drucker saw the corporation as the entity that provided a healthy, socialized community. But the corporation failed in that specific endeavor. In the mid-sixties and remainder of the century, Drucker discovered that the megachurch would suitably fit as the answer to providing a healthy, socialized community. Prior to that, Drucker had no particular interest in the church regardless of its size.

Suddenly it occurred to him that the community's need for support with life struggles, retirement issues, and services that create a healthy community could best be realized through the church. The bigger the better; and the megachurch had the ability to get things done. Such a church could incorporate the necessary means, with a strong benevolent base and vast volunteer army, to make a happy and caring socialized community.

Drucker was intrigued with the megachurch from a specifically sociological and economical point of view. Any megachurch would do just fine; as long as it was pragmatically meeting the felt needs of people. The spiritual beliefs of a particular megachurch were really not a concern for Drucker. So it made sense to him that the ambiance of the megachurch should be, above all, seeker friendly. After all, his personal pursuit of spirituality was fulfilled in Kierkegaard and Eastern mysticism.

The downhill ride on the slippery slope picked up more influential people in America and evolved into a most ominous unbiblical Emerging Movement, all of which I will be addressing. For inerrancy believers, it will be shocking and disappointing to discover that there is a connection between this seminary's departure from inerrancy, the corporate humanistic guru, Peter Drucker, the megachurchman, Rick Warren, and the highly deceptive Emerging Church Movement.

Next you'll observe the slippery slope downward where two paths crossed when Peter Drucker and Rick Warren came together. It appeared to be a marriage made in postmodern heaven. New people and new ways were coming out of the Fuller nest. Warren discovered a mentor who could help him grow his church. Drucker found a protégé who could be molded into a model leader that would propel the Purpose Driven megachurch movement forward. Or, from the New Testament perspective, was it a slippery slope downward?

CHAPTER EIGHT FOOTNOTES

1 George M. Marsden, *Reforming Fundamentalism: Fuller Seminary and the New Evangelicalism* (Grand Rapids, MI: Eerdmans, 1995), p. 302.

2 Arnold L. Cook, *Historical Drift* (Camp Hill, PA: WingSpread, 2007), p. 35.

3 C. Peter Wagner, *The New Apostolic Churches* (Ventura, CA: Regal Books, 1998), Introduction.

4 Ibid.

5 Arnold L. Cook, *Historical Drift* (Camp Hill, PA: WingSpread, 2007), p. 61.

6 Otto Helwig, "Inspiration and/or Outreach?" Billy Graham Center Archives, Wheaton, IL. Harold Lindsell Collection 192, Folder 6-20LL, Item 5.

7 C. Peter Wagner, Evangelical Theological Society Meeting held Novemver 9, 1974 at Fuller Seminary. Notes at Billy Graham Center Archives, Wheaton, IL, Harold Lindsell Collection 192, Folder 1-12KK, Item 2.

8 Ibid.

9 Harold Lindsell to Chris Crossan. Letter at Billy Graham Center Archives, Wheaton IL. Harold Lindsell Collection 192, Folder 1-12CC, Item 2.

10 Carl F.H. Henry, *God, Revelation and Authority* (Wheaton, IL: Crossway Books, 1999), Vol. 4, pp. 211-219.

11 Eddie Gibbs and Ryan K. Bolger, *Emerging Churches: Creating Christian Community in Postmodern Cultures* (Grand Rapids, MI: Baker Academic, 2005), excerpted from Donald G. Hocking, *The Emerging Church – Is It Biblical?* (Tustin, CA: HTF Publications), p. 7. Fifty-five pages, including review of Gibbs and Bolger's book and other emergent writers.

12 Ibid.

13 Ibid.

14 Dan Kimball, *The Emerging Church* (Grand Rapids, MI: Zondervan, 2003), p. 175.

15 Eddie Gibbs & Ryan K. Bolger, *Emerging Churches* (Baker, 2005), p. 28.

16 Ibid, p. 70.

17 Ibid, p. 48.

18 Ibid pp. 192, 205, 44, 54, 62.

19 Ibid p. 91.

20 Peter F. Drucker, *The Future of Industrial Man* (Piscataway, NJ: Transaction Publishers, 1995).

THE SLIPPERY SLOPE

The apostle Paul said that his apostolic authority came,

"... not of men, neither by man, but by Jesus Christ, and God the Father, who raised Him from the dead ... I marvel that you are so soon removed from Him that called you into the grace of Christ unto another gospel" (Galatians 1:1, 6).

Harold Lindsell and Francis Schaeffer both warned that when any Christian institution leaves their position on the inerrancy of Scripture, they seldom return to their original position. Paul saw another gospel emerge in his own lifetime. In my lifetime, I've witnessed an alarming abandonment of the doctrine of inerrancy. The downhill ride on the slippery slope has taken us into the valley of another gospel that is emerging before our eyes.

RICK WARREN AND PETER DRUCKER

Two very important American personalities came together on this slippery slope: Rick Warren and Peter Drucker. They appeared from surprisingly diverse backgrounds. Worlds apart in origin, their meeting of the minds laid a subtle groundwork for a one-world mentality.

Richard Duane Warren, born January 28, 1954, probably needs no introduction. Rick Warren is the founding pastor of Saddleback Church, Lake Forest, California. It is considered one of the ten largest churches in this country. He authored two highly read books, *The Purpose Driven Life* and *The Purpose Driven Church*. Warren graduated from California Baptist University, Riverside, California. He earned a Master of Divinity degree from the Southern Baptist school, Southwestern Theological Seminary, Fort Worth, Texas. He earned his doctor of ministry degree under C. Peter Wagner at Fuller Seminary. Warren named Billy Graham and Peter Drucker as his two mentors. Warren is labeled and considers himself an evangelical; and he has immense influence.

Rick Warren credits the spectacular numerical growth of his Saddleback Church to his Purpose Driven model, an organizational and marketing strategy primarily inspired by Peter Drucker.

In corporate America, Peter F. Drucker (1909-2005) was the foremost twentieth century management guru. He achieved fame and fortune as a consultant to numerous Fortune 500 companies, including General Motors and General Electric. His goal was to obtain optimum community in America wherein an individual's needs are met from the cradle to the grave. Along the way a person's worth is determined by a calculated system of accountability which assigns value that measures achievement.

Drucker was completely committed to the existential philosophy of Danish writer Kierkegaard. Drucker was so engrossed with the Dane that he learned the Danish language in order to better absorb Kierkegaard's philosophy. The platform of Kierkegaard's thinking was built solidly on the writings of German philosopher, Immanuel Kant.

Thus, Drucker philosophically bought into and built upon Kant's two-story view of reality. The lower story involves the five senses in space, time, and history. The upper story is where existential faith resides which has nothing to do with space, time, and history. In this belief structure, Christ's virgin birth, miracles, resurrection, and second coming belong only to an upper story mystical faith because they did not happen, nor could they happen, in the lower story of space, time, and history.

Drucker was also fascinated with Eastern mysticism. He was a brilliant man with a widely accommodating eclectic belief system. Driven by social engineering, Drucker pragmatically viewed the megachurch as the best sociological change agent for the community's greater good.

Drucker's quest for optimum sociological community that would impact the entire nation led him to focus on the megachurch phenomena. Warren was the one who first sought out Drucker. Drucker quickly eyed the high achieving young pastor as a protégé he could coach for his corporate systems management paradigm. Warren was the promising young talent that would be molded into Drucker's paradigm leadership image, all for the good of the country and even the world. Drucker and Warren bonded professionally and personally. Warren's Fuller Seminary studies expanded his borders of accommodation. Warren publicly boasted that Drucker had been his mentor for over twenty years.[1]

Rick Warren believed that he was on the crest of the wave of a new reformation. While the first reformation was about beliefs, Warren saw that this new one was about behavior. Hearts pounded in the chests of new evangelical postmodern Emergent churchmen as they fled from the New Testament epistles to the primacy of the Sermon on the Mount. The diverse threads in the fabric of new evangelicalism were being sown tightly together. Fuller Seminary, as an educational institution, had provided a nest for aberrant practice.

The Purpose Driven model originated from some radical philosophies about the nature of man and societies. This model is bent on transforming the nature of man and society. It was reduced to its lowest common denominator in order to carry out the most widespread worldwide appeal. The Warren message remains uniform and prefabricated to the point where Saddleback Church reports that thousands of pastors weekly download Warren's canned Purpose Driven sermons from his website to preach and promote their church growth hopes. This is preceded by the protégé pastors having every member of their church buy and read *The Purpose Driven Church*, accompanied by a congregation-wide forty-day march through the Warren philosophy for church growth.

What lies behind the Purpose Driven philosophy? It is primarily fueled by what Warren learned from Drucker and Fuller Seminary. The new evangelical seminary trains men and women to take a traditional church and mold it into a postmodern accommodating mindset that will reach a postmodern culture.

Humanists have developed and driven the definition of postmodernism; and sadly, many Christian churchmen have uncritically bought in. Postmodernism is a philosophy that says much of what we know, epistemologically, is shaped by the culture in which we live, and is controlled by emotions, aesthetics, and heritage. In fact, postmodernism can only be intelligently held as part of a common tradition without any overbearing claims to being true or right. Postmodernists reject absolutes and propositional statements of truth.

Drucker believed that the leap of faith for the traditional church meant it must become a postmodern church to accommodate and reach the postmodern culture. The culture was seeking something; but not absolute answers based upon absolute truth. Supposedly the postmodern culture would respond to a seeker friendly postmodern church if such a church would omit heavy Bible content messages from the pastor on Sunday mornings.

Drucker's view of general systems organization and management theory has been rapidly spreading through Christian seminaries this past decade. The old traditional model was New Testament based—with expository preaching and teaching from the Bible about the nature of God, man, sin, repentance, judgment, and God's plan of redemption—relying upon the power and ministry of the Holy Spirit. The new model has fixated on the megachurch as being the sociological change agent wherein man transforms himself by addressing felt needs in a community and society.

The Purpose Driven model comes straight out of the business world. It appeals to a wider audience with its common sense, seeker friendly, soft-sell approach. The Purpose Driven model has success-fully integrated Drucker's systems theory into postmodern church theology and practice worldwide.

It is not surprising that the philosophical foundation of General Systems Theory would become part of the new church model. The evolutional aspect of systems theory easily corresponds with this notion that the bride of Christ must perfect herself on earth structurally, as well as spiritually, before Jesus returns. This system works hand in hand with computer system models and is applied to human systems development as a way to measure a person's growth.

As a result, state-of-the-art methods from the computer age are becoming an indispensable part of postmodern Christianity for completing the Great Commission. A parallel doctrine teaches that the historical church was grossly inefficient, and now that we have these high tech tools we can expedite building the kingdom of God.

A new pragmatism has emerged in church circles. As long as an activity purports to produce spiritual fruit, it can be adopted as an acceptable tool for furthering the kingdom of God on earth. If there is a measure of success, then marketing such programs is acceptable since the end justifies the means.

Financial assistance is available for producing successful results from the Dallas-based Leadership Network, a Drucker inspired group. But what does James 4:4 teach?

> "Do you not know that friendship with the world is enmity with God? Whosoever therefore will be a friend of the world is the enemy of God." (NKJV)

The secular Lilly Foundation granted funds to be used at Rick Warren's extension campus of the Golden Gate Seminary, located on the Saddleback Church grounds. The grant funded a computer system to track the worldwide growth of all Purpose Driven protégé church participants. The previous generation justified a similar type of activity when it integrated psychology and sociology into theology. This has made modern management theories and techniques originating from the humanistic social sciences more acceptable in today's church growth craze.

I pray that the Holy Spirit will help us discern the issues and hold firmly to the centrality of teaching the truth from God's Holy Word and allow the Lord to build His church. God's revealed and inerrant Word must remain our sole guide. We must know that there are values and practices that are right and those that are wrong. We must remember that God has given us His Word by which we can measure truth. Just as Eve was deceived, so can any one of us. Satan is ever so subtle with distorting truth. The slippery slope includes merchandising church growth, an emerging one-world church, and a new world order.

RESISTANCE TO NEW EVANGELICALISM

Even as evangelicalism was sliding down the slippery slope into new evangelicalism, the Lord was giving birth to a movement that would be founded upon the twin sufficiencies: the sufficiency of the inerrant Bible and the sufficiency of the work and ministry of the Holy Spirit. This work of the Lord began during the mid 1960s in Calvary Chapel, Orange County, California, pastored by Chuck Smith.

The Emergent Church Movement, Purpose Driven model promoters, and associated change agents have been attempting to penetrate into and identify with the Calvary Chapel Movement of churches.

Calvary Chapel has been a God-blessed phenomenon originating from a true outpouring of the Holy Spirit among the hippies. That outpouring was known as the Jesus People Movement, a marvelous work of God that defies human explanation. We witnessed unchurched young people coming to hear the Word of God simply taught simply, verse by verse, chapter by chapter from Genesis through Revelation.

This was a movement of the Holy Spirit through faithful teaching from the Bible. There were no marketing strategies. These spiritually hungry kids heard by word of mouth that the Lord was graciously changing lives. They simply came and experienced the loving work of the Lord. Hippies came by the thousands. They repented of their sins, asked God for forgiveness, accepted Jesus Christ's finished work on the cross as punishment for their sins, and then continued to thirst for a deeper walk with the Lord and an understanding of His inerrant Word. They wanted all that the Holy Spirit would give them. The media dubbed them Jesus People and Jesus Freaks.

Some began to express this work of God with lyrics of praise unto the Lord. It was music that expressed gratitude after having experienced what Jesus called being born again (John 3:3). A new genre of praise and worship songs was born that began to spread across the country into innumerable churches. The traditional church quickly called it contemporary Christian music.

Historically, when you witness a surprising work of God, it is often loosely structured. When you try to find the cause or dynamic behind it, you end up with one surprising answer. It's a marvelous and gracious work of God! It is something you cannot duplicate or make into a marketable product. There is no humanistic key with a manual on how to franchise it. It is God-derived and not the application of some new corporate-tested systems management theory. It is difficult to deal with the many entrepreneurs who are ready to organize what is a true work of God.

This special work of God that the church experienced in the 1960s is something that human hands can't manufacture, and we must allow the Holy Spirit to continue His glorious and miraculous work. When we look at the book of Acts, it is really a record of the consistent inconsistencies of the apostles truly being led by the Holy Spirit. We've been given the ingredients: the inerrant Holy Bible and the Holy Spirit. But the book of Acts does not give us the precise recipe; that would make it all mechanical and faith would not be necessary.

The book of Acts records how Simon, the sorcerer in Samaria, believed and was baptized under Philip's preaching. Peter immediately followed up with those new believers so that through the laying on of hands, they received the Holy Spirit. Simon saw a franchising opportunity. For Simon, here was a style, strategy, event, model, or paradigm that could be duplicated! Simon offered Peter money so that he, Simon, could perform that ministry too. Peter's rebuke could not have been stronger—telling this terribly misguided entrepreneur that his money would perish with him. He needed to repent because his heart was not right in the sight of God (Acts 8:9-24).

There is also the story of the prophet Balaam in Numbers chapters 22-24 and Joshua 24:9-10. A warning of the seriousness of using gifts from God, for making profit in the things of God, is mentioned three times in the New Testament. Balaam is referred to in 2 Peter 2:15, Jude 11, and Revelation 2:14. Sending out His disciples Jesus said,

> "As you go, preach, saying, 'The kingdom of heaven is at hand.' Heal the sick, cleanse the lepers, raise the dead, cast out devils: freely you have received, freely give" (Matthew 10:7-8).

Surely Jesus knew that one day small groups of believers would grow in size to a couple of thousand or more in a single location. Jesus' words, "Freely you have received, freely give," would have to be mightily stretched to include an expanded guideline for the successful megachurchman to include: Write and sell a book on your effective model; hold seminars for potential protégés; design an organizational flow chart; provide a detailed manual for duplication of the model; enforce strict accountability to the mother church; and purge sheep in the protégé's church who are not cheerfully compliant with the newly adopted model's purposes and practices.

Is the centrality of the Word of God and the sovereign, gracious work and ministry of the Holy Spirit missing here?

I remember when a talented group of men wanted to organize Calvary Chapel into a denomination. Some of the concepts they came up with made a lot of sense to the natural man. They proposed to grab hold of the rising star, Calvary Chapel, and ride it to the top of what they diagrammed as a bell curve; to ride its growth to the high point of the curve before the rising star would begin to fade into its memorial stage. This concept is well presented in Arnold Cook's book, *Historical Drift*.[2]

JOHN WIMBER—EMPHASIS UPON SPIRITUAL EXPERIENCE

John R. Wimber (1934-1997) was one of those who wanted changes in the Calvary Chapel Movement. After his conversion to Christ, his spiritual search for church identity led him from the Quakers to a short stay in Calvary Chapel, and then to organizing the Vineyard churches with Ken Gulliksen. Alongside C. Peter Wagner at Fuller Seminary, Wimber taught a very popular class, Signs and Wonders. Through the Charles E. Fuller Institute of Evangelism and Church Growth, Wimber led church growth seminars all over the U.S. and the world. He personally explained to me the Bell Curve concept.

Highly charismatic, Wimber wanted Pastor Chuck Smith to put a greater emphasis on spiritual experiences and the supernatural gifts of the Holy Spirit. Pastor Chuck would not move from his primary commitment to teach chapter by chapter, verse by verse through the Bible with full dependence on the leading of the Holy Spirit. Wimber also tried to convince Pastor Chuck to steer the Calvary Chapel Movement into a formal denomination.

Each year a group of Calvary Chapel pastors would meet for prayer and guidance as they planned for the June Pastors' Conference. It was during the March 1981 two-day planning session at the Twin Peaks Conference Center when Wimber finally realized that Pastor Chuck was adamant and did not want Calvary Chapel to become a denomination. It would remain a fellowship of pastors with a common vision of feeding the flock by teaching through the Bible verse by verse.

Wimber was determined to start a denomination. After the June 1981 Pastors' Conference, Wimber sent a letter to all the Calvary

Chapel pastors inviting them to join him in Morro Bay, California. The intent was to move forward into becoming a denomination. He also held special face-to-face meetings with some of these pastors explaining his plan. Wimber envisioned changes that would take place and accused Pastor Chuck Smith of quenching the Spirit. At that time there were about 350 Calvary Chapel fellowships. About forty of those pastors decided to join John Wimber and Ken Gulliksen in the small group of Vineyard churches.

Tom Stipe, who was at one point in line to assume leadership of the Vineyard Movement, said,

"The most famous thing—or infamous thing—that John [Wimber] ever said to me is [when] we were in Australia in Melbourne and we had begun to share the platform with Paul Cain. And it was as though anything spiritual had disappeared. And John says to me backstage … and we were charging eighty-five bucks a head … he said, 'Man, it's hard to have a Signs and Wonders conference when there aren't any.'"[3]

A few days after the 1981 Pastors' Conference, I called Pastor Chuck and asked if we could plan a conference for the pastors where they would be built up and encouraged in the Word by men who had been serving the Lord for years, men who taught the Bible verse by verse in expository sermons. Chuck asked who I would suggest for speakers. I answered, Nathaniel Van Cleave, J. Edwin Orr, and Armin Gesswein. Gesswein had organized pastor prayer groups and he was part of a surprising work of God in Europe. Pastor Chuck gave the green light.

It was precious to see how the main focus of the Calvary Chapel pastors continued to hold fast to the sufficiency of God's inerrant Word and the sufficiency of the Holy Spirit to provide church growth.

It is certain that men called to serve our Lord can follow either God's way or man's way in the pursuit of church growth. Since it is His church and Jesus said, "I will build My church" (Matthew

16:18), I would encourage young pastors to follow God's way. The failure of one generation to communicate its faith to their children results in the loss of personal experience with a living God. When a church work starts in the Spirit, sadly it can end in the flesh and become a human organization. Over time, it can depart from its original beliefs, purposes, and practices. The result is the loss of real Holy Spirit vitality.

The apostle Paul said,

> "Are you so foolish? Having begun in the Spirit, are you now made perfect by the flesh?" (Galatians 3:3).

CALVARY CHAPEL POSITION LETTER NUMBER ONE

Immediately on August 17, 1981, Pastor Chuck responded to the Wimber episode with the first Calvary Chapel position letter. In it he said,

> "It has been drawn to my attention that some of the pastors feel that I have been guilty of quenching the Spirit of some of the Calvary Chapels or their ministers. We want to assure you that we have no desire to quench the work of the Holy Spirit. I believe that the real power of the church is found in the Holy Spirit working through the Word of God in the lives of the believers in God. I do believe that if you have only the Word of God working in the lives of believers, that you are missing a very vital ingredient. I also feel that if you have the Holy Spirit working in the believers of God without the Word, that you also are missing a very important ingredient.

> "I feel that it is important that we recognize that Calvary Chapels are not another Pentecostal church. If you desire to emphasize the experience aspects of the work of the Holy Spirit, it would probably be well if you would seek an affiliation with Pentecostal churches, Assemblies of God, Foursquare, or Church of God, because they seem to have more experience-oriented type of ministry, where I believe that Calvary Chapel has basically been established by God to fill the broad gap between the Baptist and the Pentecostal churches. We have the Spirit of God working, but the real emphasis is on the solid foundation of

the Word being the basis through which the Spirit works as He confirms the Word with signs following. But, when you reverse the order where the experience and the signs become the primary thrust, then you are moving more toward the Pentecostal position, and you should seriously consider dropping the affiliation or relation with Calvary Chapel, especially dropping the use of the Calvary Chapel name.

"We pray for each of you, that God will guide you in your ministries, and will continue His blessing on your churches and upon your own walk and relation with Him....

Yours in Him, Chuck Smith"[4]

Another failed attempt to promote Calvary Chapel into a new denomination without Chuck Smith's knowledge was called the Christianity Today Project. While Pastor Chuck was out of the country teaching the Word to a group of missionaries, advertising material was sent to the magazine. The plan was to bring pastors to Costa Mesa who were interested in joining a fast-growing, mildly charismatic organization. Interested pastors were asked to write to "Maranatha! Missions Development" for further information. The editor of *Christianity Today* sent back a letter saying that the program did not sound like Pastor Chuck Smith. And it wasn't. The project did not materialize.

CALVARY CHAPEL POSITION LETTER NUMBER TWO

On June 5, 2006, Pastor Chuck Smith responded to the Emerging Church Movement with a second Calvary Chapel position letter. It read,

"The time has come for us to restate the position of Calvary Chapel on a number of issues. We do this because Calvary Chapel has become known to represent a fairly definable entity in its approach to sound biblical teaching and approach to biblical doctrine. It's not that we believe we have the best or only way; it's simply the way we approach God's Word within Calvary Chapel. And likewise, if a different approach is to be taken, then all we ask is that the name Calvary Chapel not be attached to it.

"First of all, Calvary Chapel is not a denomination, but rather a movement. We often receive inquiries as to whether or not Calvary Chapel is a member of some national or international group affiliation. We answer such inquiries with our stated position that each church is independent and has established its own set of bylaws. We are ministers who hold basic common beliefs, and maintain them within a range of practices. We believe that every minister is responsible to Jesus as the Chief Shepherd, and will ultimately answer to Him for his ministry and not to us. We love and respect each other and rejoice with those that rejoice, and weep with those who weep. As with the apostle Paul, we do not feel that we have apprehended that for which we were apprehended, neither are we perfect, but this is what we seek to do—forgetting those things which are behind and reaching for those things that are before, we press toward the mark for the prize of the high calling of God in Christ Jesus.

"Secondly, we hold to the supremacy of Jesus as the head of the body, His church. We look to the Holy Spirit to guide and direct each decision in the building up of the body of Christ. Having begun in the Spirit, we do not seek to be made perfect in the flesh, but seek to continue to be led by the Spirit. We believe that the Bible is the inspired Word of God and is infallible and the final authority for our faith and practice. We believe that God established the model for the church in the book of Acts, and seek to follow that model as much as is possible. We feel that church history is, for the most part, a sad commentary of the failure of men who sought by human genius and resources to perfect that which began in the Spirit. The messages of Jesus to the churches in Revelation 2 and 3 reveal early in the history of the church that those problems that needed to be repented of began to be manifested. So much for church history, but something that we must not simply disregard, we must realize that it shows us so clearly how the enemy has, is, and will continue the attacks upon the church and upon our individual ministries. How our heart grieves for the many who have started the race but have failed to complete it.

"In the book of Acts we see that the activities of the church were described as:

"1. Continuing steadfastly in the apostles' doctrine, which we understand to be a systematic teaching of the Bible.

"2. Fellowship, which we understand to be a loving and caring relationship with each other. As John wrote, 'That which we have seen and heard, we declare unto you, that you may have fellowship with us: and truly our fellowship is with the Father, and His Son Jesus Christ.'

"3. The breaking of bread. This to us is a tangible representation of the unity that we share in Christ for we understand that the bread speaks to us of the body of Christ which was broken for us. As we all eat the bread and it is assimilated into our bodies, we are spiritually united through Jesus with each other in the fact that the bread that is nourishing me and is becoming a part of me is also nourishing you and becoming a part of you. Thus, we are united together in Christ. He dwells in me; He dwells in you.

"4. Prayer. Through prayer we unite our hearts with the heart of God that we might see His will accomplished in the church and throughout the world.

"We believe that when the church will make these four things the major activities of the church, which happened in the book of Acts, the Lord will add daily to the church such as should be saved. Thus, we do not look to the myriad of church growth programs that are being promoted for the building of the church but to Jesus Himself, who said that He would build His church. We do watch as the many programs come and go in which man by his wisdom tries to do the work of God more effectively, but rather than entering into the programs of man, seek to continue to be led by the Spirit of God.

"We realize that the Scriptures warn us of aberrant doctrines that would come into the church, even going so far as to deny our Lord Jesus. Second Peter chapter 2, verse 1 tells us,

> 'But there were false prophets also among the people, even as there shall be false teachers among you, who privately shall bring in damnable heresies, even denying the Lord that bought them, and bring upon themselves swift destruction.'

"Likewise in Jude, verse 4, we read,

> 'For there are certain men crept in unawares, who were before of old ordained to this condemnation, ungodly men, turning the grace of our God into lasciviousness, and denying the only Lord God, and our Lord Jesus Christ.'

"We see a tendency toward this in what is commonly called the Emergent church teachings. Some of the concerns that we have are with the speculations and positions that they are suggesting:

"1. That Jesus is not the only way by which one might be saved. It seems that they are postulating a broader gate and a broader path to heaven, sort of 'all roads lead to heaven.' That good people by every religious persuasion may be received into heaven. We feel that this goes against the plain teaching of the Scriptures and negates the need of the cross for the expiation of our sins. Paul wrote of those men in his letter to the Philippians and called them enemies of the cross of Christ. Jesus said, 'I am the way, the truth and the life, no man can come to the Father but by Me.' This is not relative truth, but absolute truth.

"2. The soft peddling of hell as the destiny for those who reject the salvation offered through Jesus Christ. There are suggestions of universalism in their teaching that all will ultimately be saved.

"3. We have difficulty in their touchy-feely relating to God, where the experience of certain feelings become the criteria for truth rather than the Word of God.

"4. We have great problems with the use of icons to give them a sense of God or the presence of God. If they want to have a tie with the historicity of the church, why not go back to the church in Acts, which seems to be devoid of incense, candles, robes, etc., but was filled with the Spirit.

"5. We do not believe that we should seek to make sinners feel safe and comfortable in church. Is it right for me to speak comfortable words to a man who is going to hell unless he turns from his sin? If I fail to warn him of the consequences of his sin, and he dies and goes to hell, will God require his blood at my hand? When is godly sorrow and conviction of sin such a wrong thing?

"6. Should we seek to condone what God has condemned, such as the homosexual lifestyle? Should we tell them that their problem is a genetic disorder rather than a blatant sin that God condemns over and over in the Bible? How long before they tell us that they have discovered that rapists, pedophiles, and adulterers have a genetic disorder and need to be understood rather than condemned?

"7. Should we look to Eastern religions with their practices of meditation through Yoga and special breathing techniques or repeating a mantra to hear God speak to us? If this is needed to enhance our communication with God, why do you suppose that God did not give us implicit instructions in the Scriptures to give us methods to hear His voice? Is it the position of my body or my heart that helps me to communicate with Him?

"8. The great confusion that exists in the divergent positions of the Emergent church results from their challenging the final authority of the Scriptures. When you no longer have a final authority, then everyone's ideas become as valid as the next person's, and it cannot help but end in total confusion and contradictions.

"There are those who say that [the] Emergent Movement has some good points, but so does a porcupine. You are better off if you don't get too close!

"So, let us not turn to our own understanding, but rather return to our own first love; and teach that the Bible is indeed the true Word of God; and teach it in its entirety; nothing less and nothing more.

Chuck Smith"[5]

The heretical problems with the Emergent or Emerging Church Movement have been analyzed by D.A. Carson, Robert R. Congdon, R. Scott Smith, and J. David Winscott.[6] The full doctrinal distinctives of the Calvary Chapel movement can be found in the book, *Calvary Chapel Distinctives*.[7]

What does the church of Jesus Christ look like when it becomes postmodern, Drucker-structured, Purpose Driven, and Emerging-minded? Let's take a look.

CHAPTER NINE FOOTNOTES

1 Rick Warren, interview held during the Biannual Faith Angle Conference on Religion, Politics and Public Life, Key West, Florida, May 2005. www.pewforum.org/Christian/Evangelical-Protestant-Churches/Myths-of-the-Modern-Megachurch.aspx.

2 Arnold L. Cook, *Historical Drift* (Camp Hill, PA: WingSpread, 2007).

3 Charles E. Fromm, "Textual Communities and New Song in the Multimedia Age: The Routinization of Charisma in the Jesus Movement," (Thesis presented to Fuller School of Intercultural Studies, Fuller Theological Seminary, Fuller 2006), p. 283.

4 Chuck Smith, letter sent to all Calvary Chapel pastors, July 17, 1981.

5 Chuck Smith, letter distributed in the Calvary Chapel Pastors' Conference folders, June 5, 2006.

6 D.A. Carson, *Becoming Conversant with the Emerging Church: Understanding a Movement and Its Implications* (Grand Rapids, MI: Zondervan, 2005); Robert R. Congdon, *The European Union and the Supra-Religion* (Longwood, FL: Xulon Press, 2007); R. Scott Smith, *Truth and the New Kind of Christian: The Emerging Effects of Postmodernism in the Church* (Wheaton, IL: Crossway Books, 2005); J. David Winscott, *From Which Well Are You Drinking?* (Santa Ana, CA: Calvary Chapel Outreach Fellowship, 2007).

7 Chuck Smith, *Calvary Chapel Distinctives* (Costa Mesa, CA: The Word for Today, 2000).

THE PURPOSE DRIVEN EMERGENT CHURCH

The Emergent Church Movement embodies a shared commitment to being postmodern in order to reach the postmodern culture. That movement certainly is not interested in advocating, let alone defending, the inerrancy of the Bible. The movement is diverse with a variety of models for a local church.

These models include the Bill Hybels seeker sensitive model at Willow Creek; Randy Frazee's Connecting Church; Robert Lewis and the Church of Irresistible Influence; and the Perimeter Church of Atlanta. The list grows. Because of modern technology, many are now expanding their influence with satellite locations in neighboring communities and distant states through the use of jumbo video screens. The pastor is seen on the big screen and is accompanied by live music at the satellite location. Nevertheless, harnessing technology can certainly be used in a Christ honoring way.

SECOND GENERATION CHUCK SMITH JR.
INTO EMERGING CHURCH

Chuck Smith Jr. has nested in the Emerging Church Movement and has been very attracted to Rick Warren and the Leadership Network. The following is an extensive quote from Chuck Smith Jr.:

"As far back as 1970, Lawrence Richards was calling for *A New Face for the Church* and in 1975 Howard Snyder pointed out *The Problem of Wineskins*. The student revolution of the 1960s marked the beginning of change in Western society, and prescient believers were already discovering that the church would have to alter some of its structures in order to recast biblical community in the new world, still forming. The recommended changes of the sixties, however, had to do more with tweaking existing structures rather than calling the entire structure, right down to its foundation, into question.

"In the last decade of the twentieth century, a small group of Christian leaders were drawn together by their mutual conviction that evangelicalism had produced a subculture that was no longer the best possible representation of Christianity. The world that had given birth to North American evangelical institutions (established basically through the 1940s to the 1960s) had disappeared by 1990. These believers realized that pushing the same methodologies (perhaps even the idea of methodology) and striving to salvage the old worldview would increasingly alienate popular culture and future generations of Christian youth.

"The group that met together to discuss these issues was fortunately blessed with astute and theologically informed thinkers like Brian McLaren and Tony Jones; ecclesiastical innovators like Todd Hunter, Chris Seay, and Brad Cecil; advocates of worship renewal like Sally Morgenthaler; and world-Christians like Andrew Jones. Scholars who had been discerning the times—Len Sweet, Stanley Grenz, N.T. Wright, Robert Webber, and Dallas Willard, to name a few—forged a biblical vocabulary that enabled the early team to converse intelligently on issues that were their passion. All of them shared two basic beliefs: Western culture had radically changed since the 1950s, and the church desperately needed renovation to respond to cultural changes.

"The more the original crew talked among themselves, the more the numbers grew. In the early 1990s, Leadership Network provided the initial platform for them to generate more discussions and host conferences. Later they adopted the name The Terra Nova Project, and when Leadership Network withdrew its support, they became Emergent, which Brian McLaren insists is a conversation rather than a movement."[1]

Brian McLaren confirmed this history in an interview that answered the question: How did all of this get started?[2]

BOB BUFORD AND LEADERSHIP NETWORK

In 1984, Leadership Network was organized by Bob Buford when there were about 100 megachurches in the U.S. It served as a resource broker that supplied information to and connected leaders of innovative churches. Buford admitted that Drucker was the unquestionable intellectual father and moving force behind his organization.[3] In 2009, Leadership Network had a staff of sixty and a nine-million-dollar budget, and that year there were over 5,000 megachurches.

In the early 1960s, Buford took over the family business, Buford Television, Inc. in Tyler, Texas. It was Drucker's writings on business management that inspired Buford to seek Drucker for business consultation. Their friendship grew over the years as they talked about management and the phenomenon of the large pastoral church. Both recognized the potential for these churches to re-energize Christianity in this country and address societal issues that neither the public nor private sectors had been able to resolve. *Forbes Magazine* quoted Drucker as saying,

"The pastoral megachurches that have been growing so very fast in the United States since 1980 are surely the most important social phenomenon in American society in the last thirty years."[4]

In 1988, Buford, along with others, convinced Drucker to lend his name, great mind, and occasional presence to create The Drucker Foundation. Through conferences, publications, and partnerships, the Foundation would help social sector entities focus on their mission, achieve true accountability, leverage innovation, and develop productive partners. Frances Hesselbein was involved as she took Drucker principles to the Girl Scouts of the USA.

Buford founded the Leadership Training Network in 1995, where Drucker's principles were applied to peer coaching of megachurch pastors who were to energize the twenty-first century Emerging church. Buford modestly boasted that he was the legs for Drucker's brain.

By 1999, Drucker's voluminous writings had been archived at the Claremont Graduate University in California. In 2008, the university formed the Drucker Institute with Buford named as chairman of the board. Drucker had been applying management principles to nonprofit organizations for years, donating half of his consulting time. He believed the nonprofit social sector would be the greatest means of export to the rest of the world.

Drucker's widow, Doris, affectionately reported via video that her husband kept no file correspondence from his General Motors and General Electric consulting days. However, there was a big file in his cedar closet named "Buford." Doris shared a letter her late husband wrote to Bob and Linda Buford on the occasion of his ninetieth birthday. The letter said,

> "But above all, this is a letter of profound thanks for what you, Bob, have done for me and for the third half of my life, the last fifteen or so years. It is through you and your friendship that I have attained, in my old age, a new and significant sphere of inspiration, of hope, of effectiveness—the megachurches. You cannot possibly imagine how much this means and has meant to me and how profoundly it has affected my life. I owe you so very much for your generous willingness to allow

me to take a small part in your tremendously important work. I can't even begin to tell you what your confidence in me and your friendship means and has meant for me.

With warm and affectionate gratitude,

Peter Drucker"[5]

Bob Buford was Drucker driven. When Drucker died at age ninety-five, Buford told a newspaper reporter, "I've long since ceased trying to determine what thoughts are mine and which come from Peter." The article went on to say, "Mr. Buford credits his mentor with transforming management into the 'alternative to tyranny.' He says that's largely responsible for 'the peace and prosperity of the second half of the twentieth century.'"[6]

What in the world happened to the peace and prosperity of the second half of the twentieth century? America has more Drucker-driven megachurches. But where is the peace and prosperity?

What are the spiritual presuppositions that underlie Drucker-driven church growth principles? Listen to the master's own words:

"Society needs a return to spiritual values—not to offset the material but to make it fully productive. Mankind needs the return to spiritual values, for it needs compassion. It needs the deep experience that the *Thou* and the *I* are one, which all higher religions share."[7]

Again the reader cannot help but note the Hegelian dialectic. The thesis is the "Thou." The antithesis is the "I." And the synthesis is the "One." This really appeals to the protégés of the McGavran and Wagner Fuller Seminary Emergent church teaching, whose paradigm shift has moved from the individual to the homogeneous group. How can a group be born again, contrary to what Jesus taught in John 3:3?

DRUCKER ADMITS: "I AM NOT A BORN AGAIN CHRISTIAN"

In an interview, Peter Drucker admitted,

> "I am not a born again Christian. I went to church and tithed. But no, I am not a Christian. I taught religion at Bennington College every other semester for five years; out of which the essay on Kierkegaard came after I had stopped teaching there."[8]

Drucker drank deeply from Zen and German mysticism when he said, "The parts exist in contemplation of the whole."[9]

Authors J.S. Bowman and D.L. Wittmer said of Drucker in the *Journal of Management History*,

> "Convinced of the overall importance of Confucian ethics, he claims that if ever there is a viable 'ethics of organization,' it will almost certainly have to adopt the key concepts of Confucian theory: clear definitions of relationships, universal rules, focus on behavior rather than motives, and behavior that optimizes each party's benefits."[10]

Drucker was Rick Warren's mentor for developing and implementing the Purpose Driven model for the church. It was a major paradigm shift from the Lord's New Testament pattern to a Drucker driven pattern whose presuppositions were steeped in Kierkegaardian, Zen, Confucian, and postmodern thinking. The spiritual deception is overwhelming and sad beyond words!

The Drucker Foundation, under Buford's leadership, organized a symposium in December 1996 called "Emerging Partnerships: New Ways in a New World," sponsored by The Rockefeller Brothers Fund. The Drucker Foundation leadership, along with Rick Warren, advanced the idea that a healthy society requires three vital sectors: a public sector of effective governments; a private sector of effective businesses; and a social sector of effective community organizations. This is what Drucker called his three-legged stool.

The mission of the social sector is to change lives. The need for the change stems from the fact that we are now living in a postmodern era. The new leaders are the change agents and they are loosely identified as Emergents. They must think and be postmodern in order to reach postmoderns. If the mission is to change lives, why depart from Jesus' teaching that to be born again is what truly changes lives? Is it because culture has become postmodern that the grace of God, working in the born again experience, no longer works?

DRUCKER, BUFORD, WARREN, CHUCK SMITH JR., AND CHUCK FROMM

Chuck Fromm arranged for me to spend three days at the Hilton Hotel in Ontario, California in the mid-eighties, where Peter Drucker addressed a group of church leaders and seminary professors. Bob Buford sponsored the meeting. At that meeting Buford explained to us that leadership communities are small groups of innovators and thought leaders pursuing a common ministry outcome, sharing ideas, developing strategy, and benchmarking measurements in the context of authentic relationships. Leadership Network discovers Emerging ministry initiatives and carefully invites strategic leaders into these communities of peers who are seeking to improve their personal and organizational performance in the focused outcome areas.

Drucker and Buford mentored my nephews, Chuck Smith Jr. and Chuck Fromm. They have become leading change agents in the Emergent Movement and they have drawn particularly close to Rick Warren. Both have spent hours in consultation with Drucker and Warren. Chuck Fromm claims to have assisted Buford with his book, *Halftime*. Chuck Smith Jr. wrote *The End of the World … As We know It: Clear Direction for Bold and Innovative Ministry in a Postmodern World*. He claims to have received counsel from Drucker while writing the book.

DRUCKER-WARREN PURPOSE DRIVEN MODEL AND FULLER SEMINARY

Warren's Purpose Driven model has expanded worldwide and appears to be, by sheer size, the leading model within the Emergent Movement. Rick Warren continues to maintain strong ties with Fuller Seminary and Edmund Gibbs, both of whom help distribute Warren's Ministry Toolbox for protégé pastors.

The philanthropic, humanistic Lilly Foundation has funded projects for both Drucker and Warren. The Saddleback Church is an extension campus for the Golden Gate Seminary in Mill Valley, California. Lilly has donated $300,000 which is being utilized by the church for computer equipment and the training of students to use digital tracking technology to monitor Purpose Driven pastors, congregations, and their development around the world.

The Purpose Driven model will only reproduce successfully if the blueprint and manual are followed precisely. Exact steps and strict accountability must be unwaveringly enforced. Protégé pastors and congregations must be committed to change from their so-called unsuccessful traditional ways of doing things. Church members who resist will be culled from the congregation early on. They will be shown the door.

The Purpose Driven model comprises a new legalism which is monitored carefully by the mother church via computer tracking. If the protégé pastor and congregation move through the transition, in lock step, they can be assured of becoming a transformed postmodern Emergent church. Whatever happened to the work and ministry of the Holy Spirit in the church?

THE POSTMODERN EMERGING CHURCH

When Gibbs addressed the students at Golden Gate Seminary, he said,

"The evangelical church in North America must undergo radical change with new kinds of leadership in order to fulfill its redemptive mission in the postmodern context of the next century…. This ongoing process of dying in order to live should not be as if we are reading the Scriptures right, for crucifixion is at the very essence of the ministry of Christ.

"Churches must embrace transitions or forfeit the possibility of exercising a transformational ministry within changing cultures. In the shift from a modern era emphasizing rationality and unified progress to a postmodern era, characterized by pluralism, ambiguity, and relativism, the church is facing a context in which the former concepts of self-identity and purpose are being challenged. The church itself will need to go through a metamorphosis in order to find its new identity in the dialectic of gospel and culture. This new situation is requiring churches to approach their context as a 'missional' encounter.

"The cultural changes with which church leaders must grapple are: Global. There is nowhere to run to. Rapid. There is no time to reflect. Complex. There is too much information to absorb. Comprehensive. They affect every area of life."[11]

The fair question to ask Fuller Professor Gibbs is this: What does the idea of a metamorphosis of the church have to do with the redemptive substitutionary crucifixion of our Lord? Can we add anything to what Jesus has already accomplished when He said on the cross, "It is finished"? It seems obvious that what Gibbs was presenting is a purely humanistic agenda. The Emergent church folks, aka new evangelicals, are looking for a new church identity in the postmodern culture rather than in the handbook of our Creator God, which is the inerrant Bible.

The word "dialectic" has been imported from the realm of philosophy. The original Greek word *dialektos* is used in the New Testament to refer to a language or tongue spoken, from which we get the English word "dialect." The philosophical notion of dialectic originated in ancient Greece and was popularized by Plato in his Socratic dialogues. Unresolved tension and paradox is embedded in a variety of dialectic forms of thinking from Socratic, Hindu, Buddhist, Medieval, Hegelian, Marxist, and even Talmudic.

THE EMERGING CHURCH HUMANISTIC DIALECTIC TENSION

New evangelicals learned about the word "dialectic" from Karl Barth and neo-orthodoxy. Conveniently, that word is in the vocabulary of the postmodern philosophers and Emergent churchmen. When you dismiss absolute truth that comes from the inerrant Bible and turn to unresolved dialectic tension, you fall into the arms of confusion where there are no ultimate answers.

Gibbs used the word "dialectic." He said: "The church must go through a metamorphosis in order to find its new identity in the dialectic of gospel and culture." The church is the bride of Christ: the household of the faithful, the body of the redeemed. It is that specific body of believers that Jesus promised to build and the gates of hell would not prevail against it (Matthew 16:18). That promise for the church rested upon the twin sufficiencies: the inerrant Bible, and the work and ministry of the Holy Spirit. Culture stands in stark contrast to the church. Culture consists of unsaved, unredeemed sinners. From the Tower of Babel the Lord scattered the unsaved. One language became many; many with diversified cultural people groups.

Where in the New Testament are we told that the church is to change; that the gospel is to change and find a new identity in culture in order to reach that culture? Since we live in a fallen and broken world, all cultures are comprised of unsaved people dominated by Satan who is the prince of this world (John 12:31; 14:30). Until Jesus comes again there will always be a tension between cultures, on the one hand; and the gospel and the church on the other.

The solution has remained unchanged. Only the grace of God releases the tension between the sinner and the timeless gospel message delivered to him from a faithful servant of the Lord using the inerrant Bible texts. The Holy Spirit works where one (who is a part of the bride of Christ) uses the inerrant Bible. This is the compelling reason why it is individuals who are born again, one by one, not homogeneous groups.

RICK WARREN BOASTS THAT PETER DRUCKER IS HIS MENTOR

Alluding to his lectures at the Harvard Kennedy School and the Law School, Rick Warren reports that he began those lectures with this quote coming from Peter Drucker:

> "The most significant sociological phenomenon of the first half of the twentieth century was the rise of the corporation. The most significant sociological phenomenon of the second half of the twentieth century has been the development of the large pastoral church—of the megachurch. It is the only organization that is actually working in society.
>
> "Now, Drucker has said that at least six times. I happen to know because he's my mentor. I've spent twenty years under his tutelage learning about leadership from him, and he's written it in two or three books, and he says he thinks it's the only thing that really works in society."[12]

The Bible teaches that man has status and significance because he was created in the image of his Creator God; even in his fallen condition. However, in today's postmodern church, "to social planners such as Peter Drucker, man's status and significance is based upon what economic value he has to society."[13]

The former view is God-centered; the latter view is man-centered. If a disabled child or adult cannot make an economic contribution to society, are they then considered without status and significance? This bankrupt, man-centered view is completely void of compassion from either God or man!

Drucker said of the individual,

> "In spite of his need and search, Christianity and the churches have been unable to provide a religious social solution. All they can do today is to give the individual religion. They cannot give a new society and a new community. Personal religious experience may be invaluable to the individual; it may restore his peace, may give him a personal God and rational understanding of his own function and nature. But it cannot re-create society and cannot make social community life sensible."[14]

The Purpose Driven model depends heavily upon human devised self-assessments and group assessments to measure and monitor its activities and progress. This is how the General Systems Theory operates, from a feedback mechanism. Buford has developed what is called the Christian Life Profile to measure the spiritual maturity of a church member.

The Drucker Foundation offers a Self-Assessment Tool workshop for an organization or community which guides them through a process to transformation. Warren has a Purpose Driven Life Health Assessment, which is a subjective self-assessment of a believer's spiritual condition and progress.

These self-assessment instruments purport to measure the things of the mind and/or spirit. They are hardly reliable and highly variable. Human behavior is difficult to measure, quantify, qualify, or predict. Multiple conflicting schools of psychology and psychiatry attest to this. Many of these self-assessment instruments rely upon vanity, flattery, improper self-disclosure of an intimate nature, and even dishonesty.

The prophet Jeremiah declared,

> "The heart is deceitful above all things, and desperately wicked: who can know it?" (Jeremiah 17:9).

Paul warned,

> "For I say, through the grace given unto me, to every man that is among you, not to think of himself more highly than he ought to think; but to think soberly, according as God has dealt to every man the measure of faith" (Romans 12:3).

The Drucker driven and Purpose Driven humanistic tools for self-assessment are mechanical; they are in the flesh. They reintroduce the church members to a new legalism.

The inerrant Bible abounds with many practical and spiritual guidelines from our Creator Redeemer for self-assessment. The Psalms, Proverbs, the New Testament Gospels, book of Acts and the Epistles are loaded with material to help disciples assess their behavior. The rest of the Scriptures are laced with innumerable examples of how to act and how not to act, drawn from the real history of men reacting and responding to their Creator and each other. These are examples that transcend cultures and time.

The beauty of God's plan is that it is grounded in the twin sufficiencies: the inerrant Word provides the guidelines, and the work and ministry of the Holy Spirit provides the gracious power of God that enables disciples to succeed for His glory. Moses understood this when he wrote,

> "The secret things belong unto the Lord our God: but those things which are revealed belong unto us and to our children forever, that we may do all the words of this law" (Deuteronomy 29:29).

Ezekiel understood this when he wrote,

> "And I will put My Spirit within you, and cause you to walk in My statutes, and you shall keep My judgments, and do them" (Ezekiel 36:27).

Jesus assured His disciples of this when He said,

> "But you shall receive power, after that the Holy Spirit is come upon you: and you shall be witnesses unto Me both in Jerusalem, and in all Judea, and in Samaria, and unto the uttermost part of the earth" (Acts 1:8).

Jesus comprehensively anticipated all cultures. Or was Jesus short-sighted? Was He unaware that in the latter decades of the twentieth century, humanists and beguiled Emergent churchmen would start declaring their culture to be postmodern? And would that alarming declaration render our Creator Redeemer's plan from before the foundation of the world to be no longer effective?

Paul understood this when he said,

> "But you are not in the flesh, but in the Spirit, if so be that the Spirit of God dwell in you. Now if any man have not the Spirit of Christ, he is none of His" (Romans 8:9).

Importing Confucian, Zen, and Kierkegaardian-soaked principles and plans into the body of Christ is disturbingly serious stuff. Paul made it ever so clear when he said,

> "For other foundation can no man lay than that is laid, which is Jesus Christ" (1 Corinthians 3:11).

The aging apostle John understood this when he said,

> "These things have I written unto you concerning them that seduce you. But the anointing which you have received of Him abides in you, and you need not that any man teach you: but as the same anointing teaches you of all things, and is truth, and is no lie, and even as it has taught you, you shall abide in Him" (1 John 2:26-27).

This is not complicated. Satan through humanists seduces. The Lord anoints His disciples through the Holy Spirit. We are to abide in His truth, the inerrant Word of God.

Next we will consider how the new evangelical Emergent church is positioning itself to become a part of Satan's end-time new world order.

CHAPTER TEN FOOTNOTES

1 Chuck Smith Jr., "What Is Emerging?" *Worship Leader Magazine* (March/April 2005), p. 22.

2 Brian McLaren, interview on July 15, 2005. www.pbs.org/wnet/religionandethics/week846/interview.html.

3 Robert P. Buford, "Long Obedience in the Same Direction, Leadership Network's 25th Anniversary Celebration, 2009." LN Archives, Dallas, TX.

4 Peter Drucker, *Management Challenges for the 21st Century* (New York, NY: HarperCollins, 1999), p. 29.

5 Robert P. Buford, "Long Obedience in the Same Direction, Leadership Network's 25th Anniversary Celebration, 2009." LN Archives, Dallas, TX.

6 *Dallas Morning News*, November 15, 2005.

7 Peter Drucker, *Landmarks of Tomorrow* (Piscataway, NJ: Transaction Publishers, 1996), pp. 264-265.

8 Drucker Archive, Claremont College Digital Library, http://ccdl.libraries.claremont.edu/cdm4/item_viewer.php?CISOROOT=/dac&CISOPTR=2176&CISOBOX=1.

9 Peter Drucker, *Landmarks of Tomorrow* (Piscataway, NJ: Transaction Publishers, 1996), p. 6.

10 James S. Bowman and Dennis L. Wittmer, "The Unfashionable Drucker: Ethical and Quality Chic," *Journal of Management History* (2000, Vol. 6. Issue 1), p. 17.

11 Dr. Edmund Gibbs, speaking at annual meeting of the American Society For Church Growth at Golden Gate Seminary, Mill Valley, CA, November 12-14, 2009.

12 Rick Warren, "Myths of the Modern Megachurch," Biannual Faith Angle Conference on Religion, Politics and Public Life, Key West, Florida, May 2005. www.pewforum.org/Christian/Evangelical-Protestant-Churches/Myths-of-the-Modern-Megachurch.aspx.

13 Lynn D. Leslie, Sarah H. Leslie and Susan J. Conway, *The Pied Pipers of Purpose* (Ravenna, OH: Conscience Press, 2004), p. 21.

14 Peter Drucker, *The End of Economic Man: The Origins of Totalitarianism*, 1939, reprinted (Piscataway, NJ: Transaction Publishers, 1995).

NEW EVANGELICALS IN THE NEW WORLD ORDER

From secular humanists to Bible-believing Christians, globalization is the hot topic. Our planet has many crises. Poverty, famine, disease, food and water shortages, natural disasters, economic downturns, moral chaos and wars impact people's consciousness worldwide. Today, news is instantaneous. Anxiety, hopelessness, and anger shroud the masses.

Even in developed countries the economic rug has been pulled out from under those who are clinging to a seemingly favored middle class status. Apart from the few wealthy elite, everyone else has been pushed out of his or her comfort zone. The near poor are moving toward poverty. The poor continue to be poor and their numbers are increasing. Sadly they are a vast growing number of people worldwide.

The humanistic social engineers believe that the solution is a world-wide redistribution of wealth, a single global currency, and a one-world government body of laws that runs everything in this global village. Such is the clarion call for this new world order. They believe the United Nations is the model that needs to be perfected. Both open and covert advocates have been beating this drum for years.

PROPONENTS OF THE NEW WORLD ORDER

Founded in 1921 in New York City, the Council on Foreign Relations has functioned as an elite super think tank. It is not an official U.S. government entity; but an autonomous council that gives advice on our nation's foreign policy and seeks to personally inform and persuade elected public officials and cultural social change agents of influence. The Council has been a strong advocate of a new world order or what is now being referred to as world governance.

Influential change agents in the United States government, military generals, world leaders, and popes have been advocating the advantages of a new world order for many decades. Take a look at just a sampling of those advocating a new world order.

1962 – Council on Foreign Relations member, Nelson Rockefeller, gave a lecture at Harvard University saying that there is "a new and free order struggling to be born.... There is a fever of nationalism ... but the nation-state is becoming less and less competent to perform its international political tasks.... These are some of the reasons pressing us to lead vigorously toward the true building of a new world order ... with voluntary service.... Sooner perhaps than we may realize ... there will evolve the bases for a federal structure of the free world."[1]

1967 – Pope Paul VI wrote the encyclical, *Populorum Progressio*, wherein he stated:

"Who can fail to see the need and importance of thus gradually coming to the establishment of a world authority capable of taking effective action on the juridical and political planes? Delegates to international organizations, public officials, gentlemen of the press, teachers and educators—all of you must realize that you have your part to play in the construction of a new world order."[2]

1973 – *The New York Times* published "From a China Traveler" by David Rockefeller, who wrote about Communist China:

> "One is impressed immediately by the sense of national harmony.... There is a very real and pervasive dedication to Chairman Mao and Maoist principles. Whatever the price of the Chinese Revolution, it has obviously succeeded not only in producing more efficient and dedicated administration, but also in fostering high morale and community purpose. General social and economic progress is no less impressive.... The enormous social advances of China have benefited greatly from the singleness of ideology and purpose.... The social experiment in China under Chairman Mao's leadership is one of the most important and successful in history."[3]

How many millions were put to death to achieve this cultural revolution?

1973 – The Trilateral Commission was founded by David Rockefeller as another elite independent think tank focusing initially on foreign policy issues related to the U.S., Europe, and the Far East. It has been widely viewed as a counterpart to the Council on Foreign Relations with the goal of one-world governance.

1977 – *The Atlantic Monthly* published "The Trilateral Connection" by former *Washington Post* columnist, Jeremiah Novak, in which he stated, "For the third time in this century, a group of American scholars, businessmen, and government officials is planning to fashion a new world order."[4]

1979 – Barry Goldwater wrote,

> "In my view, the Trilateral Commission represents a skillful coordinated effort to seize control and consolidate the four centers of power—political, monetary, intellectual, and ecclesiastical. All this is to be done in the interest of creating a more peaceful, more productive world community. What the Trilateralists truly intend is the creation of a worldwide economic power superior to the political governments of the nation-states involved. They believe

the abundant materialism they propose to create will overwhelm existing differences. As managers and creators of the system they will rule the future."[5]

1987 – Pope John Paul II wrote the encyclical, *Sollicitudo rei socialis*, which commemorated the twentieth anniversary of Pope Paul VI's 1967 encyclical, *Populorum Progressio*.

1988 – George H.W. Bush ran for the presidency of the United States, and *The Washington Post* quoted David Rockefeller as remarking, "He's [Bush] one of us [the establishment].... If he were president, he would be in a better position than anyone else to pull together the people in the country who believe that we are in fact living in one world and have to act that way."[6]

1988 – Mikhail Gorbachev spoke at the United Nations. *The Boston Globe* reported, "He called for a new world order founded not on force but on dialogue."[7]

1989 – President Bush, the elder, gave the commencement address at Texas A&M University and said, "Ultimately, our objective is to welcome the Soviet Union back into the world order.... Perhaps the world order of the future will truly be a family of nations."[8]

1990 – Mikhail Gorbachev spoke at Stanford University and was quoted by *The Sentinel* as he called for the United States and Soviet Union to be partners in building a new world order.... "Tolerance is the alpha and omega of a new world order."[9]

1990 – President Bush, the elder, delivered an address to Congress titled, "Toward a New World Order," regarding the crisis in the Persian Gulf after Iraq invaded Kuwait. Then he addressed the UN and spoke of the "collective strength of the world community expressed by the UN ... a historic movement towards a new world order."[10]

1991– The Council on Foreign Relations co-sponsored an assembly on the topic of "Rethinking America's Security: Beyond Cold War to a New World Order." It was attended by sixty-five prestigious members of government, labor, academia, media, military, and other professions from nine countries.

Later, several of the conference participants joined some 100 other world leaders for another closed door meeting of the exclusive international Bilderberg Group. As another group of elite financiers, bankers, and politicians, this exclusive organization was founded in 1954 in the Netherlands. The Bilderbergers exert considerable clout in determining the foreign policies of their respective governments. They too promote a one-world system.

In a speech there, David Rockefeller said,

> "We are grateful to the *Washington Post*, the *New York Times*, *Time Magazine*, and other great publications whose directors have attended our meetings and respected their promises of discretion for almost forty years. It would have been impossible for us to develop our plan for the world if we had been subjected to the lights of publicity during those years. But the world is now more sophisticated and prepared to march towards a world government."[11]

1993 – Confirmation hearings were held for Warren Christopher's nomination to be Secretary of State. He was a member of the Council on Foreign Relations. Christopher and Senator Joseph Biden discussed the possibility of NATO becoming a peacekeeping surrogate for the UN "to foster the creation of a new world order."[12]

1993 – General Colin Powell received the United Nations Global Leadership Award, and he remarked, "The United Nations will spearhead our efforts to manage the new conflicts [that afflict our world].... Yes, the principles of the United Nations Charter are worth our lives, our fortunes, and our sacred honor."[13]

1993 – In case there is any doubt about whether President Clinton, a Council on Foreign Relations member, supported world government, he signed a letter to the World Federalist Association congratulating Strobe Talbott, also on the Council on Foreign Relations, upon receiving the World Federalist Association's first Norman Cousins Global Governance Award. The WFA is a leading force for world federal government. Clinton wrote, "Norman Cousins worked for world peace and world government ... Strobe Talbott's lifetime achievements as a voice for global harmony have earned him this recognition.... He will be a worthy recipient of the Norman Cousins Global Governance Award."[14]

1993 – Council on Foreign Relations member and Trilateralist, Henry Kissinger, wrote in *The Los Angeles Times* concerning NAFTA, "What Congress will have before it is not a conventional trade agreement but the architecture of a new international system ... a first step toward a new world order."[15]

1994 – President Clinton signed Presidential Decision Directive 25, which strengthened the UN and described how American soldiers will serve under foreign commanders. PDD25 was only released to top administration officials and a few members of Congress; the general public was refused access at that time.[16]

1995 – Billionaire financier, George Soros, at the World Economic Forum at Davos, Switzerland, said "the world needs a new world order ... I am here to alert you that we are entering a period of world disorder."[17]

1996 – Serving for nineteen years as anchorman for CBS Evening News and often cited as "the most trusted man in America," Walter Cronkite wrote in his autobiography, "If we are to avoid catastrophe, a system of world order—preferably a system of world government— is mandatory. The proud nations someday will ... yield up their precious sovereignty."[18]

2009 – Pope Benedict XVI wrote the encyclical, *Caritas in veritate*, wherein he reiterated many of the themes from *Populorum Progressio* by Pope Paul VI in 1967.[19]

Many of the fundamentalist and evangelical segments of the Christian church have resisted alignment and involvement with humanists and religionists who are pursuing a unified new world order. This is primarily because of their allegiance to the uniquely exclusive authority of the Bible, wherein Jesus claims to be the only way to the Father.

Believers in the inerrant Bible have been committed to the priority of preaching and teaching men the gospel of the love of Jesus Christ. This is the good news that can save them for all eternity. It can prepare them for a grace-filled and peaceful experience with King Jesus in His new heaven and earth, where righteousness will reign and there will be no more war. In this present age, the Bible clearly teaches that Jesus-rejecting, rebellious sinners will not be able to live in harmony. History and reality confirm this.

The Christian missionary endeavor has resulted, along the way, in good works of kindness where hospitals, orphanages, and the basic social and physical needs of the poor have mercifully been provided for in the name of Jesus. In the past two millennia more benevolent ministries have been launched by followers of Jesus to the sick, hurt, and hungry around the world than by any other religious, humanitarian, or government entity. It was and is accomplished by His grace and for His glory.

These same historic evangelicals have fully and literally embraced the end-time prophetic Bible teachings found in Matthew 24, Luke 21, 1 & 2 Thessalonians, Revelation, Daniel, Ezekiel, and Zechariah. We are living in the last days as God's full redemptive plan of salvation continues to unfold. God has fulfilled every prophetic promise He has ever made in the Bible. There is no reason to doubt that His prophecies concerning the latter days leading up to Jesus' literal physical second coming will not be fulfilled.

Satan has been deceptive from the garden of Eden onward. Jesus and the New Testament writers warn us that Satan's deception will continue to be relentless and intense. We have clearly seen how a deceptive wedge was driven into the evangelical movement. The new evangelical movement has resulted in a departure from belief in the inerrancy of the Bible.

Postmodernism is a tool of Satan which has lured away these new evangelicals causing them to fabricate an Emergent church. The fabric of new evangelicalism consists of many threads: Fuller Seminary, Peter Drucker, Bob Buford, Rick Warren, the Emergent churches, all tightly woven together. And they all want to go global, but with the social gospel instead of the good news described in the New Testament.

RICK WARREN'S GLOBAL PEACE PLAN

On May 27, 2008, *Time Magazine* declares, "Rick Warren Goes Global." Seventeen hundred pastors met with Warren for three days. They were told that over the past four years Saddleback Church had beta-tested Warren's Purpose Driven plan by sending out some 8,000 members of the church to establish the plan in 68 nations. Their flagship project has been in Rwanda, whose president, Paul Kagame, has declared his intention to make his country the world's first Purpose Driven nation. Does this sound like a rerun of Emperor Constantine and the Holy Roman Empire?

The *Time Magazine* article continued to report that Warren is envisioning 200,000 missionaries being mobilized for his Global PEACE Plan. He is sending DVDs to the 30,000 protégé churches that have participated in his rigorous "40 Days of Purpose" initiation program. Rick Warren further claims that his website will stream to the half-million church leaders that he has trained and hopes to capture for this bold program. Billy Graham endorses this plan as the "greatest, most comprehensive and most biblical vision for world missions I've ever heard or read about."[20]

UNITED NATIONS' MILLENNIUM GOALS AND WARREN'S GLOBAL PEACE PLAN

The shared objectives of Warren's Global PEACE Plan and the United Nations Millennium Development Goals program are beyond remarkable. When Warren first unveiled the plan, the first letter in the acronym PEACE stood for Plant Churches. In time, Warren wanted to enlarge his tent to be inclusive beyond the borders of the Christian church. Now the first letter stands for Promote Reconciliation. After all, if you're going to go global let's partner with anyone or any group who will join in. When you are a postmodernist, it is very easy to morph. The acronym continues with: Equip Servant Leaders, Assist the Poor, Care for the Sick, and Educate the Next Generation.

This begs a substantial question. How can sinful humans be reconciled with each other without first being reconciled to the Creator God through the finished work of Jesus on the cross? Would not the gospel of grace have to be clearly explained to all who want to promote reconciliation?

The UN Millennium Development Goals include:

1. Eradicate extreme poverty and hunger.

2. Achieve universal primary education.

3. Promote gender equality and empower women (this will be a big one in the Muslim countries).

4. Reduce child mortality.

5. Improve maternal health.

6. Combat HIV/AIDS, malaria, and other diseases.

7. Ensure environmental sustainability.

8. Develop global partnership.

The UN website says, "We can end poverty [by] 2015."[21]

Emergent church leader, Leonard Sweet, is often quoted in Warren's Ministry Toolbox. Sweet says,

> "A sea change of transitions and transformations is birthing a whole new world…. Postmodern culture is a change-or-be changed world … reinvent yourself for the twenty-first century or die. Some would rather die than change."[22]

Warren writes a glowing endorsement that appears on the front cover of Sweet's book.

Emergent church leaders are focused on unity and a worldwide oneness reflected in the growing union between Eastern and Western cultures and thinking. Sweet's online book, *Quantum Spirituality*, sheds revealing light on the envisioned global church for the twenty-first century. In his view, the offense of the cross has been replaced with a passion for interfaith peace and possibility thinking.

Sweet quotes Thomas Merton, the new age popular Roman Catholic author who popularized mysticism and died in Asia plumbing the depths of Tibetan Buddhism.

> "We are already one. But we imagine that we are not. And what we have to recover is our original unity."[23]

RICK WARREN SELECTS KEN BLANCHARD AS PEACE PLAN LEAD TRAINER

Ken Blanchard has been selected by Warren to be the PEACE Plan senior leadership trainer. Blanchard is an author and a highly sought-after motivational speaker and business consultant. He co-authored *The One Minute Manager* which has appeared in almost every airport bookstore in this country.

While he attests to being a Christian, questions do bubble to the surface when one sees Blanchard's raving endorsement of Deepak Chopra's book. Blanchard effuses,

> "*The Seven Spiritual Laws of Success* make wonderful guiding principles for anyone attempting to create a productive and satisfying life or human organization."[24]

Deepak Chopra grew up in India. As a medical doctor he became a leading Ayurvedic physician. He totally absorbed Transcendental

Meditation and became a top assistant to the internationally famous Maharishi Mahesh Yogi, who awarded Chopra with the title *Dhanvantari*, which means Lord of Immortality, the keeper of perfect health for the world.

Questions continue. Why would Rick Warren entrust the worldwide leadership training for his Purpose Driven PEACE Plan to Ken Blanchard, whose wide borders of inclusive accommodation embrace practitioners of transcendental Eastern mysticism?

In the Great Commission, do we see Jesus instructing His followers to link arms with unbelievers and humanistic organizations for the purpose of doing good in the world? No. Was Jesus simply shortsighted and unable to anticipate how postmodernism would uniquely challenge His church in the beginning of the twenty-first century? No. If you believe Jesus is not omniscient, then you do not believe in the Jesus described in the Bible. Believers expect, under the leading of the Holy Spirit, discernment from their leaders.

In his call to action, Rick Warren said,

> "The last thing many believers need today is to go to another Bible study. They already know far more than they are putting into practice. What they need are serving experiences...."[25]

Surveys significantly dispute the depth of Bible content knowledge possessed by the average American church member.[26]

Postmodern and Emergent churchmen do not value having their congregations steeped in the knowledge of the Bible. Since they view the Bible as laden with error, then it is far easier to leave its divisive issues behind and press forward in a more accommodating posture for the widespread achievement of unity with many religious groups.

Warren's PEACE Plan fits right into the global march toward social solidarity. The widening web of community systems envisioned by his mentor, Drucker, is increasingly embraced by pastors, politicians, and local and national leaders around the world.

Warren's search for alliances and volunteers took him to the United Nations and the Council on Foreign Relations where he spoke in September 2005. He and Bob Buford have attended meetings of the Council on Foreign Relations. Both powerful organizations are determined to unify the world under a new set of social rules and systemic controls. It is a heady and ego-pumping experience to rub shoulders in this rarified elitist CFR atmosphere of the intellectual who's who of power and money; the self-anointed aspiring puppet masters.

Alarmingly, both the CFR and the UN pursue a peaceful transformation that wants to stifle the divisive, exclusive truths of the gospel of Jesus Christ. UNESCO's Declaration on the Role of Religion is the lens through which the UN promotes unity and inclusiveness of all the world's religions.[27]

The Washington Times featured an article entitled, "Rick Warren Envisions Coalition of Faith" describing Warren as "one of America's best-known evangelical Protestant pastors." At an address he gave at the annual convention of the Islamic Society of North America on July 4, 2009, Warren "pleaded with about 8,000 Muslim listeners on Saturday night to work together to solve the world's greatest problems by cooperating in a series of interfaith projects."[28]

RECONCILIATION REPLACES PLANT CHURCHES— APPEAL TO MUSLIMS

Standing before those 8,000 Muslims, Pastor Warren declared that his deepest faith is in Jesus Christ. But that was as far as Warren went. Every Muslim in that room believes Jesus was a prophet. The apostle Paul would never have missed the opportunity to tell that crowd about the nature of Jesus, the love of the Father, the purpose of the cross, the response of the sinner; and to invite those Muslims to believe, repent, and accept Jesus Christ as their Lord and Savior.

The world's greatest problem is that all men are lost and headed for a Christless eternity. Only when a sinner repents, believes in Jesus, and trusts solely in what He accomplished for the sinner on the cross, can there be any assurance of eternal life in heaven. Jesus explicitly indicated that poverty is not the greatest problem. The greatest problem is that all sinners are alienated and in rebellion against their Creator God. Poverty is a terrible consequence of that; and sadly, poverty will be with us until Jesus comes again (Matthew 26:11).

It becomes disturbingly apparent why Warren took the "P" in the acronym PEACE and changed it from "Plant Churches" to "Promote Reconciliation."[29] But this doesn't surprise us when we understand how Warren was deceived by Satan who lured him to be Drucker-driven with his postmodern Purpose Driven plan.

Rick Warren would protest saying that his church does believe the Bible is inerrant. When you go to the Saddleback Church's website and click "About Us" and then click again "What We Believe," you'll read "About The Bible" which states:

> "The Bible is God's word to all men. It was written by human authors, under the supernatural guidance of the Holy Spirit. It is the supreme source of truth for Christian beliefs and living. Because it is inspired by God, it is truth without any mixture of error."[30]

One has to wonder whether or not Pastor Rick Warren thinks that this statement is his "Get Out of Jail Free" card in his accountability before the Lord. We don't know his heart; but we surely know what he has disclosed to us. The most we can do is inspect his fruit and pray for him. Are there any of his peers who can confront, in the love of Christ, his misguided ways? When a man is catapulted into fame and celebrity status, are there any peers left that he will listen to? Who would have ever thought thirty years ago that a Southern Baptist-trained young pastor would today be a main player on the world stage, actively orchestrating a religious unity that will indeed promote a new world order as prophesied in the Bible?

Today in Fuller Seminary's PhD program at the School of Intercultural Studies, the students must recognize the globalization of the church and the end of Western Christendom. For these students, embracing postmodernism is assumed for the training of the twenty-first century Emergent churchmen.

CHANGING TIMES

I believe that most Americans, and even our own CIA, were taken by surprise with the implosive collapse of the Soviet Union in 1991. Older women were selling family heirlooms to buy food. Mikhail Gorbachev was welcomed to the U.S. and given use of our government's Presidio in San Francisco for the purpose of advancing globalization strategies. In 1994, an article appeared in a United Nations Development Report titled, "Global Governance for the 21st Century." Written by Jan Tinbergen, a Nobel Prize winner in economics from the Netherlands, he believed that we needed a world government; and this can best be achieved by strengthening the United Nations.

Pulitzer Prize winning Watergate journalist, Carl Bernstein, disclosed that his own father and mother had been members of the Communist Party during the era of the 1950s when controversial and feisty Senator Joe McCarthy was on an anti-Communist crusade in the U.S. Senate. In 1989, while Bernstein was doing research for his book, *Loyalties: A Son's Memoir*, his father alarmingly commented,

"You're going to prove Senator Joseph McCarthy was right ... I'm worried about the kind of book you're going to write about cleaning up McCarthy. The problem is that everybody said he was a liar; you're saying he was right ... I agree that the Party was a force in our country."[31]

Globalization was a major focus of Communism.

England's Prime Minister Tony Blair said,

"We are all internationalists now, whether we like it or not ... On the eve of a new millennium we are now in a new world. We need new rules for international cooperation and new ways of organizing our international institutions ... Globalization has transformed our economies and our working practices. But globalization is not just economic. It is also a political and security phenomenon."[32]

Shortly after leaving office, Blair joined the Roman Catholic Church.

In 2008 at Davos, Switzerland, The World Economic Forum hosted a "Faith and Modernization" session moderated by Tony Blair that included a prominent Catholic, Jew, Muslim, and Protestant, Rick Warren. Globalization was the focus.[33] Rick Warren was representing and promoting reconciliation with his Global PEACE Plan. There is no doubt that he was receiving high visibility on the world stage.

When the apostle Paul stood before Felix, Festus, and Herod Agrippa, Paul talked to them about Jesus; His death and resurrection (Acts 24-26). Paul witnessed to them about the good news regarding Jesus. Paul did not appeal to them in order to promote reconciliation between the Jews, Christians, and Romans whose empire included many ethnicities and religions. Paul was an ambassador for Jesus Christ.

As an ambassador, Paul was both the theologian and practitioner of reconciliation.

> "To wit, that God was in Christ, reconciling the world unto Himself, not imputing their trespasses unto them; and has committed unto us the word of reconciliation. Now then we are ambassadors for Christ, as though God did beseech you by us: we pray you in Christ's stead, be reconciled to God. For He has made Him to be sin for us, who knew no sin; that we might be made the righteousness of God in Him" (2 Corinthians 5:19-21).

Was Rick Warren an ambassador for Jesus Christ when he stood before the Harvard Kennedy School, Harvard Law School, United Nations, Council on Foreign Relations, the Islamic Society of North America, and the World Economic Forum in Davos, Switzerland? Did he beseech those audiences, as Paul would have, "in Christ's stead, [to] be reconciled to God"? We don't know. Maybe he did. We only know what was reported.

Is the next generation automatically immune to drifting away from God's truth? Are we seeing a prophetic "last days" new world order emerging in this new evangelical drift into humanistic postmodernism? Let's see what we can discover next.

CHAPTER ELEVEN FOOTNOTES

1 Nelson Rockefeller, Lecture at Harvard University, 1962. (Wm. Grigg, *The New American Magazine*, p. 5, February 10, 2003).

2 Pope Paul VI, *Populorum Progressio*, Papal Encyclical, 1967.

3 David Rockefeller, "From a China Traveler" (*The New York Times*, August 10, 1973).

4 Jeremiah Novak, "The Trilateral Connection" (*The Atlantic Monthly*, July 1977).

5 Barry Goldwater, "With No Apologies—The Personal and Political Memoirs of United States Senator," 1979. http://quotes.liberty-tree.ca/quote_blog/Barry.Goldwater.Quote.OF6B.

6 David Rockefeller, *The Washington Post*, February 10, 1988.

7 Mikhail Gorbachev, *The Boston Globe*, December 8, 1988.

8 George H.W. Bush, address at Texas A&M University, (*Arizona Daily Star*, May 12, 1989).

9 Mikhail Gorbachev, address at Stanford University. (Sentinel Wire Service. June 5, 1990).

10 George H.W. Bush, address to Congress, "Toward a New World Order," followed by an address to the United Nations, October 1, 1990.

11 William Grigg, *The New American Magazine*, p. 5. February 10, 2003. (First reported by French news agencies).

12 Warren Christopher confirmation hearings by President William J. Clinton, (Clinton Presidential Library, Little Rock, AR, January 13, 1993).

13 Colin Powell, United Nations Association, U.S.A.'s Global Leadership Award. April 21, 1993, United Nations Association U.S.A. Archives.

14 William J. Clinton, Letter congratulating Strobe Talbott as first recipient of the Norman Cousins Global Governance Award. June 22, 1993.

15 Henry Kissinger, *Los Angeles Times*, July 18, 1993.

16 William J. Clinton signed Presidential Decision Directive 25. May 3, 1994.

17 George Soros, Davos, Switzerland World Economic Forum, January 27, 1995.

18 Walter Cronkite, *A Reporter's Life* (New York, NY: Ballantine Books, 1996).

19 www.usccb.org/caritasinveritate.

20 *Time Magazine*, May 27, 2008.

21 www.un.org/millenniumgoals.

22 Leonard Sweet, *Soul Tsunami* (Grand Rapids, MI: Zondervan, 1999), pp. 17, 34, 75.

23 Leonard Sweet, *Quantum Spirituality: A Postmodern Apologetic.*

24 Deepak Chopra, *The Seven Spiritual Laws of Success: A Practical Guide to the Fulfillment of Your Dreams*, 1994. Back cover.

25 Rick Warren, *Purpose Driven Life* (Grand Rapids, MI: Zondervan, 2002), p. 231.

26 R. Albert Mohler Jr., "The Scandal of Biblical Illiteracy: It's Our Problem," article based upon Gallup and Barna research, www.crosswalk.com (2005).

27 United Nations UNESCO Declaration on the role of religion at www.unesco.org.

28 *The Washington Times*, "Rick Warren Envisions Coalition of Faith," July 5, 2009.

29 www.thepeaceplan.com.

30 www.saddleback.com.

31 Carl Bernstein, *Loyalties: A Son's Memoir* (New York, NY: Simon and Schuster, 1989). Russian KGB archives release of VENONA intercepts verified that in the 1950s Senator Joseph McCarthy was right. The Soviet NKDV had 221 agents in the Roosevelt administration in April 1941.

32 Tony Blair, "The Blair Doctrine." Chicago Economic Club, April 22, 1999.

33 Tony Blair, Faith and Modernization session at the World Economic Forum. Davos, Switzerland, 2008.

THE NEXT GENERATION DRIFTS AWAY

The second generation sons of fundamentalists and evangelical pastors who have gone astray include: Daniel Fuller, Frank Schaeffer, Rick Warren, and Chuck Smith Jr. In addition to the problem of fully valuing the doctrine of the inerrancy of the Bible, could it also be a problem with how they interpret end-time events? When principles of hermeneutics are viewed through the postmodern lens of deconstruction, then we are sadly reminded of the Israelites' similar situation in the Bible.

> "When also all that generation were gathered unto their fathers: and there arose another generation after them, which knew not the Lord, nor yet the works which He had done for Israel" (Judges 2:10).

Insight from this Scripture helps us to understand that as each generation moves further away from God's inerrant truth, the conversation or dialectic creates greater general confusion, except in the minds of the elite participants. It appears to gratify the young participants as they give new meaning to historical words that had historical definitions, which have long been used in our Christian biblical vocabulary.

The new evangelical hermeneutic has become a useful tool for hiding their new belief system; excusing them from the demanding examination of what the whole Bible teaches. They can use words which once had an accepted definition, but now have been redefined. Yet the average person in the pew is unaware of the change. The Emergent church is merging into the broad path that leads to destruction.

The Bible speaks of many false prophets who come using the name of our Lord, but they only bring confusion and cause a virus within the body of Christ. Many believers have lost their resistance to the destructive cells that are multiplying within the church body. Many have turned away from the plain truth of the Bible. They can no longer discern between cells that are destructive and normal cells that provide true abundant life in Christ. Normal healthy cells are not affected. They remain immune from the destructive cells by refusing to apply the Hegelian dialectic to God's absolute truth in the Bible. Only by accepting truth from God's inerrant Word can a person be set free from Satan's devices.

To remain healthy and strong, it is imperative to daily feed on the inerrant Word of God. Paul encourages us,

> "For this cause also we thank God without ceasing, because, when you received the word of God which you heard of us, you received it not as the word of men, but as it is in truth, the word of God, which effectually works also in you that believe" (1 Thessalonians 2:13).

ONE-WORLD RELIGION AND BIBLE PROPHECY

Now what does all this commotion about a new world order or world governance mean for Bible-believing evangelical Christians? For many, Bible prophecy that suggests the diverse religions of the world will find common ground and adopt a one-world religion seems far-fetched. Yet, in our day, we are witnessing prophecy in Revelation 13 unfold. It clearly declares a time when the whole world would merge together politically and religiously.

On June 26, 2000, there was a great interfaith celebration of the signing of the Constitution for the United Religions Initiative. Some of the faiths represented include: Hindu, Zoroastrian, Christian, Jewish, Muslim, Buddhist, Taoist, Wiccan, Baha'i, Sikh, and Indigenous Peoples. It was envisioned that this would do for the religions of the world what the United Nations was created to accomplish for the nations of the world—consolidate and unify. Above all, it would remove divisiveness and exclusiveness. Tolerance must reign via the road of accommodation and inclusiveness.[1]

The apostle Paul reminds the church that they are the "called out" people of God. They are not blended with the other religions of the world which are described as darkness destined for destruction.

> "But of the times and seasons, brethren, you have no need that I write unto you. For you know perfectly that the day of the Lord so comes as a thief in the night. For when all shall say, Peace and safety; then sudden destruction comes upon them, as travail upon a woman with child; and they shall not escape. But you, brethren, are not in darkness, that that day should overtake you as a thief. You are all as children of light, and the children of the day: we are not of the night, nor of darkness" (1 Thessalonians 5:1-5).

The Bible teaches that the Antichrist spoken of in Revelation 13 and Daniel 8:23-25 will use a false peace to deceive many. Today many are looking for a "savior" to usher in world peace and prosperity, without moral accountability. The Antichrist will promise the world such a peace if they follow him, but we have been warned that his intentions are misleading and sinister.

The move toward a global government will encompass the nations of the former Roman Empire, which is present-day Europe. These nations will be revived and eventually dominate the world. The European Union has steadily moved forward in its attempt to unite Europe politically and economically. It has succeeded in creating a European parliament, court, and common currency.

In Ezekiel 38 and Revelation 20:8, we learn of the eventual over-throw of Magog. Who is Magog? First century AD Roman-Jewish historian, Flavius Josephus, identified these people as Scythians. Fifth century BC Greek Historian, Herodotus, located these peo-ple north of the Black Sea as well as in the region of Persia. These Scythians appear to be the progenitors of the Russians, who many scholars identify as Magog. These ruthless warriors were referred to as northern barbarians.

Prophetical accounts in Ezekiel, Daniel, Zechariah, and Hosea depict judgments prior to the end of the church age. The nations listed in Ezekiel will join with Magog. This army will lead the Muslim-ruled nations listed in Ezekiel 38. They will launch a sur-prise attack upon the modern divinely regathered and reconstituted Nation-State of Israel. Mesheck, or New Testament era Asia Minor which is now Turkey, will be part of this coalition that attacks Israel. Other nations involved include Iran (Persia), Sudan (Cush), and Libya (Put). In 2002, Turkey elected a pro-Islamic party to govern their country. Anti-Semitism in the Arab world is peaking today.

THE ERROR OF REPLACEMENT THEOLOGY

The sixteenth century Protestant Reformers had given up on the nation of Israel coming back to their land since the Jews had been dispersed for 1,500 years. Influenced by Roman Catholic eschatol-ogy, the Reformers developed what is called replacement theology. They concluded that the Old Testament promises to Israel were now for the church because God was finished with Israel. This made end times theology confusing to those who failed to believe what the Bible said about the literal divine regathering and restoration of Israel. Now that Israel is again a nation, the prophecies of Ezekiel have significant meaning in today's world, especially with the pre-dicted new world order materializing before our eyes.

Every detailed prophetic prediction that God gave concerning Jesus' first coming was fulfilled, without exception. Because the Creator God does not breathe error when He communicates, we can safely assume that every detailed prophetic prediction concerning Jesus' second coming will, likewise, be fulfilled without exception.

The prophecies surrounding Jesus' first coming were literal and not allegorical. Nowhere does the Bible indicate that large sections, even entire Bible books, informing us about Jesus' second coming, are now to be interpreted allegorically. As the Creator God controls predicted history, He wants us to understand what He will literally yet accomplish.

In the Bible, God predicts what will take place in the "last days." Genesis 19 and Luke 17:28-30 indicate the flaunting of homosexuality. Ask your grandparents if there were such things as Gay Pride parades in their day.

In Revelation 3:14-16, we are told that many of those in the "last days" church would be lukewarm, wealthy, complacent—and would be vomited into the coming tribulation period. Sadly, many professing Christians do not believe that the Bible is the inspired Word of God and that Jesus Christ is God.

Revelation 13:8, 12 tells us that there will be a move toward a one-world religion. The widespread global impacting interfaith dialogues promoting tolerance and inclusiveness have already been documented.

The twenty-first century postmodern man worships and serves the creature rather than the Creator. He has taken a Kierkegaardian existential leap of faith. He has immersed himself into Eastern mysticism. He is caught up in himself. A stubborn, unreasonable mind, a rebellious heart, and a godless culture characterize both the twenty-first century and first century man as he is outside of Jesus Christ.

Both are the objects of Paul's stern words, inspired by the Holy Spirit,

> "For the wrath of God is revealed from heaven against all ungodliness and unrighteousness of men, who hold the truth in unrighteousness; because that which may be known of God is manifest in them; for God has showed it unto them. For the invisible things of Him from the creation of the world are clearly seen, being understood by the things that are made, even His eternal power and Godhead; so that they are without excuse: because that, when they knew God, they glorified Him not as God, neither were thankful; but became vain in their imaginations, and their foolish hearts were darkened" (Romans 1:18-21).

Jesus warned,

> "Wherefore if they shall say unto you, Behold, He is in the desert; go not forth: behold, He is in the secret chambers; believe it not" (Matthew 24:26).

According to Roman Catholic tradition, once the elements of the Eucharist are consecrated by the priest, they become the literal body and blood of Christ. The host is kept in the monstrance for adoration and then moved into the tabernacle, or secret chamber, for sanctified protection. Every Catholic church on earth contains a tabernacle or secret chamber.

Jesus also warned that this fraud would be accompanied by great deceptive signs and wonders (Matthew 24:23-27). Currently eucharistic miracles are reported around the globe. Roman Catholicism believes Peter was the first pope. However, Peter, writing in his own New Testament book, doesn't see Jesus in these secret chambers after His resurrection and ascension. Peter writes that Jesus "is gone into heaven, and is on the right hand of God; angels and authorities and powers being made subject unto Him" (1 Peter 3:22).

Revelation 17 and 18:7 tell of a woman who is an imposter, whom some would worship as queen. She would head up a global counterfeit church in the "last days." Tens of millions today follow the apparitions of Mary, claiming she is the Mother of the Church, the Lady of All Nations, the Co-Redemptrix, and the Queen of Heaven and Earth.[2]

The prophet Zechariah said that in the "last days," this wicked woman would go out over the face of the whole earth. She would be associated with a global curse. Her final destination would be Babylon, in the land of Shinar. Interestingly, the Catholics who believe in the apparitions of Mary claim that she will soon travel through the entire world saving those who look to her (Zechariah 5:7). Isaiah declares the lady of kingdoms would deceive God's people (Isaiah 47:5). Ultimately the Lord will expose her true identity.

Revelation 9:21 reveals that an epidemic use of drugs will occur. The Greek word *pharmakeia* is translated "sorceries" in English. It refers to illegal and mind-altering drugs. Sorcery refers to witchcraft, magic, and occult practices; it is used to enchant and deceive. They are anticipated in the "last days" as mentioned in Revelation 18:23.

Revelation 13:17; 18:3, 11, 19, 23 foretold that a global economic system would exist in the "last days." Today, globalists in every level of government in many nations are seeking to unite the world. We have seen leaders in the new evangelical branch of the church seek to become more involved in this globalization movement.

First century humanism was premodern. Twenty-first century humanism is postmodern. What do they have in common? Their cultures consist of sinful human beings, who are creatures in rebellion against their Creator; they are in desperate need of a Savior. In His eschatological discourse on the Mount of Olives, Jesus linked the time continuum between the first and the twenty-first centuries. He answered His disciples' questions about the future. He told them what to expect. He told them that the generation which sees the things He had prophetically described will know that the time of His second advent is near, even at the door. Then He said, "Heaven and earth shall pass away, but My words shall not pass away" (Matthew 24:35).

Would Jesus preserve His words from passing away if they contained error? Jesus' words are God-breathed. They are without error. Today it is heartbreaking to see second generation gifted men drift astray from the full confidence and trust in the whole counsel of God recorded in His inerrant Bible.

Supporters of a new world order are left with a critical choice:

(1) Put your trust and hope in the hands of the humanist elite who believe they know what is best for mankind; or (2) put your trust and hope in the Creator God and what He has promised to accomplish in the last days, as recorded in the inerrant Bible and which may soon take place in our time or in the near future.

I appeal to these twenty-first century second generation men who have drifted into new evangelical postmodernism to return to Jesus. Through cunning spiritual warfare Satan opened a frontal attack on the first century church at Corinth. To those who had gone astray, Paul appealed,

"Be not unequally yoked together with unbelievers: for what fellowship has righteousness with unrighteousness? And what communion has light with darkness? And what concord has Christ with Belial? Or what part has he that believes with an infidel? And what agreement has the temple of God with idols? For you are the temple of the living God; as God has said, I will dwell in them, and walk in them; and I will be their God, and they shall be My people. Wherefore come out from among them, and be separate, says the Lord, and touch not the unclean thing; and I will receive you, and will be a Father unto you, and you shall be My sons and daughters, says the Lord Almighty" (2 Corinthians 6:14-18).

The same cunning attack continues today in the twenty-first century.

If you've drifted astray, come back. Our loving God is gracious. He wants you back.

If you've dabbled in the deceptions of new evangelical postmodernism, I invite you to return and fully rest in the confidence of God's inerrant Word.

In the Appendix, we will examine what the Bible has to say about the kingdoms of light and darkness.

CHAPTER TWELVE FOOTNOTES

1 www.uri.org/about_uri/charter.

2 www.marypages.com.

THE KINGDOMS OF LIGHT AND DARKNESS

In this world there is a spiritual kingdom of light and a spiritual kingdom of darkness. Many Christians like to believe that God's kingdom is on earth now and that He determines everything that happens; so in their minds, this is God's world and not Satan's. However, the righteousness, justice, and peaceful characteristics of God's kingdom, described in the books of Isaiah, Psalms, Daniel, Ezekiel, Zechariah, and the Gospels, have obviously not yet appeared. Our prayer today remains, "Thy kingdom come. Thy will be done in earth, as it is in heaven" (Matthew 6:10).

Too many Christians live in a bifurcated world, where the particulars of daily life don't harmonize with their worldview. The New Testament says that Satan claimed authority to appoint rulers over "the kingdoms of the world" (Luke 4:6) and Jesus did not dispute it. If Satan's offer in the wilderness was not true, the kingdoms of this world would not have been a temptation to Jesus. This implies that the governments of this world are part of Satan's world system.

The idea that God's kingdom presently rules the earth can be traced back to Augustine's (354-430 AD) influence on the Roman Catholic Church. That erroneous tradition developed the concept that the pope rules now as the vicar of Christ. This was taught during the medieval period by Bernard of Clairvaux (1090-1153 AD) and Thomas Aquinas (1225-1274 AD). The divine right of kings became church dogma.

Italian Dante Alighieri (1265-1321 AD), in his *La Divina Commedia*, popularized the inferno idea that Satan is bound in hell at the center of the earth. In his magnum opus, the epic poem *Paradise Lost*, Englishman John Milton (1608-1674 AD) popularized the idea that Satan rules over hell in the underworld and torments those who are there. The Bible does not teach that Satan is bound in an underworld hell. He is very much at work in our world today. Satan will probably occupy a prominent position in the final and everlasting hell that follows the great white throne judgment of Revelation 20. So Dante, Milton, and a host of pagan occult myths have contributed to considerable confusion.

In the Bible, the English word "hell" is translated from the Hebrew word *sheol* and two different Greek words, *hades* and *gehenna*. *Hades* and *sheol* represent a temporary place with two separate compartments. One for Old Testament age believers in the comfort of Abraham's bosom; and the other for unbelievers where punishing torment happens. With Jesus' resurrection and ascension, the believers were immediately transported to paradise into the presence of their Savior. Jesus describes *hades* eleven times in the New Testament—Matthew 11:23; 16:18; Luke 10:15; 16:22-23; Acts 2:27, 31; Revelation 1:18; 6:8; 20:13-14.

The Greek word *gehenna*, used twelve times in the New Testament, is formed from the Hebrew wording that describes "the valley of the son of Hinnom" which alludes to a place of fire. The actual valley was located south of Jerusalem where the Old Testament Israelites defiantly practiced the evil abominations of the nations in the sight of the Lord. There they sacrificially burned alive their unwanted babies (postpartum abortion) on the white-hot flaming arms of a figurine of the pagan pleasure god, Molech. There they practiced witchcraft and sorcery through mediums and spiritists (2 Kings 23:10; 2 Chronicles 28:3; 2 Chronicles 33:6). In later years, the Valley of Hinnom became the constant site of garbage, trash, and refuse where perpetual fires burned and the worms of decay fed.

This Greek word *gehenna* describes the permanent eternal place, also called the lake of fire, that was created for the punishment of Satan and the fallen angels (Isaiah 30:33; 66:24; Revelation 20:11-15). Jesus uses *gehenna* when He describes "hell fire" (Matthew 5:22, 29-30; 10:28; 18:9; 23:15, 33; Mark 9:43-47). James uses the same word when he describes the "fire of hell" (James 3:6). It is clear that this finality is held in check, until God proves His goodness and fairness in His judgment, against the rebellious created angels. Sadly, for many humans this will also be their final eternal abode, as John recorded, "And whosoever was not found written in the book of life was cast into the lake of fire" (Revelation 20:15).

The seeds of Augustine's theology also sprouted in many Reformation churches where texts in the Bible were arbitrarily viewed as allegory rather than literal. This resulted in replacement theology, which views the church as replacing Israel in God's plan. It also resulted in allegorizing much of the book of Revelation. Amillennialism became the belief that the one thousand-year reign with Christ (Revelation 20) was not to be viewed as literal. Such allegorizing impacts about one-third of the Bible. There is no propositional truth in an allegory.

THE KINGDOM OF DARKNESS

When God created Adam and Eve in the garden of Eden, He created them in His own spiritual image as moral and reasoning creatures. God placed them in a perfect environment in a sinless state of perfection (Genesis 1:26, 27, 31). He gave them only one negative command. Nothing else was forbidden. This was the test of man's volition as a free will creature, just like the angels. Contrary to Augustine's teaching, volition is the one thing mankind has in common with the angelic order.

It is clear that God expected Adam and Eve to obey Him, and He held them accountable. This expectation is part of God's plan to show His justice and righteousness in condemning fallen angels to the lake of fire (Isaiah 30:33; Matthew 25:41; Revelation 19:20; 20:14, 15; 21:8). In the garden of Eden, God said to Adam,

> "And the LORD God commanded the man, saying, Of every tree of the garden you may freely eat, but of the tree of the knowledge of good and evil, you shall not eat of it: for in the day that you eat thereof you shall surely die" (Genesis 2:16-17).

Then Satan attempts to defeat God's plan,

> "Now the serpent was more subtle than any beast of the field which the LORD God had made. And he said unto the woman, Yea, has God said, You shall not eat of every tree of the garden?" (Genesis 3:1).

Today Satan continues to try to defeat God's plan.

Satan is presented in the Genesis narrative, without any explanation, as indwelling the serpent. We know that the serpent must be a reference to Satan from other biblical references (Job 2:1-7; Zechariah 3:1-2; 1 John 3:8). However, the identity of the serpent is not definitely and clearly revealed until Revelation 12:15; 20:2. Bible scholars believe that the Jewish rabbis in the first several centuries of the Christian era clearly identified the serpent of Genesis 3 with Satan.

> "And the great dragon was cast out, that old serpent, called the Devil, and Satan, which deceives the whole world" (Revelation 12:9).

Lucifer wanted to become "like the Most High" God (Isaiah 14:14). The battle scene is described:

> "And there appeared another wonder in heaven; and behold a great red dragon, having seven heads and ten horns, and seven crowns upon his heads. And his tail drew the third part of the stars of heaven, and did cast them to the earth: and the dragon stood before the woman which was ready to be delivered, for to devour her child as soon as it was born … And there was war in heaven: Michael and his angels fought against the dragon; and the dragon fought and his angels, and prevailed not; neither was their place found any more in heaven" (Revelation 12:3-4, 7-8).

Jesus came to destroy the works of the Devil (1 John 3:8).

Satan was able to persuade one third of the angels to follow him and revolt against God. To achieve this he first drew their allegiance away from God. Satan didn't try to move the angels immediately from worshiping Jehovah to worshiping himself. He knew they wouldn't buy that. He deceived them into thinking that they, too, could be like God. He used the same tactics with man. Satan first got them to move away from Jehovah's influence. If you are like God, then why should you worship God? You can just worship yourself. That is what humanism and Eastern mysticism tell us today. Lucifer slandered God by implying that God was trying to deceive the angels. This is what he did with Eve in the garden.

Lucifer was wooing the angelic order away from God; and they were faced with a decision. This grand deceiver was saying something quite different from what God was saying. When there is moral conflict, who are you going to believe—God or one of His created beings? Those angels who sided with Lucifer against God chose to believe Lucifer's lies rather than God's truth.

Mankind is faced with exactly the same conflicting moral issue. Who do you believe, God or Satan? If the Creator God is deceptive, then all is lost and there is no hope whatsoever. Thankfully, our Creator God has disclosed Himself to be loving, holy, just, and truthful. His supernatural power assures both His ability to create and communicate. Thankfully, we have His inerrant Word that tells us everything He wants us to know for our own good. The Creator God tells us about Himself, ourselves, and the world in which we live.

Most people think that the governments of the world are independent and exist as a result of accidental circumstances of history. Most Christians think that the rulers and governments of the world exist at the express will of God. However, we must distinguish between the directive will of God and the permissive will of God. We must realize that not everything that happens in the world is because of the directive will of God! God permits man to make choices, and many of those choices are not morally good and they have bad consequences.

The interpretation of Romans 13 that states God directly appoints all of the rulers of this world is incorrect. The point of this chapter is that God has established human government in this world to enforce morality because the sinful nature of man needs to be restrained. Unfortunately, many governments are immoral and enforce unrighteousness.

Today, as well as over the past centuries and millennia, Satan has chosen and goaded wicked leaders around the globe to impose untold suffering upon the human race. Satan specializes in suffering. He is the source of all suffering. He is the first cause of all suffering. Satan will reign in the final place of nonstop suffering. *Gehenna*, the lake of fire, which is the final hell, will be total and complete separation from the Creator God and His grace. All sinful men, who reject the love of Jesus Christ and His finished work on the cross, will spend all eternity in conscious unmitigated suffering in the presence of Satan and his fallen angels.

When our first parents listened to Satan rather than to God, they forfeited the title deed of the earth to our evil archenemy. From that time forward, Satan chose the wicked world rulers, both spiritual and physical. Therefore, Paul describes him as "the prince of the power of the air, the spirit that now works in the children of disobedience" (Ephesians 2:2). Paul describes our spiritual struggle by saying,

> "For we wrestle not against flesh and blood, but against principalities, against powers, against the rulers of the darkness of this world, against spiritual wickedness in high places" (Ephesians 6:12).

This verse describes the hierarchy of the angelic rule in Satan's kingdom. The English word "principalities" comes from the Greek word *arche*, which literally means "first ones," referring to the first or fallen archangels in Satan's highest council. The English word "power" comes from the Greek word *exousias*, referring to superhuman demonic authorities ruling with a variety of wicked expressions in particular regions on earth. The Greek word *kosmokrator* speaks of world dictators of darkness. They are national rulers such as are alluded to in Daniel 10:13, 20.

Kosmokrator is found in the Orphic Hymns of Satan, in Gnostic writings of the Devil, and on an inscription of the Roman Emperor Caracalla (188-217 AD). The apostle Paul uses this word to refer to the demons who rule the world system of darkness through men who appear to be the rulers of the nations.

The "spiritual hosts of wickedness" constitute the front line of the lower level of demonic hosts, who manipulate our minds and deceive mankind on a day-to-day basis (Mark 4:15; Luke 22:3; John 13:27; Acts 5:3; 1 Corinthians 7:5; 2 Corinthians 2:11; 4:4; 1 Thessalonians 3:5). The problem is that many believers and unbelievers are unaware of this spiritual warfare that Satan and his forces are using to influence their destiny. Satan is not going to be very effective if everyone knows what is going on. His success is based on deceit and stealth (John 8:44; 2 Corinthians 4:3; 11:14; 2 Peter 5:8).

These demonic rulers impose their will on the nations of the world through many occult and pagan false religions, Gnostic secret societies, and interconnected organizations (Psalm 12:3-4); and their control of politics via control of finance and commerce (1 Timothy 6:10; Revelation 17). Mankind is deceived through the manipulation of their minds by a lower order of demons. That is why the apostle Paul urged the church in Rome to "be not conformed to this world: but be transformed by the renewing of your mind" (Romans 12:2).

In modern times, think tanks capture the best solutions from the brightest humanistic minds to be applied to all apparent problems. Just as Satan deceived humans from the beginning and deceived world rulers throughout history, he also deceives today through supposedly democratic processes. During the millennial reign of Jesus, Satan will be bound and cast into the bottomless pit "that he should deceive the nations no more, till the thousand years should be fulfilled: and after that he must be loosed a little season" (Revelation 20:3).

Jesus clearly described Satan as the prince or ruler of this world (John 12:31; 14:30; 16:11; 17:15). John says that the "whole world lies in wickedness" (1 John 5:19). That is why the world hates Jesus and His believers (John 15:18-19).

Satan's rule has dominated the world through a succession of historical world empires. Genesis records, "Nimrod: he began to be a mighty one in the earth" (Genesis 10:8). Nimrod founded the original city of Babylon. The historical succession of world empires through which Satan has dominated the earth has been described in the books of Daniel and Revelation.

Daniel explains the meaning of Babylonian King Nebuchadnezzar's (605-562 BC) dream about the great image as representing the succession of world empires. The dream or vision prophetically portrays the Babylonian Empire, the Medo-Persian Empire, the Greek Empire, and the Roman Empire.

In Daniel chapter 7, Daniel explains his vision of the four "beasts" (Daniel 7:3) that he saw in the first year of Belshazzar (553 BC), who ruled Babylon in the absence of Nabonidus, his father. The term "beast" is used because those world empires devoured and destroyed people just like predatory animals in their quest for power and wealth. The dream parallels the dream of Nebuchadnezzar, which Daniel recounts in chapter 2. The "lion with eagle's wings" represents Nebuchadnezzar, who is given a man's heart, indicating he became a believer (Daniel 4:4, 17).

The bear raised up on one side with three ribs in its mouth represents the Medo-Persian Empire (Daniel 7:5). The leopard with four wings and four heads represents the Greek Empire (Daniel 7:6) under Alexander the Great which was divided between his four generals after his death. The fourth beast described as dreadful, terrible, with huge iron teeth, and different from all the others because it had ten horns (Daniel 7:7, 19, 23-24) represented the Roman Empire, which was founded as a republic rather than a monarchy.

These empires progressed from absolute autocratic rule to democratic idealism. They were inclusively described by Jesus as "the times of the Gentiles" (Luke 21:24; Revelation 16:19). These empires will be consummately destroyed by Jesus Christ (Daniel 2:31, 34, 35); and He will then inaugurate His kingdom of heaven on earth, which shall stand forever (Daniel 2:44-45; Luke 1:33).

The world system on earth is Satan's kingdom and not God's. If it were God's world, it would not have been an enemy of Christ Jesus!

Note the activities:

> Luke 4:5-6; John 8:44; 14:30; 15:18-19; 16:8-11; 17:6, 9, 12-18,
> 25-26; 2 Thessalonians 2:3-10; 1 Peter 5:8; 1 John 2:16; 4:3; 5:19.

Satan continues to deceive the nations (Revelation 13:14; 20:3, 10)
and his plan is simply to keep man from knowing the truth; the
only reliable source is God's inerrant Word, the Bible (John 1:1;
17:17).

THE KINGDOM OF LIGHT

The presence of God's kingdom is characterized by light:

> Psalm 27:1; 119:105; Proverbs 29:13; Isaiah 2:5; 9:2; 60:1; Matthew
> 4:16; Luke 16:8; John 1:4; 9; 3:19-21; 8:12; 12:46; 2 Corinthians
> 4:6; Ephesians 5:8; 1 Peter 2:9; 1 John. 1:5, 7; Revelation 21:23.

Satan's kingdom is characterized by darkness:

> Psalm 107:10-11; Luke 22:53; John 3:19; Ephesians 5:8; 6:12;
> Colossians 1:13; 1 Peter 2:9.

There are two divine kingdoms mentioned in the Bible: the kingdom of God and the kingdom of heaven. The kingdom of God
is the practical sphere of God's rule (Psalm 22:28; 145:13; Daniel
4:25). That is the place where God's will is always done. This is
a spiritual kingdom rather than a physical kingdom, and believers
are the subjects of this spiritual kingdom. However, this physical
earth and its immediate heavens are the scene of universal rebellion
against God (1 John 5:19; Revelation 11:15-18; 12:13).

Therefore, the actual sphere of God's rule is wherever His rule is
acknowledged; it is in the highest heaven and in the hearts of His
believing children. It is not coerced. It includes the angels that did
not rebel and born again people who belong to God. God's rule
has been acknowledged in the hearts of His children throughout
the ages. This kingdom now is really a spiritual kingdom, in that it

exists spiritually and not materially. It includes all those who have acknowledged the rule of God through faith in Jesus Christ and His finished work on the cross for their sins.

Jesus said,

> "But the hour is coming, and now is, when the true worshipers shall worship the Father in spirit and in truth: for the Father is seeking such to worship Him" (John 4:23 NKJV).

The expression "kingdom of heaven," or literally, "of the heavens," is one that is peculiar to Matthew's gospel. It refers to the rule of the heavens, i.e., the rule of the God of heaven over the earth as illustrated in Daniel (2:44; 4:25, 32). The kingdom of heaven is similar in many respects to the kingdom of God and is often used synonymously with it; though emphasizing certain features of divine government. When contrasted with the universal kingdom of God, the kingdom of heaven includes only men on earth, excluding angels and other creatures.

The kingdom of heaven is the earthly sphere of people who profess faith in Jesus. It includes those designated as wheat and tares; the latter are cast out of the kingdom (Matthew 13:41). The kingdom of heaven is also compared to a net containing both the good and bad fish which are later separated (Matthew 13:47).

The kingdom of heaven is revealed in three aspects. First, it is "at hand" (Matthew 4:17). The kingdom is offered in the person of the King, of whom John the Baptist was the forerunner (Matthew 3:1).

Secondly, this kingdom is being fulfilled in the present age. The kingdom of heaven is presented in seven mysteries (Matthew 13), revealing the character of the rule of heaven over the earth between the first and second coming of Jesus.

Thirdly, this kingdom is fulfilled after the second coming of Jesus. The kingdom of heaven will be realized in the future millennial

kingdom predicted by Daniel (Daniel 2:34-36, 44-45) and cov-
enanted to David (2 Samuel 7:12-16; Zechariah 12:8). This millennial form of the kingdom of heaven will be wholly future and
will be set up after the return of Jesus (Matthew 24:29-25:46; Acts
15:14-17).

The kingdom had been prophesied to Israel for over a thousand
years before the first advent of Jesus Christ (2 Samuel 7:11-17;
Psalm 89:20-37). The Jews looked forward to the kingdom which
God had promised to them (Matthew 11:12; Luke 1:33; 12:32;
Acts 1:6; Hebrews 12:28). Many Jews were expecting the immi-
nent appearance of their Messiah just prior and during the time that
Jesus was born (Luke 2:25, 36-38; 23:51).

A large body of extra-biblical apocalyptic literature was written by
Jews during this period. Jewish sects, like the Essenes, sprang up in
Israel during this time. These writings show that the Jews expected a
literal physical kingdom to be inaugurated by God; when the nation
of Israel, with Jerusalem, would be the center of world rule by the
Messiah.

Even a vocabulary had developed regarding the kingdom age in the
first century BC. The term "eternal life" or "everlasting life" was well
known during the time of Jesus' earthly ministry. Nowhere is this
term defined in Scripture; nor was Jesus ever asked what He meant
by it. We can conclude that everyone in Israel knew the term.

God had prepared that age for the advent of the Messiah in many
ways (Galatians 4:4). This term "eternal life" is found in the Jewish
rabbinical writings and is basically eschatological in outlook. The
rabbis used it to refer to the "life in the age that is eternal," referring
to the kingdom age and the eternal state. Life in the kingdom age,
or in the age to come, is eternal in quality, free from the limitations
of time, decay, evil, and sin.

The prophesied kingdom was offered to Israel by Jesus (Matthew 3:2; 4:17, 23; Mark 1:15) at His first advent. But they rejected Him as Messiah; and so rejected the kingdom as well (Matthew 23:37-39). Referring to Himself as the King, Jesus said to the Jews, "The kingdom of God is in the midst of you" (Luke 17:21). The "you" in the Greek is plural, which rules out the meaning that the kingdom is inside each of you, singular.

Paul clearly stated that God has not cast away His people, Israel (Romans 11:1-2). Thus, the church cannot be the replacement for Israel. Christians must be careful not to expropriate promises made to the nation of Israel for themselves or the church! That is the error of replacement theology.

The covenants still belong to Israel (Romans 9:4). Israel is only temporarily set aside because of their unbelief (Romans 11:20). In the future millennial kingdom, God will deal with Israel as a nation and fulfill the promised Old Testament covenants with them (Romans 11:26-27). The Abrahamic covenant is the dominant covenant of Scripture (Genesis 12:1-3; 13:14-17; 15:4-6, 12-20; 17:1,2; Romans 4:13-25; Hebrews 11:8-22, 39-40) and is superior to the Mosaic covenant.

The very name Israel means "governed by God" (Genesis 32:28-30). So when Paul says, "For they are not all Israel, which are of Israel" (Romans 9:6); Paul is saying not all Jews are governed by God; even if they use the name Israel. Jews who are governed by God have put their faith in the finished work of Jesus Christ, their Messiah. Paul said,

> "It is of faith, that it might be by grace; to the end the promise might be sure to all the seed; not to that only which is of the law, but to that also which is of the faith of Abraham; who is the father of us all" (Romans 4:16).

Therefore, the apostle could also say, "And so all Israel shall be saved" (Romans 11:26) because Jews who believed in Jesus Christ as their Messiah were governed by God. The Jews who were not saved used the name Israel even though they were not truly governed by God. Today this is still true of the Jews.

JESUS CHRIST'S RETURN

The New Testament clearly teaches that Jesus can return at any moment (Acts 1:11; Titus 2:13; James 5:8; 1 Peter 4:7). Jesus' return is imminent because there are no prophecies that need to be fulfilled for that to happen. Jesus said that the Father had appointed Him a kingdom in which the disciples will "eat and drink" with Him (Luke 22:29-30). The disciples thought that the kingdom was to appear immediately (Luke 19:11). Just before Jesus ascended into heaven some of His disciples asked Him, "Lord, will You at this time restore again the kingdom to Israel?" His answer was that it was not for them to know the times or the seasons of the kingdom (Acts 1:6-7).

This Messianic kingdom was yet future because these believing Jews were about to become part of the church, the body of Christ, which began at Pentecost (Acts 1:4-5) by means of the baptism of the Holy Spirit (1 Corinthians 12:13). The church age intervenes to postpone the kingdom. The church was never prophesied in the Old Testament. It was a mystery (Ephesians 3:3-11). It was never said of the nation of Israel that they were part of Christ's body, the church! After ascending into heaven, two angels addressed the disciples and said, "This same Jesus, which is taken up from you into heaven, shall so come in like manner as you have seen Him go into heaven" (Acts 1:11).

Previous to this, Jesus had told them about the kingdom of heaven (Matthew 25:1) and the kingdom of God (Mark 1:14); and what would happen when He returned, saying,

"When the Son of Man shall come in His glory, and all the holy angels with Him, then shall He sit upon the throne of His glory: and before Him shall be gathered all nations: and He shall separate them one from another, as a shepherd divides his sheep from the goats: and He shall set the sheep on His right hand, but the goats on the left. Then shall the King say unto them on His right hand, Come, you blessed of My Father, inherit the kingdom prepared for you from the foundation of the world" (Matthew 25:31-34).

In Daniel's vision of the progression of world kingdoms, four kings are symbolized as beasts; with the fourth one slain (Daniel 7:11), then Daniel saw the Son receive the kingdom from God the Father.

"I saw in the night visions, and, behold, one like the Son of Man came with the clouds of heaven, and came to the Ancient of Days, and they brought Him near before Him. And there was given Him dominion, and glory, and a kingdom, that all people, nations, and languages, should serve Him: His dominion is an everlasting dominion, which shall not pass away, and His kingdom that which shall not be destroyed" (Daniel 7:13-14).

"I beheld, and the same horn made war with the saints, and prevailed against them; until the Ancient of Days came, and judgment was given to the saints of the Most High; and the time came that the saints possessed the kingdom. And the kingdom and dominion, and the greatness of the kingdom under the whole heaven, shall be given to the people of the saints of the Most High, whose kingdom is an everlasting kingdom, and all dominions shall serve and obey Him" (Daniel 7:21-22, 27).

The millennial kingdom that God's saints will receive will be an earthly kingdom:

Psalm 2:8; Isaiah 11:9; 42:1-4; Jeremiah 23:5; Zechariah 14:9.

Messiah will rule the world in justice:

Isaiah 9:4-5; Jeremiah 23:3-6; 33:15-21.

From Jerusalem:

Isaiah 2:1-3; Zephaniah 3:15-17; Zechariah 8:1-3; 14:4.

He will return to the Mount of Olives where He left the earth:

Zechariah 14:4; Acts 1:11.

Creation will be returned to the state it was before the fall:

Isaiah 9:6-7; 11:6-9; 35:1; 65:18-25.

Those who die at age 100 will be considered children:

Isaiah 35:5-6; 65:20.

God will recall the Jews a second time from all the lands of their dispersion back to Israel:

Isaiah 14:1-3; Jeremiah 23:6-8; 32:37-40; 33:7-9; Ezekiel 36:16-38; 37:22-25.

He will rebuild the temple:

Zechariah 6:12-13.

Christ will come in judgment:

Psalm 96:13; Isaiah 63:1-6; 65:15-16; Malachi 3:1-4; Revelation 19:11-21.

He will root out all causes of sin:

Matthew 13:41.

Satan and the fallen angels will be put in prison so that they can't deceive anyone during the kingdom age:

Isaiah 24:21-23; Revelation 20:2-3.

Theological knowledge will be common:

Habakkuk 2:14.

The new nation or millennial kingdom of Israel will be born in one day:

Isaiah 66:7-9.

The church will reign with Christ during this kingdom age:

1 Corinthians 6:2-3; 2 Timothy 2:11-12.

Nowhere does the Bible teach that Jesus' second coming will take place after the world has become a better place because ostensibly most people will eventually be converted to Christianity. This post-millennial eschatological view was developed by Daniel Whitby (1638-1726), a wayward Unitarian clergyman of the Church of England, and embraced by the modernists of the late nineteenth century. This idea was also used to sell World War I to Americans as "the war to end all wars."

Jesus said,

"And you shall hear of wars and rumors of wars: see that you are not troubled: for all these things must come to pass, but the end is not yet" (Matthew 24:6).

And as I've stated before, Paul warns,

"This know also, that in the last days perilous times shall come. For men shall be lovers of their own selves, covetous, boastful, proud, blasphemers, disobedient to parents, unthankful, unholy, without natural affection, trucebreakers, false accusers, incontinent, fierce, despisers of those that are good, traitors, heady, highminded, lovers of pleasure more than lovers of God; having a form of godliness, but denying the power thereof: from such turn away" (2 Timothy 3:1-5).

Significant influences in changing people's biblical beliefs began with the European Renaissance. It was the arts, theatre, music, media, and public education which touched and remolded the thinking of the masses. The masses weren't touched directly by philosophy.

Philosophical humanism was birthed in the academic halls attended by the elite; and it was called higher education. Things are not what they appear to be!

Satan and his demons have been so effective in disguising and camouflaging his schemes. Most Christians are just as deceived as unbelievers as to how his evil strategies work in this world. First century believers were seriously warned by both Peter and Jude (2 Peter 2:1; 3:16-17; Jude 4).

Through the ages, Satan's deliberate lies and deceptions have often neutralized Christians in this world. Until the Lord says, "Enough," Satan will continue his grand deception. Twenty-first century existential postmodern humanism has been used by Satan to beguile both unbelievers and new evangelicals. The latter have recast their own image so that they have now become postmodern in their misguided attempt to reach the postmodern culture! There is nothing new under the sun.

However, no matter how dark things may get on earth for God's people, never forget that Jesus is coming again to rescue His church prior to His tribulation judgment. This judgment will be upon a sinful and Christ-rejecting world that chooses to live in Satan's kingdom of darkness. This tribulation period is the last seven years of the 490 years, the seventy sevens spoken of by Daniel, which God gave to the nation of Israel to conclude precisely accurate prophesied world history (Daniel 9:24-26).

The church is "caught up" and gathered to our Lord (2 Thessalonians 2:1) prior to this tribulation period:

> Acts 1:6-7, 11; 1 Corinthians 15:51-52; 1 Thessalonians 4:15-18; 5:9;
> 2 Thessalonians 2:1-4; Revelation 3:10 with Revelation 14:8, 19; 15:l;
> Revelation 16; Revelation 19.

God's purposes through the tribulation period (Daniel 9:24-26) are to:

1. End the church age with the rapture.

2. Conclude the age of Israel with Messiah Jesus Christ's second advent.

3. Judge the peoples of this world for their crimes (2 Peter 3:10-13; Revelation 8-19).

4. Destroy Satan's kingdom on earth (Daniel 2:34-35).

5. Bring in Jesus Christ's kingdom and its righteousness; He will physically and literally return to earth to judge and inaugurate His kingdom at His second advent:

> 1 Chronicles 16:31-33; Psalm 9:8; 82:8; 96:13; 98:9; Isaiah 24:1, 21-23; 26:21; 66:15-16; Zechariah 14:1-5; Malachi 3:1-5; Matthew 13:41; 24:30-31; 25:30; Acts 1:11; 1 John 2:28; Revelation 19:11-21; 22:12.

The kingdom of heaven on earth will come with the sounding of the seventh angel:

> "The kingdom of this world has become the kingdoms of our Lord and of His Christ, and He shall reign forever and ever" (Revelation 11:15b; Daniel 2:44; 7:21-22).

At the end of the millennial kingdom age, Satan, his demons, and all unbelievers will be cast into the lake of fire, which is the second death; it is spiritual and eternal separation from God (Revelation 20:10, 14-15).

How glorious it will be when we hear a loud voice from heaven saying,

> "Behold, the tabernacle of God is with men, and He will dwell with them, and they shall be His people. God Himself shall be with them, and be their God. And God shall wipe away every tear from their eyes; and there shall be no more death, nor sorrow, nor crying. There shall be no more pain, for the former things have passed away" (Revelation 21:3-4 NKJV).

"Therefore, comfort one another with these words" (1 Thessalonians 4:18 NKJV).

Obviously, what is happening in the world today is the dark work of Satan, the god of this world, who is nearing his day of judgment.

"But thanks be to God, which gives us the victory through our Lord Jesus Christ. Therefore, my beloved brethren, be steadfast, immovable, always abounding in the work of the Lord, forasmuch as you know that your labor is not in vain in the Lord" (1 Corinthians 15:57-58).

INDEX